PARS IN PRACTICE
MORE RESOURCES AND STRATEGIES FOR ONLINE WRITING INSTRUCTORS

Practices & Possibilities

Series Editors: Mike Palmquist, Aimee McClure, Aleashia Walton, and Karen Moroski-Rigney

The Practices & Possibilities Series addresses the full range of practices within the field of Writing Studies, including teaching, learning, research, and theory. From Joseph Williams' reflections on problems to Richard E. Young's taxonomy of "small genres" to Adam Mackie's considerations of technology, the books in this series explore issues and ideas of interest to writers, teachers, researchers, and theorists who share an interest in improving existing practices and exploring new possibilities. The series includes both original and republished books. Works in the series are organized topically.

The WAC Clearinghouse, Colorado State University Open Press, and University Press of Colorado are collaborating so that these books will be widely available through free digital distribution and low-cost print editions. The publishers and the series editors are committed to the principle that knowledge should freely circulate. We see the opportunities that new technologies have for further democratizing knowledge. And we see that to share the power of writing is to share the means for all to articulate their needs, interests, and learning into the great experiment of literacy.

Other Books in the Series

Mary Ann Dellinger and D. Alexis Hart (Eds.), *ePortfolios@edu: What We Know, What We Don't Know, And Everything In-Between* (2020)

Jo-Anne Kerr and Ann N. Amicucci (Eds.), *Stories from First-Year Composition: Pedagogies that Foster Student Agency and Writing Identity* (2020)

Patricia Freitag Ericsson, *Sexual Harassment and Cultural Change in Writing Studies* (2020)

Ryan J. Dippre, *Talk, Tools, and Texts: A Logic-in-Use for Studying Lifespan Literate Action Development* (2019)

Jessie Borgman and Casey McArdle, *Personal, Accessible, Responsive, Strategic: Resources and Strategies for Online Writing Instructors* (2019)

Cheryl Geisler and Jason Swarts, *Coding Streams of Language: Techniques for the Systematic Coding of Text, Talk, and Other Verbal Data* (2019)

Ellen C. Carillo, *A Guide to Mindful Reading* (2017)

Lillian Craton, Renée Love & Sean Barnette (Eds.), *Writing Pathways to Student Success* (2017)

Charles Bazerman, *Involved: Writing for College, Writing for Your Self* (2015)

Adam Mackie, *New Literacies Dictionary: Primer for the Twenty-first Century Learner* (2011)

PARS IN PRACTICE
MORE RESOURCES AND STRATEGIES FOR ONLINE WRITING INSTRUCTORS

Edited by Jessie Borgman and Casey McArdle

The WAC Clearinghouse
wac.colostate.edu
Fort Collins, Colorado

University Press of Colorado
upcolorado.com
Louisville, Colorado

The WAC Clearinghouse, Fort Collins, Colorado 80523

University Press of Colorado, Louisville, Colorado 80027

© 2021 by Jessie Borgman and Casey McArdle. This work is licensed under a Creative Commons Attribution-NonCommercial-NoDerivatives 4.0 International.

ISBN 978-1-64215-114-5 (PDF) | 978-1-64215-115-2 (ePub) | 978-1-64642-181-7 (pbk.)

DOI 10.37514/PRA-B.2021.1145

Library of Congress Cataloging-in-Publication Data

Names: Borgman, Jessie, 1980- editor. | McArdle, Casey, 1974- editor.
Title: PARS in practice : more resources and strategies for online writing instructors / edited by Jessie Borgman and Casey McArdle.
Description: Fort Collins, Colorado : The WAC Clearinghouse, [2021] | Series: Practices & possibilities | Includes bibliographical references.
Identifiers: LCCN 2021003523 (print) | LCCN 2021003524 (ebook) | ISBN 9781646421817 (paperback) | ISBN 9781642151145 (adobe pdf) | ISBN 9781642151152 (epub)
Subjects: LCSH: English language—Composition and exercises—Web-based instruction.
Classification: LCC PE1404 .P374 2021 (print) | LCC PE1404 (ebook) | DDC 808/.0420285—dc23
LC record available at https://lccn.loc.gov/2021003523
LC ebook record available at https://lccn.loc.gov/2021003524

Copyeditor: Don Donahue
Designer: Mike Palmquist
Cover and Interior Photos: Courtesy of Jessie Borgman and Casey McArdle
Series Editors: Mike Palmquist, Aimee McClure, Aleashia Walton, and Karen Moroski-Rigney

The WAC Clearinghouse supports teachers of writing across the disciplines. Hosted by Colorado State University, and supported by the Colorado State University Open Press, it brings together scholarly journals and book series as well as resources for teachers who use writing in their courses. This book is available in digital formats for free download at wac.colostate.edu.

Founded in 1965, the University Press of Colorado is a nonprofit cooperative publishing enterprise supported, in part, by Adams State University, Colorado State University, Fort Lewis College, Metropolitan State University of Denver, University of Colorado, University of Northern Colorado, Utah State University, and Western Colorado University. For more information, visit upcolorado.com.

Contents

Foreword: Turning Research into Practice ix
    Heidi Skurat Harris

Introduction: PARS and Online Writing Instruction 3
    Jessie Borgman and Casey McArdle

Glossary 13

Section 1: Design 15

Chapter 1. Online Writing Instructors as Strategic Caddies: Reading Digital Landscapes and Selecting Online Learning Tools 19
    Kristy Liles Crawley

Chapter 2. My Online Instruction Mulligan: How PARS Transformed My Technical Writing Community College Course 31
    Thomas M. Geary

Chapter 3. Strategic, User-Centered Design for a Globally Distributed, Condensed Format, Online Graduate Course 47
    Mary K. Stewart

Chapter 4. The Literacy Load is Too Damn High! A PARS Approach to Cohort-Based Discussion 71
    Alex Sibo

Chapter 5. People, Programs, and Practices: A Grid-Based Approach to Designing and Supporting Online Writing Curriculum 83
    Allegra Smith, Libby Chernouski, Bianca Batti,
    Alisha Karabinus, and Bradley Dilger

Section 2: Instruction 97

Chapter 6. Finding the Sweet Spot: Strategic Course Design Using Videos 101
    Christine I. McClure and Cat Mahaffey

Chapter 7. Designing a More Equitable Scorecard: Grading Contracts and Online Writing Instruction 119
    Angela Laflen and Mikenna Sims

Chapter 8. Not a Laughing Matter: Creating a Humor-Centric User Design in OWI 141
    Nitya Pandey

Chapter 9. Confronting Ableist Texts: Teaching Usability and
Accessibility in the Online Technical Writing Classroom 153
    Cynthia Pengilly

Chapter 10. Negotiating the Hazards of the "Just-in-Time" Online
Writing Course.. 167
    Theresa M. Evans

SECTION 3: ADMINISTRATION 181

Chapter 11. Create, Support, and Facilitate Personal Online Writing
Courses in Online Writing Programs 185
    Rhonda Thomas, Karen Kuralt,
    Heidi Skurat Harris, and George Jensen

Chapter 12. Using PARS to Build a Community of Practice for Hybrid
Writing Instructors..209
    Lyra Hilliard

Chapter 13. Preparing Graduate Students and Contingent Faculty for
Online Writing Instruction: A Responsive and Strategic Approach to
Designing Professional Development Opportunities 225
    N. Claire Jackson and Andrea R. Olinger

Chapter 14. Online Writing Instructors as Web Designers: Tapping
into Existing Expertise...243
    Jason Snart

Chapter 15. PARS for the Course: Using PARS to Teach PARS in an
Online Graduate Seminar 255
    Lydia Wilkes

SECTION 4: USER EXPERIENCE (UX) 273

Chapter 16. The Bottom End: Transposing Online Bass Lessons to
Online Writing Instruction..277
    Dylan "Too Fresh" Retzinger

Chapter 17. Ensuring High-Quality Student User Experiences: PARS
and the Technical Communication Online Writing Class 293
    Guiseppe Getto

Chapter 18. Usability Testing for OWI Instructors 305
    Joseph Bartolotta

Chapter 19. Aiming for the Sweet Spot: A User-Centered Approach to Migrating a Community-engaged Course Online 317
    Erica M. Stone

Chapter 20. PARSing out the Course: User-centered Design through HyperDocs in Online Writing Instruction 337
    Kathleen Turner Ledgerwood

Conclusion: Moving Day! 353
    Jessie Borgman and Casey McArdle

Afterword: Re-Mapping the Global Context for Online Education 355
    Kirk St.Amant

Contributors 361

Foreword: Turning Research into Practice

Heidi Skurat Harris
UNIVERSITY OF ARKANSAS, LITTLE ROCK

In his foreword to *Personal, Accessible, Responsive, Strategic: Resources and Strategies for Online Writing Instructors*, Scott Warnock (2019) described Jessie Borgman and Casey McArdle as hard working, creative & spirited.

"They are *doers*," Scott wrote (p. vii). With their first book and in their OWI Community website, Jessie and Casey invited online instructors into their classrooms, and now they've done it again with their second book, the collection you are now either holding in your hands or reading on the screen. In *PARS in Practice: More Strategies and Resources for Online Writing Instructors*, Jessie and Casey bring together online writing instructors, scholars, and administrators to share practical ideas for how they implemented the PARS approach in their classes, programs, and departments.

In Spring 2020, the phrase "we are all online writing instructors" took on a new meaning (Borgman & McArdle, 2019, p. 3) as educators moved to emergency remote instruction (Hodges et al., 2020). Although this book was not planned for the spring move to remote learning, it could not be more timely. While some students and instructors made the transition seamlessly, others were caught totally unprepared. The shift from brick-and-mortar to remote learning, and the lack of adequate online professional development at most institutions, highlighted the urgent need for collections such as this one.

Their second book, coming only a year after their first one, extends the hospitality, humor, and good will that they have established in The Online Writing Instruction Community (owicommunity.org) and through free professional development activities, such as the OWI Symposiums in August and September of 2020 (owicommunity.org/owi-symposium.html). These symposiums brought together 27 experienced online instructors to share expertise in the form of Ignite talks (ignitetalks.io/) supported with slide decks and handouts posted on the OWI Community website.

In fact, the story of how the OWI Symposiums began exemplifies the spirit Jessie and Casey have created through the OWI Community. They noted the need for professional development that would inject new ideas and energy into writing teachers on the precipice of an uncertain fall semester. They sent out a call to see if anyone would be interested in presenting an idea to new online instructors, expecting seven to ten responses. To their surprise, over 30 people responded to their impromptu call for volunteer presenters, and Jessie and Casey changed the one-day symposium to a two-day, two symposium series. Over 500 people registered for the first August Symposium, and over half of registrants had less than one year of teaching experience in online classes. Jessie and Casey invited those teaching writing online into a community with a shared purpose: making online learning personal, accessible, responsive, and strategic (their PARS approach).

Whether you have taught online for 20 years or are just getting started, the ideas in *PARS in Practice* extend the initial PARS approach through case studies and examples of online writing instruction and administration that reaches students and refreshes faculty. The authors in this collection are like the competitors at the U.S. Open who aren't all pros—they are graduate students, adjunct faculty, tenure-track and tenured professors, WPAs, graduate coordinators, deans, and independent scholars. They teach freshman composition, technical writing, online writing instruction. They study accessibility, gender, digital rhetoric, user experience (UX), creative nonfiction, linguistics, anti-racist practices, hybrid learning, multimodality, and labor practices. They are web designers, non-designers, and multimedia designers.

Just skimming the credentials of the authors in this book shows that *PARS in Practice* is a model of how to build community. That community extends from major conferences (like *CCCC* and *Computers and Writing*), to virtual spaces (the OWI Community webpage and symposium), and now to the classroom.

The PARS approach aligns golf concepts with learning to teach online. As Jessie and Casey mention in their first book, golf is a sport in which you compete against yourself. I played golf with my family, picking up my first golf club at the age of 12, and by the age of 22, I had become a less than stellar golfer but a seasoned putter hurler. I never mastered the sport, or even came close. But some of my fondest memories from the golf course are those where my family bonded around our shared love of the sport, in spite of our lack of mastery.

I had 10 years of preparation to play golf, but I had only three days of preparation to teach online. I no longer play golf (although I have clubs in the garage), but I do still teach online, where for almost two decades, I have been an active part of the group of scholars and teachers who, much like me, improved their online teaching game slowly. Just like my time golfing, my classes might have landed in the weeds more often than not, but the company I've had along the way has more than made up for the blisters.

I am honored to have the opportunity to be a part of this collection and of the OWI Community. Thank you to all of you for your dedication to online instruction. I look forward to many years of sharing online teaching success with all of you.

References

Borgman, J. & McArdle, C. (2019). *Personal, accessible, responsive, strategic: Resources and strategies for online writing instructors.* The WAC Clearinghouse; University Press of Colorado. https://doi.org/10.37514/PRA-B.2019.0322.

Hodges, C., Moore, S., Lockee, B., Trust, T. & Bond, A. (2020, March 27). The difference between emergency remote teaching and online learning. *Educause Review*, https://er.educause.edu/articles/2020/3/the-difference-between-emergency-remote-teaching-and-online-learning.

Warnock, S. (2019). Foreword. In J. Borgman & C. McArdle (Eds.), *Personal, accessible, responsive, strategic: Resources and strategies for online writing instructors* (pp. vii–x). The WAC Clearinghouse; University Press of Colorado. https://doi.org/10.37514/PRA-B.2019.0322.

PARS IN PRACTICE
MORE RESOURCES AND STRATEGIES FOR
ONLINE WRITING INSTRUCTORS

Introduction: PARS and Online Writing Instruction

Jessie Borgman
ARIZONA STATE UNIVERSITY

Casey McArdle
MICHIGAN STATE UNIVERSITY

In 2015, we decided that the field of online writing instruction (OWI) needed a "go to" resource where administrators and instructors with varying levels of experience could access the myriad of available OWI resources in a space where everyone could feel a part of something. We had both taught online for a long time and we recognized that sometimes it can feel isolating and oftentimes, universities don't provide enough training or enough resources.

Having been involved in OWI research and having attended multiple conferences while working with some foundational OWI scholars, we noticed over and over that attendees would ask for resources or a central hub for online writing instructors. Prior to 2015, no such resource existed.

So we decided to do something about it.

Upon returning from a conference in 2015, we created The Online Writing Instruction Community (owicommunity.org), a free online space full of resources for online writing instructors and administrators. We figured since no one had done it before, it might as well be us!

In an effort to give our site ethos, we created our own approach to online writing instruction—an approach that covered the main pillars of OWI research and practice outlined in the CCCC 2013 *A Position Statement of Principles and Example Effective Practices for Online Writing Instruction (OWI)*. Our website included a page on the PARS approach to OWI where we explained that PARS stands for personal, accessible, responsive, strategic. PARS encompasses all of the elements we feel make instructors and administrators successful at designing, instructing, and administering online writing courses. To offer our website visitors a more comprehensive discussion of the PARS approach, we released our first co-authored book, *Personal, Accessible, Responsive, Strategic: Resources and Strategies for Online Writing Instructors* in 2019.

To be clear, the PARS approach is not a checklist—it is a holistic approach to online instruction that acknowledges the complexity of course design and its facilitation in digital spaces. Other, more profit-motivated systems are grounded in checklists, but not PARS. We recognize the value of participatory online writing courses (OWCs) and reiterate the sentiment from Oswal and Melonçon (2017) that "moving away from checklists, which promote an ideology of normalcy, and toward participatory curriculum design affords programs a way to think of OWC design in terms of an ideology of inclusion" (p. 73).

The PARS approach provides a framework to make the complex dynamics of design and instruction and administration more accessible to both novice and experienced online instructors and administrators. Because PARS is grounded in user experience (UX), it allows instructors, designers, and administrators to understand how to create and facilitate online courses, whether they have extensive or minimal experience. The accessibility and inclusion that grounds the PARS approach allows *all* users to participate in the experience of the online course.

In our first book, each of the PARS letters had its own chapter and each of the individual chapters discussed aspects of online course design, instruction, and administration.

We've illustrated a few key points of each of the PARS letters here, but for an extended discussion, please see our first book at wac.colostate.edu/books/practice/pars/.

P=Personal

- Show your students you are a human! Writing is personal and teaching is personal so make it that way in your OWC.
- Make a connection beyond content delivery and course grades.
- Build community and foster instructor/student & student/student connections.

A=Accessible

- Remove barriers to learning.
- Think beyond ADA compliance (though that is important!).
- Take advantage of the affordances of a digital learning environment. Don't just put content built for F2F into an online space.

R=Responsive

- Establish guidelines for how you're going to respond to your instructors/students and when you're going to respond to your instructors/students.
- Set real expectations about = turnaround times for responding to students (grading, emailing, etc.).
- Create a routine and set boundaries.

S=Strategic

- PARS = it all comes together with Strategy!
- Be strategic! Strategy is the biggest part of being an online instructor and creating and facilitating an online student user experience.
- Focus on the student user experience (UX). After all, students are our primary users!

As noted, PARS spans three layers: *design*, *instruction*, and *administration*. When these layers are combined, they equal the user/student experience. If you attend to all of these layers within each letter, you get a unique user experience where students and instructors can engage in an enriched online space. Essentially, this equation is a simple one: PARS + UX = OWI. This is a visual representation of how we see the PARS framework:

P A R S	Design	
	Instruction	User Experience
	Administration	

These big picture items of design, instruction, and administration are complex and at times tedious, but PARS makes them feel less so. The flexibility of PARS allows new and experienced online instructors and administrators to focus on one or multiple aspects of their teaching or administration style at a time, but by default, they end up attending to other areas, too.

For example, if an instructor were new to online teaching, they could place focus on being **personal** for the fall semester and keep **personal** at the front of their mind as they design the course or interact with the students. By being more **personal** in their class, this instructor is also by default being more **accessible, responsive**, and **strategic**. Or, as another example, if an administrator wanted to focus on being **responsive**, they could plan out *how* and *when* they will respond to their instructional staff and by doing so, they are also being more **personal, accessible,** and **strategic.** As you focus on one PARS element, you will see how they are all interconnected!

What PARS does is filter out the complexity and reduce the urge to feel overwhelmed when thinking about all of the moving parts in an online course, or all of the moving parts of running an online writing program. By focusing on one or all element(s) of PARS, instructors and administrators are able to improve their courses and interactions.

Online Writing Instruction and the Game of Golf

As we noted in the first book, the PARS approach was born out of a shared passion for the game of golf. We both play, attend, and watch Professional Golf Association (PGA) events on television. In golf, a par score is the number of strokes a golfer is expected to take on any given hole. Shooting a par score is a goal for many experienced and inexperienced golfers. Golf is a game people play for life. It's a game that takes a lot of practice and people who play golf long enough begin to excel at the game and a PAR on a hole can become a reality. Golf is unique because you are both part of a community of golfers but you are also competing with yourself.

We feel the same can be said for online writing instruction, administration, and course design. When we play (teach, administer or design an OWI course) and get small "wins," we want to improve. We feel that no one needs to be an expert going into distance education, but everyone can improve their online teaching/administration/course design game with proper support and a great approach, like PARS.

PARS for the win!

Collection Overview

Inspiration

As we noted in the final chapter of our first book ("The 19th Hole"), we see PARS based in, and influenced by, user experience (UX) research, principles and practices (Buley, 2013; Colborne, 2011; Garrett, 2011; Getto & Beecher, 2016; Goodman et al., 2013; Hart-Davidson, 2015; Norman, 1988; Potts & Salvo, 2017; Still, 2011; Still & Crane, 2016). However, we also see a lot of opportunities for OWI and UX in the future. To us, the application of UX principles and practices is a burgeoning opportunity for OWI scholars. This collection illustrates some of the opportunities to apply foundational UX principles and practices to foundational concepts of OWI, which were outlined in the CCCC 2013 *A Position Statement of Principles and Example Effective Practices for Online Writing Instruction* (OWI).

An early attempt at recognizing the complementary nature of these fields was made by Blythe (2001) who argued that online instructors must be both instructors and designers, yet rarely are they trained to be designers (p. 329). Blythe (2001) noted that in order to combat a lack of training, instructors could follow principles of User-Centered Design (UCD). Other scholars picked up on the possibility for examining the user experience in online writing classes (almost two decades later in 2018) with the release of a *Computers and Composition* special issue (edited by Bartolotta & Bourelle), which focused on online writing instruction and UCD. Many of the pieces in the special issue explore how UCD can improve online writing instruction pedagogy or course design (Bjork, 2018; Borgman & Dockter, 2018; Greer & Skurat Harris, 2018; St.Amant, 2018; Vie, 2018). That same year, Warnock & Gasiewski (2018) co-authored a book that explored their respective user experiences as instructor (Warnock) and student (Gasiewski) in an online writing course. Now, turning to this edited collection, many of the chapters touch on the student, instructor, or administrator's user experience and offer insightful ideas to enrich these experiences. We hope that the chapters in this collection offer readers inspiration to continue to explore connections between UX, UCD, and OWI in future research.

Audience

The audience for this collection is threefold: scholar, instructor, and administrator. Due to the wide range of topics in this collection, we see these chapters being used for a variety of purposes. If you're a scholar, we see the possibility for you to use part or all of this collection to further your work in OWI or UX. The collection offers many ideas that scholars like you could expand on in order to generate new scholarship in the field. If you are an instructor, you might be inspired by the various options for expanding your pedagogy, and with the practical application focus, you may use some of the concepts in these chapters in your own online writing courses. If you are an administrator, you will likely find this collection useful in thinking through some of the bigger questions surrounding your own writing program as several of the chapters offer useful and applicable moves you could implement such as professional development, training, and supporting instructors. We've outlined target audiences in each of the section introductions.

Structure

As we noted above, the last chapter of our first book drew connections between user experience (UX) and PARS, and working on this collection we noticed some great connections that allowed us to continue exploring the PARS layers (design/instruction/administration) and resulting user experiences through the various chapters. This collection picks up where our first book left off but brings forward new and existing scholarly voices who wanted to share their experiences with the PARS approach to OWI.

This collection contains 20 chapters across four sections based on the layers of PARS and the end goal, UX. The sections are: Design, Instruction, Administration, and User Experience (UX). The chapters apply PARS in various ways with some emphasizing one PARS element like **strategic**, while other chapters look at the entire application of PARS. Within the chapters you will find examples and suggestions for using various approaches, skills, and ideas in your online classrooms and in your administrative philosophy.

As noted above, the PARS approach is interconnected so topics within each of these four sections may overlap with other layers (for example how chapters in the UX section talk about design and instruction too), but that is because PARS is fluid. While elements of PARS can be isolated and explored individually, the whole approach is bound by usability and user experience (as St.Amant eloquently notes in the Afterword to this collection).

Author Style

While reading this collection, keep in mind that all golfers have different approaches to the game and have different playing styles. Players in golf admire other golfers and their unique approaches, just as scholars admire other scholars. This collection recognizes different styles and approaches to sharing ideas in academia. Golf swings are like voices—no two are ever the same.

Now while our CFP made it clear this was a practice-based book, we purposefully didn't give our authors a lot of direction in how they were to shape their chapters. We told them to write as if they were having a conversation with the reader and to feel free to use a more informal tone in their writing in order to be accessible to readers. Essentially, we asked them to be **personal** in their writing!

We also suggested the authors to take a "citation lite" approach to their chapters because we didn't want readers to be bogged down by long literature reviews. Instead, we wanted readers to be inspired by the ideas, practices, and explorations each of the authors discuss in their chapters. This book is for practicing instructors, administrators, and scholars. It's a book you read and feel like you are chatting with a friend who has been doing some amazing things in their online classroom and they really want to share everything with you!

Lastly, as you read and take in this collection, you will see that some of the authors picked up on our golf metaphor. We also did not require them to do this, but some chose to have fun and try something new—echoing the risks they took in the classroom. And as a result, and just in case, we've included a glossary of common golf terms at the end of this introduction.

Usability/Usefulness

This collection provides practical application where authors share what they do in their own OWCs, their own professional development, their own administrative roles, and reflect on what they learned from these experiences. This book is important to your practice because it operationalizes the foundational principles and practices of OWI research.

Respecting the Game

No golf course is immune to redesign and change. The game of golf evolves, and while the goal of the game is the same, how we play it echoes the agile nature of human ingenuity. New golfers bring new approaches with new swings, which are supported by new technologies that allow them to play courses differently than they were played by previous generations. This does not imply how the game used to be played was wrong. In fact, it affords us the opportunity to appreciate prior skills as we develop new ones. We apply this golf concept to OWI as well. OWI is not immune to redesign and change. In fact, its very nature (technology!) makes it susceptible to continual redesign and change.

So, when we look at the extensive body of research in OWI that comes before this work, it gives us the good fortune to situate this collection as a space for some new and experienced voices to showcase their skills while sharing the same goal of helping and educating students in online classes. This collection, and subsequent collections, are perfect examples of peer-to-peer learning and they represent the redesign and change that can occur in an academic field of study through building on foundational scholarship and embracing technological advances.

Thus, this collection recognizes and respects the contributions of the foundational texts of OWI and encourages readers who are unfamiliar to read them. Some of these texts that have impacted our work and the work of the authors in this collection are early books on OWI and the work contributed by the CCCC Committee for Effective Practices for Online Writing Instruction (2007–2016).

Early texts specific to OWI:

- The Online Writing Classroom, Susanmarie Harrington, Michael Day, and Rebecca Rickly (2000)
- Preparing Educators for Online Writing Instruction: Principles and Processes, Beth Hewett and Christa Ehmann (2004)
- Online Education Global Questions, Local Answers, Kelli Cargile Cook and Keith Grant-Davie (2005)
- Teaching Writing Online: How and Why, Scott Warnock (2009)
- The Online Writing Conference: A Guide for Teachers and Tutors, Beth Hewett (2010)
- Hybrid Learning: The Perils and Promise of Blending Online and Face-to-Face Instruction in Higher Education, Jason Snart (2010)
- Online Education 2.0 Evolving, Adapting, and Reinventing Online Technical Communication, Kelli Cargile Cook and Keith Grant-Davie (2013)

And the *CCCC* OWI Committee work:

- Report of the State of the Art of OWI, CCCC Committee for Effective Practices for Online Writing Instruction (2011)
- A Position Statement of Principles and Example Effective Practices for

- Online Writing Instruction (OWI), CCCC Committee for Effective Practices for Online Writing Instruction (2013)
- Foundational Practices of Online Writing Instruction, Beth Hewett and Kevin DePew (2015)

In addition to the foundational texts mentioned above, we also acknowledge all of the authors and texts not mentioned and encourage readers to review the vast amount of OWI scholarship available on *The Bedford Bibliography of Research in Online Writing Instruction*. This resource compiled and edited by Heidi Skurat Harris, Mahli Mechenbier, Sushil Oswal, and Natalie Stillman-Webb was updated in 2019. We also encourage readers to access The Global Society of Online Literacy Educators adapted version of the 2013 *CCCC OWI Position Statement*, which is called *Online Literacy Instruction Principles and Tenets* and was released in 2019.

Taking into account all of these texts, we want to point out that we have moved beyond validating OWI as a field. This collection is about the future of OWI and the new voices and new ideas that can contribute to, and build upon, this foundational research. With this collection, we are hoping to usher in a new approach to OWI scholarship and while our authors may or may not heavily cite these texts in their chapters, it does not mean they don't recognize their contributions.

You are Now on the Tee!

After the first book was released, we received multiple notes from people across the country indicating how much our book had helped them. The simplicity of the PARS approach was accessible to readers and aided them in thinking about some of the more sophisticated aspects of designing and facilitating their online courses. We began receiving invitations to speak at professional development events and to hold OWI workshops centered on PARS. We were humbled. We are still humbled. But we were/are also overjoyed because helping people who have very little OWI training or access to OWI resources has always been our goal.

Neither of us had any training when we began teaching online and so we know first-hand how lonely and challenging it can be to self-instruct and be a good online instructor at the same time. We've been very excited about the energy and inspiration we've given people, especially experienced online writing instructors and administrators who have embraced PARS as an opportunity to continue to work on their pedagogy and management skills.

As this collection illustrates (and as Skurat Harris eloquently writes in her Foreword to this book), we've assembled quite a community of online writing instructors, administrators, and scholars. One of our goals for this collection was to expand the community of OWI by inviting new and existing voices to contribute to the research on OWI and we feel we've accomplished that goal. We invited scholars at all levels to be considered for this collection and we are very pleased with the variety of voices we are able to share with you.

As we close out this collection introduction, it is also important to note that while we were working on this collection, the COVID-19 pandemic started. In fact, the month we sent out the CFP, was the start of the pandemic and the book will likely be released as infection rates are climbing even higher. We recognize that because of the pandemic many people were catapulted into online teaching with little or no training. We know from first-hand experience how difficult this is! We hope that for those of you who are new to OWI this collection serves as an introduction to some exciting possibilities for your online courses.

We are delighted to bring you this collection that illustrates the various ways that the PARS approach can be applied to online writing courses. We hope that you will find the chapters useful and that you will be inspired to attempt some of the activities and strategies contained within them. We also hope that this collection inspires you to use the PARS approach as you design, instruct, and administer your own online writing courses/programs. And finally, if you have not already done so, we invite you to please join our community!

Website: owicommunity.org
Facebook Group: facebook.com/groups/owicommunity
Twitter: @theowicommunity
Google Group Discussion Forum: TheOWIC@googlegroups.com

References

Bjork, C. (2018). Integrating usability testing with digital rhetoric in OWI. *Computers and Composition, 2018*(4), 4–13.

Blythe, S. (2001). Designing online courses: User-centered practices. *Computers and Composition, 18*(4), 329–346.

Borgman, J. & Dockter, J. (2018). Considerations of access and design in the online writing classroom. *Computers and Composition, 2018*(4), 94–105.

Borgman, J. & McArdle, C. (2019). *Personal, accessible, responsive, strategic: Resources and strategies for online writing instructors.* The WAC Clearinghouse; University Press of Colorado. https://doi.org/10.37514/PRA-B.2019.0322.

Buley, L. (2013). *The user experience team of one: A research and design survival guide.* Rosenfield.

Cargile Cook, K. & Grant-Davie, K. (Eds.). (2005). *Baywood's technical communication series. Online education: Global questions, local answers.* Baywood.

Cargile Cook, K. & Grant-Davie, K. (Eds.). (2013). *Baywood's technical communication series. Online education 2.0: Evolving, adapting, and reinventing online technical communication.* Baywood.

Colborne, G. (2011). *Simple and usable: Web, mobile, and interaction design* (2nd ed.). New Riders.

Conference on College Composition and Communication Committee for Best Practices in Online Writing Instruction. (2011). *Report of the state of the art of OWI.* http://www.ncte.org/library/NCTEFiles/Groups/CCCC/Committees/OWI_State-of-Art_Report_April_2011.pdf.

Conference on College Composition and Communication Committee for Best Practices in Online Writing Instruction. (2013). *A position statement of principles and example effective practices for online writing instruction (OWI)*. http://www.ncte.org/cccc/resources/positions/owiprinciples.

Goodman, E., Kuniavsky, M. & Moed, A. (2012). *Observing the user experience: A practitioner's guide to user research* (2nd ed.). Morgan Kaufmann.

Garrett, J. (2011). *The elements of user experience: User-centered design for the web and beyond*. New Riders.

Getto, G. & Beecher, F. (2016). Toward a model of UX education: Training UX designers within the academy. *IEEE Transactions on Professional Communication, 59*(2), 153–164.

Greer, M. & Skurat Harris, H. (2018). User-centered design as a foundation for effective online writing instruction. *Computers and Composition, 49*, 18–24.

Harrington, S., Day, M. & Rickly, R. (2000). *The online writing classroom*. Hampton Press.

Hart-Davidson, B. (2015). The turn to learning: A view of UX project management as organizational learning practice. *International Journal of Sociotechnology and Knowledge Development (IJSKD), 7*(30), 4–52.

Hewett, B. (2015). *The online writing conference: A guide for teachers and tutors*. Macmillan.

Hewett, B. & DePew, K. (2015). *Foundational practices of online writing instruction*. The WAC Clearinghouse; Parlor Press. https://doi.org/10.37514/PER-B.2015.0650.

Hewett, B. & Ehmann, C. (2004). *Preparing educators for online writing instruction: Principles and processes*. National Council of Teachers of English.

Norman, D. (1988). *The design of everyday things*. Basic Books.

Oswal, S. & Melonçon, L. (2017). Saying no to the checklist: Shifting from an ideology of normalcy to an ideology of inclusion in online writing instruction. *WPA: Writing Program Administration, 40*(3), 61–77.

Skurat Harris, H., Mechenbier, M., Oswal, S. & Stillman-Webb, N. (2017). *The Bedford bibliography of research in online writing instruction*. https://community.macmillanlearning.com/.

Snart, J. (2010). *Hybrid learning: The perils and promise of blending online and face-to-face instruction in higher education*. Prager.

St.Amant, K. (2018). Contextualizing cyber compositions for cultures: A usability-based approach to composing online for international audiences. *Computers and Composition, 2018*(4), 82–93.

Still, B. (2011). Mapping usability: An ecological framework for analyzing user experience. In M. Albers & B. Still (Eds.), *Usability of complex information systems: Evaluation of user interaction* (pp. 89–109). CRC Press.

Still, B. & Crane, K. (2016). *Fundamentals of user-centered design*. CRC Press.

Vie, S. (2018). Effective social media use in online writing classes through universal design for learning (UDL) principles. *Computers and Composition, 2018*(4), 61–70.

Warnock, S. (2009). *Teaching writing online: How and why*. National Council of Teachers of English.

Warnock, S. & Gasiewski, D. (2018). *Writing together: Ten weeks teaching and studenting in an online writing course*. National Council of Teachers of English.

Glossary

Golf Terms

Ace: A hole-in-one. Hitting the ball into the hole in one stroke.

Birdie: One stroke under par.

Bogey: One stroke over par.

Bunker: (A hazard) usually a hole of sand.

Caddie: The person who carries a golfer's clubs.

Double Bogey: Two strokes over par

Drive: A golfer's first stroke from the tee box on every hole.

Eagle: Two strokes under par.

Fore!: A warning shouted when the ball is heading toward a person or object.

Fairway: A long stretch involving a neatly maintained grass which runs between the green and the tee box.

Green: The smooth grassy area at the end of a fairway especially prepared for putting and positioning the hole.

Handicap: A system used to rate the average number of strokes above par a player scores in one round of golf.

Hazard: Anything on a golf course that is designed to be hazardous to one's score.

Moving Day: Saturday of a golf tournament. The day you make your move to win on Sunday.

Mulligan: A second chance (do over) to perform an action, usually after the first chance went wrong through bad luck or a blunder.

Par: The number of strokes a golfer is expected to need to complete the play of one hole on a golf course.

Putt: Any shot taken by a putter when you are on the green.

Putting from the green: Getting the ball to the green is a goal because it makes the putting easier and reduces one's overall score.

Putting from the rough: Is more challenging than putting from the green because traditionally the rough is higher grass and a more challenging shot.

Rough: The taller grass that borders the fairway.

Sweet Spot: A specific area of the clubface, found within the perimeter defined by the grooves. It represents the precise area where the golf ball should be hit for optimal results.

Online Writing Instruction Terms

OWI: Online writing instruction or instructor
OWC: Online writing course
OL: Online learning or online learner
OWPA: Online writing program administrator

Other Terms

LMS: Learning management system
CMS: Content management system
GTA: Graduate teaching assistant
WPA: Writing program administrator
F2F: Face-to-face
UX: User experience
XA: Experience architecture
UCD: User-centered design

Section 1: Design

Welcome to the Design section of this collection! We selected the above golf course picture to illustrate how challenging a course can be and how one has to be strategic not to land in the sand! The golf image also illustrates how golf course designers are strategic in their choices. They plan their golf courses to be challenging and rewarding.

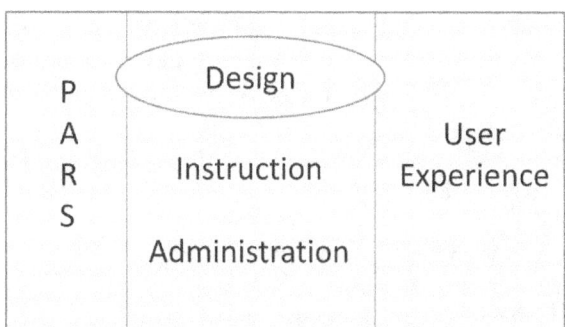

This is our goal for you when you think about designing your online writing courses, go for both challenging and rewarding, but always keep access in the front of your mind! This section has chapters that focus mostly on the challenges of course design and the choices we make as instructional designers. As Blythe (2001) pointed out, often online writing instructors are forced into a dual role of instructor and designer with very little professional training. The chapters in this section address this duality head on and share with you some useful tips and tricks for mitigating some of the challenges that come with designing online writing courses or programs. The audience for the chapters in this section is both instructors who may have to design and teach their own courses, and administrators who may be looking to design the courses in their writing programs. The chapters in this section are applicable to both novice and experienced course designers. As discussed, design is one of the PARS approach layers and your course design needs to be personal, accessible, responsive and strategic.

Design is one of the first things your students will see when they log into a course. **Personal** design is important. You can make your course design more personal by doing a few quick things:

- Use colors and images on the content pages in the learning management system
- Create an intr.oduction video.
- Put your picture on the syllabus along with your content information.
- Ensure your tone is upbeat/friendly/inviting in the text you write throughout the course including announcements, assignments, and discussion prompts.

Accessible design builds on ADA compliance (ada.gov) and allows students to better connect with content, and connect with you and with their peers. A few quick things you can do to ensure an accessible design are:

- Simplify the navigation in the LMS (learning management system) and reduce the number of clicks it takes a student to find things.
- Make sure your videos are closed caption with a written script available and that the video length is close to or under five minutes.
- Ensure you create (or adapt) assignments that allow for flexible submission formats as some students may be working only from their cell phones.
- Consider how students will access the course content and re-imagine and test assignments for digital spaces.

Responsive design ensures open lines of communication are maintained between you and the students. It also ensures that your students know how and when to contact you so that you don't have to work 24/7.

- Tell students how/when/where the class meets and if it is asynchronous, synchronous.
- Post office hours, days off and email response times—work-life balance is important!
- Post a course calendar so you and your students can plan ahead for major writing assignments and smaller assignments.
- Convey to students how you'll grade and post response times for grades.

Strategic design pulls everything together.

- Map out your course goals and how you're going to accomplish them by using a consistent weekly or module layout, which might include things such as a week/module overview, objectives, readings, lessons/lectures, discussion, and the writing assignment.
- Be strategic about what tools from the learning management system you plan to use, and what other external technology tools you're going to use in your class.
- Review your course materials to ensure you are providing information through various channels and including all learning styles.
- Plan out your assignments so that they are not all due at one time or due during a busy week in your personal life.

The chapters in this section model these practices and offer you ideas on how you can implement them. Crawley's chapter, for example, asks you to use Shipka's "statement of goals and choices" (2011) as a strategic framework to think about your technology tools and how you use them in your online writing courses. Geary's chapter illustrates how to design an accelerated technical writing course with the PARS framework in mind to create a course that is structured, accessible, outcomes focused, and facilitates connection among students and the instructor. Stewart's chapter addresses the challenge of time zones and digital spaces and how to design a course that is more responsive to students' needs. Sibo's chapter argues for instructors to consider reducing the literacy load of their online courses as they design and to utilize the small student cohort model in order to expand student collaboration and peer to peer learning. And lastly, Smith, et al.'s chapter illustrates how designing an online writing course using a grid-based approach to scaffolding and customizing assignment sequences can benefit instructors and administrators in a myriad of ways.

References

Blythe, S. (2001). Designing online courses: User-centered practices. *Computers and Composition, 18*(4), 329–346.

Shipka, J. (2011). *Toward a composition made whole*. University of Pittsburgh Press.

Chapter 1. Online Writing Instructors as Strategic Caddies: Reading Digital Landscapes and Selecting Online Learning Tools

Kristy Liles Crawley
FORSYTH TECHNICAL COMMUNITY COLLEGE

Abstract: With so many tools to choose from such as listservs, discussion boards, video conferencing apps, blogs, podcasts, and Second Life, instructors' decisions become complicated and research or trial and error become cumbersome ways to pinpoint obstacles or flaws in online learning tools. To streamline the online tool selection process, in this chapter, I utilize Jody Shipka's statement of goals and choices (SOGC) (2011) as a strategic framework for choosing an appropriate online learning tool for specific goals and audiences. I focus on key questions adapted from SOGC to examine learning goals, audience, context, and online learning tools' capabilities and limitations. To illustrate the efficacy of SOGC, I apply SOGC to determine if I should use a discussion board forum or Zoom, a video conferencing tool, in my composition class to interrogate the tools' alignment with my students' needs and learning goals for a peer response session. Through my application of SOGC, I argue that SOGC assists instructors in strategically aligning online learning tools with students' needs and learning goals. Overall, SOGC prompts instructors to articulate their reasons for using specific learning tools. With new learning tools constantly emerging, SOGC serves as a sound framework for strategic online tool selection.

Keywords: strategic, online learning tools, statement of goals and choices, Jody Shipka, peer response, Zoom, discussion boards

In hopes of coaching their players to victory, caddies strategically calculate yardage, select the best club, and ponder ideal body mechanics conducive to a flawless swing while considering obstacles such as wind speed, hills, water, bunkers, and sand traps. Of course, in movies like Caddyshack (1980), they also worry about pesky, dancing gophers. Like contemplative caddies, online writing instructors strategically select tools to help students achieve specific goals. With so many tools to choose from such as listservs, discussion boards, video conferencing software, blogs, podcasts, and Second Life (secondlife.com), instructors' decisions become complicated and research or trial and error become the only ways to pinpoint obstacles or flaws in online learning tools. To limit the overwhelming task of sampling numerous tools, instructors often experiment with a few tools or default to the primary tools built into their college's LMS.

To avoid a default or "trial and error" method when selecting tools, instructors, like caddies, need a strategic approach. For caddies, each shot calls for the strategic approach of reading the greens. Serving as composers when recording their observations, they provide a clear reading of the landscape as they consider goals and obstacles before they choose the best club for the shot. Although a similar reading process takes place for instructors, how do instructors read the digital classroom landscape to determine the best learning tools for a specific audience's goals?

In this chapter, I utilize Jody Shipka's (2011) statement of goals and choices (SOGC) as a framework for choosing an appropriate online learning tool for specific goals and audiences. SOGC fits into the PARS (personal, accessible, responsive, strategic) framework due to its focus on personal and strategic. Below I have adapted Shipka's SOGC's questions so that each question focuses on digital tools:

1. "What, specifically, is this piece [tool] trying to accomplish . . . ? In other words, what work does, or might this piece [tool] do? For whom? In what contexts?"
2. "How did you end up [using this tool] as opposed to others . . . ? How did [this tool] allow you to accomplish things that other [tools] would not have?" (p. 114).

The first question focuses on goals, the tool's capabilities, audience, and context. The second question prompts instructors to reflect on the tool's weaknesses and strengths compared to others. To illustrate the efficacy of SOGC, I apply the aforementioned questions to determine if I should use Zoom (zoom.us), a video conferencing tool, as opposed to a discussion board forum in my composition class for peer response sessions. I apply SOGC to Zoom in order to interrogate the tool's alignment with my students' needs and learning goals. Because tools of the same type such as Blackboard's Collaborate (blackboard.com), a similar video conference tool, possess only slight differences, it is not worthwhile to apply SOGC due to their almost identical approaches to student learning. Obviously, there are not correct answers to SOGC's guiding questions. SOGC provides a foundation for making an informed decision. Through my application of SOGC, I argue that SOGC assists instructors in strategically aligning online learning tools with students' needs and learning goals.

The Strategic Caddy: Reading the Landscape via SOGC

Each year Callaway, Ping, Cleveland, and so many other brands release new golf clubs on the market with the promise of driving distance and accuracy. Caddies strategically fill bags with clubs aligned with their players' needs in mind.

Acknowledging a player's slow swing speed, a caddy selects an ultralight hybrid club with high-strength stainless steel to enable the player to powerfully launch the ball without being encumbered with a heavy club. With an in-depth knowledge of their players' strengths and limitations, caddies thoughtfully advise players.

Similarly, instructors' knowledge of students and context aids in online tool selection, a process best performed with SOGC. While I am using Shipka's SOGC as a framework for strategic tool selection, Shipka's SOGC originally focused on student writers' detailed statements of their goals and choices. In the classroom, Shipka (2011) asked students to "detail how, why, and "under what conditions they made their rhetorical, technological, and methodological choices" (p. 113). For example, students pondered the following questions: Is the composer successful in communicating his or her message? Why did the composer choose to include a hyperlink near the bottom of the page? What tools did they use to create their work? Why did they use these tools? By formulating answers to the aforementioned questions, students become aware of the choices that the composer made, and when students create their own texts, they too will be conscious of the choices that they make. When they deliberately reflect on their choices or others' choices, they recognize the importance of audience because all choices are tied to audience. Because they are considering their choices, students' revisions will also be meaningful. If they cannot articulate a specific choice, they may find that another choice assists them in communicating their message more effectively.

Keeping Shipka's emphasis on choices, I adapted Shipka's SOGC to reflect the choices instructors make in the process of online tool selection. To begin the process of tool selection, I address the first set of SOGC questions: "What, specifically, is this piece [tool] trying to accomplish...? In other words, what work does, or might this piece[tool] do? For whom? In what contexts?" (Shipka, 2011, p. 114). By responding to SOGC questions, I focus on audience and context. For example, if I were using a peer review tool, I would ask myself what this tool is trying to accomplish. The answer would be peer review, and then I would consider the work the tool would do for my students in the context of our course. With audience and context in mind, instructors strategically select tools when designing an effective online writing course.

Audience

When selecting online tools, I envision the work tools perform for specific users under unique circumstances. In other words, I read the digital classroom landscape to determine the best learning tools for a specific group of students. Part of exploring the digital landscape involves course mapping that assists instructors in designing a course. While this chapter does not focus on creating course maps, SOGC's concern for audience aligns with course design considerations addressed in Borgman and McArdle's (2019) Personal, Accessible, Responsible, Strategic:

Resources and Strategies for Online Writing Instructors. According to Borgman and McArdle (2019), "The main thing to consider when creating a course design is who are your student users. How will they be accessing the content? How comfortable are they with technology? What do they need to learn to move on to the next course?" (p. 72). SOGC builds on these useful design questions by further examining audience and context for online learning tools. Considering most community colleges and universities possess diverse student populations, I included concerns related to audience and context below as a guide for interrogating tools.

Age

It is easy to label students in their teens or twenties as tech savvy digital natives and older adults as technologically challenged. Do not let misleading assumptions persuade you to think certain tools will be challenging or easy to use for some students. Often students rely on the same transferable knowledge they utilize in new writing situations. Downs and Wardle (2012) underscore the important role transferable knowledge plays in new learning situations:

> While we may not be able to teach students transferable writing skills, we can provide them with transferable writing knowledge that they can take with them to help them work through any writing/communication assignment. As different writing situations offer different answers, the transferable knowledge is not the answers but the questions: not "how to write," but how to ask about how to write. (p. 134)

When confronted with new tools, students often rely on their prior knowledge. Their previous technological experiences help them shape questions and expedite their learning. For instance, when I assist advisees with registering for classes for the first time, they frequently say, "Is this like adding items to an Amazon shopping cart?" Students draw connections between learning technologies and the technologies they experience in the military, in their workplace, or in their personal lives such as gaming or shopping. Their transferable knowledge accelerates the learning process. Likewise, classroom peers enhance the learning process by serving as mentors to those struggling with new tools.

Academic Standing

Freshman composition students may have their first LMS experience in your classroom whereas in an advanced composition class, students have completed more than one college-level class. For freshman or returning students who are re-taking FYW in a digital environment, they may rely on their personal experiences with technology and peer mentoring, as noted in the previous section on age. For advanced composition students, your FYW class in conjunction with the other classes afforded them experience with your college's LMS as well as specific online learning tools. Even for students taking all face-to-face classes for multiple years, their LMS use is likely because many instructors utilize an LMS as a supplemental resource. Although freshmen and advanced composition students never experience all online learning tools, their transferable knowledge increases with multiple classes' use of different online learning tools.

Accessibility

When considering the work that online learning tools perform for students, instructors must consider accessibility. Tools with closed captioning and screen readers assist those with hearing and visual impairments as well as benefit students in other ways. In a 2014 study, Berg et al. observed that "students commented that the captions made it easier to take notes, improved understanding by watching and reading, helped them learn the spellings of words, enabled them to watch the videos with the sound turned off, and enabled them to follow the videos more closely, as the captions helped focus attention" (p. 5). While captions potentially enhance all students' understanding, captions seem especially beneficial for second language learners to see and hear words to reinforce their understanding of words they may encounter for the first time or words that appear unclear due to a speaker's accent, rate of speech, volume, or pitch. As an accessibility feature, captions aid in diminishing language barriers to help level the playing field so that native English speakers do not have an advantage over ESL speakers.

Additionally, accessibility features coincide with students' lifestyles. A student in my class once mentioned that she loved the closed-captioned feature because she could silently read the text of the video while her children slept. Another student shared his experience with listening to course lectures on his cell phone when driving or working around the house. Both examples undergird the importance of online tools' accessibility features.

Social Class

Seeing students on their cell phones, tablets, and laptops around campus makes it appear like all students have unlimited access to devices and the internet. However, deep concerns emerge when one considers the materiality of writing technologies. Wysocki (2004) notes that materiality may be

> understood more broadly to refer to a host of socioeconomic conditions contributing to writing production, such as the availability of certain kinds of schooling, number of students in writing classes, student financial aid (and the need for it), public health, access to time and quiet. (p. 3)

Students' limited time and resources weigh heavily in the decision to incorporate certain tools. In some instances, when possessing minimum wage jobs and supporting families, students rely on financial aid to cover educational expenses. Such considerations prompt instructors to reflect on economic challenges and thoughtfully respond to the following questions: Do students rely on borrowing campus computers or using computers in a campus lab? Are students' access to computers restricted to certain times? Do these devices support the tools that you want to use? How much does the learning tool cost? Will the cost be considered as course materials that will be covered by financial aid? Some tools have free versions but require users to pay for more advanced features. Will the university pay for a campus-wide subscription? Can the tools perform with slower internet speeds and function efficiently on various devices and operating systems?

The aforementioned questions overlap with the important considerations noted above in my discussion on accessibility. By ensuring that each student has access to technology, instructors avoid the scenario that only those with extensive funds have access to technology others cannot afford. To guarantee access, SOGC questions focus on how online learning tools perform work for specific users. Acknowledging students' diversity and specific needs, instructors can employ SOGC questions to ignite conversations between faculty, administrators, students, and financial aid representatives to ensure accessibility.

Context

While students' personal characteristics inform tool selection, the context of the course in terms of timing and modality influence tool selection as well. In the past, colleges subscribed to the quarter or semester system, but now instructors teach a wide spectrum of shorter classes throughout the year from eight-week or four-week classes to self-paced classes with rolling registration dates. Varying time frames prompt instructors to consider several points. For shorter lengths of time, do students have enough time to learn to use a specific online tool effectively? Does this tool play a role in participation or coursework throughout the semester or will this tool be used only one time? Your answers to questions concerning time, cost, and use prove whether a specific tool is a worthwhile investment.

Similar questions connected to context involve synchronous and asynchronous online components. Prior to registration, course descriptions disclose the expectation of synchronous or asynchronous online participation. When selecting tools, consider whether the tool functions best in a synchronous or asynchronous setting. If the class does not have synchronous meetings, is it feasible to ask students to collaborate synchronously through online learning tools on their own time for group work? Considering students' outside commitments to family and employers, tools geared toward synchronous interactions can be punitive when students are unable to interact with their classmates in a timely manner to collaborate and complete assigned work.

Strategically Aiming for a Hole in One: Applying SOGC to Zoom Peer Response Sessions

In order for readers to see SOGC in action, I am applying it to Zoom, a free video conferencing tool that I am using for the first time in a peer response session in my synchronous online composition class. For clarity, I am reposting the SOGC questions above my responses.

> What, specifically, is this piece [tool] trying to accomplish . . .?
> In other words, what work does, or might this piece[tool] do?
> For whom? In what contexts? (Shipka, 2001, p. 114)

Prior to addressing what Zoom accomplishes in an online peer review session, I will first describe the students and specific context. My freshman composition class is made up of twenty-two students at Forsyth Technical Community College in Winston-Salem, North Carolina. With only four students older than thirty, the majority of the class, eighteen students, was under thirty. In an informal discussion, I gathered information about the students' familiarity with Zoom. None of the students mentioned using Zoom or similar apps in other classes. With most of them being in college for only one or two semesters, their potential for in-class experience is limited. A few students used Zoom for personal interactions prior to our peer response session while the majority of the class depended on their knowledge of Skype or similar apps for understanding Zoom's features. Only three students claimed they did not have any knowledge of Zoom or similar apps. Due to students' varying levels of knowledge, I created a voiceover PowerPoint video with captions to demonstrate how to access and use Zoom's basic features. With the majority of students relying on financial aid to cover educational expenses, Zoom's basic plan with free unlimited meetings eliminated any financial obstacles involving financial aid or out of pocket costs.

In terms of Zoom's performance, Zoom's video, screen-sharing, chat feature, and recording capabilities make the work involved in online peer review possible. Because students conveyed their comments orally, the chat feature was not used. However, students desiring to use the closed captioning feature were able to do so. Prior to beginning their meeting, the groups activated the record feature to ensure that I was able to watch their session and they were able to listen to the recording when revising their work. Having access to peer response questions and their peers' papers prior to the meeting, groups of four students met via Zoom. Due to the small group size, the students' images were not minimized to tiny thumbnails. Instead, students could clearly see their peers' facial expressions and hear their tone of voice throughout the session. They periodically shared their screen when they needed to revisit the peer review questions typed on a Microsoft Word document. Likewise, students shared screens when referring to specific passages within their peers' papers and used the annotation tools to underline certain phrases or circle particular words.

> How did you end up [using this tool] as opposed to others...?
> How did [this tool] allow you to accomplish things that other [tools] would not have? (Shipka, 2001, p. 114)

Prior to using Zoom for a peer response session, I utilized Blackboard's discussion board for peer response sessions. Craving interactions akin to those in a face-to-face peer response session, I turned to Zoom's features to accomplish more effectively the goal of students participating in an active writing community. Some discussion board posts often consist of short, unsupported points such as "Great job!" or "I liked your paper. It is interesting." Frequently, discussion board responses did not include a conversation between the author and responders. After the responders posted their comments, authors rarely posed follow-up questions or comments.

Although the question sheet provided a guide for responders, the groups appeared to engage in authentic conversations about writing. The screen sharing feature allowed responders to be more specific. Instead of mentioning that the author needed to elaborate on a certain point, the screen sharing feature enabled responders to physically point to a specific passage that needs additional examples. Through pointing, drawing, and describing, authors' engagement and interest increased as I noticed more authors commenting in response to their peers' suggestions. Some comments consisted of clarification questions such as "Are you saying that the fourth paragraph should be the first body paragraph?" Other comments seemed appreciative or reaffirming as in "That makes sense now." Additional comments outside of advice for improvement surfaced during Zoom sessions underscoring the idea of community. Because papers focused on problems in their chosen profession, some students briefly conveyed their own personal stories related to the author's topic.

Despite strides in creating an active writing community through building personal connections through interactions, reserved students and unprepared students, in some cases, struggled to articulate their responses in the conversations unfolding over the fifty-minute class meeting in which only forty of the minutes could be dedicated to Zoom because its free basic plan only allows forty minutes for meetings with more than three participants. Often when shy or reserved students paused to gather their thoughts, extroverted students' voices frequently filled the silence. The timed meetings failed to provide responders with time for reflection. For those unprepared for the meeting, the timed peer response session did not allow them to stop and read their peers' papers. Instead their brief comments highlighted their minimal participation while prepared responders shared their substantive comments. Acknowledging this challenge in Zoom peer response sessions inspires me to ponder solutions for equal participation opportunities and recognize that tools such as asynchronous discussion boards do provide time for reflection and space for all voices to be heard as students write their responses in a limitless space. Similarly, questions of the quality of comments in a synchronous conversation via Zoom offer little room for careful planning and expansion. In his discussion of asynchronous discussion boards, Warnock (2009) stated, "I find that the natural delay helps conversations on the boards achieve a level of sophistication beyond many, if not most, onsite class discussions" (p. 70). Warnock's astute observation motivates instructors to consider online learning tools' roles in encouraging or stifling in-depth, sophisticated responses. High stakes and low stakes assignments often determine the level of sophistication needed in the phases of working on specific projects.

Solutions such as establishing roles and rubrics allow for further improvements in Zoom peer responses. In an eCampus News article, Stansbury (2008) pointed to rubrics as a possible solution, as she highlighted that for "real learning to occur in an online setting, virtual-school educators must establish clear rubrics and enforce rules for participation" (par. 1). Likewise, the roles that instructors typically play in an online course can be transferred to students. Roles such as facilitator or moderator offer students the ability to pace their discussion. The aforementioned suggestions serve as potential solutions. In some cases, reserved and unprepared students may not participate, but through rubrics and clearly defined roles, students become aware of expectations tied to participation and accountability. These potential solutions serve as a starting point as I ponder strategies for revision.

Final Thoughts and Application

At the end of a round of golf, caddies with their players often gather in the clubhouse to congratulate today's winners and enjoy refreshments. Amidst the jovial atmosphere, caddies and players reflect on how they initially read the greens and how the greens actually played. With insights gained through experience, caddies revise strategies to assist players in executing skilled shots in tomorrow's game.

Similarly, after classes utilize online learning tools, instructors celebrate their victories and reflect on strategies for improvement. Through reflecting on SOGC, instructors carefully consider how online learning tools align with their students' needs as well as the course's context and objectives. In other words, SOGC's emphasis on the personal and strategic, two of the key elements of the PARS approach to online teaching, assists instructors in making informed decisions. In the peer response example above, Zoom's features performed the work needed for students to engage in an active writing community, and the synchronous nature of the course made the Zoom meeting possible, but revisions, as illustrated by my SOGC responses above, need to be made in terms of extending time for the sessions and encouraging reserved and underprepared students to participate.

Furthermore, a different context and a different set of students transform SOGC responses and bring about new areas for revision. In terms of context, an asynchronous class poses logistical challenges as students must agree to a time to meet, which differs from engaging in a peer review session during a synchronous class meeting that happens on a weekly basis. Similarly, other obstacles emerge in a different context.

When changing the context to one involving Zoom being used for a large class discussion, differences in participation and sense of community arise. Reed (2020) noted,

> Some professors argued, correctly, that it's disheartening in Zoom to talk to a bunch of black boxes with names in them. Cold-calling those black boxes often result in silence, strongly implying that the student isn't actually there. Good discussions—one of the affordances of synchronous technology—require that people are actually tuned in. (para. 3)

The black boxes and unresponsive students, in some cases, allude to a disconnect between the goal of active class participation and Zoom's minimization of students' presence. Tanya Joosten further confirms the disconnect between a large class discussion via Zoom and engagement: "Video conferencing tools end up encouraging 'teacher-centered learning,' Joosten says. While these platforms are meant to facilitate multiway interaction, she says, they effectively collapse into one-way communication after a certain number of people join in" (as cited in Supiano, 2020, para. 11). Joosten's description of teacher-centered learning via Zoom illustrates the importance of SOGC's final question: "How did [this tool] allow you to accomplish things that other [tools] would not have?" (Shipka, 2001, p. 114). In this case, Zoom's features fail to perform work that other tools are able to do. Discussion boards outshine Zoom in terms of large groups' participation, for discussion boards afford all students space to participate through their written posts. Unlike a timed Zoom meeting, an asynchronous discussion board forum allows time for reflection.

The large group discussion example above highlights SOGC's ability to affirm one's reasons for utilizing a specific learning tool or acknowledge the tool's limitations that keep it from satisfying students' needs and aiding students in meeting course objectives. There are never right or wrong answers for SOGC. Overall, SOGC replaces random trial and error with a strategic approach to online learning tool selection involving the following steps:

- Identify the work a tool performs for a specific audience and context.
- Recognize reasons for using a tool in light of a project's goals.
- Pinpoint how a tool enables you to accomplish goals that other tools do not. (Shipka, 2001, p. 114)

When following the steps listed above, instructors soon discover SOGC is not a flawless approach to tool selection. Sometimes instructors have clear goals and choices for a tool, but the tool does not function as planned, so revisions become inevitable. Results vary with differing contexts, students, and learning objectives. Considering all learning tools possess limitations or weaknesses, SOGC prompts instructors to articulate their reasons for using specific learning tools. With new learning tools constantly emerging, SOGC serves as a sound framework for strategic tool selection.

References

Berg, R., Brand, A., Grant, J., Kirk, J. S. & Zimmerman, T. (2014). Leveraging recorded mini-lectures to increase student learning. *Online Classroom, 14*(2), 5.

Borgman, J. & McArdle, C. (2019). *Personal, accessible, responsive, strategic: Resources and strategies for online writing instructors.* The WAC Clearinghouse; University Press of Colorado. https://doi.org/10.37514/PRA-B.2019.0322.

Downs, D. & Wardle, E. (2012). Reimagining the nature of FYC: Trends in writing-about-writing pedagogies. In K. Ritter & P. K. Matsuda (Eds.), *Exploring composition studies: Sites, issues, and perspectives* (pp. 123–144). Utah State University Press.

Ramis, H. (1980). *Caddyshack* [film]. Orion Pictures.

Reed, M. (2020, May 13). Should showing faces be mandatory: A new question posed by technology. *Inside Higher Ed.* https://www.insidehighered.com/blogs/confessions-community-college-dean/should-showing-faces-be-mandatory.

Shipka, J. (2011). *Toward a composition made whole.* University of Pittsburgh Press.

Stansbury, M. (2008). Online insight: Challenges beat cheerleading. *eSchool News.* https://www.eschoolnews.com/2008/05/08/online-insight-challenges-beat-cheerleading/.

Supiano, B. (2020, April 2). "Zoomed out": Why "live" teaching isn't always the best. *The Chronicle of Higher Education.* https://www.chronicle.com/newsletter/teaching/2020-04-02.

Warnock, S. (2009). *Teaching writing online: Why and how.* National Council of Teachers of English.

Wysocki, A. F. (2004). Opening new media to writing: Openings and justifications. In A. F. Wysocki, J. Johnson-Eilola, C. L. Selfe & G. Sirc (Eds.), *Writing new media: Theory and applications for expanding the teaching of composition* (pp. 1–41). Utah State University Press.

Chapter 2. My Online Instruction Mulligan: How PARS Transformed My Technical Writing Community College Course

Thomas M. Geary
Tidewater Community College (Virginia Beach, VA)

Abstract: In this chapter, I will delve into the affordances of PARS-informed (personal, accessible, responsive, strategic) online writing instruction in an accelerated technical writing course for an underserved, two-year college population. Influenced by user-centered design and Borgman and McArdle's (2019) PARS approach, I transformed what had previously been a stale and frustrating online course into a dynamic, participatory community tailored to my students' unique needs. The redesigned course emphasized structure, connection, and accessibility to ensure student success and completion of learning outcomes. This chapter closes with remaining challenges in efficient online writing instruction and potential applications of my strategies.

Keywords: OWI, online writing instruction, online learning, technical writing, community colleges, two-year colleges

In 2019, I taught an online writing course for the first time in several years. I was optimistic but cautiously so because despite much success in my face-to-face instruction (e.g., teaching awards and positive evaluations), certifications to teach online, and comfort operating in our learning management system and other digital spaces, I had avoided returning to what was previously an unmitigated disaster. My previous online writing courses (OWCs) were riddled with slow feedback, poorly received activities, and a loss of connection to my students. It was a lot of work—many hours of preparation and labor for both the students and me—and it was not nearly the same as my vibrant face-to-face classes. The "Position Statement of Principles and Example Effective Practices for Online Writing Instruction" (2013) developed by the Conference on College Composition and Composition (CCCC) OWI Committee highlighted as its fourth principle that the appropriate teaching strategies "should be migrated and adapted to the online instructional environment," yet my pedagogy, activities, and assignments translated poorly, if at all (para. 5). Even my personalized touches felt stiff and forced. I had underestimated how much my pedagogical strategies and my course would need to change to achieve a thriving online environment.

Yet I knew the importance of persisting and bettering myself at online writing instruction (OWI). Many students at my institution—Tidewater Community College (Virginia)—prefer or need asynchronous learning to meet their busy schedules, and I wanted to both challenge myself and dispel notions that online instruction isn't as lively or engaging. Though many may expect first-year learners at the two-year level to struggle in adapting to online learning, Shea and Bidjerano (2014) found in a National Center for Education Statistics study of 18,000 community college participants that students taking online courses experience a "boost to degree completion" and are more likely than their peers to earn a credential (p. 110). They write, "Online learning appears to represent a new path that for some students is far more efficient and effective in allowing access to and graduation from college" (Shea & Bidjerano, 2014, p. 110). If I wanted to help guide my Tidewater students to stronger professional writing habits that would benefit them across the curriculum, I had to return to my failed venture into online instruction. What I needed was an effective philosophy to aid in the redesign of my online course.

When my accelerated, eight-week Technical Report Writing class moved online due to enrollment concerns, I researched and implemented user-centered design and Borgman and McArdle's (2019) PARS (personal, accessible, responsive, strategic) approach, transforming what had previously been stale and overwhelming into a dynamic, participatory course. The results were better than I had anticipated, and this student-first course design has influenced all of my instruction, remote and in-person. In this chapter, I will detail my OWI mulligan, golf terminology for a chance at redemption after an initial blunder. I will share my experiences and analyze practical strategies and affordances for each of the PARS elements as well as limitations for implementing the philosophy in a fast-paced course designed for the often-underserved two-year college population. After establishing the unique needs of the students in my community college courses, I will review successes and perceived failures in personalizing my instruction, making my courses more accessible, becoming more responsive, and implementing strategies that foreground student success.

Community College Students

The first step to effectively designing any user experience, particularly one that involves students in a writing classroom, is to know the audience. Though many online teaching strategies may be intended as universal, what works in one situation—for example, for advanced students—may fall flat for others—like those for students who lack experience or confidence in their abilities. My OWC is designed for those who most need a meaningful connection, a clear sense of structure, and consistent guidance: two-year college students.

With many adult learners, first generation students, parents, full-time and part-time workers, and active and retired military, Tidewater Community

College in Virginia enrolled 33,000 students in 2017–2018, making it the second-largest community college in the state ("About TCC," 2020). Tidewater's student population is not unlike many two-year institutions across America with many students historically disadvantaged and/or facing food, job, transportation, or housing insecurity. A 2019 report by ITHAKA, an educational non-profit organization with a focus on digital preservation and increased access and affordability, revealed students struggling to balance basic needs with academic and professional responsibilities (Blankenship et al., 2019). A survey of 10,844 currently enrolled community college students found that over half of respondents—56 percent of whom are first generation, 32 percent born outside the United States, and 75 percent working adults—identified difficulty balancing school responsibilities with jobs, family life, and basic needs (Blankenship et al., 2019). The increased challenges faced by two-year students, including access, lack of academic preparation, and necessary resources, put them at a disadvantage in succeeding in higher education, particularly when an online course—especially a technical writing course needed by many students seeking a career in medical fields, business, engineering, or the sciences—is poorly designed or lacking in engagement.

Community college degree and certificate attainment has risen since the 1990s, yet many are failing to complete their goals. Mullin (2011) reports that 630,000 associate degrees were awarded in 2009–2010,—with 40 percent in the humanities or liberal arts and sciences—an increase of 86 percent from 1989–1990. Community college students regularly enroll to advance in the workplace and earn licenses and credentials, yet the vast majority fall short. The Century Foundation (2019) reports, "Only 38 percent of students entering community college complete a degree or certificate within six years. While 81 percent of students entering community college say they aspire to eventually transfer and receive a four-year degree, only 15 percent do so after six years" (p. 1). This dire situation has been the impetus for guided pathways restructuring, needs assessments and initiatives to address food and housing insecurity, and pushes for compassionate pedagogy.

For OWI strategies to be tailored to community college students and aid students in becoming stronger academic and technical writers across the curriculum, they must reach this under-represented population. They must also be easily utilized by faculty whose workload is 30 credits (15 credits, or five three-credit courses, per semester) minimum, with many instructors at Tidewater and other two-year institutions taking on overload credits each semester. Successful online writing strategies for my mulligan needed to be straightforward, easy to tailor and implement, and designed for the underserved. Borgman and McArdle's (2019) *Personal, Accessible, Responsive, Strategic: Resources and Strategies for Online Writing Instructors* meets that criteria as it carefully considers a wide range of students and faculty entering digital spaces and builds on user experience design principles.

PARS: Personal, Accessible, Responsive, Strategic

To use a golf metaphor, as frequently used in Borgman and McArdle's (2019) text, the problem for many community college students—especially those in fast-paced eight-week courses—is not that they are failing to sink their putts. The issue is that many have never been to a golf course. They do not even know how to hold a driver let alone get a ball on the green. Thus, the rhetorical design of the PARS approach centers on the audience. It is tailored to guiding online instructors to pay close attention to user experience: one that is highly structured yet loose and accommodating for the students. A practical application of a user-centered approach, created from years of collective experience of observations and feedback from students, rather than the systems-design too often utilized (Eyman, 2009), the PARS approach focuses course design and delivery on ensuring student success and completion of learning outcomes.

Contemporary user experience design, according to Greer and Harris (2018), aims to build a culture with three steps: "user research, iterative design, and collaboration" (p. 2). User research is gathered from useful insights and not simply likability, and iterative design "assumes and requires that products and platforms be revisable, flexible, and dynamic" (Greer & Harris, 2018, p. 3). Collaboration occurs between designers, instructors, and students, with the latter entering after a course is designed; Greer and Harris (2018) argue for student involvement early in the process. In the PARS approach, student feedback is solicited early in the course and the instructor both gets to know the students and collaborates with them to develop a dynamic class through personalization of the content.

Personal

Foregrounding unique, personal practices ensures that the student is central to all decision-making; in implementing user experience design and PARS elements, I paid close attention to these student necessities for the ideal digital learning environment and then aimed to meet those needs. Among the personal touches added to my Technical Report Writing course are the inclusion of a course overview, multimedia, and one-on-one connections.

Martinez et al. (2017) note in their national survey of students in online writing courses the need for a tutorial or online orientation. A brief overview of the main areas of the digital space was an important first step in breaking any communication barriers. In addition to a Canvas learning management system orientation quiz, in my course modules area, I set up a "how to navigate the course" table with descriptions of each tab (course area) for students. Each course content module, which I keep limited to seven and aligned with

My Online Instruction Mulligan 35

major topics and assignments, has an overview, learning objectives, and clearly labeled headings (e.g., readings, videos, assignments). Finally, the home page of the course features images that link students directly to the most often visited course areas: the syllabus, course information, an "about your instructor" page, the learning modules, and online support.

To further establish myself as personable and welcoming, I follow Borgman and McArdle's (2019) advice to "create learning opportunities that appeal to the various senses" (p. 20) by integrating a Prezi (prezi.com) "about me" with embarrassing facts of my guilty pleasures (see Figure 2.1) to highlight that I am also human. Sure, it builds credibility to read about my doctoral studies and 15+ years of teaching experience, but I want students to reach out to me any time in a conversational manner, and if they know of my awful childhood photo (see Figure 2.2) or aversion of mayonnaise or my love of The Bachelor television series, I am more likely to gain their attention. My Prezi introduction blends images, video, audio, and text to appeal to students, and it's the first of many multimodal readings. Students can likewise create their own Prezi introductions, post audio or video greetings, or attempt something creative to bridge the gap of the personalization lost when not in a face-to-face class. I encourage each student to make themselves more than just a name—and perhaps an avatar—on a discussion board.

Figure 2.1. Prezi likes and dislikes.

Figure 2.2. An unflattering childhood photo.

I also post weekly overview videos and short personal "shout outs" to students through the Canvas Studio (community.canvaslms.com) tool. These personalized videos (see Figure 2.3) let students know that my video recordings are not generic but individualized to respect the organic nature of every class. The recordings, as per Borgman and McArdle's (2019) recommendation and awareness of two-year student challenges with consistent computer access and/or reliable access or bandwidth, are typically at four minutes or less, though weekly overviews tend to run a bit longer (up to eight minutes at most) as I connect stories and strategies to readings and assignments. For example, I elaborate on the importance of a unique cover letter by sharing one of my own failures during a job search while in college. If students comment on the video and find that narrative engaging, I might extend the next week's video on designing instructions. I aim to connect with each class uniquely the same way that a performer does at comedy shows, reading the room to improvise and build on what works.

My Tidewater students have remarked on many occasions that they have not enjoyed English courses in the past—possibly due to struggles with the course content—but the unique video recordings result in positive feedback and encouraging course evaluations. These personal connections cannot fully replicate the face-to-face class, but the short video clips demonstrate to students that I care about their access, an important factor for the students at my institution.

Figure 2.3. Canvas Studio video uploads.

Accessible

The second strategy in the PARS approach, accessible, is defined by Borgman and McArdle (2019) as removing obstacles to learning online as "the isolated nature of working online creates enough barriers for students, so navigating your course and finding what they need to be successful should not be an additional barrier" (p. 38). Accessibility involves understanding the target audience and continuous reflection, the process of assessing one's own instruction, including technology usage, and design throughout and after a semester (McCabe & Gonzalez-Flores, 2017). I strive to foster an accessible classroom through open educational resources, a needs survey, and visual clarity and general flexibility, taking into account Bjork's (2018) strategies for blending user experience design and digital rhetoric.

For six years, I have relied entirely on open educational resources (OERs) to keep the cost of course materials free for students. With students already facing many financial hardships, the cost of a textbook should be the least of their concerns. I was an early adopter of Tidewater's Z Degree (zero cost textbook) initiative, in which all courses use OERs or public domain material, and the move from costly textbooks to Creative Commons licensed resources has allowed me the flexibility and freedom to find resources of various modalities for my students, including but not limited to articles, videos, and podcasts. Hutchins (2020) contends that OERs pair well with student smartphones, increasingly used for educational purposes, and enhance experiences for students with disabilities. I have found that nearly all students prefer using OERs because of the reduced cost and flexibility. Hutchins (2020) adds that although OERs remain underutilized with under 10 percent of college instructors adopting them, "the benefits of OER [are] not only cost savings but also accessibility, efficiency, [and] time savings" (p. 304). If a resource that I find is not highly accessible for all students—including closed captions for videos, easy navigation, and optimization for any device—then I can find and adopt a new resource at any point. A few high-quality OER repositories for composition and technical writing instructors include OER Commons (oercommons.org), Writing Commons (writingcommons.org), and Saylor Academy (saylor.org). These collections have significantly improved accessibility of course content in my Z Degree courses.

Early in the semester, I also disseminate a technological needs survey (see Figure 2.4) to determine what concerns exist regarding internet connectivity, buffering of videos, types of devices available, and other possible concerns community college students might face in an OWC. The survey has been beneficial thus far, revealing issues my Tidewater students face, such as slow WiFi and a lack of webcam availability for synchronous learning, recording of presentations, and/or office hours visitation. I plan to add a follow-up needs survey in future semesters regarding the course design and content to further gauge student concerns and provide data for my continued reflection.

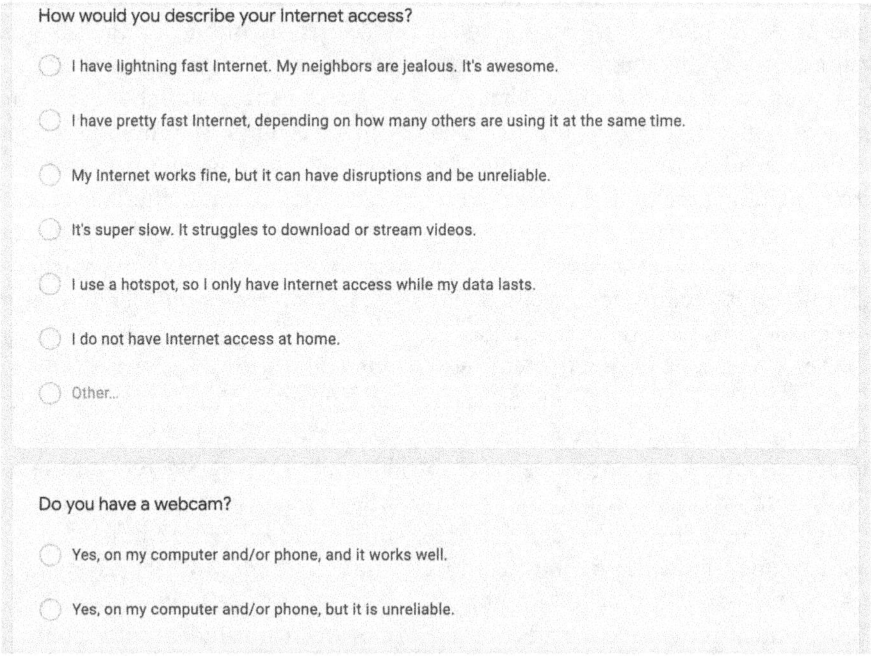

How would you describe your Internet access?

○ I have lightning fast Internet. My neighbors are jealous. It's awesome.

○ I have pretty fast Internet, depending on how many others are using it at the same time.

○ My Internet works fine, but it can have disruptions and be unreliable.

○ It's super slow. It struggles to download or stream videos.

○ I use a hotspot, so I only have Internet access while my data lasts.

○ I do not have Internet access at home.

○ Other...

Do you have a webcam?

○ Yes, on my computer and/or phone, and it works well.

○ Yes, on my computer and/or phone, but it is unreliable.

Figure 2.4. Technology needs survey.

The design of content in my courses is intended to be visually consistent and appealing. Document design principles in user experience aid in reading comprehension and demonstrate concern regarding student accessibility of content, particularly with my open educational resources replacing a textbook. Jones (2018) highlights the importance of collaboration and input from students in syllabus design, and those principles similarly apply to the design and delivery of a learning management system's course content. Jones (2018) notes, "headings, density of text, and white space can work along or against other design elements to increase accessibility of information or to cause readers to disengage with the text" (p. 2). The consistency of weekly announcements that use bulleted lists and avoid underlined text (to avoid URL link confusion) as well as the use of graphics and calendars comfort the reader and make for a more enjoyable, accessible online experience. Adding a final review for the effective application of design principles prior to publishing a course or new content can help in improving readability and visual consistency; this step was key to my successful mulligan in online instruction.

Bjork's (2018) student-centered perspective to OWI combines usability with rhetorical implications. His heuristics for mixing user experience design and digital rhetoric include an emphasis on awareness of all student-users including those who are marginalized or with disabilities, the development of community rather than task completion, and an understanding "that tasks are never neutral acts and . . . the subject positions of student-users impact how they navigate these tasks" (2018, p. 8). Consideration of students of all backgrounds, their experiences, and their needs aids greatly in building a more accessible space for dynamic learning. We might not be able to eliminate all aspects of the digital divide, but incorporating OERs, needs surveys, and visual consistency can make for an improved user experience and more attention paid to the course content and instructor feedback from the student perspective.

Responsive

Responsiveness—the third PARS element—was essential to transforming my bogey (a bad course) into a birdie (a successful course). Though in my previous efforts I felt overwhelmed by grading and constant discussion replies, Borgman and McArdle's (2019) advice about setting boundaries and providing quick responses changed my mindset. By implementing well-designed rubrics (see Figure 2.5) and quick, holistic feedback, almost an "ungrading" method as opposed to lengthy walls of text that could intimidate, I found my feedback as a conversation with the students.

What I had been experiencing in my earlier online courses was not unusual. Borgman and McArdle (2019) elaborate on the challenge of adapting to the workload of an online course and knowing how to set limits: "Just because something exciting is available all of the time, doesn't mean being a part of it all the time is healthy or productive. Online instructors run the risk of being overly responsive" (p. 54). My eagerness to get involved in every student discussion and to offer ample feedback to each activity and assignment had burned me out, and I needed new strategies for handling the heavy workload of a two-year college instructor. I wanted to connect with each student and provide thoughtful commentary, whether in discussions, minor activities, or major assignments, but with six or seven classes of 20–25 students, it just wasn't possible.

The incorporation of a rubric and a fast, holistic set of comments saved me. It still provides students with feedback and opens a dialogue regarding their work, which can be continued during office hours or via email, without inundating them with many sentence-level remarks (or me with grading). Inspired by writing center pedagogy, comments on grammar, mechanics, and/or style are usually reserved for only the first page of a longer submission with patterns identified rather than each specific instance marked. The rubric (e.g., the Project Proposal categories of content, design, grammar and style, and Gantt chart) visually shows students where they can focus during revisions, and it allows for flexibility of a grading range for each category. Pairing the rubric with brief, timely feedback initiates an immediate conversation with the student, an important but easy to overlook aspect of teaching at the two-year college. Students can become overburdened with family, career, and coursework, but keeping them invested in their learning is more likely when feedback is unintimidating and timely.

Project Proposal

Criteria	Ratings			Pts
Content	20.0 to >15.0 pts **Strong Content** — The proposal establishes a clear rhetorical situation and feasible Technical Report topic with ample depth and research to support claims. It not only meets the assignment, but demonstrates a fully developed sense of the scope of the project. References are included.	15.0 to >8.0 pts **Average Content** — The proposal meets the assignment's objectives but lacks a strong sense of audience, topic, limitations, scope, and/or purpose. The proposal does not demonstrate sophisticated thought or a strong grasp of the target audience and may be lacking recommended sections. One or two references are included.	8.0 to >0 pts **Poor Content** — The proposal fails to meet the assignment by lacking an appropriate rhetorical situation or purpose. It does not meet length or content requirements and may not establish a clear Technical Report issue. No References are included.	20.0 pts
Design	10.0 to >8.0 pts **Strong Design** — The Project Proposal is consistent and visually appealing for the target audience. Bullet points, hierarchy of information, and appropriate white space are utilized appropriately.	8.0 to >4.0 pts **Average Design** — The Project Proposal includes some effective design elements to guide the target reader but is inconsistent. The design may impact the readability of the document.	4.0 to >0 pts **Poor Design** — Little to no attention is paid to the design elements of the Project Proposal. The target audience might struggle in understanding the document due to its poor readability.	10.0 pts
Grammar and Style	10.0 to >8.0 pts **Strong Grammar/Style** — The prose is clear and memorable. The proposal contains few, if any, grammatical or mechanical errors and illustrates the group's control of diction for the target audience.	8.0 to >4.0 pts **Average Grammar/Style** — The proposal displays weaknesses in grammar, mechanics, or punctuation through consistent but not egregious errors such as fragments, missing commas, or spelling. The vocabulary resembles a conversation and not a well thought-out professional proposal for the target audience.	4.0 to >0 pts **Poor Grammar/Style** — Excessive errors of grammar, spelling, or punctuation cause the reader to struggle to comprehend the proposal. Meaning is unclear due to incomprehensible sentences.	10.0 pts
Gantt chart	10.0 to >8.0 pts **Strong Gantt chart** — A clean and easy to comprehend Gantt chart is included with the Project Proposal. It establishes a realistic timeline for the Technical Report and includes a variety of components of the final project.	8.0 to >4.0 pts **Average Gantt chart** — An effective Gantt chart is included with the Project Proposal but it might be struggle to engage the viewer due to concerns with readability or feasibility of the timeline components. Aesthetic concerns might impact the chart.	4.0 to >0 pts **Poor Gantt chart** — No Gantt chart or a very poorly constructed Gantt chart is included with the Project Proposal. It may be very difficult to understand, not resemble a timeline chart, or demonstrate no realistic timeline for the project.	10.0 pts

Figure 2.5. Rubric for a Project Proposal.

Shivers et al. (2018) advocate for low-stakes weekly activities, and even in an accelerated course, this advice can assist the student in building confidence to tackle major assignments. Early low-stakes activities—like a professional email and memorandum in my Technical Report Writing course—can familiarize students with the grading system, use of rubrics, and revision process. It also can guide them seamlessly from one assignment to another, which aids in how a student "reads" the course. That type of strategic design might seem effortless, but it requires much intentionality and effort.

Strategic

Strategic design, the fourth of the PARS elements, is defined as "approaching the online course in a way that makes you think about designing an entire experience for a very specific user" (Borgman & McArdle, p. 72). The move from the low-stakes efforts toward major assignments, a linear, cumulative design, along with careful alignment with announcements and videos, guides the student to a firm, scaffolded grasp of the content and, in my class, toward a polished ePortfolio for a public audience (Shivers et al., 2018). Earlier Technical Report Writing assignments like the resume and cover letter, project proposal, instructions or manual, and memoranda can be highlighted on the digital platform of their choice to demonstrate students' professional writing abilities, and students apply all that they have learned regarding design principles to polish their websites. By showing students from day one of the semester how all of these assignments build and lead to a cumulative portfolio, I hope to set a clear, reasonable expectation for the semester and avoid miscommunication, which Borgman and McArdle (2019) note is frequent in OWI: "[O]ften a lot of the headaches that occur in online courses happen because of the gap in understanding of what is expected from each party involved, instructor and student" (p. 74). A well-structured map might not come naturally and could even necessitate an overhaul of a course, but it is key to ensuring a positive course experience for students.

My own audience-focused strategies also take into account Wiggins and McTighe's (2005) backward design, "a map for how to achieve the 'outputs' of desired student performance" (pp. 5–6). Working from learning outcomes and objectives back to assignments, activities, readings, and tools used ensures that the process is one that was well thought out from the student's experience. My own content grid for the Technical Report Writing course (see Figure 2.6) labels first the module and the appropriate course learning outcomes. Then, I create learning objectives based on Bloom's taxonomy, list assessments and learning activities for that module and the open educational resources utilized, and estimate the time spent to complete everything at a satisfactory level. The content grid aided my (re-)development of the course from bogey to birdie and ensured that the backward design principle was carefully implemented to maximize student success.

Module	Learning Outcomes	Learning Objectives	Assessments & Learning Activities	Learning Materials	Time on Task
Module 1: Memos, E-mails, Summaries	Revise and edit effectively in all assignments, including formal media such as e-mail messages to the instructor. Develop professional work habits, including those necessary for effective collaboration and cooperation with others. Recognize, explain, and use the formal elements of specific genres of organizational communication: white papers, recommendations and analytical reports, proposals, memorandums, web pages, wikis, blogs, business letters, and promotional documents.	• Students will develop and utilize strategies for starting the writing process. • Students will identify the aspects of a rhetorical situation in a recall quiz. • Students will review memorandum samples and compare and contrast strengths and weaknesses of the samples. • Students will compose a well-designed, error-free 1-page memorandum that addresses a target audience of the instructor's choice. • Students will assess and evaluate each other's memos by completing a draft worksheet.	Discussion: E-mails (student-student interaction, student-content interaction) Discussion: Memos (student-content interaction, student-instructor interaction) Discussion: Summaries (student-content interaction, student-instructor interaction) E-mail Assignment (student-content interaction, student-instructor interaction) Memo Draft Workshop (student-student interaction) Group Memo Assignment (student-content interaction, student-student interaction, student-instructor interaction) Daily Summary Assignment (student-content interaction, student-instructor interaction) Review Quiz (one quiz that spans multiple modules, but I'll put it here and Module 2) (student-content interaction, student-instructor interaction)	• Read: Audience Analysis https://www.arksmnet.com/~hcquires/textbook/aud.html ("Audience Analysis" by David McMurrey) • Read: Effective E-mail Communication: https://learn.saylor.org/mod/page/view.php?id=5576 ("Effective E-mail Communication" by Saylor Academy) • Read: Memorandums and Letters: https://saylordotorg.github.io/text_business-communication-for-success/s13-02-memorandums-and-letters.html ("Memorandums and Letters" by Saylor Academy) • Read: Organization by Saylor Academy: https://saylordotorg.github.io/text_business-communication-for-success/s13-03-organization.html • Read: Writing Summaries from Sources by Rick Dollieslager: http://community.tncc.edu/faculty/dollieslager/Writsums2.html • Read/Browse: Sample Formal Reports and Sample E-Portfolios (posted under Modules) • Watch: Video (see below)	12 hours

Figure 2.6. Course content grid.

Though I have yet to share my course content grids with Tidewater students, a step that I feel could both increase transparency and result in useful student input, the impact is felt in the course design in our Canvas LMS. The modules that take shape in the course content grid are the organizing units of the course, and each one contains the learning objectives and resources as well as additional material that students might find useful. Assignments, announcements, and videos are hyperlinked both in the modules as well as their separate areas in the course. A course architecture that seamlessly guides students from one activity to the next can be time consuming on initial setup, but it functions as a virtual hand holding and a reliable, consistent design that welcomes students of any level of preparation. Strategic instruction is perhaps the most essential element of the PARS approach for two-year college instructors to incorporate into their OWI.

Limitations

Though the implementation of PARS and user-centered design principles resulted in a successful redesign of my technical writing course, the process was not without some bogeys, which is to be expected in an accelerated two-year college technical writing course. Among the limitations that I faced were a heavy workload, constant notifications—both for the instructor and students,—a difficulty in sustained conversations, and a failed group memorandum assignment.

Though the responsive strategies in the PARS approach, including setting limitations, using rubrics, and opening with low-stakes activities, cut down on the heavy grading load, there were still relentless submissions and notifications from the learning management system. I have adapted to a constant heavy grading load as a community college instructor with a 30-credit hour obligation, but it is a challenge when the number of students in each course exceeds that which is recommended by the Conference on College Composition and Communication. Its ninth principle of OWI is, "OWCs should be capped responsibly at 20 students per course with 15 being a preferable number" ("A position statement," 2013, para. 10). My technical writing course remains capped at 25 students with overloads welcome. The myriad student works to grade were paired with constant updates by Canvas of new submissions, on the web and the mobile app as well as emails, a reminder that I would never be caught up. Students similarly faced the heavy workload: at least one assignment and several readings and discussions each week can be grueling.

Sustained conversation with and between students via discussions is recommended by McCabe and Gonzalez-Flores (2017) as important to online courses as they build community. In my experience, however, I tapered off the number of replies to students after the first half of the semester, focusing on grading their work and providing one-on-one feedback. What this left was a course that felt disconnected, especially after an early group memorandum assignment. Though I advocate for group work because of its importance in many businesses and areas in which technical writing is common, the group assignment has not been favored by students, who find it difficult to work with one another on differing schedules. Group work of any type, including in-depth peer review, has been a struggle in my eight-week courses. Even when I have implemented mid-week deadlines, there does not seem like there is enough time for students to truly engage one another unless they can meet synchronously. A nationwide survey by Martinez et al. (2019) similarly found that some online writing activities "were not always implemented in ways that improve student writing, rendering them somewhat ineffective" ("Implications," para. 2). Even as a low-stakes assignment, the memorandum was viewed was one of the most disliked assignments of the semester, leaving me to reconsider the inclusion of a collaborative document in such a fast-paced course with a unique population of working adults and active military students who might not be available to log in several times a week.

Final Thoughts and Application

In spite of a few drawbacks, I am satisfied with the transformation of my Technical Report Writing course through the use of the PARS approach and user experience design guidelines. In future semesters for all of my courses, I plan to involve students even more in the design process through inquiries, additional needs surveys, and potentially focus groups. To continue to utilize the same approach and rest on my laurels might be easy, but it fails to incorporate those that my decisions impact the most: the students. Jones (2018) writes, "While instructors often develop the content for their courses based on programmatic student learning outcomes, established course objectives, vetted scholarship on teaching and learning ... there is little to no collaboration or input from students, the end-users of the [syllabus] document" (p. 3). Creating a dialogue with my community college students and consistently returning to reflection of what worked will ensure that all documents, OERs, activities, assignments, and design and delivery choices have been vetted.

Any writing instructor who plans to implement the PARS approach in their OWI should consider these three points as the foundation of their conversion:

- Know your students. It's hard to personalize your content, make a course accessible, or strategize student completion if you are not aware of their needs, which can vary at each institution and even class. Use surveys, course evaluations, and student feedback as opportunities to learn what works for them.
- Put yourself in your students' shoes. Many students prefer OERs and bite-sized videos (four minutes or less) because they increase accessibility. Which other student-focused changes can you make to your course content? Review the visual design of your course. Can the readability be improved for students?
- Be open to change. It's hard to admit that a pedagogical strategy, activity, or trusted assignment is not working. But it's even harder for your students to succeed if they're being set up for a frustrating experience. Adaptability is key.

When properly applied, the PARS elements guide students and serve as a virtual caddie, a golfer's trusted assistant and advisor. Like any good caddie, the PARS approach provides us with the tools and insights needed to be successful. It reminds us to treat our course material as revisable and flexible and to foreground the student experience. Combined with an orientation, clearly structured information, and a personalized one-on-one connection, this student-friendly approach not only gets students on the course but also teaches them the basics. Instead of forcing the marginalized and underserved to match our golf handicap, we can meet them where they are and level the playing field.

References

Bjork, C. (2018). Integrating usability testing with digital rhetoric in OWI. *Computers and Composition, 49*, 4–13.

Blankenstein, M., Wolff-Eisenberg, C. & Braddlee. (2019, September 30). Student needs are academic needs: Community college libraries and academic support for student success. *ITHAKA*. https://sr.ithaka.org/wp-content/uploads/2019/09/Ithaka-SR-Report-Student-Needs-Are-Academic-Needs-Report-9302019.pdf.

Borgman, J. & McArdle, C. (2019). *Personal, accessible, responsive, strategic: Resources and strategies for online writing instructors.* The WAC Clearinghouse; University Press of Colorado. https://doi.org/10.37514/PRA-B.2019.0322.

The Century Foundation. (2019, April). *Recommendations for providing community colleges with the resources they need*. https://production-tcf.imgix.net/app/uploads/2019/04/25171942/recommendation_commcollege_2019.pdf.

The Conference on College Composition and Communication Committee for Best Practices in Online Writing Instruction. (2013, March 13). *A position statement of principles and example effective practices for online writing instruction (OWI)*. http://www.ncte.org/cccc/resources/positions/owiprinciples.

Eyman, D. (2009). Usability: Methodology and design practice for writing processes and pedagogies. In S. Miller-Cochran & R. Rodrigo (Eds.), *Rhetorically rethinking usability: Theories, practices, methodologies* (pp. 213–228). Hampton Press.

Greer, M. & Harris, H. S. (2018). User-centered design as a foundation for effective online writing instruction. *Computers and Composition, 49*, 14–24.

Hutchins, C. E. (2020). Creating and using open educational resources (OER) in reading and writing classes. *Teaching English in the Two-Year College, 47*(3), 297–311.

Jones, N. N. (2018). Human centered syllabus design: Positioning our students as expert end-users. *Computers and Composition, 49*, 25–35.

Martinez, D., Mechenbier, M. X., Hewett, B. L., Melonçon, L., Skurat Harris, H., St.Amant, K., Phillips, A. & Bodnar, M. I. (2019). A report on U.S.-based national survey of students in online writing courses. *Research in Online Literacy Education, 2*(1). http://www.roleolor.org/a-report-on-a-us-based-national-survey-of-students-in-online-writing-courses.html.

McCabe, M. & Gonzalez-Flores, P. (2017). *Essentials of online learning: A standards-based guide*. Routledge.

Mullin, C. M. (2011, October). *The road ahead: A look at trends in the educational attainment of community college students* (Policy Brief 2011-04PBL). American Association of Community Colleges.

Shea, P. & Bidjerano, T. (2014). Does online learning impede degree completion? A national study of community college students. *Computers and Education, 75*, 103–111.

Shivers-McNair, A., Phillips, J., Campbell, A., Mai, H. H., Yan, A., Macy, J. F., Wenlock, J., Fry, S. & Guan, Y. (2018). User-centered design in and beyond the classroom: Toward an accountable practice. *Computers and Composition, 49*, 36–47. https://www.sciencedirect.com/journal/computers-and-composition/vol/49.

Tidewater Community College (2020.) *About TCC*. Tidewater Community College. https://www.tcc.edu/about-tcc/.

Wiggins, G. & McTighe, J. (2005). *Understanding by design* (2nd ed.). Association for Supervision and Curriculum Development.

Chapter 3. Strategic, User-Centered Design for a Globally Distributed, Condensed Format, Online Graduate Course

Mary K. Stewart
CALIFORNIA STATE UNIVERSITY SAN MARCOS

Abstract: This chapter presents a case study of engaging in strategic, user-centered design for a globally distributed online course that aimed to train first-year writing instructors in hybrid and online pedagogy. The fifteen graduate students in this course represented six time zones, from California to China. Drawing on the Community of Inquiry framework, I analyze my design decisions and demonstrate how I initially designed the course to be responsive to my particular student population, and how I adapted the design in response to student feedback as the course progressed. My goal is to provide an example that can inform how other writing instructors design flexible and responsive online writing courses.

Keywords: online writing instruction, user-centered design, globally distributed learning, community of inquiry, teaching presence

Writing instructors have always been instructional designers, even if they don't use that term. Our task is to create spaces where students learn about writing through talking with peers, reflecting on their practice, and responding to feedback with revision. Writing instructors, then, must not only be subject matter experts, but also community builders. And community building requires more than "throwing students together with their peers with little or no guidance" (Bruffee, 1984, p. 652). Writing instructors must make careful "moves that create an environment of safety and inquiry that allow learning to take place" (Sackey et al., 2015, p. 116). In other words, strategic instructional design is embedded into composition pedagogy.

Online writing instruction (OWI) scholars are particularly attentive to instructional design because, in addition to making decisions about what digital and non-digital tools will facilitate student-student, student-instructor, and student-content interaction, online writing instructors also build the learning environment (Blythe, 2001). Unfortunately, while many instructors are trained in composition pedagogy, few are explicitly trained to be instructional designers, and even fewer are trained in the technical skills required to build virtual learning environments. Consequently, OWI scholars advocate for training instructors as instructional designers (Breuch, 2015) and call for purposeful, pedagogy-driven course design (Harris et al., 2019).

Jessie Borgman & Casey McArdle's (2019) emphasis on strategic design in *Personal, Accessible, Responsive, Strategic: Resources and Strategies for Online Writing Instructors* responds to those calls. This chapter applies the PARS approach to a globally distributed online graduate course, particularly focusing on the S in PARS: strategic.

Strategic, User-Centered Design

Borgman & McArdle (2019) advocate for "a strategy focused on the user experience of the students" (p. 71). Too often, they contend, "user feedback is only gathered at the end of the course or upon degree completion" (2019, p. 89), resulting in course designs that are not responsive to the unique needs of the students. Instructional design models that focus primarily on outcome alignment exacerbate this issue. James Porter (2014), for example, argues that course evaluation programs' (e.g., Quality Matters) intense focus on mapping activities to assignments to outcomes often neglects

> the importance of instructional *context*. "The course" is imagined from a formalist frame as a well-made urn, an aesthetic object that can be evaluated, like a well-made essay, apart from its particular context, abstracted from the both rhetor (the instructor) and audience (particular students). (p. 25)

When instructional design neglects context, the course essentially functions as a tightly aligned textbook that does little to facilitate the types of student-student and student-instructor interactions that are required for the socially situated learning that writing studies values. The strategic, user-centered design for which Borgman & McArdle (2019) advocate offers an alternative.

Stuart Blythe (2001) defines user-centered design in contrast to "systems design," arguing that if writing instructors follow a systems approach, they "set specifications (e.g., course goals and technological means for meeting those goals) and then begin creating a Web-based course to meet those goals" (p. 334). To instead follow a user-centered approach, instructors should gather information about their students before determining specifications, such as students' access to and familiarity with course tools and goals for taking the course. Because the digital environments that support online learning are often unfamiliar to students, online instructors might additionally perform formal user-experience testing by observing students as they navigate the course site. Once the course begins, instructors should continually solicit student feedback and be prepared to make adjustments in response. Doing so places "the student experience at the heart of the course" and creates "responsive, flexible, experience-based and reflective online learning" (Greer & Harris, 2018, p. 22). In the language of PARS, being responsive to students during strategic design facilitates personal and accessible learning (Borgman & McArdle, 2019).

Michael Greer & Heidi Skurat Harris (2018) additionally maintain that user-centered design is more than a set of practices: it is a mindset that instructors must adopt if they wish to uphold the CCCC OWI Principles (cccc.ncte.org/cccc/resources/positions/owiprinciples). This mindset is particularly important for OWI Principle #1: Access. Jessie Borgman & Jason Dockter (2018) articulate this argument as they advocate for a "definition of access that extends beyond accessible course materials" (p. 95). Definitions of access must also recognize the varied devices students use and the range of factors that influence how they interpret materials such as prompts and instructions. In practice, this means that, in addition to following web accessibility guidelines (i.e., captions for videos, headings in documents, alternative text on images), writing instructors should engage in user-design practices such as: polling students before the course begins, offering frequent opportunities for student reflection, presenting instructional materials through multiple modes, and creating a variety of ways for students to access and interact with the content, their instructor, and their peers.

Collin Bjork (2018) takes these arguments a step further, advocating for augmenting theories of user-centered design with theories of digital rhetoric. Through this lens, instructors consider not only how students use and access online courses, but also how they use them rhetorically. This perspective builds upon scholarship that recognizes that interfaces are never ideologically neutral (Arola, 2010; Gallagher, 2015; Hawisher & Selfe, 1991). Accordingly, any analysis of a user's experience must account for "the social, cultural, political, and ideological stakes" of participating (Bjork, 2018, p. 7). User-centered design thus helps us account for the humans involved in education, and digital rhetoric helps us account for the social contexts and power dynamics that inform how those humans approach and interpret the tasks of teaching and learning.

Globally Distributed OWI

Accounting for social context as well as technological access is particularly important in a globally distributed online writing course, such as the one I will describe in this chapter. As the CCCC Statement on Globalization (cccc.ncte.org/cccc/resources/positions/globalization) notes, writing instructors need to design courses that "take into account students' prior literacy experiences across languages and dialects, valuing students' ways of life, ways of knowing, and ways of making meaning" (2019, p. 685). The statement also recognizes the potential of cross-cultural education for showcasing "differences in language and culture in the teaching and practice of writing" (CCCC Statement on Globalization, 2019, p. 686).

Specific to globally distributed online writing instruction, scholars explore strategies for teaching students to write for global audiences (Rice & St.Amant, 2018; St.Amant & Rice, 2015) and discuss pedagogies for facilitating online courses that consist of globally distributed students (Cleary et al., 2019). These scholars emphasize the importance of thinking about both cultural differences and technological logistics when working with geographically distributed students. They also note the value of exposing students to international audiences and diverse cultural perspectives, as well as the challenges of coordinating interactions across time zones and among students with varied access to course tools. In this chapter, I build upon that scholarship to explore how the PARS approach can guide the strategic, user-centered design of a globally distributed online graduate course.

The Community of Inquiry Framework

In addition to the PARS approach, I draw on the Community of Inquiry (CoI) framework (Garrison, 2017), which is another instructional design heuristic. Like PARS, CoI situates learning in the context of student-student and student-instructor relationships (Gillam & Wooden, 2013; Stewart, 2017). The CoI framework additionally identifies specific elements of "teaching presence," which has helped me apply strategic (and personal and accessible and responsive) design to specific teaching tasks, like setting up the course site, responding to students, and coordinating group work.

In a CoI, the goal is to facilitate interactive learning and knowledge co-construction, which CoI scholars call "cognitive presence." In order to achieve cognitive presence, instructors need to intentionally establish both "social presence" and "teaching presence." Social presence emerges when students establish sufficient relationships to sense a common purpose in the learning community and thus engage in interactions that lead to collaboration. Teaching presence creates the foundation of a community of inquiry, as the instructor designs the course and facilitates student interactions in ways that support both social and cognitive presence. For example, when an instructor intentionally designs a peer review activity in a way that helps students establish trust and engage in reader response feedback, the teaching presence (activity design) supports social presence (trust) that leads to cognitive presence (revision in response to reader response feedback).

In this chapter, I will focus on teaching presence, which CoI scholars further categorize into three instructor actions: Design & Organization, Direct Instruction, and Facilitating Discourse (see Table 3.1). In what follows, I will describe the ways I applied the PARS approach as I engaged in the three categories of teaching presence. My goal is to provide a detailed example of *strategic*, user-centered design that can help other writing instructors create *personal*, *responsive*, and *accessible* online writing courses that meet the needs of diverse, global learners.

Table 3.1. Categories of teaching presence

Teaching Presence Categories	Example Instructor Actions
Design & Organization typically occurs before the course begins and is what most people refer to when they talk about "instructional design."	Envisioning the course arc Drafting the syllabus Creating major assignments Building the course shell
Direct Instruction occurs when the instructor provides clarifications and resources that deepen students' engagement with the course concepts.	Posting assignment instructions Writing activity prompts Posting announcements Sending emails Providing feedback on student work
Facilitating Discourse occurs when the instructor puts students in situations where they will explore multiple perspectives and engage in negotiation that leads to knowledge co-construction.	Facilitating discussion forums Coordinating peer review workshops Conferencing with small groups Inviting multiple perspectives Posing problems that require negotiation

Designing a Condensed-Format, Globally Distributed, Online Graduate Course

The doctoral program for which I was teaching at the time of this writing aims to train teacher-scholars in composition and applied linguistics, and most students are experienced composition and/or language instructors. Typically, the students come to campus for two months in the summer, taking two four-week courses in June and two four-week courses July. However, in the summer of 2020, the COVID-19 pandemic mandated that our courses be offered online. Consequently, in March 2020, I began the task of designing my course, Hybrid & Online Writing Pedagogy, for online delivery.

From a PARS perspective, strategy and access should guide course Design & Organization. Consequently, I began the design process by surveying my students. I asked about: prior experience with online learning, concepts and projects of particular interest, time zone, year in the program, technology access, and preferences for asynchronous or synchronous learning. I also included an open-ended question inviting students to share concerns or challenges they anticipated facing because of the online format.

I learned that the 15 enrolled students represented six time zones, from California to China. Approximately half (46%) reported previous experience with teaching hybrid or online courses, while the other half (54%) explained that their only experience with online learning was emergency remote instruction in Spring 2020. All but one student indicated that they would prefer some synchronous interaction throughout the four-week course, though several noted that their internet connection was not reliable. I also learned that the students were in their second or third summers of the doctorate program, which meant that they had a shared experience as students, including prior experience with negotiating cultural differences among cohort members.

After the course was complete, I invited the students to participate in an IRB-approved research study that allowed me to analyze the weekly reflections they wrote for the course and that included a demographic survey. Fourteen students consented to participate in the study, and eleven provided demographic information. Of those 11, 82% identified as female and 18% identified as male, 45% identified as domestic (U.S.) and 55% identified as international (primarily Near or Middle Eastern). All but one student identified as multilingual (the majority spoke two languages). At the time of the course, the students' ages ranged from 32–47.

As I began to envision the course, which aimed to immerse face-to-face composition instructors in the theories and practices of OWI, I started with a syllabus designed for a 14-week version of the course. Were I to teach the four-week version face-to-face, I would have had assigned readings followed by in-class discussion four days a week (Monday–Thursday). The global distribution of my students, and the concerns about internet connectivity, meant that this design could not be replicated via video chat. Instead, I decided to limit synchronous interactions to once a week, on Fridays. To accommodate multiple time zones, I hosted two (recommended, but not required) chats every Friday, one at 8 a.m. ET and one at 12 p.m. ET. Students were welcome to attend either chat, and they had the option to watch the recording if they were unable to attend.

I also re-imagined the course as four units rather than fourteen weeks, ultimately designing weekly modules that included four types of tasks: Projects, Reading Responses, Group Activities, Video Chats, and Reflections. In the LMS, I organized these into Reading Responses and Activities/Projects (see Figure 3.2).

Table 3.2. Interaction in and modality of activities

	Interaction	Modality
Projects	1:1, instructor-student, student-content	asynchronous, multimodal
Reading Responses	1:many, instructor-students, student-students, student-content	asynchronous, textual
Group Activities	1:group, student-students, instructor-students, student-content	synchronous, multimodal
Video Chats	1:many, instructor-students, student-students	synchronous, multimodal
Reflections	1:1, instructor-student	asynchronous, textual

Strategic, User-Centered Design 53

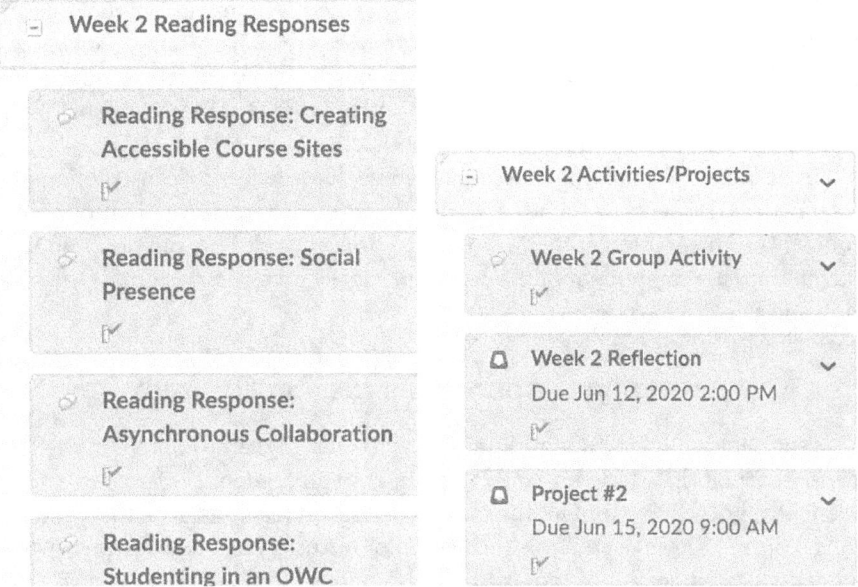

Figure 3.1. Weekly modules.

As I envisioned each element of the course, I followed recommendations in the literature to create a set of activities that balanced one-to-one and one-to-many student-student, student-instructor, and student-content interactions (Moore, 1989), as well as a combination of asynchronous/synchronous (Mick & Middlebrook, 2015) and textual/multimodal (Rankins-Robertson et al., 2014) components (see Table 3.2).

The remainder of this chapter analyzes my application of the PARS approach to strategically design and facilitate each of the five course components.

Projects

The course Design & Organization gave students a choice between two final projects: a pedagogical portfolio or a scholarly article. Regardless of the final, Projects 1 and 2 involved designing instructional materials and interactive activities for an online course. Project 3 was either a revision of those materials or a proposal for the scholarly article. All of my Summer 2020 students opted for the pedagogical portfolio, which included a critical analysis of the materials they created throughout Projects 1–3. The Projects were due on Mondays at 9 a.m. ET because that is when I intended to begin reading student work. In the spirit of being personal and responsive, I was transparent about this reasoning and frequently discussed both instructor and student workload throughout the course. See Appendix A for project descriptions.

My Direct Instruction for the projects included assignment instructions and feedback. Following the PARS emphasis on being responsive, my feedback was primarily formative, making recommendations for how students could revise their materials from project to project, or commenting on how students might re-imagine their final projects for publication.

In terms of Facilitating Discourse, some knowledge co-construction was intended as students responded to feedback during revision. I also created moments for peer interaction during a final project workshop, but designing and facilitating this component of the course primarily involved Design & Organization and Direct Instruction.

Reading Response Discussion Forums

This summers-only doctoral program aims to offer the same content in the condensed format that students would encounter in an academic-year course. Consequently, I opted to maintain the 12 sets of assigned readings from the semester-long course. These were transformed into reading response forums, where students posted an initial response every Monday–Thursday by 2 p.m. ET and then responded to two peers by 5 p.m. ET. I selected 2 p.m. ET as the due date to give myself time to read and respond to the forums each day. See Appendix B for an example prompt.

Figure 3.2. Video announcement synthesizing reading response forums.

I initially intended to achieve Direct Instruction through responding in writing to each post. In practice, the literacy load proved unsustainable—in the first forum, 108 posts were created within 24 hours. I felt overwhelmed as I waded through the responses, and several students noted that they were struggling to keep up with the ideas dispersed across so many threads. Consequently, I made two changes to the design. I made the requirement for students to respond to peers optional. Then, instead of responding to each student individually, I read through the posts, took notes, and created a video that synthesized the students' contributions, taking care to directly quote or paraphrase each student in my verbal response. To account for the internet connectivity difficulties that I knew many students were encountering, I posted a PDF script for each video. This revision was responsive to student and instructor workload, made the assignment more personal because the students received a multimodal message from me every day that directly acknowledged their individual contributions to our learning community, and accounted for accessibility via the script. Figure 3.2 is a screenshot of the first video response.

This decision had a major impact on both Direct Instruction and Discourse Facilitation. Had I responded individually to each student, the Direct Instruction would have been primarily one-to-one, as my response would address the individual author, and perhaps the peers who responded to that author. Shifting to a video response changed my Direct Instruction to one-to-many; I was now creating one holistic response instead of 15 individual responses. My students' reflections indicate that this shift increased our collective sense of the course as a community. As one student wrote, the videos "tricked" her brain into thinking we'd met as a class; as another student put it, "the video posts provide a sense of community and connectedness to the course." On the other hand, this decision meant that students were not responding to each other's posts. Some students regretted this, noting that the lack of responses lessoned the opportunity for Discourse. Other students indicated that they were benefiting from reading their peers' posts, suggesting that the bulletin-board forum still facilitated knowledge co-construction even if there was not written evidence of it. Of course, my context is important—I'm working with highly motivated graduate students who are likely to read each other's posts even if responses are not required. That might not be the case in first-year composition.

Weekly Group Activities

Unlike the reading response forums, the group activities were intentionally designed to facilitate back-and-forth negotiation and conversation. In week 1, I divided the students into five groups of three, based on time zone; each group met to discuss a particular concept from the week's readings and then collaboratively created a multimodal presentation. I also created Google Documents for each group that included graphic organizers with spaces for individual and group notes, and I asked the groups to email me early in the week with a description of their plan for approaching the project and distributing the work.

My hope was that students would meet synchronously and benefit from talking with their peers, both for the purposes of knowledge co-construction and for gaining a sense of connection with classmates (Aragon, 2003). In practice, this activity became a stressful exercise in logistics as the groups struggled to find time to meet. Context is again important—I learned that most of my students were simultaneously enrolled in a research methods course that required them to interview and be interviewed several times (one student had nine interviews that week). This understandably increased their anxiety around scheduling the group meetings for my course. The multiple time zones were also complicated to navigate. I attempted to mitigate this by grouping students who were in similar time zones, but, as one student wrote, it remained "time-consuming to collaborate online with everyone's differing schedules, responsibilities, and time zones." Furthermore, as another student explained, "my group members who live in the same time zone as me work on completely different schedules than I do, so I might as well have been in another time zone."

When the groups did meet, they were more focused on producing the required presentation than on negotiating or connecting. As one student explained,

> I knew that our goal as a group was to engage in a conversation about what we found and build on each other's ideas. However, due to time constraints and the need to produce a deliverable, it just ended up being a narration of what each person found and the rest was planning what we needed to do next.

I wanted students to connect and negotiate, but I also required proof of their collaboration via a graded product. This product became their sole focus, and they unanimously reported in their reflections that the activity did not lead them to connect with their peers or with the content in the way I intended.

In response, I revised the Week 2 group activity. My original plan was to have five groups of three who each identified an online academic community and then analyzed their community through a unique lens. I re-grouped the students into three groups of five, and, instead of each group focusing on one lens, one person within the group represented a lens. The students posted their unique analysis to the forum and then responded to their peers, bringing back the asynchronous responses that some students missed from the reading response forums, and also creating a more manageable literacy load since the students only saw the responses from their small groups.

Figures 3.3 and 3.4 present the initial and revised group activity instructions for Week 2. You'll notice that the instructions use bullet points, indentation, bold font, and purple font; this visual design, and the writing style, aims to enact Beth Hewett's (2015) recommendations for writing readable instructional materials. The Initial Week 2 Group Activity Instructions are found below.

Week 2 Group Activity (Initial)

Discussion Topic

Due June 12 at 2:00pm

The activity for this week will involve each group conducting a rhetorical analysis of two digital communities: one academic (a D2L course you are currently taking or another formal learning environment you can find online, such as a MOOC) and one non-academic (any interface that everyone in your group has access to, such as a social media platform). Here are you group assignments and associated Google Docs:

- Group 1 (tbd after week 1)
- Group 2 (tbd after week 1)
- Group 3 (tbd after week 1)
- Group 4 (tbd after week 1)
- Group 5 (tbd after week 1)

Step 1: Reach out to your group and create a plan for how you will complete the work this week. Email Mary with a summary of your plan. I recommend reaching out to your group on Monday and emailing Mary on Tuesday.

You are welcome to request a group meeting with Mary at this point. to discuss your plans and clarify expectations. However, this is not required; we can just as easily talk over email.

Step 2: Determine what academic and non-academic digital communities your group will analyze, and then individually access the two interfaces from multiple devices, including at least one mobile device.

Step 3: Meet with your group to discuss your experiences, using the information in the Group Google Document to guide your discussion. How you meet is completely up to you, and it can be synchronous or asynchronous.

Step 4: As a group, create a multimodal presentation that summarizes what you and your group learned. This could be an infographic, a PowerPoint or Prezi with voice-over, a podcast or recorded video of you interviewing group members about their experience with online learning, etc. Your primary goal is to teach the other groups about your assigned principle.

Your multimodal presentation should be posted to D2L by Friday, June 12 at 2 p.m. ET. Then, by Friday at 5 p.m. ET, please review the other groups' presentations and post a response to at least one group.

The Revised Week 2 Group Activity Instructions are found below.

Week 2 Group Activity (Revised)

Discussion Topic

Due June 12 at 2:00pm

We're going to try a new strategy for the group assignment this week. Week 1 was primarily designed to be synchronous group work because you needed to negotiate and co-author. This week is designed to be more asynchronous, where each group member is in charge of bringing a particular piece of knowledge to the group, and then you co-construct knowledge as you read, reflect on, and respond to the individual contributions.

Instead of five groups of three, we'll have three groups of five (larger groups are typically better for asynchronous knowledge construction, while smaller groups are important for managing the logistics of synchronous co-authoring):

Group 1: [student names]

Group 2: [student names]

Group 3: [student names]

I've set this up using the Groups feature in D2L, which means that you will only see your small group's posts to the discussion forum. The deadlines are set up as the same as last week: post due Friday at 2 p.m. ET and replies due Friday at 5 p.m. ET; however, you and your group can set different deadlines, if you'd like.

The activity for this week will involve each group conducting a rhetorical analysis of an online, academic communities. This could be a D2L course from IUP or another formal learning environment you can find online, such as a MOOC or a Kahn Academy class. Each group member will be assigned to analyze that community through a particular lens: (1) social presence, (2) accessibility, (3) asynchronous interaction, (4) literacy load, and (5) usability.

Step 1: Reach out to your group and decide: (a) what academic community you will analyze, (b) who will be assigned to what lens, and (c) if you want to stick with the Friday deadlines or propose something else. Email Mary by 5 p.m. ET on Tuesday with a summary of your plan.

Step 2: Individually access the interface from multiple devices, including at least one mobile device, and draft a 500–600 word discussion forum post or a 5–7 minute video that analyzes the community through your assigned lens. Your initial post is due by Friday at 2 p.m. ET.

Below you'll find some guidance for each lens. You do not have to account for every question I'm posing; this is just meant to get you started. If you'd like to be put in contact with the people from other groups who are also assigned to your lens, let me know.

Lens #1: Social Presence. Referring to the readings by Rourke et al., Aragon, and Rendahl & Breuch, consider: Did you see evidence of the three categories of social presence in the academic community? Did you see evidence of social presence in support of satisfaction and/or in support of learning? Was the social presence you observed hindered or supported by the type of interaction (asynchronous or synchronous; textual or multimodal)?

Lens #2: Accessibility. Referring to the readings by Oswal and Rodrigo, consider: How was your experience in the community impacted by the device(s) you are using and your internet connection? How are your experiences impacted by your previous experiences with the online communities or your assumptions about what constitutes "successful" communication or participation in this community? How are your experiences influenced by larger sociocultural factors, e.g., the relationship between your individual identity and the community?

Lens #3: Asynchronous Interaction. Referring to Warnock & Gasiewski, consider the asynchronous interactions you observed. What tools are people using to communicate in the community? Is the communication all textual or multimodal? What makes a particular type of communication effective in this space?

Lens #4: Literacy Load. Referring to Warnock & Gasiewski, consider: How do people participate in the academic community? How is this participation different from "attendance" in a face-to-face class or from being physically present at a non-academic event? What literacies (reading, writing, multimodal communication, multitasking . . .) are required to support that participation? How does that literacy load compare to what you would expect from equivalent face-to-face interactions? Beyond technical access, what factors influence who is invited to participate and who has a voice/authority in the community?

> Lens #5: Usability. Referring to Bjork, consider: What was your user experience with the platform? How was your experience impacted by your access to technology or cultural identity? What evidence of user design do you see in the platforms? Who seems to be the intended user? How does the interface invite particular uses?
>
> **Step 3**: Respond to each of your group members, contributing at least one reply to each member's thread. Your responses should reflect on how their lens relates to or departs from or deepens your understanding of your own lens or other group members' lenses. Your responses to peers are due by Friday at 5 p.m. ET.

The students responded far more positively to this design, and some groups reported in their reflections that they engaged in negotiation of multiple perspectives and achieved a sense of connection with peers. For example:

> This updated design does not require having to go through too many organizational steps and gave us the chance to focus on engaging with the content itself. We still had highly useful conversations through Whatsapp while the forum replies to each other deepened our understanding of the various lenses.

However, other students reported that the intended social learning was not achieved: "My group interacted via WhatsApp to try and coordinate things. Since everything is asynchronous, it's not really feeling like a group work project, and I think it might have worked equally as well as a discussion post."

Consequently, I once again revised the group activity. In Week 3, I asked my students to meet for half an hour in small groups for what I called a "Non-Deliverable Synchronous Activity." They emailed me early in the week explaining when and how they planned to meet, and they reflected on the experience in their Weekly Reflections. The Week 3 Group Activity instructions follow.

> **Week 3 Group Activity**
>
> Discussion Topic
>
> Due June 19 at 2:00pm
>
> This week, we're going to try what I call a Non-Deliverable Synchronous activity. Each group will meet for 30 minutes and discuss the teaching presence within an online course (you can discuss our course, another IUP course you are currently taking, or one of the Coursera, Kahn Academy, or Facebook environments you looked at last week). There will be no deliverable—you are just on your honor system to get together and talk for 30 minutes.
>
> I've sorted you into the same groups that you worked with in

Week 1:

Group 1: [student names]

Group 2: [student names]

Group 3: [student names]

Group 4: [student names]

Group 5: [student names]

Step 1: Reach out to your group and determine (a) what online course you will focus on and (b) when you will meet. Email Mary with an update on your plans.

Step 2: Prior to meeting with your group, explore the online course and look for examples of the three elements of teaching presence: Design & Organization, Facilitating Discourse, and Direct Instruction.

Step 3: Meet with your group and discuss the course. The goal is to deepen your understanding of teaching presence through applying the theory to concrete examples. If you want to dig a little deeper, consider reflecting on one or more of the following:

- **Response to writing**. What evidence did you see of formative v. summative or group v. individual feedback in the course? Which of the teaching presence categories (design & organization, direct instruction, and facilitating discourse) inform, or should inform, response to writing? How does the key role of response in writing pedagogy inform your definition of teaching presence?
- **The student's role in teaching presence**. What evidence did you see of students participating in the facilitation of teaching presence in the course? How can you imagine students contributing to each of the three teaching presence categories (design & organization, direct instruction, and facilitating discourse)? What about writing or language instruction makes the student role in teaching presence particularly important (or not important)?
- **Accessibility**. To what extent do the Quality Matters Rubric and the Community of Inquiry Framework account for teaching presence? If you were using these instruments to analyze the course that you toured, how do you think you'd describe the level of design & organization, direct instruction, and facilitating discourse in the course? To what extent do you believe using teaching presence as a design heuristic would contribute to or detract from creating an accessible

and high-quality online course? What other elements would you recommend designers take into account?

- **Multimodal instruction.** What evidence did you see of multimodal teaching presence in the course site? How can you imagine using multimodal instruction to facilitate each of the three teaching presence categories (design & organization, direct instruction, and facilitating discourse)? One argument for online writing courses is that the form of the course reinforces the content as students have to write and read in order to participate in the course. A similar argument argues for multimodality in online courses because it can reinforce digital literacy as a learning outcome. Did you see any evidence of this in the course you toured? Do you agree or disagree that multimodal instructional materials can facilitate digital literacy in an online writing course?

You are not required to submit any kind of deliverable as a result of this activity. However, if your group runs into questions or ideas that you want to discuss with Mary, feel free to email her. You might engage in an email exchange with Mary, or ask her to add something that came up in your group to the Friday chat agendas, or ask her to schedule a separate meeting with you and/or your group.

The students responded well to this task. Most reported that they had engaging conversations and expressed relief at the lack of deliverable, noting that they were able to focus on each other instead of on a graded product. As one student wrote,

> I believe that I have learned the most from this week's group activity compared to the past two weeks. I feel like when there was a deliverable, we were too tense and too much focused on the deliverable itself and the "task distribution" rather than on discussing our understandings of the readings and the concepts in them. This week, we discussed the theories we struggled with. We compared our understandings of the same theory or text.

Another student noted, "the discussion we had this afternoon, not tied to an assignment, was the type of interaction I and my group members wish we could have engaged in more frequently over the past few weeks."

These students are motivated learners who had a tangible sense of community with their peers based on our time together in the course and their prior knowledge of one another. I do not know how a non-deliverable activity would work in another learning context, but the experience has caused me to seriously rethink the role of deliverables that accompany synchronous interactions. Moving forward, I plan to integrate a combination of asynchronous and non-deliverable synchronous collaborative activities in my courses.

The evolving Design & Organization of the group activities was responsive to information I was gaining from student reflections, and strategically sought to make the activities more accessible given students' personal contexts. At the same time, the learning outcomes remained consistent, and the content of the activities (essentially discussion prompts) were largely unchanged. My approach to Direct Instruction was similarly consistent—it occurred via assignment instructions, email exchanges with the groups, and responses to the work they posted in the forums—but the deliverables I was expecting (or not expecting) were substantially revised. The most interesting element of this experience was the quest for Discourse Facilitation. Ultimately, the students found ways to connect and negotiate with each other, but it was critical for me to understand the course from their perspectives before I was able to design an activity that effectively facilitated that discourse. The PARS approach put me in a situation where I was soliciting sufficient student feedback to engage in those adaptations.

Synchronous Video Chats

I held two synchronous video chats every Friday, 8–9 a.m. ET and 12–1 p.m. ET. Students could choose which chat to attend and if they were unable to attend, they could watch the recording and email me with questions or schedule a one-on-one meeting. Most students attended a chat every week, and the two students who did skip a chat only missed one week each.

The goal of these chats was threefold: (1) to reinforce our sense of community and the personal nature of online learning, (2) to give students the opportunity to ask questions and thus make the course more accessible, and (3) to discuss concepts from the forums and activities that week. These chats proved effective for Facilitating Discourse; the students were lively participants and much of our time was spent reflecting on how their experiences as online students illuminated or departed from concepts in the readings. We also engaged in "off topic" conversations about the impact of current events on their personal lives. My Direct Instruction primarily took the form of offering clarifications or insights from OWI scholarship based on questions and comments from students. This responsive instruction style was supported by the Design & Organization of the chats. I opened the chat with a full group discussion of the course logistics and invited questions about projects or assignments. I then moved students into break out rooms where they generated a list of topics that they wanted to explore in more depth, which guided our subsequent full group discussion.

Reflections

The final and perhaps most critical component of this course was an individual reflection that students submitted every Friday by 2 p.m. ET. I relied on these reflections to revise the course as it progressed, thus strategically working to make the course both responsive and accessible. See Appendix C for an example prompt.

My Direct Instruction for the individual reflections was one-to-one. The feedback was conversational, enacting the PARS emphasis on personal as I empathized with students who reported struggling with the realities of a condensed format online course. If the student chose to reflect on what they learned, then I provided more content-specific feedback as I shared my own interpretations of the course concepts. The individual reflections created important opportunities for student-instructor dialogue, which may have led to some knowledge co-construction, but these activities were not intentionally designed to Facilitate Discourse.

Final Thoughts & Application

The goal of this chapter is to offer an example of how I applied the PARS approach to engage in strategic, user-centered design for a condensed format, online graduate course. My hope is that the level of detail will provide other instructors with a starting point for what things to consider and what questions to ask when engaging in strategic design. Ideally, we are designing courses that offer a balance of one-to-one and one-to-many student-student, student-instructor, and student-content interactions that guide students towards co-constructing knowledge within a cohesive course community. The PARS approach facilitates a design that includes both structure and flexibility, so that students have a clear sense of the course goals and expectations, and also have the opportunity to express when the design is misaligned with their needs and contexts. More specifically, I recommend the following steps to implement strategic, user-centered design in online courses:

1. Survey students before the course to learn about their technological access and any issues that may hinder their ability to participate in the course.
2. Integrate frequent opportunities for student reflection on what they are learning and how the course is (or is not) facilitating that learning.
3. Modify course logistics (due dates, required interactions, assignment details) in response to student feedback.
4. Critically examine the required deliverables and question if that those deliverables are necessary to support student learning.

The PARS approach illustrates that there is not one "right" or "best" way to design a course; instead, successful course design accounts for the social context of both students and the instructor, including their workload, technological access and familiarity, and lives beyond the course. This requires the instructor to invest time into the course design, and also be willing to adapt the plan as the course proceeds. In the language of PARS, strategically designing accessible and personal learning environments requires that we are responsive to our students.

In closing, I must acknowledge that I am in a privileged position as a tenure-track faculty member trained in both instructional design and theories of learning, and those privileges influence the time I have to dedicate to course design and facilitation, as well as my approach to those tasks. In other contexts, the "mandated use of LMS platforms and out-of-the-box design principles like Quality Matters," alongside administrative mandates for quickly-built online courses staffed primarily by contingent faculty, and academic assumptions that online learning is necessarily inferior to face-to-face, create institutional, economic, and cultural barriers to strategic, user-centered design (Greer & Harris, p. 22, 2018). It is imperative that institutions intentionally and ethically account for the social contexts of both their students and their teachers if they intend to offer high-quality online courses that rely on strategic, user-centered design.

References

Arola, K. L. (2010). The design of web 2.0: The rise of the template, the fall of design. *Computers and Composition, 27*(1), 4–14.

Aragon, S. R. (2003). Creating social presence in online environments. *New Directions for Adult and Continuing Education, 100,* 57–68.

Bjork, C. (2018). Integrating usability testing with digital rhetoric in OWI. *Computers & Composition, 49,* 4–13. https://doi.org/10.1016/j.compcom.2018.05.009.

Blythe, S. (2001). Designing online courses: User-centered practices. *Computers and Composition, 18,* 329–346.

Borgman, J. & Dockter, J. (2018). Considerations of access and design in the online writing classroom. *Computers & Composition, 49,* 94–105.

Borgman, J. & McArdle, C. (2019). *Personal, accessible, responsive, strategic: Resources and strategies for online writing instructors.* The WAC Clearinghouse; University Press of Colorado. https://doi.org/10.37514/PRA-B.2019.0322.

Bransford, J. D., Brown, A. L. & Cocking, R. R. (2000). *How people learn: Brain, mind experience, and school.* National Academy Press.

Breuch, L. K. (2015). Faculty preparation for OWI. In B. Hewett & K. E. DePew (Eds.), *Foundational Practices of Online Writing Instruction* (pp. 349–388). The WAC Clearinghouse; Parlor Press. https://doi.org/10.37514/PER-B.2015.0650.2.11.

Bruffee, K. A. (1984). Collaborative learning and the "Conversation of mankind." *College English, 46*(7), 635–652. https://doi.org/10.2307/376924.

CCCC statement on globalization in writing studies pedagogy and research. (2019). *College Composition and Communication, 70*(4), 681–690.

Cleary, Y., Rice, R., Zemliansky, P., St.Amant, K. & Borgman, J. C. (2019). Perspectives on teaching writing online in global contexts: Ideas, insights, and projections. *ROLE: Research in Online Literacy Education, 2*(1). http://www.roleolor.org/perspectives-on-teaching-writing-online.html.

Gallagher, J. R. (2015). The rhetorical template. *Computers and Composition, 35*(1), 1–11.

Garrison, R. D. (2017). *E-learning in the 21st century: A community of inquiry framework for research and practice* (3rd ed.). Routledge.

Gillam, K. W. & Shannon R. (2013). Re-embodying online composition: Ecologies of writing in unreal time and space. *Computers and Composition 30*, 24–36. https://doi.org/10.1016/j.compcom.2012.11.001.

Greer, M. & Harris, H. S. (2018). User-centered design as a foundation for effective online writing instruction. *Computers & Composition, 49*, 14–24. https://doi.org/10.1016/j.compcom.2018.05.006.

Harris, H. S., Melonçon, L., Hewett, B. L., Mechenbier, M. X. & Martinez, D. (2019). A call for purposeful pedagogy-driven course design in OWI. *ROLE: Research in Online Literacy Education, 2*(1). http://www.roleolor.org/a-call-for-purposeful-pedagogy-driven-course-design-in-owi.html.

Hawisher, G. E. S. & Cynthia, L. (1991). The rhetoric of technology in the electronic writing class. *College Composition and Communication, 42*(1), 55–65.

Mick, C. S. & Middlebrook, G. (2015). Asynchronous and synchronous modalities. In B. L. Hewett & K. E. DePew (Eds.), *Foundational practices of online writing instruction* (pp. 129–148). The WAC Clearinghouse; Parlor Press. https://doi.org/10.37514/PER-B.2015.0650.2.03.

Moore, M. G. (1989). Three types of interaction. *The American Journal of Distance Education, 3*(2), 1–6.

Porter, J. E. (2014). Framing questions about MOOCs and writing courses. In S. D. Krause & C. Lowe (Eds.), *Invasion of the MOOCs: The promises and perils of massive open online courses* (pp. 14–28). Parlor Press.

Rankins-Robertson, S., Bourelle, T., Bourelle, A. & Fisher, D. Multimodal instruction: Pedagogy and practice for enhancing multimodal composition online. *Kairos: A Journal for Teachers of Writing in Webbed Environments 19*(1). http://kairos.technorhetoric.net/19.1/praxis/robertson-et-al/index.html.

Rice, R. & St.Amant, K. (2018). *Thinking globally, composing locally: Rethinking online writing in the age of the global internet*. Utah State University Press.

Sackey, D. J., Nguyen, M.-T. & Grabill, J. T. (2015). Constructing learning spaces: What we can learn from studies of informal learning online. *Computers and Composition, 35*(1), 112–124.

St.Amant, K. & Rice, R. (2015). Online writing in global contexts: Rethinking the nature of connections and communication in the age of international online media. *Computers and Composition, 38*, v-x.

Stewart, M. K. (2017). Communities of inquiry: A heuristic for designing and assessing interactive learning in technology-mediated FYC. *Computers and Composition, 45*, 67–84. https://doi.org/10.1016/j.compcom.2017.06.004.

Appendix A. Project Descriptions

3. Projects

Throughout the semester, you will submit three projects.

Project #1: Design a Unit: Create a draft of a syllabus that includes a lesson plan for one unit of an online course (3–4 weeks). Your design should include the *weekly* *topics* and the *assignment sheet* for the culminating project. Compose a reflective cover letter that introduces the materials, explaining what they are and how they enact the theories we've been reading. See the assignment sheet for more details.

Project #2: Interactive Activities: Design the interactive student-student activities associated with the unit you designed for Project #1. This might involve discussion, peer review, group work, collaborative writing, etc. The interaction could take place within an LMS (i.e., discussion forums, synchronous chat) or outside of the LMS (i.e., social media, other online tools or apps). At minimum, you will need to include *one asynchronous activity and one synchronous activity*. Compose a reflective cover letter that introduces the materials, explaining what they are and how they enact the theories we've been reading. See the assignment sheet for more details.

Project #3: Preparing for the Final Project: The goal of Project #3 is to prepare you for the Final Project, so you will have options of how you approach it. If you are creating a pedagogical portfolio for your final project, then Project #3 will involve *creating instructional materials* to introduce and evaluate the activities you designed for Project 2, and also composing a reflective cover letter that introduces the materials, explaining what they are and how they enact the theories we've been reading. If you are writing a scholarly article or creating a response to the COVID-19 pandemic, then you will *draft a project proposal*, which will include a reflective element. See the assignment sheet for more details.

4. Final Project

Option #1 = Pedagogy Project: You will submit a final portfolio that includes revised elements from Projects #1, #2, and #3. The final product should include: (a) a syllabus with the course schedule fully developed for one unit and (b) a collection of the activities, instructional materials, and assessment artifacts presented in an LMS or a course website that you design (see Projects 1–3 for more details on what's expected). You will additionally submit a 4–5 page critical analysis essay that analyzes how your materials reflect current theories and best practices for hybrid and online writing instruction. This paper should engage with at least one major theory/concept from this course (i.e., social presence, accessibility, multimodal instruction, etc.), and should build an argument for why others should also consider this concept/theory when designing their own courses.

Note: You will receive instructor feedback on Projects 1, 2 & 3, and it is expected that you use this feedback to inform your final portfolio, if you choose this option.

Option #2 = Scholarly Article or Pandemic Response: Draft a scholarly article that responds to the some of ideas we've talked about this semester, and/or responds to higher education's response to the COVID-19 pandemic. This could be a theoretical article, an empirical article (if you already have data to work with), a teaching article, or a more creative project (i.e., a webtext or an autoethnography or an artistic response). As long as you are engaging with the theories of online and hybrid pedagogy, or pandemic pedagogy, then the project will be accepted. You'll write a proposal for Project #3 and receive instructor approval.

Please also identify a journal in which you wish to publish this article, and use the author guidelines to inform the article parameters (word count, genre, etc.). You might consider journals such as: Computers & Composition, Research in Online Literacy Education, Journal of Online Learning, The Internet and Higher Education, or British Journal of Educational Technology.

Appendix B. Social Presence Reading Response Prompt

Discussion Topic

Due June 9 at 2:00pm

After you've done the reading, compose a response. Your initial post (due Tuesday at 2 p.m. ET) should be 300–400 words, or a 3–5 minute audio/video, and it should respond to one of the discussion prompts below:

- Option #1: Social Presence. In response to Rourke et al., which is a seminal article that introduced social presence as an element of the Community of Inquiry Framework, define "social presence" and "immediacy," and reflect on why these elements are important for learning. Please also differentiate between the three elements of social presence: interpersonal/affective communication, open communication, and group cohesion, offering examples of when you have experienced these phenomena, and in what educational context. You might also reflect on how things have changed since this article was published in 1999.
- Option #2: Social Presence for Satisfaction v. Learning. In response to Aragon, differentiate between social presence that supports student satisfaction and social presence that supports student learning. Please also reflect on his recommended strategies and consider how you could apply them in Project #2. In that consideration, discuss why you might use different modalities (asynchronous/synchronous) to facilitate a particular type of social presence at a particular moment in your course.
- Option #3: Social Presence in OWI. Rendahl & Breuch's literature review summarizes an important concern in OWI: can students engage in the collaboration and interaction that composition theory says is critical for learning? In other words, the field has been asking, can we establish sufficient social presence in an OWC? Should we? With this in mind, define "engagement" and "participation" and reflect on how these behaviors might look in a regular online course and/or in a pandemic pedagogy course.

Appendix C. Individual Reflection Prompt

Week 2 Reflection Assignment

Due June 12 at 2:00pm

Please write a 400–500 word individual reflection on your experience with the activities this week and submit it to this Assignment Folder by Friday at 2pm. Your response should:

- Offer a general reflection on your experience this week. How are you handling the workload of a summer [program] course while living at home?
- What's the number one takeaway you have from the readings and activities?
- How was the group work? What did you notice about the different designs from last week to this week? What are the benefits and drawback to each approach?
- What's your plan for Project #2? Any questions or things you want to run by me?

This is an appropriate place to ask me questions or express any concerns about the course.

Chapter 4. The Literacy Load is Too Damn High! A PARS Approach to Cohort-Based Discussion

Alex Sibo
PENNSYLVANIA STATE UNIVERSITY, UNIVERSITY PARK

Abstract: This chapter demonstrates how a cohort-based model of student discussion can ameliorate student and instructor literacy loads within the current paradigm of online course enrollments that often exceed the recommendations of the CCCC. The PARS approach to online writing instruction offers a framework for understanding and designing a model of discussion that encourages quality over quantity for low stakes student engagement and that lowers the stakes for instructor engagement in student discussion. The focus of this chapter emphasizes the role student collaboration and peer to peer learning and assessment in online learning. Readers of this chapter will learn how to develop personalized cohorts, strategically administrate cohort-based discussion, and provide accessible and responsive assessment of student engagement within cohorts.

Keywords: online writing instruction, literacy load, assessment, discussion, discussion boards

As a former online English student and current online English instructor, I am quite guilty of skimming discussion boards, hoping to find a quick intervention or a place to insert an easy, helpful comment. The cause of this phenomenon, the cumulative amount of reading and writing one must perform in a course, has been labelled "literacy load" by June Griffin and Deborah Minter (2013). According to Griffin and Minter's (2013) report, "the reading load of the online classes was more than 2.75 times greater than the face-to-face courses" (p. 153). What for Scott Warnock (2009) is the very virtue of online writing courses, that students and instructors "write, write, and write some more" (p. 69), is what leads Griffin and Minter to conclude that "online courses as they are often configured can overtax students, particularly academically underserved and ELL [English Language Learner] students" (2013, p. 153). Quantity of writing and reading has been a point of emphasis in advocating for the validity of online writing instruction (OWI). However, the literacy load required by quantity-focused OWI pedagogy leaves both students and instructors "stretched," according to Lisa Melonçon and Heidi Skurat Harris (2015), often at the expense of learning outcomes. How can we as online writing instructors mitigate the detrimental effects of a high literacy load on us and our students without sacrificing the rich interactions that take place in online writing courses?

For the past three years I have managed to mitigate the literacy load in my online writing courses (OWCs) through cohort-based discussion. Simply put, cohort-based discussion revolves around student discussion in small groups over the course of an entire class term. If most OWC discussions are analogous to the one big class-wide discussion favored by face-to-face (F2F) instructors, cohort-based discussions are analogous to the breakout group discussions also used in F2F and other synchronous courses. Working with a limited number of peers allows students to develop more intimate, trusting relationships with one another while still learning from other and opposing perspectives. As the research team of Cunningham, Hilliard et al. (2019) have demonstrated, stronger relationships among discussion participants in OWCs equates to better outcomes from discussions and peer review sessions. But perhaps the most important conclusion put forth by Cunningham et al. (2019) is that smaller class sizes correlate to a stronger sense of community within the class. We may not be able to rely on our institutions to do the right thing and institute lower course caps, but we do have control over how we structure discussion (i.e., creating small discussion cohorts) and therefore how large and how strong the peer communities are.

My use of cohort-based discussion extends the research and application of group discussions in OWI, a pedagogical method that is currently underutilized in OWCs. For example, Carmen Kynard (2007) has described a hybrid model of first-year writing in which she used group-based Blackboard discussions in tandem with F2F class wide discussion. Also using a form of cohort-based discussion, Ken Gillam and Shannon R. Wooden (2013) have endorsed an ecological model of writing in OWCs where students collaborate in small groups for a single assignment cycle in order to balance cognitive and communal writing outcomes. The logical next step from both Kynard (2007) and Gillam and Wooden (2013) is to implement cohort-based discussion in a fully online course for an entire semester. Fewer peers means greatly reduced literacy loads, allowing for deeper reading and more meaningful conversation among peers. A greater emphasis on socially constructed knowledge and collaborative learning creates a more student-centered online classroom, allowing instructors to take a more "hands off" approach to discussion. By providing less direct feedback and focusing more on discussion monitoring and facilitation, instructors can reduce a significant amount of their writing load.

In the remainder of this chapter, I will lay out practical guidelines for how to implement cohort-based discussions in an OWC. For instructors, there are three areas to focus on when implementing cohort-based discussions: *development*, *administration*, and *assessment*. Each of these areas incorporate aspects of the PARS approach and are informed by my own experience and observation of previously conducted courses, and feedback and interviews with former students participating in cohort-based discussions.

Design: Personalized and Accessible

Putting together cohorts should be a collaborative process between instructors and students. Cohorts can naturally reduce literacy loads for students just by reducing the number of peers they interact with, and strategic decisions regarding cohort development can help increase the quality of interaction between students. While cohort development can add some extra work for instructors at the beginning of the course term, they can help reduce instructor literacy load in the long term. Rather than just randomly putting a certain number of students into a virtual pod together, it is best to make sure that cohorts have some common ground and some rationale for why peer cohorts have been selected. In other words, cohorts should be personalized.

As Jessie Borgman and Casey McArdle (2019) suggest, icebreaker activities in the first week of a course are a great method for personalizing the online classroom. Naturally, an icebreaker or introductory discussion is the best place to begin the process of selecting cohorts. In order to learn more about them, and to have their peers do the same, have students self-identify their areas of study, paper topic interests, educational/professional background, and personal information (that they are comfortable disclosing) in these introductory discussions. Personal disclosures allow students to see their peers both as fellow humans and allows them to make personal connections with one another. These interactions are vital for instructors to see who gets along with whom and can be an important set of data for constructing cohorts.

In addition to instructor observation, it is a good practice to solicit student input for such an important decision as deciding who they are going to be stuck with for the next six to 14 weeks. As Jessie Borgman and Jason Dockter (2018) have persuasively argued, online student populations have a variety of needs that can be met through the concept of user-centered design (UCD). One such tool for instructors to tailor their courses to their students' learning needs, Borgman and Dockter (2018) suggest, are private polls and surveys for students to communicate their "learning preferences, expectations and experiences as online students" (p. 98), information that is also useful for cohort construction. Instructors should be explicit about what these surveys will be used for and solicit student input on what type of experience they wish to get out of a cohort: are they looking to interact with disciplinarily like-minded people, or are they more interested in a supportive group with whom they a share a number of personal interests? By soliciting and collecting this information, instructors can ensure a personalized and *accessible* cohort experience.

Once all this information is collected within the first week, it is time to organize students into cohorts. For starters, it is important to make sure there are the right number of participants in each cohort. The key is to balance reducing literacy loads for students, while ensuring that there is still a lively community where discussion is taking place. Too many participants and there is not much benefit to the reduced cohort number and students will not have the same recognition of their peers; too few and the discussion boards will feel like a ghost town, which can be further exacerbated by mid-semester enrollment attrition. Ideally, a cohort should have just enough members that they can survive a student dropping the course and that each student can name their peers off the top of their head (which will be important for assessment). I have found the magic number to be six for my purposes. That number could easily be expanded to eight, depending on student and instructor preference.

Once cohort sizes are established, it is time to sort students into cohorts. I have found that cohorts can operate very similarly to discourse communities, so putting students into cohorts based on similar majors or areas of study, like fine arts and IT majors, has been very successful. Combing students with similar topic interests (like in Gillam and Wooden's 2013 study) has also been effective, whether students have been interested in writing about sports or social justice. Similarly, students who have similar educational and professional backgrounds, like military veterans and returning students, have been able to draw on their shared experiences and really come together to build some lively connections and conversations.

Of course, there are some cohort construction methodologies to avoid. For example, Paul Kei Matsuda (2006) warns against linguistic containment, the isolation of multilingual students from their monolingual peers. Instructors need to be mindful of cohort demographics, including race, gender, linguistics, (dis)ability, and so forth. As Josephine Walwema (2018) asserts, in an online learning environment "dialogue with people of other cultures helps build social responsibility and the goodwill to promote the wellbeing of all people" (p. 31). It is important to remember that students who benefit from white cultural hegemony are both the ones who need to be educated about other cultures and who are often resistant to such learning. For this reason, students from currently marginalized and historically underrepresented backgrounds should not be made to carry the burden of educating their more privileged and recalcitrant peers. Whenever student information is available, instructors should avoid containing students to homogenous cohorts or relying on tokenism to "diversify" cohorts.

---

1. What did you already know about the subject of this week's reading?
2. What did you learn from this reading?
3. What do you not understand from the reading?
4. How can you use this reading to help you complete the next assignment?

Figure 4.1. Reading response questions.

Instruction: Personalized and Strategic

Having assembled the discussion cohorts, the literacy load should begin to lessen for students and instructors. In order to separate cohort discussion spaces, instructors can create separate discussion boards for each cohort. Depending on the course management system (CMS) being used there are some shortcuts to creating multiple discussion boards for different cohorts. Some CMSs have a built-in "group" function that facilitates the use of discussion cohorts. However, CMSs are not always desirable to use, so there are ways to bootstrap discussion cohorts in any online space. For example, instructors could simply create multiple versions of the same discussion prompt, labelled for each individual cohort. Although less ideal, discussion could continue to be conducted in one single message board, but students would only be responsible for interacting with members of their cohort.

Once the discussion boards are made, it is time to think about discussion prompts. One type of prompt that has benefitted the most from the cohort-based discussion, in my experience, is a reading response discussion. Students are asked to answer the four questions listed in Figure 4.1 in response to the week's assigned reading and respond to one another based on their answers. These questions (adapted from Cheryl Glenn's teaching practice for an online context) allow students to reflect on their own reading and synthesis of course material, while also inviting students to deliberate over difficult concepts.

Moreover, discussion boards in a cohort environment function as a site of collaboration and knowledge construction, as a result of fewer discussion participants. As Kenneth A. Bruffee (1984) and John Trimbur (1989) suggested several decades ago, collaborative learning is an integral part of composition pedagogy and the "democratization" of learning. As personalized cohorts and communities of practice, discussion participants are likely already familiar with the topics and concepts that their peers are working with, more so than the instructor. Since instructors know more about writing concepts than about the disciplinary content of students' interests, the personalization of cohorts enables students to take charge on matters of content. For this reason, discussion boards in many cases can be turned over almost exclusively to the students as "their" space. It is, of course, recommended for instructors to continue reading through student discussions, but instructor input can be kept to a minimum through some early discussion modelling, along with conflict resolution and thought provocation when necessary.

In keeping with the strategic instruction advocated by Borgman and McArdle (2019), instructors need to be strategic about how they interact with students in discussion, which can be aided by collaboration. Whenever a member of the cohort has a question about the reading, their peers are prompted to answer the question and help explain more difficult concepts to one another collectively. Rather than the instructor being the locus of knowledge, students are encouraged to discover their own meaning-making and knowledge-building capacities through collaborative discussion. This collaborative, meaning-making discussion is exemplified by the "Blackboard Flava-Flavin" that Kynard (2007) observed in her hybrid first-year writing courses. Trickstering and digital signifying are methods of re-constructing knowledge and the university that are culturally specific to the Black working class students in Kynard's study. However, they offer proof that students are more than capable of advanced meaning-making without the direct hand of instructor intervention.

In addition to reading responses, writing workshops also work well in cohort-based discussions. These can take the form of planning or brainstorming for the next assignment, concept exercises, or peer review of rough drafts. Like reading responses, workshops in cohort-based discussion encourage students to collaborate with one another to improve their writing through planning, exercise, and draft review. A strategic use of cohort discussion helps to mitigate instructor literacy loads by leveraging the potential of collaborative learning.

On occasion I have found that some cohorts just do not result in fruitful discussion, either because there was conflict, too many participants had to drop the course, or there was not the alignment of interests that there appeared to be at the beginning of the course. Rather than ask students to bear through it for the rest of term, redistributing the cohort members into other appropriate cohorts has proved to be surprisingly effective. If instructors have kept notes from the introductory discussion and have continued to monitor discussion, it should be quite easy to place students into new cohorts. After several weeks, many of the cohorts have been able to create congenial communities that are welcoming to newcomers rather than exclusive and reactionary. A quick explanation and introduction should be more than enough to add a new member to a cohort and to keep it running smoothly.

Assessment: Accessible and Responsive

When Borgman and McArdle (2019) talk about responsiveness, they discuss determining the how and the when of giving feedback to students. Cohort-based discussions present new opportunities for instructors to assess and provide feedback on student participation in discussion. In typical discussion environments, instructors can assess participation based on completion, which does not provide much holistic feedback, or on the instructor's sense of a student's contributions to discussion, attended by a burdensome literacy load. Students can also be asked to provide self-reflections and self-assessments, but this individualistic look at discussion can ignore the rich social and cognitive interchanges that occur in discussion boards. With cohort-based discussions, students can be asked to reflect on their own contributions to discussion, as well as that of their peers. These reflections can in turn be used by instructors to assess the quality of participation and to offer feedback for improvement and encouragement.

This instructor-proctored peer assessment can best be performed using surveys, as seen in Figure 4.2. Each student can receive the following survey questions, repeated for the number of peers in their cohort (e.g., if there are six students in each cohort, individual students will need to answer the assessment questions five times). The questions in Figure 4.2 help instructors to assess individual student participation through the experience of their peers, while helping to mitigate instructor literacy load during assessment. Students not only help instructors wade through discussion boards by highlighting specific strengths and weaknesses throughout the instructional unit, they offer their own feedback for peers that can be curated, anonymized, and distributed to the student.

---

1. Which of your peers are you assessing?
   a. How well did this classmate contribute to your learning in this unit?
   b. They were an excellent resource for myself and others.
   c. They were an active and helpful participant.
   d. They were not a very helpful participant.
   e. They actively prohibited my learning (explain why below).
2. What is the best example of this classmate's helpful participation during this unit? Be specific.
3. What could this classmate do to be a more helpful participant in the course? What specific things would be helpful to yourself or others?

Figure 4.2. Peer assessment survey.

Turning to the individual questions in the survey, Question 2 asks students to provide a holistic assessment of their peers' contributions to discussion. I have found this method makes assessment *accessible* to students, because they have a seat at the table for assessing a space that is more theirs than the instructor's, particularly since standards of assessment have historically placed the instructor as the arbiter of "good" and "bad" participation. Student answers to Question 2 can be used as a rough heuristic for assigning letter grades. For example, the student who is "an excellent resource" has earned an A, whereas the student who was "not very helpful" has earned a C. It is of course helpful to scaffold this practice of grading for students beforehand. Instructors who practice ungrading can still use the holistic assessment as a heuristic to identify students that need more support. Option d ("they actively prohibited my learning") allows students the opportunity to disclose issues in discussion that they had not previously brought to the instructor's attention or were not readily apparent to the instructor. As one example, I have had a student recognize that one of her peers was frequently plagiarizing her posts and responses in discussion. The student she accused was changing the language enough that I was unable to recognize what he was doing, but as the original author of the posts, the first student recognized this pattern of her own ideas being passed off in another's words. By bringing this to my attention, I was able to privately intervene.

Question 3 of the survey asks students to provide evidence and a rationale for their holistic assessment of each peer. This question not only helps students practice analytical writing by requiring them to support their original claim, but it also allows them to calibrate their response to Question 2. If they selected option a for one of their peers but are having difficulty identifying a particularly helpful post or behavior from that peer, this allows them to rethink their original assessment. Furthermore, this question helps instructors to identify the strengths of an individual students' participation without having to review every discussion board in every cohort.

Question 4 acts similarly to Question 3, by asking students to reflect on how their peers could improve their contributions to discussion. Even students that instructors may perceive as helpful and insightful contributors to discussion can improve as peers. For example, I have had an excellent student with previous writing experience who I thought was a very helpful and insightful contributor in discussion. However, a few of her peers who were less experienced writers observed that her comments to them, particularly in peer review, could be overwhelming and even intimidating. Thanks to their input, I was able to remind this student of her audience and her responses quickly became more amenable and helpful to her peers.

In addition to allowing students a moment of reflection, the peer assessment surveys allow instructors to be more *responsive* when assessing discussion. As Beth Hewett (2015) reminds us, "minimal, yet personalized response sets boundaries that ease the instructor literacy load" (p. 105) By curating students' reflections into a single assessment comment, the literacy load is further eased. Once students complete the surveys, I go about collating the responses for each student, reading all the encouraging and constructive comments that students have provided on their cohort mates. From these responses I write up a brief comment for each student that summarizes the assessment of the discussion participation, highlighting the areas of excellence and suggestions for improvement. This process allows peer feedback to be anonymized, so that students can speak honestly about their peers; students do not feel pressure to keep quiet about issues for fear of personal blowback, and instructors can filter out unwarranted comments about a student.

In my experience, such comments typically come from students who are perpetuating linguistic racism against their peers who use Black Language (Baker-Bell, 2020) or Global Englishes (Canagarajah, 2013). Such comments can offer a moment for instructors to push back against students' prejudices and advocate for what April Baker-Bell (2020) defines as "Linguistic Justice," a pedagogy that "affords Black [and other non-white] students the same kind of linguistic liberties that are afforded to white students" (p. 7). It goes without saying that comments that perpetuate linguistic racism in peer assessment should not be used to negatively affect grades of the students targeted by these comments.

As an example of successful instructor-proctored peer assessment, this was my feedback in the first unit for the abovementioned student whose participation was excellent, but was at times overwhelming for her peers (names changed to protect the innocent):

The people loved your contributions to discussion, Hannah! One thing that came up is that your comments can be a little overwhelming and intimidating for others to engage with, given your ethos as someone with previous writing experience. Something worth keeping an eye on as you modulate your participation to suit your audience of peers.

I have found that sometimes students perfectly describe someone's contributions better than I could and are worth quoting in my feedback. For example,

One of your peers referred to you as a "rockstar." Keep on rocking, Andrew.

Discussion cohort assessment gives students access to the structure of power entailed through assessment and allows for responsive feedback based on the principles of collaborative learning.

Final Thoughts and Application

As I have illustrated in this chapter, cohort-based discussion greatly mitigates the burden of student and instructor literacy loads associated with discussion and assessment. An additional benefit of reduced literacy load is that discussion boards no longer emphasize the quantity of reading and writing students need to perform, but rather emphasize the quality of peer interaction. Moreover, cohort-based discussions are demonstrably practical through an adherence to the PARS approach: they offer personalized discussion spaces and feedback for students, follow existing recommendations of accessibility and universal design, are responsive while managing instructor literacy load, and offer a strategic way to structure an OWC.

Students themselves have spoken to the perceived benefits of using cohort-based discussion, not only for managing the literacy load they experience, but for helping develop their writing skills and making class more enjoyable. According to one student, "the fact that there were [only six people in the cohort,] we were not exactly overwhelmed . . . trying to give so many people feedback on what they were doing." Another student expressed his favor for cohort-based discussion by observing that for him, "the smaller the size [of participants in discussion], the less trepidation" about participating. Some students attributed the improvement of their writing and that of others to the cohorts. One stated that "small group sizes were by far the best format in my opinion to develop basic writing skills," while another observed that "using cohorts for discussion is an effective way to help the students better their writing." But perhaps most importantly, several students graced cohort-based discussion with the epithet, "enjoyable."

As an instructor, my observations also support student claims about their own development through cohort-based discussion. Students have made more substantial connections with their peers and have turned out higher quality writing through discussion cohorts than through other discussion models I have used. Furthermore, student attrition has been curbed significantly, perhaps as a result of students' increased learning or even enjoyment. Whereas previously only around 70 percent of students had completed the course, students in the cohorts now complete the course closer to 90 percent of the time now. My job as an instructor has also changed and improved in some ways. Using cohorts allows me to better keep track of who individual students are because of how the cohort divisions group students. Most importantly it has lightened my literacy load in terms of responding to students in discussion and in feedback. As a result, reading through student discussion has become less of a chore and more of a rewarding experience.

As observed throughout this chapter, cohort-based discussions still need to consider issues that can arise from intercultural and linguistic engagement, especially when it comes to assessment. Certainly, there is further work to be done to adequately address linguistic racism within cohorts-based discussion. With that being said, my hope is that this chapter, to put it in Borgman and McArdle's golf metaphor, can help instructors avoid the bunkers as they assemble their own cohort-based OWCs.

References

Baker-Bell, A. (2020). *Linguistic justice: Black language, literacy, identity, and pedagogy*. Routledge.

Borgman, J. & McArdle, C. (2019). *Personal, accessible, responsive, strategic: Resources and strategies for online writing instructors*. The WAC Clearinghouse; University Press of Colorado. https://doi.org/10.37514/PRA-B.2019.0322.

Borgman, J. & Dockter, J. (2018). Considerations of access and design in the online writing classroom. *Computers and Composition, 49*, 94–105.

Bruffee, K. A. (1984). Collaborative learning and the "conversation of mankind." In S. Miller (Ed.), *The Norton book of composition studies* (pp. 545–562). Norton.

Canagarajah, S. (2013). *Translingual practice: Global Englishes and cosmopolitan relations*. Routledge.

Cunningham, J., Hilliard, L., Stewart, M. & Stillman-Webb, M. (2019, March 14). *Researching communities of inquiry in blended and online writing courses: Results of a multi-institutional, mixed methods study* [Conference session]. Conference on College Composition and Communication, Pittsburgh, PA, United States.

Gillam, K. & Wooden, S. R. (2013). Re-embodying online composition: Ecologies of writing in unreal time and space. *Computers and Composition, 30*(1), 24–36. https://doi.org/10.1016/j.compcom.2012.11.001.

Griffin, J. & Minter, D. (2013). The rise of the online writing classroom: Reflecting on the material conditions of college composition teaching. *College Composition and Communication, 65*(1), 140–161.

Hewett, B. (2015). *Reading to learn and writing to teach: Literacy strategies for online writing instruction*. Bedford St. Martin's.

Kynard, C. (2007). "Wanted: Some Black long distance [writers]": Blackboard Flava-Flavin and other Afrodigital experiences in the classroom. *Computers and Composition, 24*, 329-345.

Matsuda, P. K. (2006). The myth of linguistic homogeneity in U.S. college composition. *College English, 68*(6), 637-651.

Melonçon. L. & Harris, H. (2015). Preparing students for OWI. In B. L. Hewett & K. DePew (Eds.), *Foundational practices of online writing instruction* (pp. 411-438). The WAC Clearinghouse; Parlor Press. https://doi.org/10.37514/PER-B.2015.0650.2.13.

Trimbur, J. (1989). Consensus and difference in collaborative learning. In S. Miller (Ed.), *The Norton book of composition studies* (pp. 733-747). Norton.

Walwema, J. (2018). Digital notebooks: Composing with open access. In R. Rice & K. St.Amant (Eds.), *Thinking globally, composing locally: Rethinking online writing in the age of the global internet* (pp. 15-34). Utah State University Press.

Warnock, S. (2009). *Teaching writing online: How and why*. National Council of Teachers of English.

Chapter 5. People, Programs, and Practices: A Grid-Based Approach to Designing and Supporting Online Writing Curriculum

Allegra Smith[1]
PURDUE UNIVERSITY

Libby Chernouski
PURDUE UNIVERSITY

Bianca Batti
GEORGIA INSTITUTE OF TECHNOLOGY

Alisha Karabinus
GRAND VALLEY STATE UNIVERSITY

Bradley Dilger
PURDUE UNIVERSITY

Abstract: Negotiating instructor autonomy, course consistency in student experiences and programmatic outcomes, and best practices for both instructional design and writing pedagogy can prove challenging in face-to-face classes—and these challenges are compounded in online writing instruction environments. In this chapter, we describe our strategic approach to balancing people, programs, and practices: a grid-based approach to scaffolding and customizing assignment sequences for online writing instruction at a large state research university. We share a 3 × 3 grid for structuring the learning progression in a 16-week online first-year writing course. By tracing the history of this grid's development, we provide insight into the collaboration between writing instructors, program administrators, and curriculum designers, demonstrating how educational stakeholders are balanced in the design of online writing curriculum. Providing the theory and best practices behind the design of this grid approach builds a model for other programs to adapt to their own institutional and pedagogical contexts. We then describe the grid's application for assessment and professional development in our writing program, explaining the benefits this approach provides for instructors and

---

1. Correspondence concerning this article should be addressed to Allegra Smith, Department of English, Purdue University, United States. Email: allegra.w.smith@gmail.com

administrators. We conclude by suggesting how writing program administrators could modify the grid approach to fit their own curricula—in two-course sequences or themed syllabus approaches, for example—affording transfer of these practices across institutional and programmatic contexts.

Keywords: adaptable course shells, content management, curriculum design, flexible pedagogy, professional development, scaffolding, templates

Balancing instructor autonomy and curricular standardization has long been a concern for writing programs (Carter-Tod, 2007). The demands of online writing instruction mean student success and instructor professional development must simultaneously be considered as well (Stewart et al., 2016). In this article, we share an approach to curriculum design created and led by a team of instructors from Introductory Composition at Purdue (ICaP) that balances these concerns and implements the PARS (personal, accessible, responsive, strategic) best practices for online writing instruction (OWI). Using an adaptable assignment sequence, visualized in a 3 × 3 grid, has helped online instructors approach OWI using the PARS elements of responsiveness and strategy and has made the standardized curriculum more accessible for both instructors and students. We present the assignment grid, trace its history, describe its applications, and suggest how other programs can develop their own variations modified for their institutional and programmatic contexts.[2]

Context for Course Development

ICaP is a unit of Purdue University's Department of English, directed by a professor in rhetoric and composition, with a full-time assistant director and a large team of graduate research assistants actively involved in program administration. Until recently, instructional staff were primarily English graduate students, teaching a 1:1 load of our unique four-credit course, English 106. Most undergraduates take only 106 or an equivalent; Purdue has no WAC or WID program, and only one writing course in the general education core.

Multiple changes that began in fall 2016 prompted the development of an online version of English 106: a well-publicized restructuring in the College of Liberal Arts (CLA) that introduced a competing class based on reading "great books," at the same time that CLA radically reduced the size of the Graduate Program in

---

2. The authors would like to thank instructional designer Debbie Runshe (Purdue Teaching and Learning Technologies) for her guidance and mentoring throughout the course design and assessment process. Thanks are also due to Rachel Atherton (who helped shape the form of the course when she taught one of the first sections in fall 2017 with Allegra and Libby), and Ola Swatek (who developed the course with Allegra in summer 2017). The design of ENGL 106-DIST was supported by the Department of English, the College of Liberal Arts, and Digital Education at Purdue University.

English (Cassuto, 2019); the resultant increase in adjunct and one-year instructors teaching for ICaP; and undergraduate enrollment rising so quickly that scheduling classrooms became difficult. The rapidly changing contexts of writing instruction underscored the need for flexible approaches that would respond to changing expectations, afford strategic partnerships, and create a curriculum highly accessible to both ICaP instructors and students. Thus, the then-director of ICaP (Bradley) met with Purdue's Digital Education division to propose building a fully online version of ENGL 106. He convened a team of graduate student research assistants to design a course template for piloting in fall 2017.

Developing the 3 × 3 Grid

Initially, the graduate student online course developers (Allegra and Ola) created a single master course template, with help from an instructional designer (Debbie) and the writing program administrator (Bradley). They knew that they wanted to give instructors options to assign different projects in the future—to be responsive to the diverse needs and teaching strengths of the various instructors in the introductory composition program, which included graduate teaching assistants from a variety of programs (M.A., M.F.A., and Ph.D.), adjunct instructors, continuing lecturers, and tenure-line and tenured faculty. So before designing the grid, online course developer Allegra mapped a learning progression for the first version of ENGL 106-DIST, based on a digital rhetorics theme. This learning progression included objectives for each of the three major course projects, broad themes that projects could fall under, and a preliminary list of alternative assignments that could be pursued after the first course template was tested. (See Figure 5.1, Learning Progression.)

This initial course design and learning progression moved students along a continuum of writing skills and audiences: from observing and reflecting upon their own experiences, to researching and analyzing a concept or phenomenon for a select group of like-minded readers, to finally remixing and presenting that research for an unfamiliar audience. After applying this progression and testing its fit with both the instructors and students of ICaP, the objectives have been revised into the form that the grid takes now. (See Table 5.1, Assignment Grid.)

The grid provides three units, each with three project options for instructors to choose from. These projects were shaped over time in response to feedback from instructors, fixing the three-assignment approach both for standard 16-week semesters, as well as for shortened eight-week terms (in summer and the first and second halves of full semesters). The team experimented with four-unit sequences because they were common across ICaP already, but quickly came to a consensus that a three-unit grid with more granular scaffolding was better for both instructors and students. These three units have changed slightly since the initial course design, to match programmatic outcomes and ensure consistency of objectives across sections of 106:

OBSERVE + REFLECT

DIGITAL AUTOBIOGRAPHY
- Students will write about one way in which a **digital tool, technology, or space** has affected them as a person, student, and/or citizen
- They'll **tell a story** about their experiences with a particular interface or community and connect that to their professional/career plans
- They get to **choose the best medium** to facilitate their autobiography: PowerPoint presentation, report, website, audio essay, blog, interactive story, traditional essay, etc.

ALTERNATE ASSIGNMENTS:
- Profile of a space/place
- Traditional literacy narrative
- Autoethnography
- Cultural artifact analysis

RESEARCH + ANALYZE

RESEARCHED ARGUMENT
- Students will use scholarly and popular sources to **construct a researched argument** about a technological tool, application, or phenomenon
- They will **conduct secondary research,** using Purdue Library databases and open source digital tools (such as Google Scholar), on a topic related to technology and their personal or professional interests
- They will **assess, summarize, and synthesize sources** to make a case to a community of like-minded peers

ALTERNATE ASSIGNMENTS:
- Discourse community or community of practice report
- Research paper or report
- Mapping the problem essay

REMIX + PRESENT

ADVOCACY INFOGRAPHIC
- Students will **remediate** their research project for a different, more public-facing audience
- They will **identify a specific audience** to direct their argument towards, and tailor their communication to that audience
- They will **create an infographic** for circulation in a digital space of their choice (Facebook, Pinterest, Tumblr, etc.) aimed at informing/persuading the audience they've targeted

ALTERNATE ASSIGNMENTS:
- TED talk
- Informative/advocacy web site
- Transmedia storytelling (tracing frames from a movie, TV show, book, etc.)

Figure 5.1. Learning progression for ENGL 106-DIST, showing the original design later expanded into the 3 × 3 grid.

These alterations to the learning progression foreground rhetorical thinking across all assignments, demonstrating ICaP's commitment to rhetorical education as a foundation of all first-year writing courses—and, indeed, of all *writing*. This ensures that the work in ENGL 106 courses—regardless of theme or approach—is grounded in the theory and research of rhetoric and writing studies, and builds a similar toolkit for students across sections.

Table 5.1. Assignment grid

ENGL 106-DIST Assignment Grid			
Instructor chooses one project from each row.			
Unit	Option 1	Option 2	Option 3
Unit 1: Rhetorical Thinking + Analysis	Digital Interface Analysis	Rhetorical Analysis	Scholarly Article Analysis
Unit 2: Research + Argument	Primary Research Report	Mapping the Problem Essay (Lit Review)	Researched Argument
Unit 3: Remediation + Multimodal Rhetoric	Podcast	TED Talk	Research Poster or Infographic
Unit 4: Reflection	Portfolio		

Table 5.2. Changes in grid units over time

Version 1	Version 2	Rationale
Observe and reflect	Rhetorical thinking and analysis	Match ICaP's first learning outcome, "demonstrate rhetorical awareness of diverse audiences, situations, and scenarios"
Research and analyze	Research and argument	Respond to instructor feedback about the program's fifth learning outcome, "perform research and evaluate sources to support claims"
Remix and present	Remediation and multimodal rhetoric	Align strategically with disciplinary research on remediation (Davis et al., 2010; DePalma, 2015; Fraiberg, 2010; Prior & Hengst, 2010; Shipka, 2005); highlight the multiple modes that students practice throughout the course

The grid provides three assignment options for each of these three units: some more "traditional" in nature, like a primary research report or analysis of a scholarly article; while others engage more deeply with concepts of digital rhetoric and user experience (UX), like a digital interface analysis that asks students to break down components of the audience and purpose for a technology, or a podcast that presents their research project. These options support instructors by giving them a choice: a new instructor can stick with a familiar genre to test the waters of online teaching, or an experienced lecturer who's getting bored with reading the same old papers can try out a new assignment to add to their repertoire.

ICaP also uses a common assignment across all sections, regardless of theme or modality (face-to-face, hybrid, or fully online), for the purpose of standardizing programmatic assessment. All students assemble a final portfolio of their work, as well as an overall course reflection, for submission at the end of the semester. This final portfolio serves as a fourth unit to the grid, highlighting students' reflective work and metacognition about their growth and skill development over the course of the semester (Jenson, 2011; Shipka, 2011; VanKooten, 2016; Yancey, 1998). The incorporation of the portfolio was also a response to instructor wishes for flexibility, in that it can be used with any assignment and the approach to reflection can be varied.

People: How the Grid Supports Instructors and Students

While the assignment grid itself gives instructors pedagogical autonomy over course design within the bounds of best practices for OWI, structuring the grid into units ensures course objectives are being met. Each unit and its associated assignments target two course outcomes specifically as unit objectives. These objectives remain the same, regardless of which assignment from the grid is selected for each unit. Units and assignments are taught sequentially, maintaining a strict learning progression that scaffolds student learning consistently. That is, students always receive grounding in rhetorical thinking and analysis before moving on to research and argumentation, advancing to remediation and multimodal composing in the third unit. While instructors may emphasize different aspects of rhetorical thinking, research, or multimodality according to the assignments they choose, student learning is scaffolded according to the overarching unit structure.

There are also programmatic benefits to the scaffolding provided by a unit-framed grid structure. If substitutes must be found for an online course, experienced online instructors will be able to more easily situate themselves in another instructor's course, thanks to the linear progression established by the unit structure. In addition, maintaining and revising course materials is more manageable when curriculum developers can work on each unit in turn, rather than considering each assignment in the grid independently. For example, a single rubric is managed for each unit, rather than for each individual assignment.

Much of online writing instruction scholarship speaks of student-users, and the need to carefully design and scaffold material for student accessibility and success. The grid approach we present here establishes a consistent rhetorical trajectory across all of the courses in the program, ensuring the achievement of established learning outcomes and a consistent learning experience for students across all sections of first-year writing. Further, the grid approach takes into account *instructor*-users, and how instructor experience and course design impacts success from their perspectives alongside those of the students.

The grid approach also embeds the work of instructional designers in curriculum, which helps manage the administrative workload. This strategic implementation in design and administration focuses primarily on instructor support and professional development, extending the PARS emphasis on enhancing the student experience in OWI through strategic administration (Borgman & McArdle, 2019). The use of a "grid approach" in online first-year writing fits with existing research that suggests template courses are a best practice for OWI (Rodrigo & Ramírez, 2017), but that writing instruction should be "personal" (Borgman & McArdle, 2019). A grid allows some standardization across a writing program—as well as the ability to work within a pre-established template for instructors who are new to teaching online—while also giving all instructors flexibility to choose and customize. This approach not only provides a consistent and well-implemented curriculum but also helps writing program administrators ethically and sustainably support instructors, providing "reasonable control over their own content and/or techniques" (National Council of Teachers of English, 2013), and facilitating the PARS element of access through access to professional development. This flexibility supports a variety of instructors, providing space to customize based on different needs while preserving consistency across program curricula.

Context is important for designing content and approaches in OWI development (Blythe, 2001; Sullivan & Porter, 1997), but context extends beyond students and must be considered from programmatic and institutional perspectives as well. The strategic development of grid modules that can be mixed and matched according to instructors' strengths and interests, as well as accompanying flexible rubrics that can apply to multiple different projects that satisfy the same learning goals, has been developed with inexperienced graduate students and contingent faculty who teach multiple sections in mind (Bourelle, 2016). Instead of having to figure it out on the fly when creating an online writing course (OWC) from scratch, instructors can choose ready-made items from the grid, reducing their workload so they can instead focus on establishing a teacherly presence in their online class and providing valuable feedback to students. This strategic intervention into course design allows instructors to select assignments they are comfortable with, then be supported with templates and other materials designed in a manner consistent with course outcomes, program goals, and best practices for online instruction.

Adapting and designing strategies for success in OWI cannot stop with considerations of student success. Instructor success is an essential component in developing OWI. New OWI instructors often feel hesitant to make direct changes or adaptations to template course shells, for fear of "messing them up" or going against established standards (Stewart et al., 2016). On the other hand, allowing complete design freedom or a very loosely structured "bare bones" course fails to provide the necessary scaffolding to ease new instructors into the digital learning environment and can cause issues of workload exploitation for otherwise vulnerable graduate instructors and untenured faculty. Thus, the flexible grid approach provides a responsive middle ground between unrestricted curriculum and rigid standardized templates, empowering instructors to personalize the curriculum, while still providing a safety net (emphasizing the "responsive" and "personal" elements of the PARS approach). A flexible grid approach, rather than cookie-cutter templates that do not allow for customization, ensures that curriculum achieves programmatic outcomes and reflects instructional design best practices, while still providing instructors autonomy over the courses they teach.

Practices: Putting the Modular Grid to Work

The grid is introduced to instructors in the training materials and resources they receive when teaching online for ICaP for the first time. The modular grid and associated units are presented as the foundational course structure, which instructors are expected to modify minimally, especially if they have not taught online previously. The work of presenting the grid and course structure to instructors is accomplished through face-to-face training (when possible), a formal instructor manual, and an online, asynchronous instructor training course that relies heavily on the PARS elements.

Additional resources and materials instructors are given refer back to and support the grid structure in order to make personalized course design manageable. The materials provided include:

- Syllabus and course calendar templates
- Assignment sheets for each project in the grid

- Outcome-based analytic rubrics (one for each unit, to be used for any assignment option in that unit)
- List of suggested readings from program-approved primary textbooks for each assignment
- Example syllabi and course calendars featuring different sequences of assignments from the grid
- LMS course shell with pre-built units that mirror the grid structure

By using program-provided materials and resources built around the grid structure, instructors are able to personalize their online course design. In asking instructors to use pre-built materials to teach online, we find it necessary to take the time to introduce and explain the grid and the course structure it supports so that instructors can make best use of the materials we provide. In addition, we strive to make clear the connections between the materials provided and best practices for OWI.

Once instructors are introduced to the grid and its supporting materials, they are asked to select their sequence of course assignments, which will form the basic structure of their online course. As mentioned previously, all supporting materials are designed with the grid in mind, giving instructors the freedom to choose an assignment from each unit that is most appealing or familiar to them.

Instructors who have taught the course previously are encouraged to try new assignments from the grid. Swapping out one assignment for another typically involves some changes to supplementary course materials and activities, but because the assignments from each unit of the grid target the same outcomes, the course structure and course calendar can remain relatively unchanged.

Responsive pedagogy is autonomous pedagogy—for both students and instructors. Just as students should be able to choose topics that fit with their professional and personal interests, so too should instructors be able to choose assignments and approaches that fit with their pedagogical values and goals. While research suggests that template courses are a best practice for *strategic* administration of online writing programs (Rodrigo & Ramirez, 2017), allowing flexibility that empowers instructors to assign projects that they care about lays the groundwork for *responsive* pedagogy. When instructors have a choice between projects, they can select the one that best aligns with their teaching style and commitments, so students create work that they are actually interested in reading and providing feedback on. The grid supports instructors, who in turn support students through their direct instruction and feedback.

Programs: Strategies for Adapting the Modular Grid to Diverse Institutional Contexts

When developing the English 106-DIST grid, the ICaP administrative team formally requested instructor feedback through a focus group discussion, where instructors and course developers talked specifically about assignments the instructors had taught and would like to teach. One way we responded to instructors was by removing assignments that they found difficult to teach online, especially in the accelerated versions of the course taught during the summer and partial semester terms (first or second eight weeks). In addition to meeting with instructors to pick their brains about how they could personalize the units through integrating their own expertise, the ICaP staff who developed the curriculum—first Allegra, then Bianca, then Libby—also taught the course itself. Thus, the individuals driving the curriculum changes and development responded to their own firsthand experiences with online writing instruction to create a better learning experience.

In the next section, we suggest ways to adapt the grid course to local contexts strategically, based on our experience at Purdue and another institution.

Adapting the Curriculum for Multilingual Writers

As ICaP is currently piloting its first version of online composition for multilingual writers, we selected an assignment sequence from the grid that experienced 106-INTL instructors agreed would help most international students acculturate to academic writing at Purdue. The instructors then collaborated to modify the assignments and added activities to provide the scaffolding necessary to support multilingual learners. Extensive use of group and individual conferencing, the hallmark of 106-INTL, was integrated into the scaffolding of assignments.

Expanding Assignment Options to Integrate Local Practices

The grid need not be 3 × 3 and can be expanded if more variety is desired given local cultures. For example, Bianca, currently a Brittain Fellow at Georgia Tech, worked with the GT Writing and Communication Program (WCP) during the spring and summer 2020 terms to develop infrastructures for online teaching during the COVID-19 pandemic. Bianca and WCP leadership drew from ICaP's modular grid approach to develop ideas for assignment sequencing for instructors teaching English courses at Georgia Tech. The local culture of the WCP at Georgia Tech is one that requires instructional flexibility, especially because instructors in the program are asked to develop their own assignments and course themes. (This is another way the grid can reflect a UX-influenced approach to administration.) WCP courses also emphasize WOVEN (which stands for written, oral, visual, electronic, and nonverbal) communication. The WCP's learning outcomes also take a slightly different approach to those of ICaP and require all English instructors to teach assignment sequences that include multimodal and collaborative projects.

To account for this flexible, multimodal pedagogy, the WCP provided summer instructors with a more extensive modular grid that provides ideas for multimodal projects that build off each other and collectively emphasize different modes of WOVEN communication. This modular grid also included ideas for scaffolding within assignment sequences, such as peer review, storyboards, outlines, and usability tests; this allowed WCP instructors not only to garner ideas for assignment scaffolding but also to have flexibility throughout the process of their course design. In all these ways, the WCP at Georgia Tech built off the modular grid approach because doing so allowed Bianca and WCP leadership to efficiently prepare instructors to teach online during the pandemic (Burnett et al., 2020).

Table 5.3. 10 × 5 Grid Adaptation

10 × 5 Grid Used by Georgia Tech Writing and Communication Program (WCP)			
Guidelines: You can create an assignment/project sequence by mixing and matching (from the columns below) in ways that reflect the outcomes of your course, the pedagogical style you want to emphasize, the technology you want to use, and/or the community partners with whom you'll work. In your short remote summer course, a single session assignment/project sequence may be sufficient-in whatever sequence supports your course.			
Select project emphasizing W (but with OVEN in the process)	Select project emphasizing O/N (but with WVE in the process)	Select process emphasizing V (but with WOEN in the process)	Design scaffolded feedback/review
Feature article	PPT with voiceover	Infographic	Peer reviews
White paper	Radio PSA	Comic strip	Checklists
Wiki article	TED talk	PSA video	Sketches
Annotated bibliography	Podcast	Poster	Storyboards
Analytical essay	Radio drama	Data visualization	Annotated drafts
Manifesto	Record an interview	Website	Outlines
Children's book	Record a discussion	Maps/story maps	Audio/video clips
Tech pamphlet	Panel presentation	Book covers	User/usability tests
Review/commentary	Museum guide tape	Visuals for lit/poetry	Track changes
Your own choice	Your own choice	Your own choice	Your own choice

Adapting the Grid to Multiple-Course Sequences

The WCP also needed to consider its two-course sequence when developing online infrastructures. Students at Georgia Tech take a two-course sequence—English 1101 and English 1102—during their first year. Instructors often develop and use different texts, assignments, and course themes depending on which English course they are teaching. This two-course sequence also contributed to Bianca and WCP leadership's decision to provide instructors with a more extensive modular grid; instructors benefit from additional assignment sequencing ideas because they make use of different assignment sequences in the different courses they teach during the academic year. Bianca further adapted these materials to prepare incoming fall 2020 instructors for a full, 16-week semester of remote teaching, and she is interested in developing multiple grids to more strategically address the needs of the different English courses WCP offers at Georgia Tech.

Integrating the Grid into WAC or WID Programs

Even though the WCP is not an explicitly WAC or WID program, their recent development of online course structures demonstrates areas that WAC and WID programs must consider when leveraging the modular grid approach; because Georgia Tech is a STEM-oriented institution, the resources that Bianca and WCP leadership developed for online and remote instruction have also had to retain the program's mission of teaching and learning communication across disciplines and curriculums. The assignment sequences represented in the program's modular grid and other instructional resources thus maintain the program's objectives in teaching writing and communication in ways that emphasize research, process, and rhetorical awareness.

The handbooks, workshops, assignment sequences, and other materials developed for WCP remote instructors have leveraged lessons learned from Bianca's work with ICaP's online students and instructors. Indeed, the development of these materials was undergirded by the same theory and praxis that informs ICaP's modular grid. The modular grid's visualization of adaptable assignment sequences provides instructors with models and frameworks to help with their course design and development—which helped WCP instructors adapt more easily to teaching online during the pandemic—while also preserving instructors' autonomy and flexibility when choosing assignments to teach. With more and more institutions and programs, like the WCP, realizing the urgency of strengthening and expanding online course offerings that respond to student and instructors' needs both during and after the COVID-19 pandemic, implementing the modular grid approach can provide programs with a strategic solution for online course design.

Final Thoughts and Application

We hope that our experiences using the PARS approach to design a grid that responds to instructor and student needs can help guide your own online curriculum development, teacher training, and program administration. To review, here are some key takeaways from the 3 × 3 grid design and implementation process:

- Personal: Providing instructors with the opportunity to select from a suite of ready-made assignment options helps them to customize the

courses they teach, while reducing the cognitive load of building an entire syllabus and calendar from the ground up.
- Accessible: Having multiple pre-designed options for course projects enables instructors to match the writing tasks they assign to the wants and needs of their students, removing barriers to learning and success in the course.
- Responsive: Implementing a flexible grid approach responds to the needs of a diverse body of instructors—offering a middle ground between cookie-cutter templates and unrestricted curricula.
- Strategic: Building multiple assignments—with their accompanying readings, lesson plans, rubrics and assessment tools, etc.—ensures a cohesive curriculum and learning experience across sections in an online writing program that is closely linked to standard learning outcomes.

We see OWI as an opportunity for instructors—particularly graduate students and postdoctoral fellows—to grow as educators and professionals. For this reason, the grid-based curriculum is presented not only as a required tool for effective instruction, but also as a resource that was developed strategically and responsively with instructor input. When training instructors in the use of the grid and other course resources in our online training site, we not only discuss the practical how-to of the grid, but the *why*. Instructors are required to read the *PARS* text in its entirety, moving chapter by chapter through asynchronous training modules based on each aspect of OWI: personal, accessible, responsive, and strategic. In addition, we explicitly address how the curriculum ICaP has developed employs and follows the *PARS* elements through module videos recorded by ICaP staff. By working through personal reflections and engaging in online discussion boards with fellow instructors, instructors learn more about best practices for OWI in ways that will hopefully enable them to extend these skills beyond their time as an ICaP instructor.

The training materials developed for ICaP's online instructors speak to the same pedagogical values that undergird our implementation of the modular grid. That is, because we want our instructors to learn the value of implementing personal, accessible, responsive, and strategic online writing pedagogy, we have made efforts to model those same principles when developing materials for instructor use. Programmatically, ICaP seeks to model the *PARS* approach in all the materials we have developed, and the modular grid is a particularly tangible representation of such modeling; just as we want students in ICaP courses to have access to *PARS*-driven modes of learning, so too do we hope to provide instructors with resources that will help them better develop and understand their own *PARS*-inspired pedagogical values. In other words, the materials we have developed—from the modular grid to our training resources—allows ICaP instructors to implement OWI best practices and allow our program to implement forward-thinking praxis that gives instructors agency over their own pedagogies as well.

References

Blythe, S. (2001). Designing online courses: User-centered practices. *Computers and Composition, 18*(4), 329–346. https://doi.org/10.1016/S8755-4615(01)00066-4.

Borgman, J. & McArdle, C. (2019). *Personal, accessible, responsive, strategic: Resources and strategies for online writing instructors.* The WAC Clearinghouse; University Press of Colorado. https://doi.org/10.37514/PRA-B.2019.0322.

Bourelle, T. (2016). Preparing graduate students to teach online: Theoretical and pedagogical practices. *Writing Program Administration, 40*(1), 90–113.

Burnett, R. E., Batti, B., Frazee, A., Hoffman, C. & Rose, M. (2020). *A writing and communication program (WCP) teaching guide: Creating remote courses for summer 2020.* Georgia Institute of Technology.

Carter-Tod, S. (2007). Standardizing a first-year writing program: Contested sites of influence. *WPA: Writing Program Administration, 30*(3), 75–92.

Cassuto, L. (2019, November 10). A modern great books solution to the humanities' enrollment woes. *The Chronicle of Higher Education.* https://www.chronicle.com/article/A-Modern-Great-Books-Solution/247481.

Davis, A., Webb, S., Lackey, D. & DeVoss, D. N. (2010). Remix, play, and remediation: Undertheorized composing practices. In H. Urbanski (Ed.), *Writing and the digital generation: Essays on new media rhetoric* (pp. 186–197). McFarland.

DePalma, M. J. (2015). Tracing transfer across media: Investigating writers' perceptions of cross-contextual and rhetorical reshaping in processes of remediation. *College Composition and Communication, 66*(4), 615–642.

Fraiberg, S. (2010). Composition 2.0: Toward a multilingual and multimodal framework. *College Composition and Communication, 62*(1), 100–126.

Jenson, J. D. (2011). Promoting self-regulation and critical reflection through writing students' use of electronic portfolio. *International Journal of ePortfolio, 1*(1), 49–60.

National Council of Teachers of English. (2013, March). *A position statement of principles and example effective practices for online writing instruction (OWI).* Conference on College Composition & Communication. http://cccc.ncte.org/cccc/resources/positions/owiprinciples.

Prior, P. A. & Hengst, J. A. (Eds.). (2010). *Exploring semiotic remediation as discourse practice.* Palgrave Macmillan.

Rodrigo, R. & Ramírez, C. D. (2017). Balancing institutional demands with effective practice: A lesson in curricular and professional development. *Technical Communication Quarterly, 26*(3), 314–328. https://doi.org/10.1080/10572252.2017.1339529.

Shipka, J. (2005). A multimodal task-based framework for composing. *College Composition and Communication, 57*(2), 277–306.

Shipka, J. (2011). *Toward a composition made whole.* University of Pittsburgh Press.

Stewart, M. K., Cohn, J. & Whithaus, C. (2016). Collaborative course design and communities of practice: Strategies for adaptable course shells in hybrid and online writing. *Transformative Dialogues: Teaching & Learning Journal, 9*(1), 1–20.

Sullivan, P. A. & Porter, J. E. (1997). *Opening spaces: Writing technologies and critical research practices.* Ablex.

VanKooten, C. (2016). Identifying components of meta-awareness about composition: Toward a theory and methodology for writing studies. *Composition Forum, 33*.

Yancey, K. B. (1998). *Reflection in the writing classroom*. Utah State University Press.

Section 2: Instruction

Welcome to the Instruction section of this collection! We selected the above golf course picture to illustrate how things may look intimidating at the start (look at that water!) but with the right instructor, anything is possible. In the picture above, a golfer must have the skills and experience to hit their ball over the water. We think the same can be true at the start of an online course. Each new online course can be intimidating, even if you're a seasoned online instructor, and new courses are especially intimidating if you're new to online instruction.

We hope the chapters in this section, which focus on pedagogy, can give you some new clubs to put in your golf bag, that is, give you some of those skills you might need to get through your online writing course. The audience for the chapters in this section is instructors who teach online writing courses, but that is not to say that others, like administrators or scholars of OWI can't glean new insights from the ideas that these authors share. The major takeaway from this selection of chapters is that if you focus on small things (Darby & Lang, 2020) in your pedagogy you can make big changes for the user experience in your course. The chapters in this section give you an opportunity to explore something new in your online courses, such as videos, grading contracts, the use of humor, focusing on accessibility, ableism, and equity in your teaching as well as what to do when you get a course at the very last minute. One of the things we stress as we talk about being a good online instructor is being personal, accessible, responsive and strategic with your students. And as we outlined in the introduction, you don't have to do these things all at one time if that feels like it's too much. Instead, you can focus on one small thing, for example, being personal, and doing that one small thing will result in big rewards for you and your students.

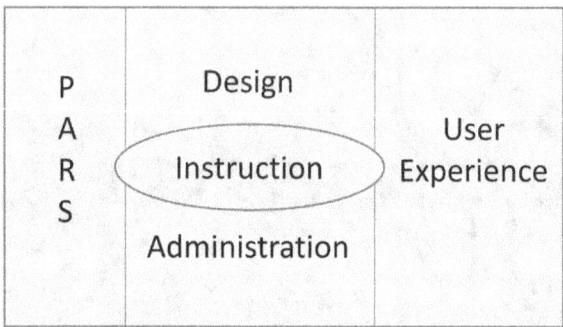

You can make your instruction **Personal** by doing little things that remind your students that you are a human being and not a computer. A few examples of ways to be a more personal instructor include:

- Being caring and compassionate in your communication with students and sharing personal information (hobbies/interests) with students in your instructor bio.
- Completing and participating in an ice breaker activity each time you meet with your class to get students talking.
- Sending weekly "check-in" emails to students.
- Contacting students by phone or via Zoom or making videos so they can hear your voice and see your face.

Accessible instruction moves beyond just ADA (ada.gov) compliance and there are many things you can do to be a more accessible instructor and create more accessible course materials:

- Make a video and walk students through where to find things in the online classroom (not every instructor organizes in the same way!).
- Ensure your course materials are ADA compliant and pay attention to students with accommodations to ensure they are getting their accommodations met.
- Post help resources for students both for your class and university wide resources (tutoring, writing center, library, advising, counseling, mental health support, etc.).
- Don't assume students know how to use the technologies in your course, show them and make them practice using them!

For **Responsive** instruction, it is important to think about *how* you will respond and *when* you will respond. When thinking about how and when you will respond, it is important to keep in mind the following considerations:

- Will you hold weekly drop-in office hours? Or email hours? Or homework hours? How will you hold these (what technology will you use)? When will you hold office, email or homework hours?

- Will you participate in the discussion boards? When will you participate in the discussions? What kind of responses will you make in the discussions? General ones to the whole class? Individual ones to each student?
- How will you respond to their writing? End comments? In-text comments? Use of LMS commenting feature? Microsoft Suite commenting? Google Docs commenting?
- How long will it take you to respond to their writing (this should be posted somewhere so the students know)? Will you return feedback in 48 hours, 72 hours, 3–5 days? How long will it take you to respond to email (again, this should be posted), 24 hours, 48 hours?

Strategic instruction brings it all together. Being a strategic instructor includes:

- Planning how your course design and you (as the instructor or administrator) will be personal, accessible, responsive and strategic.
- Planning the logistics for your synchronous course time and your asynchronous time.
- Planning out your teaching. Where in the course can you best insert yourself as a teacher and make the most impact?.
- Planning out the course content and course calendar to ensure that both meet the outcomes of the department or course.

The chapters in this section help you put these PARS based instruction practices into use. Many of the chapters in this section focus on how you can enhance your instruction by incorporating one small thing. For example, Mahaffey and McClure's chapter provides both a "how to" and a "when to" discussion of using videos. Laflen and Sims chapter illustrates how to use labor-based grading contracts to even the playing field for students. They illustrate that a student-centered approach to grading allows instructors to be more responsive. Pandy's chapter illustrates how the use of humor can enhance the personal aspects of the connection between the instructor and their students. Being an accessible instructor is the focus on Pengilly's chapter. Pengilly's chapter provides a unique perspective on both integrating and teaching usability and accessibility principles in the online technical writing classroom. Lastly, Evans' chapter illustrates through personal experience how the PARS approach works well for "just in time" or "last minute" teaching and can aid instructors in meeting the needs of their students.

References

Darby, F. & Lang, J. (2019). *Small teaching online: Applying learning science in online classes*. Jossey-Bass.

Chapter 6. Finding the Sweet Spot: Strategic Course Design Using Videos

Christine I. McClure
EMBRY-RIDDLE AERONAUTICAL UNIVERSITY, DAYTONA BEACH

Cat Mahaffey
UNIVERSITY OF NORTH CAROLINA AT CHARLOTTE

Abstract: Teaching online often means that we don't "see" our students, which makes it difficult to build the kind of strong student-teacher connections necessary for student success. We propose that videos and video conferencing allow us to re-embody ourselves and make online instruction personal and more effective. This chapter is framed around each element of PARS, using videos to enhance personal connections—between the instructor and students, as well as among students; to create accessible course content; to be responsive, including student feedback and timely course announcements; and for strategic video creation and placement within an online course. We focus on both the whys and hows of creating different types of course videos, grounding our discussion around intentional pedagogical choices that instructors can make regarding when, how, and where to do such labor. This chapter includes appendices with walkthroughs for creating videos using free open-access software—OBS, Screencast-O-Matic, Zoom and Screencastify—as well as using the auto captioning tool in YouTube to edit captions and/or create transcripts.

Keywords: personal, accessible, responsive, strategic, video making, screencasting, captions, transcripts

Designing an online course is never simple. Most instructors feel confident in their knowledge of discipline-specific content and are eager to share that knowledge with students, but they often don't know how to help students understand course content, much less keep them engaged with that content in an online environment because of lack of training in eLearning theories. When we teach face-to-face, we use visual cues to determine when/if students understand our lectures. We design interactive experiences such as incorporating clicker technology or engaging students in discussions, but how does that translate to an online experience? How do we ensure that students are engaged in "active learning," or "methods that allow students to construct their own understanding of course material and engage in the learning process" (Caviglia-Harris, 2016, p. 322)? How can we disseminate our discipline specific content knowledge in ways that allow students to actively interact with the information, "pay attention, . . . organize incoming information, . . . [and] integrate incoming information with other knowledge" (Peters, 2014, p. 23)?

Although there are multiple ways to foster active learning, some proven methods are video conferencing and instructional videos (Borup et al., 2015; Clark et al., 2015; Fiorella et al., 2018; Lamey, 2015; Peters, 2014; Thomas et al., 2017). Online instructors are likely already aware that videos facilitate enhanced presence, class community, and accessibility, but many either aren't comfortable with recording tools or aren't confident in knowing where and when to use videos. In their book, *Personal, Accessible, Responsive, Strategic: Resources and Strategies for Online Writing Instructors*, Borgman and McArdle (2019) discuss extensively how videos aid in creating more personal and accessible online writing classes. Although there are many videos already designed for online learning, such as Khan Academy, we believe that instructors should make their own videos to at least supplement outside content.

We fully recognize the increased workload, often without additional pay, support, or resources, necessary to create new content for online delivery, especially those who must first learn the basics, so for some, our call for video presence and enhanced course materials will sound daunting. To that end, this chapter focuses on both the whys and hows of creating videos. Specifically, we aim to lay out intentional pedagogical choices that instructors can make regarding when, how, and where to do such labor, and we hope to demonstrate that the benefits of creating videos for your online courses far outweigh the difficulties you will encounter. This chapter is framed around each element of PARS, as we first explore how videos enhance personal connections—between the instructor and students, as well as among students. Then we lay out the importance of accessible course content with an expanded definition of what accessibility means. The next section shares our experience of using videos as a tool for being responsive, including student feedback and course announcements. The final section puts everything together by offering best practices and how-tos for strategic video creation and placement within an online course.

Increasing Personal Connections

Teaching online generally means never seeing our students, and it also means that they never see us. This "seeing" is more than a lack of visual cues; it is also a lack of hearing, a disembodiment that affects the possibility of building a relationship with our students. This lack of relationship, or connection, is often one of the biggest difficulties in online environments (Borgman & McArdle, 2019). Since there is no "body/face/voice [the] corresponding visual/oral/aural components are gone" (Hewett, 2015, p. 60), and we are reduced to alphabetic text through the design of our courses, assignment guidelines, announcements, and feedback or static pictures that attempt to convey who we are. Most online teachers now include pictures of themselves on their bio pages, as shown in chapter one of Borgman and McArdle's (2019) book, and they also state that being disconnected physically can create a sense of insecurity in our students. In order to build personal relationships with our students and offset their insecurity, we need to re-embody ourselves. Through our face, voice, eyes via videos, we make online instruction not only more personal, but more real and tangible in a way that can't be achieved solely through alphabetic text, static pictures, or even videos created by other people/instructors.

Research suggests many benefits to instructors creating their own videos for online instruction. First, students report a sense of connection in courses where instructors regularly interact either via synchronous video conferencing or asynchronous video (Clark et al., 2015). This instructor-to-student connection is vital for student success. In fact, Borup et al. (2011) found that student interaction with their instructor was similar to that of face-to-face instruction, and the majority of students stated that video communication helped them to develop an emotional connection with their instructor and to know that they could rely on them for help. This emotional connection illustrates a deeper level of trust between instructors and students, leading students to reach out more often because they are confident that there is an actual person they can depend on beyond the interface. Some students also said that the videos contained a type of visual self-disclosure that helped them get to know their instructor (Borup et al., 2011). Students want to see who we are; they want to know that we are human. We need to stop worrying about the "mess" behind us as we record ourselves or whether we are perfect or not. Second, asynchronous videos are better for conveying complex concepts and fostering reflective engagement with ideas at a higher level (Borup et al., 2015), especially when instructors make eye contact with the camera (Fiorella et al., 2018), rather than relying solely on alphabetic text that can be misinterpreted or misunderstood. We are used to speaking to our students and clarifying ideas orally, so we should put those skills to use by creating our own content videos. We should explain to our students what we mean while looking them in the "eye."

In addition to making a connection with students and clarifying complex concepts, making our own videos lets students see our emotion—as long as we are willing to share that side of ourselves. Snart (2010) believes instructors should

> look at the computer, look at the webcam, look back at the computer, then finally say what you, um, have to, um, say . . . this all may produce a very real and approachable online identity (if a somewhat comical one), which is ultimately what we are going for. (p. 116)

In short, we should strive for authenticity and honesty in our videos because, ultimately, we want to make personal videos for our students. However, not all instructors are as emotive as others. In fact, in their study of text and video feedback, Thomas et al. (2017) determined that text feedback exhibited a higher frequency of emotion in instructor feedback than in the videos that they reviewed, but they acknowledged it was easier to code for textual emotion which was exhibited through elements such as exclamation points and all caps. Their research indicates that not all professors use their facial expressions or vocal inflection to illustrate the same level of emotion, but those professors who are more emotionless in video may show more emotion via textual feedback. Ultimately, we need to remember that although most research shows videos are important in projecting an embodied presence in our classes and in helping us to connect with our students, not all instructors have the same emotive facial or vocal tonal variations, and this is okay. We are all different, and we have different teaching styles, and this will be evident in our videos just as it is in our face-to-face teaching. Students want to see our humanness, our eyes, our face, because they want to connect with us as people. We also believe that text in the form or captions and transcripts should be included, so add those capital letters or exclamation points, if that is your style.

Increasing Accessible Course Content

In addition to embodiment issues, there are multiple accessibility concerns in online course delivery. Many instructors focus on accessibility in terms of disabilities that need to be overcome rather than removing barriers in the environment that are causing issues (Tobin & Behling, 2018). One student may have an accommodation due to being hearing impaired, but how many other students have issues not brought to the attention of Disability Services and/or issues that affect learning, such as limited access to technology or outside jobs and family? Furthermore, some students may not even be aware they have limitations, especially those that require extensive and expensive testing protocols for official documentation (i.e. hearing impairment, depression, anxiety, etc.—see Kerschbaum et al., 2017). The OWI [Online Writing Instruction] Committee for Effective Practices in Online Writing Instruction (2013) defines accessibility as the "needs of learners with physical disabilities, learning disabilities, multilingual backgrounds, and learning challenges related to socioeconomic issues (i.e., often called the digital divide where access is the primary issue)," and they argue in their position statement (cccc.ncte.org/cccc/resources/positions/owiprinciples) that the OWI environment must address issues of equity, flexibility, use, error, and technological effects so that students in writing courses can be successful. We need to realize, however, that not all students provide documentation to university disability services offices, nor do they share any outside obstacles that may affect their success in our classes. Borgman and McArdle (2019) stress that accessibility is more than just compliance. They encourage an expansion of how we define access to one that considers "the ways that [we, as teachers] might actually be impeding [our] students learning by creating barriers to the access of [our] course content (2019, p.

37). We must rethink how we approach accessibility, and focus instead on how to make our classes accessible to all learners, and we must consider course/content access in much broader terms. According to Tobin and Behling (2018), the U.S. Department of Justice's Office of Civil Rights is reframing requirements of higher education due to lawsuits brought by individuals against colleges and universities. They argue that we should no longer wait for accommodation requests from students; instead, we should provide equal access to all educational material in a timely manner, which will benefit all students and will avoid discrimination. It is our job as instructors to teach all of our students, and we must accommodate the physical, technological, emotional, and mental issues that may potentially prevent our students from succeeding and remove as many barriers as possible by providing our educational materials in multiple forms: visual, auditory, and text based.

We view our call for usage of videos in online courses as a way to fulfill the expanded definition of accessibility laid out by Mahaffey and Walden (2019):

> Accessibility refers to the ease of entry and use of a product, service, space, or text; and considers course design (navigation, layout, color scheme, font type, font emphasis), course tools (applications, discussion forums, quizzes) and course materials (instructional texts, resources, assignment descriptions, submission and evaluation guidelines). Thus, an accessible tech-mediated course is one that affords every learner the opportunity to succeed, regardless of technological skill, reading level, native language, learning preference, or physical impairment. (p. 42)

The different types of videos you can create (announcements, feedback on assignments, assignment walk-throughs, content, syllabus overviews, etc.) open up visual and auditory access to your materials that are not possible in just textual form. They allow students who are visually impaired, or those who are visual learners, the ability to understand content, connect with you, and engage in active learning. This also increases access for working students who may need to listen to a lesson while driving. It's important to note here that we are not proposing using videos exclusively since that would actually limit access. The larger goal is to encourage you to incorporate videos into your course development processes.

Furthermore, we advocate for all videos to be captioned and accompanied by transcripts. As Kerschbaum (2013) notes, "it is almost impossible to read a transcript and watch a video at the same time" (p. 62), and providing access involves more than creating a separate accessible component that exists outside of the original text. Doing so would be an example of retrofitting which is reactive rather than proactive. For example, transcripts *proactively* accommodate students who prefer reading a text to watching a video, and students with limited broadband access who are perhaps using data plans to access their courses when internet access is unavailable. Our goal is to provide students with multiple options to access content without specifically requesting it.

Increasing Responsiveness

One way to incorporate videos into your course is by responding to student work via video rather than just through text. Lamey (2015) says, "commenting on students' work in the form of a video has the potential to improve the feedback experience for both instructors and students" (p. 692), but he questions whether this is the best option for writing classes since instructors tend to include more global rather than sentence-level comments through video feedback. This is a valid concern, but this issue can be solved by being thoughtful in our approach to feedback and resisting the urge to focus on only general writing issues. Intentionally referencing specific sentences or paragraphs demonstrates a deeper commitment to student improvement. Hewett (2015) argues that video actually allows instructors the ability to "drill down into content or sentence-focused specifics because the instructor can point students to particular pages or lines in a text" (p. 191). We need to remember that it is our job to help students improve, and giving clear, specific feedback is one way to do that. While video feedback increases interactivity, video length is of concern. Lamey (2015) suggests that feedback be given in no more than four minutes, but we recommend between five to seven minutes to avoid overwhelming students while allowing ample space for specific rather than general feedback.

Instructors must also consider their own time constraints, and often writing specific feedback to each student can be time consuming, which limits the amount of individual feedback to students. As Borgman and McArdle (2019) explain, "[h]aving enough energy to provide effective feedback comes down to managing your time and resources" (p. 55). The good news is that video feedback decreases the time instructors must dedicate to grading while also increasing the amount of feedback provided (Warnock, 2009). Having said that, it's important to keep in mind that some students prefer written feedback. Borup et al. (2015) determined that written feedback was easier to access since students could easily scan the text rather than having to watch an entire video, and they could read the text anywhere, but watching a video was problematic due to sound issues or internet capabilities. They also found that instructors were more concise in their text comments than in video. Despite this, video feedback allowed students to gauge instructor "visual and vocal cues . . . [which] seemed to help in conveying the praise the instructors intended," and it also seemed to "soften criticism" (2015, p. 177). Furthermore, instructors were more conversational in their videos than in their text feedback. We believe that the findings of this study support our call for consistently providing captions and transcripts with all videos, especially instructional and feedback videos that students may need to access in multiple ways. If this can't be done in the LMS, we recommend that you bullet point your feedback in a clear and concise way in textual form so that students can easily refer back to your feedback as they revise or rewrite.

Increasing Strategic Application

We recognize that creating online courses increases workload, often without additional pay, support, or resources, so for some, our call for video presence and enhanced course materials will sound daunting. In this section, we discuss the fourth element of PARS, strategic, and offer a strategic framework for thinking about how, where, and when to invest in video creation. We think it's important to utilize open access software to minimize financial burdens on faculty, so the tools we profile are free to use with some limitations, but most of them offer paid subscriptions with enhanced features. This section will focus only on the capabilities of free tools to help you decide which tool could be utilized for your video and how to use those tools. We have included four appendices at the end of this chapter with directions on how to use each tool: OBS, Screencastify, Screencast-o-matic, Zoom. In addition, we include a final appendix with direction on how to upload any MP4 file to YouTube, and how to create and edit captions, and transcripts.

Table 6.1. Comparison of recording platforms and tools

Capabilities	Screencastify	Screencast-O-Matic	OBS	Zoom
Pause and restart	Yes	Yes	Yes	Yes
Record screen	Yes	Yes	Yes	Yes
Record webcam	Yes	Yes	Yes	Yes
Record screen and webcam simultaneously	Yes	Yes	Yes	No
Annotation and Drawing	Yes	No	Yes	Yes—on whiteboard
Shift between screen and webcam	No	No	Yes	Yes
Edit video	Trim only. Need paid subscription for advanced editing	Need paid subscription	Yes	No
Save MP4 file locally	Yes	Yes	Yes	Yes
Create captions	No	No	No	Yes
Edit/add captions	No	Yes	No	No
Time Limit	5 minutes. Unlimited with paid subscription	15 mins	None	40 minutes
Cost for more video affordances	$29/yr for educators	$19.80/yr	N/A	N/A

To emphasize our goal to situate different types of videos, along with clarifications for where, how and when to create and include them in an online course, we describe our framework through the following golf analogies: the Tee Box, the Fairway, and the Green. Like each of these areas of the golf course, tools and strategies for making videos are context specific and having shifting best practices.

The Tee Box

The tee box is typically the starting point for golfers. It's where you view the layout of the hole, the length of the fairway, and any sandpits or trouble spots. This analogy is helpful for considering how much time and energy to invest in course instructional videos. Specifically, this starting point offers instructors the opportunity to make decisions about where instructional videos might be reused across courses and/or semesters. For example, if you teach the same course often, you might want to create videos that walk students through course concepts or assignments that you're least likely to make major changes to every semester. And these longer lasting videos are wise places to invest more time and energy, especially if you expect students to learn and/or practice concepts in asynchronous learning environments.

Best Practices for Tee Box Videos

- Create or work from a transcript and include this with the video or link to the video
- Write the presentation content: PowerPoint, Google Slides, or Prezi
- Include edited captions
- Be yourself so students can sense your presence
- Speak clearly, but don't be afraid to make mistakes
- Chunk your content and make more videos rather than trying to create one long video—no more than seven minutes per video, but shorter is better

The Fairway

A successful drive from the tee box lands the ball in the fairway, the place of strategic transition between the long drive and the final putt. This analogy is helpful for thinking about what type of videos to create and/or adapt based on changes made for each iteration of a course, things like welcome, start here, and course navigation videos. The fidelity of these videos is less critical so you can feel comfortable simply recording your webcam for welcome videos and recording your course website for start here and course navigation videos.

Best Practices for Fairway videos

- Create or work from a transcript and include this with the video or link to the video

- Include edited captions
- Be yourself so students can sense your presence
- Shorter is better—no longer than five minutes

Table 6.2. Best practices for tee box videos

Tee Box Videos	Assignment Walk-throughs	Course Content
Recommended Technologies	OBS Screencast-O-Matic Screencastify Zoom	OBS Screencast-O-Matic Screencastify Zoom
Maximum Length	5 minutes	5–7 minutes
Visuals	Completed Assignment Guidelines	Completed Course Design
Transcript / Captions	Essential	Essential
Screen Capture	Essential	Essential
Webcam	Helpful	Helpful
Headset w/ Microphone	Essential	Essential

Table 6.3. Best practices for fairway videos

Fairway Videos	Welcome	Course Navigation	Instructor Introduction	Start Here/ Syllabus Walkthrough
Recommended Technologies	OBS Zoom	Screencast-O-Matic Screencastify	OBS Zoom	Screencast-O-Matic Screencastify Zoom
Maximum Length	5 minutes	5 minutes	3–4 minutes	3–4 minutes
Visuals	Webcam	Completed Course Design	Unnecessary	Completed Full Syllabus
Transcript/ Captions	Essential	Essential	Essential	Essential
Screen Capture	Unnecessary	Essential	Unnecessary	Essential
Webcam	Essential	Helpful	Essential	Helpful
Headset w/ Microphone	Recommended	Recommended	Helpful	Essential

On The Green

A good shot from the fairway lands the ball on the green, where the golfer pulls out the putter and the final putt(s) take place. The only place the putter is used, this unique space calls for a completely different strategy, one that involves reflection and keen aiming. This analogy aligns well with those course videos that you create on-the-fly, things like weekly announcements and reminders, whole-class or individual feedback, and syllabus or calendar updates. Even though these are created at the last minute, these videos are perhaps the most impactful and most important with regard to instructor presence. For this reason, instructors should attempt to get comfortable with seeing and hearing themselves on screen. The more real and less polished you are, the stronger your presence will be perceived by students.

Best Practices for On The Green Videos

- Avoid overplanning
- Be yourself so students can sense your presence
- For feedback, refer to specific sections of the student paper—give some general feedback, but give specific feedback as well

Table 6.4. Best practices for on the green videos

On the Green Videos	Weekly Announcements	Syllabus / Calendar Update	Individual Student Feedback	Whole-Class Feedback
Recommended Technologies	OBS Screencast-O-Matic Screencastify Zoom	OBS Screencast-O-Matic Screencastify Zoom	OBS Screencast-O-Matic Screencastify Zoom	OBS Screencast-O-Matic Screencastify Zoom
Maximum Length	5 minutes	2–3 minutes	5–7 minutes	5 minutes
Visuals	Weekly Overview of Coursework	Updated syllabus/ calendar	Student Submission	Student Samples or Models
Transcript/ Captions	Essential	Essential	Essential	Essential
Screen Capture	Recommended	Helpful	Essential	Recommended
Webcam	Recommended	Helpful	Recommended	Recommended
Headset w/ Microphone	Recommended	Recommended	Recommended	Recommended

Final Thoughts and Application

In order to be effective online instructors, we need to think about how we can engage with our students beyond the text, and using the PARS framework allows us to view videos in a more dynamic, inclusive way. First, through the creation of our own lecture, announcement, and feedback videos, we re-embody ourselves by including our image and voice so our students see us as human beings who want to make personal connections with them and help them succeed. Second, we should consider an expanded definition of accessibility to include not only students who have physical disabilities or accommodations through university disability services, but also those who have technological, familial, language, or other issues that could in some way impact their educational endeavors. We need to make our videos proactively accessible to the widest range of students through our choices of technology, captions, graphics, transcripts, and design. Third, creating feedback videos allows us to be responsive to students while still balancing our own (often very heavy) workloads. Fourth, we need to be strategic in our choice of technology. Remember, students do not need highly edited, complex videos with graphic overlays to help them understand course concepts. To help you in your video creation, we have included five appendices which describe how to use various technologies at the end of this chapter. As instructors, our goals are not to show off our video skills; instead, we should strive to utilize technology thoughtfully with pedagogical reasoning.

Like students, online instructors come to the "classroom" with diverse experiences, values, and talents. We fully recognize that there is no one-size-fits-all model for teaching—not for face-to-face classrooms nor online environments—and we certainly aren't advocating that videos can or should replace the real-time dynamic interactions that foster deep and transferable learning. Instead, we hope that this chapter grants online instructors knowledge of free programs and how to use them, a sense of empowerment, and an expanded vocabulary for types of instructional videos and an awareness of how and where to create and use videos in their online courses.

What we all care about is education, and we want every student to succeed. To that end, we also hope this chapter makes the case for no longer "privileging a particular set of preferences and modes of working" (Kerschbaum, 2013). Accessibility is an ever-increasing challenge, one that can be "particularly hairy (but especially important)" (Peters, 2014, p. 185). In their latest reimagining of a "set of principles and tenets for online literacy education," the Global Society of Online Literacy Educators (GSOLE) placed accessibility at the top of their list, including the following definition of access and inclusion: "Inclusion and access involve using multiple teaching and learning formats, engaging students' choices, and welcoming all students in the course" (gsole.org). We assert that strategic use of video conferencing and instructional videos are perhaps the best way to welcome and engage students into an online learning environment, while increasing instructor presence and fostering instructor responsiveness.

References

Borgman, J. & McArdle, C. (2019). *Personal, accessible, responsive, strategic: Resources and strategies for online writing instructors.* The WAC Clearinghouse; University Press of Colorado. https://doi.org/10.37514/PRA-B.2019.0322.

Borup, J., West, R. E. & Graham, C. R. (2011). Improving online social presence through asynchronous video. *Internet and Higher Education, 15*(3), 195–203. https://doi.org/10.1016/j.iheduc.2011.11.001.

Borup, J., West, R. E. & Thomas, R. (2015). The impact of text versus video communication on instructor feedback in blended courses. *Educational Technology Research and Development, 63*(2), 161–184. https://doi.org/10.1007/s11423-015-9367-8.

Caviglia-Harris, J. (2016). Flipping the undergraduate economics classroom: Using online videos to enhance teaching and learning. *Southern Economic Journal, 83*(1), 321–331. https://doi.org/10.1002/soej.12128.

Conference on College Composition and Communication OWI Committee for Effective Practices in Online Writing Instruction. (2013). *A position statement of principles and effective practices for online writing instruction (OWI).* https://www.ncte.org/cccc/resources/positions/owiprinciples.

Clark, C., Strudler, N. & Grove, K. (2015). Comparing asynchronous and synchronous video vs. text-based discussions in an online teacher education course. *Journal of Asynchronous Learning Network, 19*(3), 48–70. https://doi.org/10.24059/olj.v19i3.668.

Fiorella, L., Stull, A. T., Kuhlmann, S. & Mayer, R. E. (2018). Instructor presence in video lectures: The role of dynamic drawings, eye contact, and instructor visibility. *Journal of Educational Psychology, 111*(7), 1162–1171. https://doi.org/10.1037/edu0000325.

Hewett, B. L. (2015). *Reading to learn and writing to teach: Literacy strategies for online writing instruction.* Bedford/St. Martin's.

Kerschbaum, S. (2013). Modality. *Kairos: A Journal of Rhetoric, Technology, and Pedagogy. Kairos: A Journal of Rhetoric, Technology, and Pedagogy, 18*(1). http://kairos.technorhetoric.net/18.1/coverweb/yergeau-et-al/pages/mod/index.html.

Lamey, A. (2015). The philosopher as teacher: Video feedback in philosophy. *Metaphilosophy. 46*(4–5). 691–702.

Mahaffey, C. & Walden, A. (2019). #teachingbydesign: Complicating Accessibility in the Tech-Mediated Classroom. In K. Becnel (Ed.), *Emerging Technologies in Virtual Learning Environments* (pp. 38–66). IGI Global.

Peters, D. (2014). *Interface design for learning: Design strategies for learning experiences.* New Riders.

Snart, J. A. (2010). *Hybrid learning: The perils and promise of blending online and face-to-face instruction in higher education.* Praeger.

Thomas, R. A., West, R. E. & Borup, J. (2017). An analysis of instructor social presence in online text and asynchronous video feedback comments. *Internet and Higher Education, 33*, 61–73. https://doi.org/10.1016/j.iheduc.2017.01.003.

Tobin, J. T. & Behling, K. T. (2018). *Read everyone, teach everyone: Universal design for learning in higher education.* West Virginia University Press.

Warnock, S. (2009). *Teaching writing online: How and why.* National Council of Teachers of English.

Appendix: Step-by-Step Guides

Using OBS to Create Videos

Step 1
Download OBS Studio

Go to: https://obsproject.com/ Choose your operating system (Windows, Mac, or Linux)

NOTE: OBS requires a one-time download with no account. After that, it runs on your computer without the need for web access.

Step 2
Install OBS Studio

Find the OBS file in your Downloads folder

Double-click the file to begin the install

Select "Optimize just for recording" for Usage Information

Step 3
Run the Wizard

The auto-configuration wizard will execute a set of tests and than recommend settings for your recordings.

Click "Apply Settings" to accept them.

Step 4
Launch the OBS Application

Find the application in your files and open it.

NOTE: OBS creates a "recording window" that runs beside the "capture window." Using two monitors or a widescreen monitor works best.

Step 5
For Screen Capture

Click + in the "Sources" box at the bottom of the window.

Select "Window Capture" and then "Create new." Click OK.

Open the drop-down menu beside "Window" and select the application you want to capture (Chrome, Word, etc.). Click OK.

Step 6
For Webcam

Click + in the "Sources" box at the bottom of the window

Select "Video Capture Device" and then "Create new." Click OK.

Open the drop-down menu beside "Device" and select your webcam. Click OK.

Step 7
For Webcam and Screen

Perform Steps 5 and 6 in order, adding both options to your "Sources" area.

NOTE: Make sure "video capture" is the first source and "window capture" is the second source.

Step 8
Adjust the Capture Window

Reduce the size of your browser window, slideshow, or document window so that it all shows up in the recording window.

Step 9
Adjust the Recording Window(s)

Press "alt" to crop the screen and/or webcam.

Click and hold to move the screen and/or webcam.

Drag the corners to resize the recording window.

Step 10
Check the Audio Settings

Select "settings" in the right hand menu.

Select "Audio" and make sure your mic is selected in the "Devices" section.

Step 11
Record Your Video

Select "Start Recording" in the right-hand menu

The recording will start immediately

Step 12
While Recording

Use the "||" button to pause and restart.

Note the indicators at the bottom of the recording window that show when you're recording and when you're paused.

Step 13
End Recording

Click "Stop Recording."

The software will instantly add the recording file to a folder called "Movies."

Don't close the OBS software yet.

Step 14
Convert to MP4

OBS records in .mkv format but .mp4 is best.

With the OBS recording window active, click "File" in the menu at the top your monitor and then "Remux Recordings."

Step 15
Remux the Recording

Find the video file in your Movies folder and drag it to the left column titled "OBS Recording," then click "Remux."

The mp4 file will be in your Movies folder along with the .mkv file.

Using Screencast-O-Matic to Create Videos

Step 1

Go to Screencast-O-Matic Homepage

Go to: https://screencast-o-matic.com/

No need to create an account

Step 2

Select "Start Recording for Free"

Then select "Launch Free Recorder"

If this is your first time using Screencast-O-Matic, you'll need to download the application

Step 3

(One-Time) Download the App

Depending on your security settings, a series of pop-up windows may appear, asking for permission to access your files, webcam, and screen.

Step 4

Select Your Recording Options

Choose from Screen, Webcam, or Both

Don't adjust "Max Time" or "Size"

Click "Narration" to choose your mic

Don't adjust "Computer Audio"

Step 5

(Optional) Adjust Preferences

Take note of the various hotkeys and other options. If you're new to Screencast-O-Matic, avoid adjusting these until you gain some practice with them.

Step 6

Adjust the Recording Window

Move the window and/or increase or decrease the size using the corner and side adjustments.

If your recording window is too small, your video will be blurry when viewed via full-screen.

Step 7

Record a Test Video

Click the red "Rec" button under the recording window.

A 3-second countdown will begin.

Record a few seconds and then click "||" under the recording window to pause the recording.

Step 8

Preview Test Video

Once the video is paused, click to play to view your recording.

Check for clear audio and visuals.

If adjustments are needed, click the trashcan icon and re-adjust your settings.

Step 9

Adjust the Recording Window(s)

Press "alt" to crop the screen and/or webcam.

Click and hold to move the screen and/or webcam.

Drag the corners to resize the recording window.

Step 10

Restart Recording

Use the "|<" icon to reset the recording to 0:00.00.

Click the red "record" button.

Choose "Yes, truncate" to record over your test.

Your countdown will begin.

Step 11

Record Your Video

If you make a mistake while recording, you can pause and shift the timer back to record over your mistake.

NOTE: Everything past that point in your video will be deleted. Use caution when with this tool.

Step 12

End Recording

Click "Done."

Choose "Save/Upload."

Select "Save as Video File."

Step 13

Select Publish Options

"MP4" is recommended "Type."

Update "Filename" as desired

Select the "Folder" you want to save the file in.

Step 14

(Optional) Upload Captions

Select "Open Captions" to upload a pre-prepared transcript file.

NOTE: The file must be .txt, .sbv, or .srt.

Step 15

"Publish" Your Video

This saves the file to your local computer or uploads it according to your selection.

Finding the Sweet Spot 115

Using Zoom to Create Videos

Step 1
Open and/or Download Recording Tool

Go to: https://zoom.us/signup

Sign up for an account.

Step 2
Create a Meeting

Click "Schedule a New Meeting"

NOTE: Do not click "record the meeting automatically on a local computer" because the recording will start immediately upon entering.

Step 3
Set Zoom Meeting Options

Fill out relevant information, especially:

"When" - day/time you want to record

"Video" - Host "on"

Click **Save.**

Step 4
Enable Advanced Settings

Click "Settings" on the left side toolbar:

"Host Video" - on
"Annotations" - on
"White board" - on
"Closed Captions" - on
"Save Captions" - on

Step 5
Pre-Recording Prep

Prepare visuals- such as assignment guidelines or PowerPoint presentation, open browser windows and/or assignment documents.

Step 6
Start the Meeting

Click "Meetings" on the left toolbar.

Click "Start" for the meeting.

Step 7
Check Audio

Click the carrot next to the microphone on the bottom toolbar.

Choose your speakers & microphone.
Choose "Test Speaker and Microphone" and follow directions.

Step 8
Check Video

Click the carrot next to the video on the bottom toolbar.

Enable front camera.

Enable virtual background if you wish.

Click the video icon to turn on video.

Step 9
To Create Captions

1) You can type them.

2) Someone else in the meeting can type them.

3) You can use a third party CC Service if you have an API token.

Step 10
To Record

Click the record button at the bottom of the screen.

Warning: there is no way to rewind the video if you make a mistake.

Step 11
To Pause the Recording

Press the Pause button on the bottom toolbar or the top left of the screen.

Step 12
Share Screen

Click Share Screen on the bottom toolbar.

Click the page you would like to record.

You can pause or stop the share of your screen to go back to your webcam.

Step 13
To End the Recording

Click Stop Recording.

Click the red End button at the bottom right.

Step 14
To Finish

A window will appear alerting you that Zoom is converting your video to an MP4 file.

This may take awhile.

Save the video to your computer.

Using Screencastify to Create Videos

Step 1: Download Screencastify

This tool is a Chrome extension, so use Chrome as your browser.

Go to https://www.screencastify.com/

Click "Add to Chrome" in the top right.

Step 2: Add to Chrome

In the new window, click "Add to Chrome."

Click "Add Extension."

Step 3: Start the Setup

Click the red arrow with the camera at the very top Chrome toolbar.

Enable "Automatically save videos to Google Drive."

Sign in with your Gmail account.

Step 4: Set Permissions

Enable "Camera and Microphone."

Enable "Drawing and Annotation Tools."

Click **Next**.

Step 5: Changes to data window

Click "Allow".

"The ability to 'read and change all your data on the websites your visit'. We ask for this permission in order to embed our annotation tools and webcam into your current Chrome tab. Screencastify never monitors, stores or tracks your browsing information." from https://help.screencastify.com/article/251-why-do-you-ask-for-chrome-permissions.

Step 6: To Introduce Yourself

Click **Educator**.

Click the level of education you teach on the next screen.

Step 7: To Begin

Click the Red Arrow at the top right of the Chrome toolbar.

Step 8: Enable Options

Click the three horizontal bars to open the options window.

Enable "Google Drive."

Enable other options as you wish.

Step 9: To Begin

Click the red arrow at the top right of the Chrome toolbar again

Choose browser, desktop, or webcam

NOTE: Your webcam can be taped along with the Desktop.

Step 10: Enable Mic and

Click Select to choose Microphone and camera.

Step 11: More Options

Click "Show More Options."

Enable Countdown, Drawing Tools, and Audio.

Step 12: To Record

Press Record.

Choose what visual frame you want to record.

Click "Share" and recording countdown will start.

Step 13: To Pause

The red arrow at the top includes a red dot to show recording has started.

Use || to pause recording at the bottom left along with annotation tools.

Step 14: To End Recording

Press "Stop Sharing" bottom at the bottom of the screen.

Trim part of the video off by using the cutting tool or skip to save the video.

Step 15: Save, Download, or Publish

The screen at the right allows you to save to Google Drive, publish to Youtube, email, get an embed code, download an MP4 or audio only file.

Finding the Sweet Spot 117

Uploading to YouTube

Step 1

Create or Login to YouTube Account

Go to https://www.youtube.com/.

Click "Sign In."

Step 2

Upload a Video

Click the video camera icon with the + symbol on the toolbar at the top right.

Select "Upload Video."

Step 3

Select Video

Click "Upload Video" to open dialog box on your computer.

Drag and drop or select your video file.

Note: Keep all videos in one file locally so you can access them easily.

Step 4

Choose Details for the video

Add a clear title and description of the video, and check audience selection.

Click **Next**.

Note: Other info is optional by expanding OTHER OPTIONS feature.

Step 5

Add Video Elements

Choose "Add end screen" if you would like to point students to another video.

Choose "Add card" if you would like students to take a poll during the video.

Click **Next**.

Step 6

Choosing Visibility

Click "Private," "Unlisted," or "Public."

Click **Save**.

Note: Unlisted will allow only your students to see your video with the link you provide.

Step 7

Video Published

Copy the url or the embed code for your students.

Click **Close**.

Note: An embed code allows students to watch the video in the LMS. This is especially important if you have international students who can't access Youtube.

Step 8

Wait for Auto-captions

The process is now automatic, but it may take up to an hour depending on the length of your video.

Note: Captions are vital for accessibility.

Step 9

Find the Auto-Captions

Go to "Your Videos."

Click the blue "Edit Video" button under the video.

Click "Subtitles" in the left menu.

If the auto-caption is complete, you'll see "English (Automatic)."

Step 10

Open the Auto-Captions

Click "Duplicate and Edit."

Optional: Click "Assign Timings" if you prefer to see the video timestamps. If you want to copy this as transcript, it's best not to assign timings.

Step 11

Edit the Auto-Captions

Edit the captions in the left column.

The right column will show you what the captions look like on the video.

Look for the following errors: wrong word, missing capital letters, punctuation, etc.

Step 12

Copy the Captions

Copy the captions and paste them onto a document for your transcript.

You can clean up the text as desired for readability.

Step 13

Publish Edited Captions

Click "Publish."

Note that you now have two caption files - (1) English (video language) Published by Creator, and (2) English (Automatic). Delete the second one.

Step 14

Return to YouTube

Click the video thumbnail in the top left and click the play button.

Optional: Preview the video and repeat steps 9 through 13 if edits are needed.

Step 15

Share or Embed Your Video

Click "Share" under your video and copy the link.

Click "Embed" to generate an embed code.

NOTE: Some LMS platforms automatically embed YouTube videos via the link.

Chapter 7. Designing a More Equitable Scorecard: Grading Contracts and Online Writing Instruction

Angela Laflen and Mikenna Sims
CALIFORNIA STATE UNIVERSITY, SACRAMENTO

Abstract: In this chapter we consider how applying Borgman and McArdle's (2019) recommendations for being a responsive and strategic online instructor to labor-based grading contracts in online writing instruction (OWI) can help us develop a strategy for response aimed at making our courses more equitable for all students. Labor-based contract grading, which makes student labor in the course the basis for assessment, has been identified as a more equitable method of assessment for diverse learners, and this method of assessment also works against the assumption that some students bring to their online courses that they are "correspondence like" (Borgman & McArdle, 2019, p. 30). For these reasons, labor-based contract grading can be an appealing response strategy to use in OWI. Nevertheless, this strategy can be difficult to implement effectively in OWI due to students' unfamiliarity with contract grading and the constraints imposed by learning management system (LMS) technologies. These challenges can lead to user experience problems for students and instructors that leave students confused about course grades and instructors discouraged from using grading contracts. We contend that a student-centered design approach is necessary to use grading contracts as an effective response strategy in OWI, and we share the grading contract documents we use in our own online classes and discuss how these are designed around students and their needs.

Keywords: labor-based contract grading; response strategy; assessment; student-centered design

In this chapter, we consider two elements of Borgman and McArdle's PARS approach, responsive and strategic. We show how using these two elements along with labor-based grading contracts can make our online courses more equitable for all students. We think of our efforts to implement labor-based grading contracts in online writing instruction (OWI) as an attempt to design a more equitable "scorecard" with which to assess our students. In golf, scorecards are used to record how many shots a golfer took to complete the hole, and at the end of the round, the scores from each individual hole are added together to provide the total score for the 18 holes. Each hole also has an assigned number of shots, called par, that a proficient golfer is expected to finish in. Holes can be par 3, par 4, or par 5. For example, for a par 3, the golfer is expected to complete the hole in three shots (par), theoretically by landing on the green from the tee and finishing in two putts. Golf also has names for scores below and above par on a single hole. For example, if a golfer takes five shots on a par 4, that's one over par or a "bogey." Six shots is a "double bogey." A score of one stroke better than par (i.e., a 2 on a par 3) is a "birdie." If a golfer beats par by two strokes, they have made an "eagle." In our OWI courses, grading contracts operate similarly. These documents also help students track their progress toward meeting course requirements and assignment criteria. They employ specialized terms such as "complete" and "incomplete," with which students must be familiar in order to understand the contract and use it to measure their progress. However, while par represents a pre-established measure to which golfers aspire, grading contracts allow students to be involved in defining what "par" means in OWI, and they have multiple opportunities during a semester to meet or exceed "par." In a labor-based grading contract, "par" is associated with meeting collaboratively determined standards for labor rather than meeting some pre-determined, subjective standard of proficiency. For this reason, labor-based contract grading, which makes student labor in the course the basis for assessment, has been identified as a more equitable method of assessment for the types of diverse learners that populate online writing courses.

According to Inoue (2019), contract grading is more equitable because it makes "all final course grades more accessible to every student in the room, regardless of the languages they practice, their linguistic backgrounds, or most other social dimensions" (p. 140). Additionally, labor-based grading contracts work against the assumption that some students bring to their online courses that they are "correspondence like" (Borgman & McArdle, 2019, p. 30) since, if we value students' labor in an online course, then clearly the course is not just a checklist of tasks to complete as quickly as possible. For these reasons, labor-based contract grading can be an appealing response strategy to use in OWI. Nevertheless, this strategy can be difficult to implement effectively in OWI due to students' unfamiliarity with this assessment method and the constraints imposed by learning management system (LMS) technologies. These challenges can lead to user experience problems for instructors and students that leave students confused about course grades and instructors discouraged from using grading contracts. In this chapter, we contend that a student-centered design approach is necessary to use grading contracts as an effective response strategy in OWI, and we share the grading contract documents we use in our own online classes and discuss how these are designed around students and their needs.

Benefits of Labor-Based Grading Contracts in OWI

Labor-based contract grading is particularly well-suited for use in OWI. As the scholarship on OWI indicates, online learners are generally very diverse (Cleary et al., 2019). Borgman and McArdle (2019) explain that "[o]nline courses and degrees have an appeal that reaches diverse students—the returning full-time working student with a family, the part-time student with a family, the military student stationed overseas, the former college student dropout who is returning to school after a larger break spent working" (p. 77). In addition to diversity in age and life experience, diversity in OWI also takes many other forms including gender and ethnic diversity (Clinefelter et al., 2019), varying degrees of English speaking and preparation for college (Borgman & McArdle, 2019), differing levels of technological access and knowledge (Greer & Harris, 2018), and differences in learning styles and abilities (Borgman & Dockter, 2018). Labor-based grading contracts are a good choice for use with such diverse groups of students because they take into account and reward students for their effort. In conventional models of assessment, student labor often goes unnoticed and unrewarded as the "quality" of student work is the factor that determines student grades. As Inoue (2019) explains, although "[a]ll pedagogies ask students to labor. . . . They usually ignore the actual labor of learning in favor of systems that judge the so-called quality of the outcomes of student labor, favoring a single judge's (the teacher's) decisions about the quality of the products of labor" (p. 129). The result of prioritizing quality over labor is that "conventional grading systems . . . often are unfair to diverse groups of students," as "quality" is determined by a single measure and often represents inequitable language standardization (Inoue, 2019, p. 61).

The use of a labor-based grading contract works to remedy this. The grading contract delineates the number of tasks students must complete in order to earn their desired course grade. Essentially, the more labor a student does, the better their course grade will be. Quality is separated from the course grade; though quality remains a focus of class discussions, activities, and peer- and instructor-feedback (see Appendix A for our sample grading contract). The grading contract is also a group-authored document in which students and faculty collaboratively make assessment decisions through negotiation and class discussions. Instructors decide whether they want to extend this collaboration to a single element in the grading contract (such as participation), or into all elements of the contract (such as deciding the amount of labor required to earn a "B" in the course). We have found that involving students in assessment decision-making leads to increased investment in the course and contributes to an increased sense of community, both of which are particularly important in online courses as "[r]esearch demonstrates that classes taught with high rapport (defined as high levels of faculty/student presence and engagement) can increase retention by up to 40 percent" (Greer & Harris, 2018, p. 23). In her study of rapport-building strategies in online courses, Glazier (2019) found that "[a]lthough rapport cannot change students' level of preparedness or the personal life circumstances that may prove challenging in any given semester, rapport just may help students cope with those challenges. The data clearly show that rapport helps them to be more successful" (p. 449). Labor-based grading contracts provide opportunities to build rapport and increase engagement as instructors and students work together to define the parameters of the grading contract. These documents provide a focal point for discussing how students' work is assessed throughout the course—conversations that we encourage at the level of the whole class via LMS discussion boards focused on aspects of the grading contract and individually as students email us with questions or visit us during online office hours to discuss their progress in class.

For these reasons, contract grading has been framed as a method of assessment that encourages student learning (Danielewicz & Elbow, 2009; Inoue, 2019), furthers critical pedagogy (Shor, 1996; Thelin, 2005), and provides the opportunity to enact socially-just, antiracist assessment practices (Inoue, 2015, 2019). Inoue (2019) has further identified three primary benefits of using grading contracts in writing classes: they eliminate quality-based judgments of student performance, provide students and teachers with the opportunity to critically evaluate how language is used (and privileged) in various ecologies, and give students the space to try new things without the risk of losing points (reframing failure as something more productive). While little scholarship considers grading contracts in OWI specifically, we have found that these benefits have been maintained in our own online writing courses. Further, research has called for the use of social contracts in OWI (Mick & Middlebrook, 2015) and an emphasis on fairness in online writing assessment (Sapp & Simon, 2005). While there is a need for additional research on the degree to which grading contracts influence different diversities, we believe that the use of a grading contract works to create and maintain equitable spaces in which diverse student populations can succeed in their online courses.

Challenges to Implementing Grading Contracts in OWI

Despite the benefits of grading contracts for OWI, they can be difficult to implement effectively both because of the complexity of introducing students to a new method of grading in an online environment and because of the ways that LMSs shape and constrain grading practices. Previous research on student perceptions of grading contracts has found that in face-to-face (F2F) contexts, some students resist the use of contract grading. For example, Inman and Powell (2018) report that although students in their study acknowledged that the grading contract allowed them to focus on improving their writing and encouraged risk-taking, they still preferred receiving conventional grades on their work (pp. 39–40).

Mikenna conducted an informal survey about contract grading during the second half of the spring 2020 semester and found different results. While half of her students did express a preference for conventional grades, half of them also indicated that they preferred the grading contract. Interestingly, among those who preferred conventional grades, they indicated that this preference was due to their familiarity with conventional grading methods. Though much of students' resistance to grading contracts may be evidence of what hooks (2014) identifies as the pain associated with giving up old ways of thinking and assessment methods such as the use of points or percentages that students are used to, it does point out the need to communicate clearly with students about a new method of grading in OWI. As Borgman and McArdle (2019) emphasize, "[o]ften a lot of the headaches that occur in online courses happen because of the gap in understanding of what is expected from each party involved, instructor and student" (pp. 73–74). Communicating clearly and frequently with students via secure course and campus communication tools about how they will be assessed is always an important way for instructors to be responsive to students in OWI, and being responsive is especially necessary when using a method of assessment that is likely to be unfamiliar to students such as labor-based contract grading.

Additionally, it is crucial to be strategic in designing grading contract documents for use in OWI because the systems design approach operative in most LMSs makes it impossible to simply migrate grading contracts as they are implemented in F2F courses into OWI. Within systems design, LMS system requirements and limitations determine use of the LMS, and the result is frequently, as Harris and Greer (2017) discuss, that LMS technologies "create spaces that are constrained in particular ways that affect and often restrict student access and learning" (p. 48). In the case of grading contracts, LMS technologies narrowly limit the options that instructors have for providing grades to students in ways that strongly push instructors toward quality-based assessment. Instructors who want to implement contract grading within LMSs often resort to "hacking" their LMS's grading tools, which predictably leads to student confusion.

During May 2020, a discussion thread on the WPA listserv titled "Contract and Specifications Grading on Canvas" documented a number of difficulties that instructors have implementing contract grading in LMSs. Grover (2020) posted the initial query, explaining in his post that though he liked

> the idea of [students] being able to see their grades and access feedback whenever and however they want, in a familiar and secure interface, and I like having the assignment due dates linked to the calendar Canvas generates for them—I just don't like all the baggage that Canvas forces on me to take advantage of these things.

List members replied with a number of creative ways that they have implemented grading contracts in LMSs (not just in Canvas), but as Evans (2020) noted, many of these represented "ungrading 'hacks'" more than real solutions, leading her to conclude that "the LMS grading paradigm just can't be manipulated into a grading contract." Though instructors can and do find workaround solutions, these often confuse students as to how they are being graded, as several posters also confirmed in the listserv discussion.

Angela's efforts to make Canvas gradebook and assignment tools work with the course grading contract demonstrate both the possibilities for and difficulties of working within the limitations of the LMS. Though the workaround solutions available to an instructor will vary depending on the institutional LMS in use and an instructor's preferences, Angela adapts the Canvas settings, gradebook, and assignments tools to accommodate contract grading by taking the following steps:

Under "enabled course grading scheme" in Canvas course settings, Angela sets her own GPA scale for the course as depicted in Figure 7.1.

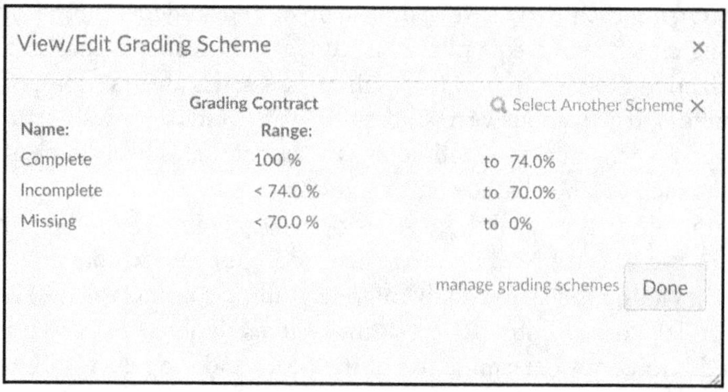

Figure 7.1. The custom grading scheme Angela sets up in Canvas settings.

In Canvas Assignments, Angela creates an assignment called "Fulfillment of the Course Grading Contract." Then she uses "assignment groups weight" in Canvas Assignments to set all of the assignment groups at 0% of total except for the Fulfillment of the Course Grading Contract assignment, which she weights at 100% of total (see Figure 7.2).

Figure 7.2. How weighted assignments in Canvas Assignments are configured so the Grading Contract is 100%.

When Angela creates an assignment in Canvas, she uses the settings in Figure 7.3. This means that when she grades students' writing, they see "complete," "incomplete," or "missing" for their assignment (see Figure 7.4).

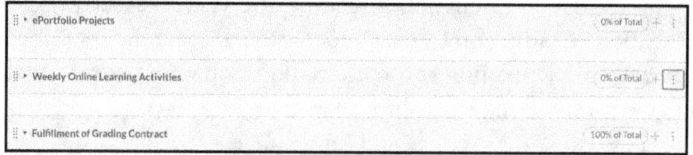

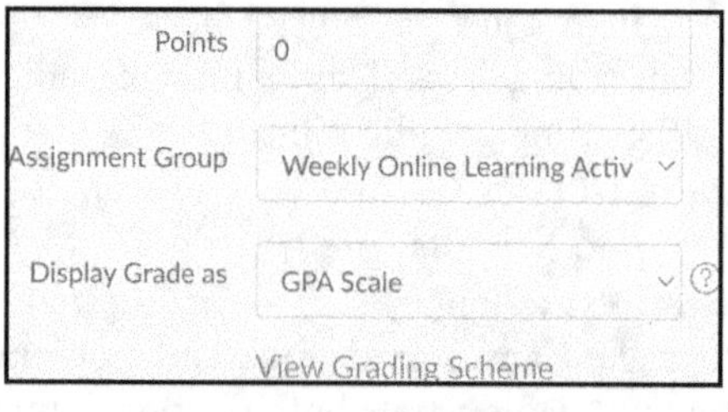

Figure 7.3. How Angela configures an assignment's settings so it uses her custom grading scheme.

Angela sets all students' grades for the "Fulfillment of the Course Grading Contract" Assignment to 85% at the beginning of the semester to reflect the fact that if they complete the grading contract they will receive a B for the course (see Figure 7.4). As the semester progresses, she adjusts this percentage as needed.

Week 15 Discussion Post Weekly Online Learning Activities	0 (missing)	0	
ePortfolio ePortfolio Projects	0 (complete)	0	
Fulfillment of Course Grading Contract Fulfillment of Course Grading Contract	85 (B)	85	

Figure 7.4. A student's view of the gradebook in Canvas after Angela implements her custom grading scheme, weights assignments so that the grading contract assignment is weighted at 100%, and sets the default grade for the grading contract at 85%.

By taking steps like these, we are able to force the Canvas gradebook to represent student grades consistent with our grading contract, but this workaround—like other workarounds we have tried—is still not optimal. This particular workaround not only requires instructors to take several non-intuitive steps in order to implement, but also still confuses students who see 0's listed for their assignments alongside the word "complete." Nevertheless, the desire to implement grading contracts within the LMS is understandable since institutions provide more technical support for LMSs than they do for external platforms (which they may not support at all), and some instructors are required to house grading within their institution's mandated LMS and to report grades from within the LMS as well. However, the poor user experience that often results from this systems design process discourages many instructors from implementing a form of assessment particularly well-suited to OWI. Consequently, even though we have found ways to make Canvas (mostly) represent grades the way we want, these "hacks" do not constitute our strategy for response in our classes. Rather, they illustrate the limitations of the systems design approach. In contrast, we advocate for a student-centered design approach that emphasizes communicating clearly with students about assessment procedures and that uses tools within and outside the LMS as needed to do so.

Developing a Strategy for Being Responsive

The technical challenges of implementing grading contracts in LMSs serve as a good reminder that, as Borgman and McArdle (2019) contend, "elements of face-to-face courses can rarely be successfully migrated into online ones" (p. 73). Instead, implementing grading contracts effectively in OWI requires an instructor to be both responsive and strategic, as Borgman and McArdle (2019) describe these elements of their PARS approach to OWI. While being responsive concerns "setting boundaries for instruction/grading/virtual availability," being strategic refers to "architecting an experience" (Borgman & McArdle, 2019, p. 3) that is "focused on the user experience of the students" (p. 71). Taken together, these two pillars of the PARS approach suggest that instructors should develop a strategy for being responsive based on their understanding of who their students are and what they need. Indeed, in OWI, having a strategy for being responsive is arguably even more important than in F2F contexts because, as Warnock (2015) explains, "feedback provides students with their most individualized teaching experience in online settings" (p. 166). Because students cannot quickly ask clarifying questions in person about feedback or course grades, it is especially important for instructors to communicate clearly with students about how and when their work is being assessed. At the same time, because students in OWI write even more than students in F2F courses, it is easy for online writing instructors to become overwhelmed by trying to respond to all of the writing that students produce in an online writing course or even to keep up with student emails inquiring about course grades and feedback. For this reason, Borgman and McArdle (2019) advise that "[t]he goal of being responsive is to help you maintain a high level of interaction with your students while not getting buried under the avalanche of emails and essays" (p. 65). In other words, being responsive means developing a clear strategy for response that will help students and the instructor have a better experience in OWI.

A student-centered design approach is necessary to develop an effective strategy for being responsive in OWI. Student-centered design, which is based on Blythe's (2001) user-centered design (UCD) approach, places students and their needs at the center of online course design rather than system requirements and limitations. Student-centered design is collaborative and recursive, as "teachers and students must be present in the time and space of the class to work within and beyond the constraints of institutional LMS platforms and design and employ learning spaces that achieve this more collaborative model of student-instructor co-creation" (Harris & Greer, 2017, p. 48). Additionally, instructors using student-centered design draw flexibly from available tools and apps to help them meet student needs rather than limiting themselves to the tools offered by one mandated LMS. As Harris and Greer (2017) explain, "[w]e are moving beyond a time when a single LMS will be workable for all students in all situations, toward a new, more flexible model that sees technology as an ecosystem of interlocking tools and applications rather than as a single, one-size-fits-all platform" (p. 51). Like UCD, student-centered design is based on our actual observations of students using technology and attempts to design online learning spaces around students' observed needs. For example, when we observe students (and instructors) struggling to understand and use LMS gradebook tools for contract grading applications, it is clear that we need to design different types of documents and processes to make contract grading more effective in OWI. The complexity of students' needs and desires when it comes to assessment also illustrates why student-centered design is not synonymous with UCD. While UCD typically emphasizes how a user completes a single task, students have complex interactions in online courses. In the case of assessment documents, students might interact with these documents to get a sense for their current grade in a course, plan what they think is necessary in the future in order to achieve the course grade they desire, understand how an instructor assesses their writing, and seek feedback that can help them to improve their performance or meet the instructor's expectations, among other reasons. In other words, we cannot simply design our courses to ensure that students can, for example, find their grade on an assignment. From our observations of and interactions with students in OWI, we know that this would only partially address students' needs and that they may need other information to help them understand what a grade means or how to use the information. Thus, though UCD provides a design process—involving user research, iterative design, and collaboration—that instructors can use to design online learning spaces for students, putting students—instead of users—at the center of design also means implementing this process within the enormously complex context of learning.

In our online courses, we have employed student-centered design to develop our strategy of using grading contracts to respond to students. Rather than designing our grading contracts based on the constraints and limitations of the LMS, we begin instead with our knowledge of our student users and their needs for timely, clear, and individualized response on their labor in our courses. To do this, we work within and outside of our institutional LMS as needed to capitalize on the strengths of different tools and applications to 1) create with students a grading contract that spells out exactly what constitutes participation and collaboration in the online course, 2) provide opportunities for our students to assess their own progress in meeting the requirements of the grading contract for each major course assignment and 3) provide a personalized grading contract for each student as a visual, interactive document that makes the different components students will be evaluated on highly visible and that records their progress throughout the semester. Together, these practices represent our strategy for responding to students in our online writing courses.

Collaboratively Authored Labor-Based Grading Contract

The labor-based grading contract document itself is the most distinctive feature of contract grading (see Appendix A for the grading contract we use). Labor-based grading contracts frequently stand apart from other assessment tools by their length. The sample grading contract that Inoue (2019) published as an appendix to Labor-Based Grading Contracts: Building Equity and Inclusion in the Compassionate Writing Classroom and has made available to other instructors as a PDF, is seven pages long (wac.colostate.edu/docs/books/labor/appendixa.pdf).

Grading contracts are lengthy because in addition to detailing required elements of the course, they must clearly educate students about this often new and unfamiliar form of grading and define exactly how students' work will be assessed in the class. The grading contract thus often explains the rationale for using labor-based contract grading, defines key terms, and details the requirements for achieving an A, B, C and so forth in the course. There are a number of ways that instructors might choose to define the terms used in their grading contracts. In his sample grading contract, Inoue (2019) uses the terms "complete and on time work" and "late or incomplete work" to distinguish between assignments (p. 332). Similarly, we generally use "complete" and "incomplete" to distinguish between assignments in need of additional revision and those that have satisfied assignment requirements. Other instructors might prefer language such as "unsatisfactory," "satisfactory," or "satisfactory plus," or the terms "needs revision/developing," "meets expectations," and "exceeds expectations."

There can be problems with presenting such important and potentially confusing information to students in a lengthy document, particularly in an online class. Online instructors are encouraged to "chunk" information to make it more readable and improve student engagement and comprehension (Malamed, 2009; Miller, 1956). Consequently, based on what we know about our students' needs for a thorough introduction to a new method of assessment along with what we know about their needs for course content to be organized into manageable chunks, we create an entire module in our online courses outlining how contract grading will work (see Figure 7.5). The module allows us to chunk information so students don't get overwhelmed by being confronted by one long contract document, to include as many details as we need to provide, and to set completion of the grading contract module as a prerequisite for other course content to open for students.

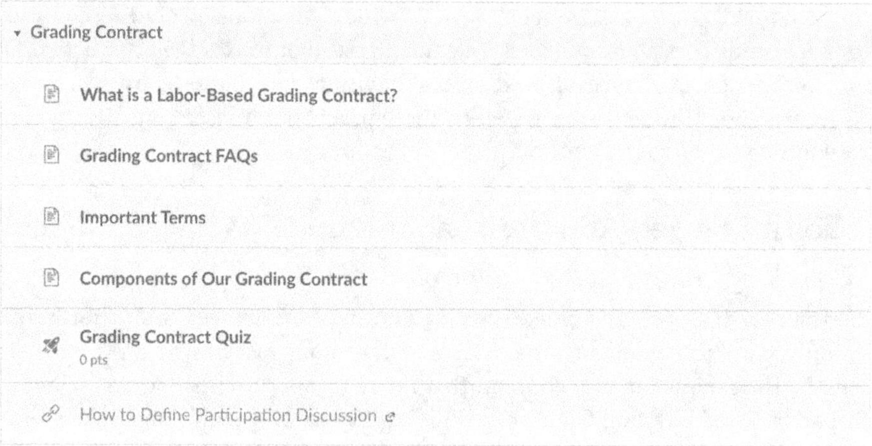

Figure 7.5. An example of a grading contract module in Canvas.

Additionally, most labor-based grading contracts include a collaborative element where students and faculty work together to define certain elements of the contract, such as participation and collaboration. In our classes, we tend to use the LMS discussion board to facilitate this collaboration, but instructors could use whatever tool they prefer to foster collaboration (Google Docs, etc.). We have collaborated with our students on defining B-level participation in the course as completing 80 percent of their weekly online learning activities, and we have defined citizenship as responding to one another with respect and compassion throughout the semester. While these collaborative elements are typically outlined at the beginning of the course, it is important to check in with the class throughout the semester or at the midpoint of the semester to see if any changes to the contract need to be made. Because this method of assessment is new to most students, they may not immediately have concerns with the contract; however, as students gain familiarity with this method of assessment, class discussions often result in the renegotiation of elements of the grading contract beyond participation and collaboration, and begin to include discussions of fair labor processes. In OWI, instructors may want to initiate these dialogues privately by way of a writing warm-up or a survey using Google Forms in order "to be sensitive to students' privacy and unease with sharing potentially personal information with the class as a whole" (Inoue, 2019, pp. 229–230), after which the conversation can move onto a more public forum, such as Google Docs or a discussion post on institutional LMS platforms.

Self-Assessment Forms

We have found that to improve student understanding of and communication around the grading contract in online classes it is not enough only to provide the contract to students at the beginning of the term. Most students are unfamiliar with grading contract assessment and benefit from opportunities to see how it is being used throughout the semester to assess their work and how criteria such as "complete" or "incomplete" are applied. To help improve student fluency with grading contract language and provide opportunities for self-assessment, we have developed a self-assessment form (see Appendix B) that we modify for each course assignment that is included on the grading contract. This helps students to gain familiarity in using the language of the grading contract and experience in assessing their own labor and performance in the course. It also helps students to create a revision plan for their assignments that they can implement to improve their writing in subsequent drafts. Students can also be involved in the process of creating the grading criteria for each course assignment, which further encourages student and faculty collaboration.

There are many ways instructors can introduce the self-assessment form to their students. In her class, Mikenna uses course communication tools both inside and outside of her institutional LMS to introduce the self-assessment form. She starts by creating a Weekly Online Learning Activity as an assignment in Canvas. For this activity, students are asked to read a sample student paper that is housed in a Google Doc. They are then instructed to review the assignment directions and grading criteria, then fill out the self-assessment form as if the paper was their own. This type of scaffolding activity gives students the opportunity to try out the self-assessment form before using it to assess their own written work, and provides instructors the opportunity to comment on how students are filling out the form and clearly communicate how the grading criteria (whether they were collaboratively constructed or not) are being applied to the writing task at hand. After this activity, Mikenna asks her students to use the self-assessment form as a cover page on the first draft of each of their ePortfolio Projects.

Individualized Grading Contract

Finally, we use the collaboratively-authored grading contract to create an interactive, individualized grading contract for each student that is updated throughout the course (see Appendix C for our sample individualized grading contract). The individual grading contract clearly shows each student where they stand in relation to completing contract requirements, allowing them to keep track of which course requirements they have completed and what they still need to spend more time on. For online courses, it can be helpful to update these weekly for the sake of clarity and clear communication, but instructors can also update them after each major assignment or at other specified times such as at midterms and again before the end of the semester—as long as students are informed ahead of time when they will receive these updates. Individual grading contracts are interactive since instructors add to them throughout the semester, but also links to assignments or instructor feedback can be added to the contract as well depending on the program the instructor uses to make them. The main concern with these documents is that instructors ensure they are private since they include student grade data. For this reason, we have found that it makes sense to create and maintain these documents using a program like Word or Pages, which allows us to save them on our secure personal computers. These programs also support hyperlinking and elements of visual design if instructors wish to make them more interactive. For example, an instructor might add a hyperlink to direct a student to a web resource related to a particular writing issue they need to work on. To share the documents with students, we upload them to the "Fulfillment of the Course Grading Contract" assignment we have created in Canvas assignments. This method ensures that students' grade information is kept secure in compliance with FERPA regulations and can also satisfy any institutional policies that grading take place within the mandated LMS.

Not only does our individualized grading contract represent a more personalized response strategy, but also a more equitable one. As previously mentioned, labor-based grading contracts are generally more equitable because they make all course grades more accessible to all students (Inoue, 2019); however, the unfamiliar contract language coupled with the limitations of LMS gradebooks often lead to student confusion. Our individualized grading contract works to remedy this while also providing students the opportunity to ask questions about course assignments and their course grade. For example, a returning full-time working student with a family might find the individualized grading contract particularly helpful because they may not have the ability to meet with their instructor during regular business hours to inquire about their progress in the course. The individualized grading contract provides such students with a quick point of reference in regard to their course grade and labor progress. It also gives such students the opportunity to review, leave comments on, and ask questions about their individualized grading contract whenever they sit down to work on their coursework—whether that be in the morning before they head to work, or late at night after their children have gone to bed. This flexibility, alongside the clarification we hope this individualized grading contract provides, works to further the equitable assessment practices we use in OWI.

Final Thoughts and Application

The documents described above represent our attempt to implement contract grading in OWI in a way that is student-friendly and helps all our students succeed, regardless of the student diversity represented in our classes. It is helpful to think of this in terms of golf and we envision the golf analogy of moving toward a more equitable scorecard for the students in our courses. In golf, obviously, the goal is to make pars, birdies, and eagles while avoiding bogeys, double bogeys, and worse. In other words, scorecards help golfers to track exactly how they are performing for each hole and to measure their performance against par. Additionally, over time, this record helps golfers to track their improvement and identify areas they need to work on. In order to work, scorecards have to be easy to understand and use. Golfers also have to understand the language of scorekeeping to appreciate that making a birdie is preferable to making a bogey. The fact that golfers use the scorecard after every hole ensures their familiarity and usefulness in helping golfers improve their performance on particular holes and their overall score through practice.

Labor-based grading contracts operate similarly in OWI. We recommend that instructors design labor-based grading contracts for easy reading and comprehension in order to communicate to students exactly how many assignments and activities a student needs to complete to succeed in the course and the criteria for successfully completing each assignment or activity (what we might think of as par for each assignment). We also suggest that students be provided with opportunities to interact with grading contract documents often enough that they become familiar with them and fluent in the assessment language used in the course—whether this is "complete and incomplete" or "still developing, satisfactory, and exceeds expectations." Lastly, we urge instructors to provide individual progress reports to students regularly as they complete the grading contract requirements as to provide feedback on both their performance on specific assignments and activities as well as on their overall course progress.

By using Borgman and McArdle's PARS elements responsive and strategic along with labor-based grading contracts, instructors can make assessment more equitable for the diverse students in OWI. Since our students bring with them a wide variety of experiences, differences, and abilities, making labor the basis for assessment helps to ensure that all our students can succeed in our courses. In OWI, it is equally important to implement this response strategy by designing grading contract documents that are student-centered and aid in comprehension. Since the documents that we provide to students in OWI constitute their experience and understanding of the course even more than they do for students in F2F courses, it is essential that those documents do not further confuse students about how they are being graded or where they stand in the course, but rather support the work of student learning.

References

Blythe, S. (2001). Designing online courses: User-centered design. *Computers and Composition, 18*(4), 329–346. https://doi.org/10.1016/S8755-4615(01)00066-4.

Borgman, J. & Dockter J. (2018). Considerations of access and design in the online writing classroom. *Computers and Composition, 49,* 94–105.

Borgman, J. & McArdle, C. (2019). *Personal, accessible, responsive, strategic: Resources and strategies for online writing instructors.* The WAC Clearinghouse; University Press of Colorado. https://doi.org/10.37514/PRA-B.2019.0322.

Cleary, Y., Rice, R., Zemliansky, P. & St.Amant, K. S. (2019). Perspectives on teaching writing online in global contexts: Ideas, insights, and projections. *ROLE Journal.* http://www.roleolor.org/perspectives-on-teaching-writing-online.html.

Clinefelter, D. L., Aslanian, C. B. & Magda, A. J. (2019). *Online college students 2019: Comprehensive data on demands and preferences.* Wiley.

Danielewicz, J. & Elbow, P. (2009). A unilateral grading contract to improve learning and teaching, *College Composition and Communication, 61*(2), 244–268.

Evans, K. (2020, May 14). *Re: Contract and specifications grading on Canvas* [Discussion post]. WPA Listserv. https://lists.asu.edu/cgi-bin/wa?A2=WPA-L;72aa3a9a.2005&S=.

Glazier, R. A. (2016). Building rapport to improve retention and success in online classes, *Journal of Political Science Education, 12*(4), 437–456. https://doi.org/10.1080/15512169.2016.1155994.

Greer, M. & Harris, H. S. (2018). User-centered design as a foundation for effective online writing instruction, *Computers and Composition, 49,* 14–24.

Grover, S. (2020, May 14). Contract and specifications on grading in Canvas [Discussion post]. WPA Listserv. https://lists.asu.edu/cgi-bin/wa?A2=WPA-L;a5468f5e.2005&S=.

Harris, H. S. & Greer, M. (2017). Over, under, or through: Design strategies to supplement the LMS and enhance interaction in online writing courses, *Communication Design Quarterly Review, 44*(4), 46–54.

hooks, b. (2014). *Teaching to transgress: Education as the practice of freedom.* Routledge.

Inman, J. O. & Powell, R. A. (2018). In the absence of grades: Dissonance and desire in course-contract classrooms. *College Composition and Communication, 70*(1), 30–56.

Inoue, A. B. (2015). *Antiracist writing assessment ecologies: Teaching and assessing writing for a socially just future.* The WAC Clearinghouse; Parlor Press. https://doi.org/10.37514/PER-B.2015.0698.

Inoue, A. B. (2019). *Labor-based grading contracts: Building equity and inclusion in the compassionate writing classroom.* The WAC Clearinghouse; University Press of Colorado. https://doi.org/10.37514/PER-B.2019.0216.

Kohn, A. (2013). The case against grades. *Counterpoints, 451,* 143–153.

Malamed, C. (2009). *Chunking information for instructional design.* The Elearning Coach. http://theelearningcoach.com/elearning_design/chunking-information/.

Mick, C. S. & Middlebrook, G. (2015). Asynchronous and synchronous modalities. In B. L. Hewett & K. E. DePew (Eds.), *Foundational practices of online writing instruction* (pp. 129–148). The WAC Clearinghouse; Parlor Press. https://doi.org/10.37514/PER-B.2015.0650.2.03.

Miller, G. A. (1956). The magical number seven, plus or minus two: Some limits on our capacity for processing information. *The Psychological Review, 63,* 81–97.

Sapp, D. A. & Simon, J. (2005). Comparing grades in online and face-to-face writing courses: Interpersonal accountability and institutional commitment. *Computers and Composition, 22*(4), 471–489.

Shor, I. (1996). *When students have power: Negotiating authority in a critical pedagogy.* University of Chicago Press.

Thelin, W. (2005). Understanding problems in critical classrooms. *College Composition and Communication, 57*(1), 114–141.

Warnock, S. (2015). Teaching the OWI course. In B. Hewett & K. DePew (Eds.), *Foundational practices of online writing instruction* (pp. 151–181). The WAC Clearinghouse; Parlor Press. https://doi.org/10.37514/PER-B.2015.0650.2.04.

Appendix A. Sample Grading Contract

This grading contract, which is an adaptation of Inoue's (2019), represents a version of a grading contract that Mikenna has negotiated with students in her first-year writing course.

Course Grading

This class is assessed using a labor-based grading contract. You will not be given a point value per assignment; instead, your grade will be entirely determined by the labor you put into your coursework. While I will not grade you based on the quality of your work, all of the feedback you receive, as well as our discussions and activities, will be about the quality of your work and how you can grow as a reader, writer, and researcher.

In this class we will also try to create a community of compassion, a group of people who genuinely care about the wellbeing of each other—and part of that caring, that compassion, is doing things for each other. It turns out, this also helps you learn. The best way to learn is to teach others, to help, to serve. So we will function as collaborators, allies with various skills, abilities, experiences, and talents that we offer the group, rather than opponents working against each other for grades or a teacher's approval.

The default grade for the class is a "B." If you do all that is asked of you in the spirit it is asked, then you will get a "B." If you turn in assignments late, forget to do assignments, etc., your grade will be lower. If you put in more labor by completing one of our two optional projects, you will get an "A."

I know this all sounds very different—it is very different than how we've been taught grades "should" work. I imagine you have some questions, so here are some FAQs to get us started:

Frequently Asked Questions (FAQs)

What is a grading contract?

A contract is "a binding agreement between two or more persons or parties" (Merriam-Webster).

A *grading contract*, then, is an agreement between the students and the instructor about the work that needs to be done in order to earn a specific grade.

What is labor?

"Labor is work the body does over time" (Inoue, 2019, p. 129).

Why do we use a grading contract in this course?

"Teachers often take for granted that students must labor in order to learn. They must read or write, take notes or discuss. However, typical grading systems rarely account for students' labor in any way. They usually ignore the actual labor of learning in favor of systems that judge the so-called quality of the outcomes of student labor, favoring a single judge's (the teacher's) decisions about the quality of the products of labor. Because labor is neglected in such conventional grading systems, they often are unfair to diverse groups of students. Labor-based grading contracts attempt to correct this problem" (Inoue, 2019, p. 129).

"Grades tend to diminish students' interest in whatever they're learning. Grades create a preference for the easiest possible task. Grades tend to reduce the quality of students' thinking. While it's true that many students, after a few years of traditional schooling, could be described as motivated by grades, what counts is the nature of their motivation. Extrinsic motivation, which includes a desire to get better grades, is not only different from, but often undermines, intrinsic motivation, a desire to learn for its own sake" (Kohn, 2013, p. 144).

Important Terms

Complete Assignments

An assignment will be considered "complete" if it meets all of the criteria listed on the assignment sheet and is turned in on time.

To earn a "B" in this class, all of your ePortfolio Projects must be "complete" after you submit the Final ePortfolio.

Incomplete Assignments

An assignment will be considered "incomplete" if it does not meet all of the criteria listed on the assignment sheet.

If you receive an "incomplete" on an ePortfolio Project, you will have the opportunity to revise for a "complete" in your Final ePortfolio; however, there must be evidence of **substantive** revision, reflection, and effort.

To earn a "B" in this class, you cannot have any "incomplete" ePortfolio Projects after you submit your Final ePortfolio.

Late Assignments

An assignment will be considered "late" if it is turned in after the deadline listed on Canvas. All of our assignments and their due dates are listed on Canvas under the "Syllabus" tab.

To earn a "B" in this class, you can turn in one ePortfolio Project late throughout the semester. However, this paper must (1) be "complete" when it is turned in and (2) be turned in within 48 hours of its original due date to avoid receiving a grade of "missing." For example, if a paper was due on Friday, May 1st at 11:59 p.m., that paper must be completed and turned in by 11:59 p.m. on Sunday the 3rd.

Missing Assignments

Any ePortfolio Projects not done period, or "missing," for whatever reason, are put into this category.

To earn a "B" in this class, you cannot have any missing ePortfolio Projects.

If any of the ePortfolio Projects become "missing," it constitutes an automatic failure of the course. Please reach out to me if you ever find yourself struggling to complete our coursework on time—we can work together to come up with a solution.

Weekly Online Learning Activities

Weekly online learning activities constitute the assignments you would complete in class if we were meeting in a face-to-face format. This includes assignments like peer review workshops, discussion posts, and informal assignments.

Weekly online learning activities cannot be made up after their deadline. If you submit a weekly online learning activity on time, it will be "complete." Even complete online learning activities will often receive feedback in order to help you improve in the future.

To earn a "B" in this class, 80% of your weekly online learning activities must be "complete."

Below is a table that shows the main components of our course contract.

Desired Course Grade	# of Complete ePortfolio Projects	# of Incomplete ePortfolio Projects	# of Late ePortfolio Projects	# of Missing ePortfolio Projects	% of Weekly Online Learning Activities Completed on Time
A (4.0)	5	0	0	0	≥90%
B (3.1)	4	0	1	0	≥80%
C (2.1)	3	1	2	0	≥70%
D (1.1)	2	2	3	1	≥60%
F (0.0)	0	4	4	2	<60%

In addition to updating our gradebook in Canvas, I will also give you an individual grading contract that will be updated once a week as we complete our course assignments. This individual contract should help you manage the assignments you need to complete to earn your desired course grade.

I know more questions will arise throughout the semester. Please, never hesitate to ask me questions about the grading contract, your standing in the class, your writing, etc. I am here to help you be successful!

Appendix B. Self-Assessment Form

This form represents one way that Mikenna reminds her students how they are being assessed in the course and helps her students to become fluent in grading contract language.

> Directions: Please fill out the following self-assessment form and submit it along with your first draft of ePortfolio Project #3. First, please comment on what you've done well and what you still want to improve on during revision. Then, tell me whether you think that the labor you have put into this paper earns a "complete" or "incomplete" grade.
>
> Note: If you have completely ignored one of the following grading criteria, your paper is likely "incomplete."

Done Well	Grading Criteria	Revision To-Do's
	Criterion #1. Did you clearly state your specific research question?	
	Criterion #2. Did you use *at least* five sources (four peer-reviewed sources and one webpage) to support your inquiry? Did you thoroughly analyze these sources?	
	Criterion #3. Did you organize your paper logically? Did you use subheadings? Remember, at a minimum you need to have: (1) an introduction section, (2) a section for your research question, (3) a problem section, (4) a solutions section, and (5) a conclusions section.	
	Criterion #4. Did you thoroughly develop all of your main points? Be sure to explain to your reader *why* your research question is important, *what* the problem is, and *how* they can solve this problem.	
	Criterion #5. Did you write a paper that is 2,000–3,000 words long? A paper that is not *at least* 2,000 words long will automatically receive an "incomplete" and is not eligible to submit in the Final ePortfolio. This does not include any images, graphs, or your Works Cited page.	
	Criterion #6. Did you incorporate peer-feedback and make substantial revisions from draft 1 to draft 2?	

Based on the above criteria, is your paper "Complete" or "Incomplete"? Explain your reasoning.

Appendix C. Example of an Interactive, Personalized Grading Contract

This individualized contract is updated weekly to help students track their progress toward meeting grading contract requirements.

Individual Grading Contract

Category	Task	To earn a "B"	Marcus
ePortfolio Projects	Project #1: Literacy Narrative	All projects must be "complete" after submitting the ePortfolio	✓
	Project #2: Book Review		✓
	Project #3: Edited Collection		
	Project #4: Final Reflection		
	Project #5: English 121 Reflections *or* Project #6: A Letter to Tara Westover	Optional to qualify for an "A"	If you are aiming for an "A," be sure to complete one of these assignments & submit it in the Final ePortfolio.
Final ePortfolio	Final ePortfolio must be "complete"	✓	
Process Work	Revision	You make substantive revisions when the assignment is to revise—extending or changing the thinking or organization—not just editing or touching up	✓ You have done a great job with your revisions between drafts! I appreciate how thoughtfully you integrate your colleagues' feedback into your writing.
	Deadlines	Submit no more than 1 late ePortfolio Project	✓

Designing a More Equitable Scorecard

Category	Task	To earn a "B"	Marcus
Weekly Online Learning Activities	Regularly complete weekly online assignments	≥80% of weekly online learning activities completed on time	✓
	Regularly complete weekly readings		✓
	Peer-Review Workshops		✓ So far, you have completed 2 of the 4 peer-review workshops.
	ePortfolio Link Checks		X I cannot access all of the documents on the "Education" page of your ePortfolio. Can you make sure your link sharing permissions are set to "anyone with link can view"? Once you make this change, your "incomplete" grade will become "complete."
	Post on our weekly discussion board & thoughtfully reply at least 2 times		X This is the fourth week you have not posted on our weekly discussion board. Is there something I can do to help you be more successful on this part of our contract? How can we make this labor more manageable?
Citizenship	Respond to one another with respect and compassion	✓	✓ Your peer-feedback shows a deep respect for your colleagues' labor and writing.

Note: I will update this document once a week so that you always know where you stand in the course. If you ever have any questions about the class, your labor, etc., please do not hesitate to send me an email or stop by my virtual office hours (W 10–11am).

Chapter 8. Not a Laughing Matter: Creating a Humor-Centric User Design in OWI

Nitya Pandey
FLORIDA STATE UNIVERSITY

Abstract: Online spaces are often viewed as cold and robotic platforms where it is difficult to cultivate human connection. Building and nurturing a virtual classroom community can be more challenging than fostering a face-to-face classroom community. Moreover, OWI deals with the teaching and learning of writing, and writing can be an immensely personal and social activity. In that sense, it is crucial that OWI classes possess an element of warmth and cordiality so that the members of the classroom community feel a sense of comfort and ease while sharing their thoughts and work with one another. This chapter presents humor as a method to promote that togetherness and sociability. It focuses on the ways to utilize pedagogical humor in OWI classes in a productive manner while cautioning about the downsides of inappropriate humor.

Keywords: online writing instruction, personal, social, pedagogical humor, fostering virtual classroom community, human connection

It is the final week of Spring 2020 semester. Due to the safety concerns owing to the surge in COVID-19 cases, the College Composition course is being taught online since March. The transition happened without much preparation, and everyone has been quite stressed out for the past few weeks. This is the last class of the final week and it is a presentation day. The teacher decides to dissipate the tension by cracking a joke. She looks at the anxious faces on her computer screen. She takes a deep breath and unmutes herself on Zoom, the platform that is being used for the class, and comments in a nonchalant voice: "Jeff, where is Cookie? Let's say Hi to her before we begin." As if on cue, the large black and white cat, Cookie, who has been a regular member of the class ever since it switched to the online platform, appears on his screen. She blinks a couple of times and mews, her face perfectly somber. The mew is loud and clear since Jeff, once again, has forgotten to mute himself. This makes everyone in the class, including Jeff and the instructor, burst into laughter. Everyone looks visibly relaxed after that little episode.

This scenario might sound familiar to many people who have been a part of online classes as students or instructors. If the class is synchronous, it is quite normal for people to attend the class from their living rooms. In these situations, pets often become a part of the classroom community. The case of Cookie, the cat, is just an example of contextual humor where a furry member of the online classroom added to the fun quotient. Apart from such spontaneous comments, there are many other ways of integrating humor into online pedagogy through written and audio-visual means. This chapter discusses them and emphasizes that despite having its fair share of challenges, humor, when incorporated into online writing instruction, can be a beneficial way to nurture human relationships in virtual classrooms.

Setting up an online instruction module can be a challenging task. There are several aspects of the class ranging from syllabus and assignments to the mode of online instruction (asynchronous or synchronous or both) that need to be considered. Jessie Borgman and Casey McArdle present the Personal, Accessible, Responsive, Strategic (PARS) framework where they emphasize on designing online writing courses with students' experiences in mind. The "P" in PARS, that stands for "Personal," can be a crucial factor in this context. When instruction takes place through online mode, there is undoubtedly more challenge involved since it is difficult to replicate the humanness that comes naturally in a face-to-face setting. But that does not mean that online classrooms need to be cold and robotic. According to Borgman and McArdle (2019), "Writing is personal, and teaching is personal—connecting with students is a way to confirm students understand various elements of the course" (p. 8). And humor can be that personal element, that binding factor, which can bring people closer, if it is used correctly.

Benefits and Challenges

Humor is an essential part of human interaction and community building. Merriam-Webster dictionary defines humor as "the mental faculty of discovering, expressing, or appreciating the ludicrous or absurdly incongruous; the ability to be funny or to be amused by things that are funny." Humor, when used appropriately, can lighten up a tense atmosphere, and an instructor who uses humor in a suitable manner comes across as amicable, personable, and warm. Shared laugher makes people less defensive and more welcoming. Humor, according to Borcherdt (2002), "breaks into people's preoccupation with what goes wrong. When you can laugh at a problem, you imply that you will prevail against it. Humor humanizes—it takes you from being a part-time professional to the realm of being a full-time human" (p. 248). Humor adds human touch to digital spaces and connects people sitting behind screens with one another.

However, while it is necessary to acknowledge the importance of humor, it is essential to recognize the ways in which it can be detrimental. Offensive or derogatory humor should be avoided in all educational settings. Moreover, it is immensely crucial that jokes are cracked while keeping the context in mind. The cat humor mentioned in the beginning of the chapter, for instance, worked well because there was already a suitable atmosphere surrounding it. Also, it was innocent, well-intentioned, and positive, and it aided to the process of instruction by minimizing the tension in the classroom. Torok et al. (2010) conducted a study investigating the use of humor in a college classroom with an aim to examine the students' perceptions towards pedagogical humor and the types of humor recommended by the students and the faculty. When asked about the limitations of classroom humor, one of the most common responses by the students was "the potential to be offensive, especially regarding issues that were ethnically or sexually precarious" (Torok et al., 2010, p. 18). A degrading remark in the guise of a joke, therefore, has a negative effect on the students' learning processes, and breaks the ethical code of classroom conduct.

An instructor can always choose the kind of humor they want to bring to their classroom. Borgman and McArdle (2019) feel that the need for this connection between the instructor and the learner is even more valuable in a writing class because writing is a personal task which is, at the same time, social. They observe that "students want a social experience, even if it's in an online course; humans are social and they want their courses online to feel social and it's not so much that a class is actually social but more that it gives off the appearance of being a social community" (2019, p. 25). Since the online classroom is a community, it gets deeply agitated when pedagogical humor turns hostile. Sometimes, even an offhand comment that was intended to be funny might sound hurtful to some people, which may spoil the learning environment. Furthermore, a jovial teacher might not be perceived as a competent instructor and as a result, the students might not end up taking the course seriously. These kinds of risks are always present, and it takes time and patience for a teacher to develop their personal sense of humor, which is simply an extension of one's teaching persona. According to Korobkin (1988), "Awareness of humor can be a gradual behavioral process in which an individual develops a personal outlook on life that sees, recognizes, and accepts rather than judges and commands" (p. 157). She maintains that infusing humor into classroom instruction requires continuous efforts and revisions that is built on thought, experience, and positive energy.

Building a Student-Focused Community

Despite these challenges, humor is still worth including in online instruction pedagogy since it enhances the virtual experience and helps build a closer-knit academic community. While transitioning online from a physical classroom, or primarily planning for synchronous or asynchronous or hybrid instruction, instructors are often looking for ways to make the experience as comfortable and convenient as a physical classroom. But at the same time, it is unfeasible to ignore the affordances of the virtual platform that the course is going to be conducted on. Humor, in this scenario, can be one of those elements that are migrated from face to face classrooms to online classrooms to fill in that gap. In the study that is previously mentioned in this chapter, Torok et al. (2004) further note that "When asked about the potential outcomes of using humor in the classroom, students mentioned that humor has the power to make teachers more likeable, facilitate understanding of course material, lower tension, boost student morale, and increase student attentiveness" (p. 18). In traditional physical classrooms, using humor for these purposes might be much easier compared to virtual academic spheres. The challenge is greater online due to the lack of physicality in human connection and at times, the inability to read facial expressions or hear the voice tone in fully asynchronous online courses. In virtual scenarios, there is a high possibility that humor is misconstrued, and that situation needs to be avoided. Shatz and LoSchivo (2006) note that while selecting humor for an online course, it is essential that the educational purpose behind the humor is considered. According to them:

> In contrast to humorists, who gauge success by laughter, educators measure the effectiveness of humor by how it promotes learning. Although humor can be used to increase students' overall enjoyment of the online experience, most of the humor incorporated into an online course should serve an instructional purpose. Otherwise, the course material and the instructor might be perceived as "fluff." (para. 9)

It is the instructor's job to determine that their humor is educational, classroom-appropriate, as well as a social lubricant. When used properly, humor can quell student anxiety, make difficult concepts clearer, and create a positive impact on teacher-student interactions and classroom relationship dynamics.

Humor can help students feel less awkward about their odd backgrounds, strange camera angles, babies and/or pets moving around, bad Wi-Fi connections along with other technological difficulties, and general exhaustion from staring at the computer screen for too long. Garner (2006) conducted a study to assesses the impact of curriculum-specific humor on retention and recall, as well as student evaluations of the course and the instructor. Although some instructors believe that humor can be disruptive, Garner states that "the use of appropriate humor in this study has been shown to enhance the learning environment and has a significantly positive impact on the retention of educational materials in a real-world academic setting" (2006, p. 179). When humor is content-focused and suitable, it makes the students feel that the instructor is making efforts to decrease anxiety and make the class more enjoyable and productive. Since the instructor is the authority, it is, for the most part, their job to create this easygoing, cheerful atmosphere by assimilating humor in their classroom. The instructors, according to Korobkin (1988), need to establish a "comedy routine" (p. 157) in the sense that they need to be aware of the subject matter, their own personality and presentation skills along with the needs of their audience, i.e., the students. Korobkin states that "the college instructor can use the instructional design process in order to promote effective and laughter-filled learning" (1988, p. 158). Instructional design, therefore, is a strategy that deals with developing instructional approaches and materials, identifying objectives, as well as analyzing activities. By incorporating humor into their instructional design, instructors can ensure that their class is inclined towards using pedagogical humor, suitably and systematically.

Instructional design is a crucial aspect of online writing courses because despite being different in terms of the medium of instruction, an online classroom, just like a physical classroom, needs to be pleasant and motivating, as the goal for both is to educate. At the same time, online spaces have their own attributes which shape the pedagogical expectations and design of the class. According to the CCCC's position statement of principles and example of effective practices for online writing instruction (2013), "Appropriate composition teaching/learning strategies should be developed for the unique features of the online instructional environment" (OWI Principle 3). Online environment is unique because it is a classroom situated in a cloud space. However, the online medium still has parallels with face-to-face instruction, such as the quality of academic performance that needs to be maintained and the level of student satisfaction that needs to be achieved. Other similarities include group meeting space, working towards the same goal, i.e., learning to write better, and community building in terms of teacher/student interaction and student/student interaction. Humor, for that matter, can be a positive addition to the online instructional design because it adds humanness to the digital space. Borgman and McArdle (2019) underscore the significance of being personal in specific areas of the course. One of the things they mention is sharing the teacher's own writing to cultivate connections with students. They maintain that "instructors should take the lead in making the online classroom a safe space to share their writing by sharing some of their own writing and inviting conversation" (2019, p. 25). For instance, the teacher could provide the students with a humorous prompt and then give them a chance to connect it to their own lives. One example could be: I once tried to think from the point of view of my cat. If she could write, what would her daily journal look like? Remember, she is a Professor Cat. So, she will be able to write complete, correct sentences and present a brilliant account of her day. What would *your* pet's journal be like? Remember, they have the thinking and writing abilities of their human, a College Student. This prompt could be followed by a brief paragraph on the instructor's own account from the point of view of their cat. This would keep things light and funny, make the teacher appear more relatable, and could be, in general, considered a good way to build mutual rapport with the students, throughout the semester.

Students, in that sense, should always be kept in mind while constructing the course with humor infused into it. When instructors design a course, they create an outline for the entire semester. They give attention to details when they plan out larger as well as smaller assignments and ways of delivering and executing them. And since students are their audience, it is vital that they remain at the forefront as the instructors make these crucial decisions. Borgman and McArdle (2019) agree when they state that

> the main thing to consider when creating a course design is who are your student users. How will they be accessing the content? How comfortable are they with technology? What do they need to learn to move on to the next course? Considering larger questions like these will help you map out a successful course design. (p. 72)

When people never meet face-to-face, the situation gets a little complicated, and as a result, communication gaps may ensue, thus causing misinterpretation of moods and information in the class. Warnock (2015) examines the foundational structure that ground online writing instruction. In his work, "Teaching the OWI Course," he claims, "in my observation of OWCs and reading student evaluations associated with them, a common disappointment that students voice is the lack of engagement in the asynchronous discussions by their instructors" (p. 164). However, just because the instructor is not commenting in detail, one cannot necessarily conclude that they are detached or disinterested. It may simply mean that there are some fissures that need to be filled.

Such cracks and gaps might be the result of dry language that is often used during these interactions or the lack of congeniality in the existing relationship between the teacher and the students. Humor, in either case, could be a good solution. James (2004) believes that as more classes are offered in the online format, the teachers and students should be aware about the advantages of humor. He states that the "teachers need to learn how to use humor to their benefit in the classroom. Humor can assume many forms, including body language, facial expressions, and tone of voice" (2004, p. 93). Here is an example of how this can be done: The day you are teaching proposal writing on Zoom, for instance, (or even recording an asynchronous lecture), show up in a formal attire but have an animal wallpaper in the background and pretend that you have not seen them yet. In the middle of the conversation, casually look behind and have a dramatic "Oops" moment. You may remark, "Hey, I didn't know that he had been standing there. Hello, buddy! Can you hear me?" You might smile, shrug, and carry on with the lecture and then at some point, acknowledge the animal again. If possible, include the animal in your conversation. Visual cues like these help in retention of past lectures. You can, for instance, refer to this lecture in the future when you are commenting on a student's work and say: "That day when I was in my best suit talking about proposals, you know, I had a guy standing behind me, do you remember we had discussed about . . ." And this could be a good connecting point to the previous lesson while providing current feedback. Instead of an animal, you may use a historical figure, a celebrity, a cartoon character, or any other remarkable figure that the students might remember for a while.

Final Thoughts and Application

To follow up on that, here are some final thoughts and application of humor in the online writing classroom.

Icebreakers

When the teacher sends out the introductory announcement notice or welcome video, they will be talking about the first assignment of the semester. According to Hellman (2007), humorous icebreakers can be an excellent way to set the tone for the rest of the period which can be immensely conducive to alleviating tensions and creating a learner-friendly environment. "On occasion, you could produce an official looking document and act as if you are about to read an important announcement. Then, tell a joke. Guerilla humor strikes!" (Hellman, 2007, p. 37). Obviously, since you would be doing it in an online class, you could probably do it on a video lecture or through written means. Similarly, you would be doing it on a screen if it is a synchronous class. Another example is if your icebreaker is a discussion board post, you might want to try an activity that includes short personal stories using hilarious images of pets or students' favorite movie scenes or cartoon strips. The teacher, however, should be mindful about not compelling the students to share stories or pictures that make them feel uncomfortable or embarrassed.

Instructional videos

These are the soul of an online class, especially if it is an asynchronous class. Instead of just reading announcements and emails that go on forever, if the students get a few minutes of audio-visual lecture from the instructor, it might make them feel more connected to the mystery person on the other side of the screen who is responsible for teaching them and grading their papers. Melanie Hibbert (2014) talks about instructional presence in her article "What Makes an Online Instructional Video Compelling?" She conducts interviews with students and puts together the responses which show that faculty presence is the key factor related to students' engagement and perceived learning from videos. "The most engaging videos for me [are] when the professors use wit and humor," (2014, para. 21) she quotes one of the interviewees. In order to add humor to the videos, the instructors can use different strategies like including deliberate, pregnant pauses, cracking jokes and sharing anecdotes.

Likewise, videos can also be borrowed from other internet platforms. There are serious topics that need to be discussed in the class and plagiarism is one of them. It is extremely crucial that the instructor and the students have the conversation about plagiarism and the repercussions of plagiarism. However, the topic can be discussed in good humor. For example, there is a short Saturday Night

Live video where a teacher is assigning grades to students who have plagiarized their essays from the internet.

youtube.com/watch?v=yDxN4c_CmpI

This is a six-minute-long video titled: "Plagiarism." It was aired on May 3, 2003. The video is humorous in terms of its content, but it holds a serious message. It is about a class where the teacher realizes that a few students have plagiarized. Some have copied from the internet, some have asked their older siblings for their essays, and some have decided to copy user reviews off of Amazon. Videos like these could bring much needed attention to the issue of plagiarism, albeit in a funny way. It is, however, important that the teacher establishes the gravity of the issue, and even this video, despite its humor, shows that the students end up getting an "F" for plagiarized homework.

Assignments

These are the major areas where humor can be at play. In addition to using humorous language to draft an assignment question or a writing prompt, humor in delivery can also help in explaining complex concepts. In addition to building relationships between instructor and students, humor can also play a significant role in solidifying connections between students.

This could be useful, for instance, in forming online peer communities. Students learn and enjoy more when they feel connected with the teacher and their peers. According to Anderson (2011), "humor enhances creative thinking; increases group cohesion; increases student attention and interest; and builds classroom climates that promotes learning" (p. 75). Students in online classes might dread any group work, for instance, peer reviews. An instructor can create an atmosphere through light-hearted discussion board posts or a common Google document where the whole class can write together. Similarly, casual jokes and humorous materials like memes or social media posts or comic strips or cartoons can help students formulate bonds during groupwork. Once the community is formed, it is easier for them to work as a team during presentations and peer reviews.

Likewise, introduction/icebreaker posts could be a method of assigning groups in an online class. The instructor might ask students to include a funny story and/or a picture that is related them. And based on the similarity of those pictures, people can be put in the same groups. The instructor can always write individual notes to the groups saying: "Hey guys, you are the Happy Campers. All three of you had hilarious stories and pictures related to camping!" The next time they give a presentation, they can be introduced as the group: "Happy Campers" and this contributes to the development of group humor which is understood and enjoyed by the entire classroom community.

Feedback

David James (2004), in his commentary, "A need for humor in online courses," cites Linda Boynton, an Oakland Community College instructor, who has taught online for several years. Boynton insists that humor is pivotal in her online classes, although humor in an online classroom looks different than humor in onsite classrooms.

According to James, Boynton's online humor is often expressed through written comments. "Boynton keeps extensive personal notes on students so she can use familiar phrases or allusions in email responses when attempting to be humorous. She warns that crafting a message like this means "going back through and editing it so it reads more casually and hopefully more 'funny'" (2004, p. 93).

Furthermore, Boynton believes in presenting students with the opportunity to be "reactively funny" online. In doing so, she shares her own personal anecdotes that are full of humor, so that the students are prompted to do the same. Although risky, Boynton believes that humor is a key component in online classroom and she successfully assimilates humor into her pedagogy through careful and thorough planning. To this, James adds: "Because humor is one of the major traits of the best, most effective teachers, it is a characteristic that all teachers should want to hone, practice, and nurture, regardless of medium" (2004, p. 94). Something as simple as a smiling emoji can work wonders in helping the student decipher the teacher's tone when reading written comments.

Visual cues

Being a part of an online class as an instructor or a student is not just about teaching or learning the contents of the course. It is also about getting acquainted with the etiquette of conversing, behaving, and interacting in the virtual world. This includes something as simple as choosing an appropriate Zoom background or one's own display picture, which might induce laughter but not offend anybody in any manner. It is important that both students and instructors use this opportunity to learn how to have fun while maintaining the decorum of an instructional platform.

Individual Conferences

This is an excellent opportunity where the instructor and the students get the opportunity to interact with one another through audio or video calls on an individual basis. In asynchronous classes, this is a valuable moment because it brings the instructor and the student in contact with one another on one-on-one level. Usually, conferences can be up to fifteen to thirty minutes in length and conducted once or twice every semester.

When students call, it is always good to start out with a casual chit-chat. Boynton's idea of maintaining a record of the student can be helpful in remembering a prior conversation you have had with a student. One can always make jokes like: Hey, the last time we talked you mentioned that you were having no luck with fishing. How did it go this weekend? Did you get a chance to go fishing at all? This conversation could be augmented by the instructor's own personal story about something hilarious that happened with them while they were on a fishing trip, fifteen years ago. Or, it could be something like this: I liked how you included that meme in your minor assignment. It was funny. You think you could do something more with memes?

Such amicable exchanges keep the students at ease and show them that you know them and remember them and genuinely care about their work.

Downsides of Using Humor

In addition to its perks, humor, as discussed above in the chapter, has its own downsides. There are a few things that can be done to avoid unsuitable humor:

- Mention it clearly in the syllabus that a "joke" that is considered sexually offensive or a "humorous" comment that is derogatory towards any gender, community, or individual will not be tolerated under any circumstances.
- The instructor should be mindful that their jolliness does not hinder their authority as an instructor. If the teacher gets too friendly, the students might start taking the course, its contents, as well as its grading schemes and late policies a little lightly. It is, therefore, necessary that healthy boundaries are drawn and followed. It should be made clear that a teacher can be friendly, but they can never be a friend.
- Maintain a strict balance between lightheartedness and solemnity when it comes to delivering lectures, instructions, and announcements in writing and through audio-visual means. A teacher is not a comedian, and although they might be funny, they are there to do their job, which is to teach.

Humor adds life to any class, specifically an online class. Innovative and inoffensive humor creates a positive teaching and learning environment which helps the students and the instructor have fun while doing their job. There can be little recurring jokes about the instructor's ancient coffee machine or self-deprecating humor about the instructor's forgetfulness that can put students at ease in a virtual classroom. If the students are comfortable with it, occasional jokes targeted towards them like the one mentioned in the beginning of the chapter, are acceptable. Likewise, humor that is purely related to the subject matter or the course content, along with accidental and situational humor, all add to the positive vibes of the class. A writing instructor is not a professional comedian. Regardless, a little effort makes a great deal of difference because a teacher is in a position of authority, and their strategic humor plays an enormous role in enhancing the overall learning experience.

References

Anderson, D. G. (2011). Taking the "distance" out of distance education: A humorous approach to online learning. *Journal of Online Learning and Teaching, 7*(1), 74–81.

Borcherdt, B. (2002). Humor and its contributions to mental health. *Journal of rational-emotive and cognitive-behavior therapy, 20*(3–4), 247–257.

Borgman, J. & McArdle, C. (2019). *Personal, accessible, responsive, strategic: Resources and strategies for online writing instructors.* The WAC Clearinghouse; University Press of Colorado. https://doi.org/10.37514/PRA-B.2019.0322.

Conference on College Composition and Communication. (2020). *Rationale for OWI principle 3.* Medium. https://cccc.ncte.org/cccc/resources/positions/owi principles/principle3rationale.

Garner, R. L. (2006). Humor in pedagogy: How ha-ha can lead to aha!. *College Teaching, 54*(1), 177–180.

Hellman, S. V. (2007). Humor in the classroom: Stu's seven simple steps to success. *College Teaching, 55*(1), 37–39.

Hibbert, M. (2014, April 7). What makes an online instructional video compelling? *Educause Review Online.* https://er.educause.edu/articles/2014/4/what-makes-an-online-instructional-video-compelling.

James, D. (2004). A need for humor in online courses. *College Teaching, 52*(3), 93–120.

Korobkin, D. (1988). Humor in the classroom: Considerations and strategies. *College Teaching, 36*(4), 154–158.

Merriam-Webster. (n.d.). Humor. In Merriam-Webster.com dictionary. https://www.merriam-webster.com/dictionary/humor.

Shatz, M. A. & LoSchiavo, F. M. (2006). Bringing life to online instruction with humor. *Radical Pedagogy, 8*(2), 8.

Torok, S. E., McMorris, R. F. & Lin, W. C. (2004). Is humor an appreciated teaching tool? Perceptions of professors' teaching styles and use of humor. *College Teaching, 52*(1), 14–20.

Warnock, S. (2015). Teaching the OWI course. In B. L. Hewett & K. E. DePew (Eds.), *Foundational practices of online writing instruction* (pp. 151–182). The WAC Clearinghouse; Parlor Press. https://doi.org/10.37514/PER-B.2015.0650.2.04.

Chapter 9. Confronting Ableist Texts: Teaching Usability and Accessibility in the Online Technical Writing Classroom

Cynthia Pengilly
CENTRAL WASHINGTON UNIVERSITY

Abstract: This chapter examines a series of integrated, pedagogical activities for addressing ableist structures, accessibility, and usability issues in the online technical writing classroom. By examining this specific case, this chapter provides a unique perspective on both integrating and teaching usability and accessibility principles in the online technical writing classroom, which has implications for OWI and PTC practitioners. The pedagogical process studied includes a description of the institutional context, the integration of Borgman and McArdle's (2019) accessible and strategic OWI principles from the PARS model, and the iterative design and revision of the online technical writing class via modeling, scaffolding, and other pedagogical strategies. This chapter extends the conversation regarding the complicit nature of technical writing classrooms in reinforcing dominant perspectives by offering an intentional pedagogy that resituates and reframes traditional PTC concepts, such as usability, and ties it explicitly to human-centered elements of accessibility, ableism, and equity.

Keywords: online writing instruction, online technical writing, ableism, usability, accessibility, iterative design

I began my academic career first teaching online as contingent faculty, only shifting to the classroom several years later. Thus, my pedagogical development has been influenced by industry experience as a technical writer and software trainer, by my experience as an online graduate student for the entirety of my master's program, and by the limited body of online teaching scholarship that existed at the time when I made the shift to university teaching (Ko & Rossen, 2003; Warnock, 2009). Indeed, each of these influences informed my approach to, comfort with, and interest in teaching online writing instruction (OWI). This passion and experience led me to a tenure-track position at Central Washington University (CWU) where I teach six out of eight yearly classes online. In the English Department, our most successful program is the Professional and Creative Writing B.A. that has over one-hundred and thirty online majors compared to just forty face-to-face majors; the degree can be completed fully online, in-person, or a combination of the two, but students must declare their modality as online or on-campus at the outset of the program. As an assistant professor of professional and technical writing, I teach more online sections of ENG 310 Technical Writing than any other course, so I focused my initial OWI redesign efforts on this course.

Several years and iterations of teaching ENG 310 were necessary for me to develop a pedagogically sound approach to addressing ableist texts, accessibility, and usability issues in the online technical writing classroom. During the redesign, I drew extensively on Hewett and DePew's (2015) guidance for integrating OWI principles alongside the digital pedagogy projects infused in my courses. (As a side note, I had the wonderful opportunity of being mentored by Dr. DePew during my doctoral studies.) Often, technical communication and professional writing instructors are tasked with teaching technology skills; however, as Walton (2006) posits, technical communication students must also learn how technologies should support human dignity and human rights and focus on the cultural and personal implications on a consumer's life. Likewise, in my classes, I want students to understand the cultural and personal implications of their documents, and the designs of those documents, on differently-abled bodies, and I also want my courses to provide students with strategies for addressing ableist practices.

In this chapter, I annotate a series of scaffolded assignments and discussion board activities intended to prepare students for the major projects in ENG 310; these annotations thereby highlight the accessible and strategic design elements that are embedded in the course and are informed by Borgman and McArdle's (2019) PARS model (personal, accessible, responsive, strategic). It takes several weeks for students to understand concepts such as usability, readability, accessibility, and universal design—common concepts in the disciplines of professional writing and OWI—but these concepts are resituated or reframed in my courses as essential to achieving usability, equity, and accessibility beyond the classroom. Jones (2016) argues that the field of professional writing and communication, "can be complicit in reinforcing which perspectives and whose experience are valued and legitimized" (p. 342), so a conscious pedagogy is necessary to infuse the human-centered elements of accessibility and equity into the technical writing classroom to avoid reinforcing and codifying such inequitable practices.

Therefore, this chapter demonstrates key aspects of the PARS model used in an online technical writing class, a class which has specific implications for OWI practitioners and the growing body of OWI scholarship. This chapter also contributes to the broader conversation about usable, accessible, and inclusive design in the composition classroom, thereby placing several academic fields or communities of practice into conversation with one another (e.g., technical communication, OWI, and composition studies). Finally, this chapter has specific implications for scholars and practitioners of professional and technical communication (PTC) because it offers metacommentary on both integrating and teaching usability and accessibility principles in the online technical writing classroom through modeling, scaffolding, and other pedagogical strategies.

Institutional Context

Central Washington University (CWU) is a small, geographically isolated, regional institution with a growing online student population. My primary teaching responsibilities as a tenure-track professor occur online, and I was chiefly hired to expand the department's online course offerings in professional and technical writing. Similar trends of growth in online student enrollments exist in other programs across campus, so even our service courses, such as ENG 310 Technical Writing and ENG 311 Business Writing, are most often scheduled in a fully online, asynchronous modality. I have taught ENG 310 for nearly fifteen years, including my time at CWU, so the iterative design aspects of the course, from a usability and student-centered design perspective, have been quite extensive and intentional (Greer & Harris, 2018).

One of the challenges of creating an accessible and strategic course design was to introspectively find ways to align the departmental or disciplinary goals (externally imposed) with my own pedagogical goals for the course (internal positioning). In the case of ENG 310, for instance, I was aware that none of the course outcomes explicitly addressed usability or accessibility, so it was necessary to strategically build these aspects into the major assignments and projects. As an additional challenge, the status of ENG 310 as a service course means it uniquely serves English and non-English majors as a required or elective course in thirteen different academic programs, most notably for business, engineering, teacher education, theatre design, and natural sciences programs. My goal became guiding students beyond the surface level understanding of usability and access that often pervades the technical communication classroom by integrating accessibility aspects into the course content as well as the course structure; this integration included a careful analysis of the learning management system (LMS), of its natural affordances, and of available system modifications for addressing accessibility concerns.

As Oswal and Melonçon (2014) point out, discussions of access are generally resisted in academia, and universal design (UD), and usability conversations taking place among industry professionals and PTC scholars often omit educational contexts. In my experience, these issues are even more frequent for online classrooms for which LMS and other technology platforms are already predetermined, hence requiring instructors to be intentional, strategic, and proactive in course design if they hope to build accessible, inclusive, and anti-ableist learning spaces. The hidden political agendas of course management systems have been addressed by other scholars and activists (Bjork, 2018; Oswal & Melonçon, 2014), and I extend these discussions with a critical examination of the Canvas LMS and its accessibility merits and of how the design of such systems can impede student success and create access barriers.

As part of CWU's institutional context, I was able to attend professional development opportunities for online teaching, which thankfully included courses in universal design (adapted through the framework of student-centered design for learning), creating accessible syllabi, and building accessible and inclusive courses, thus leading to CWU's institutional certification for Master Online Teacher. I am grateful to our Multimodal Education Center (MEC), and the MEC's Director Chad Schone in particular, for offering such specialized training and for politicizing the educational platforms and pedagogical practices that continue to reify ableist systems of power. Much of my training and intentional redesign work was focused on ENG 310, the results of which I discuss below.

Strategic and Accessible Design

The accessible and strategic course design elements examined in this chapter are drawn from Borgman and McArdle's (2019) PARS model. I begin with strategic design because it lays the foundation of the entire course, serving as a framework for the accessibility aspects of the course. According to Borgman and McArdle (2019), in strategic course design, "you're creating a user experience for your students (the users) and you need to consider/plan for all of the elements of this experience in order to make it successful" (p. 72). My own pedagogical experiences have aligned with this definition of strategic design, and I also find that advanced, intentional planning is essential for accessible course design and iterative course revisions, which is a key component of user-centered design. In short, accessibility is easier to achieve when it is strategically incorporated into the course at the initial design phase.

Accessibility can be defined in several ways, but I draw from Borgman and McArdle's (2019) definition of accessibility which involves two main aspects: accessible structure and accessible content. Borgman and McArdle (2019) define accessibility as "the little things that instructors do that impede students" (p. 37), and accessible course design asks instructors "to use materials, software, websites, or tools that are not blocked via pay walls, international laws, hardware students might not be able to afford, or any other requirements that eliminate students and their ability to participate at a level necessary for success" (p. 36). This definition of accessibility attends to structural issues in a course, which is understandably pertinent in the online classroom due to the reliance on interfaces and screens. It is Borgman and McArdle's (2019) extended definition of accessibility to include accessible content that raises the stakes for OWI practitioners. As the authors state, "It takes time to learn about creating accessible *materials* for students with diverse abilities and it takes time to create an online course that meets the needs of a diverse student population" (p. 36, my emphasis). I use this expanded definition of accessibility in this chapter, thereby identifying the strategic approach used to incorporate accessibility into both the structure and content of ENG 310.

Strategic and Accessible Structure

As previously stated, ENG 310 is an introductory level course that serves a number of majors, so effectively modeling accessible and inclusive design was necessary through my own pedagogy and key pedagogical genres, such as the syllabus and assignment prompts. I also needed to better understand the constraints and affordances of the Canvas LMS with regard to accessibility merits, including any strategies or applications that could be used to overcome barriers to access. Table 9.1 identifies the third-party tools, indeed a multifaceted approach, I used to achieve a strategic and accessible course structure for ENG 310. This table captures the most useful and prominent accessibility features for each program based on the instructor's personal experience but is not an exhaustive list.

Table 9.1. Third-party tools for strategic and accessible course design*

Accessibility Tool	Accessibility Features
Panopto	Screen reader support with structured headings Video captions and transcription: automatic and manual Automatic file conversion: from video to audio RSS feeds for video and/or audio files
Blackboard Ally	Automatic file conversion: HTML, PDF, electronic braille, audio, ePub, Beeline Reader Accessibility score for each file: uses clear percentages in color-coded format (red to green) with suggestions for improvement Accessibility report for the entire course: identifies lowest scoring files and those that are easiest to fix
Adobe Acrobat Pro	Standard features: structured headings, captions, alternate text for images, detects scanned text Acrobat Pro's Make PDF Accessible Tool: wizard that automates some steps and walks you through items that need attention Acrobat Pro's Check and Report Accessibility Tools: checks the document and produces a report with suggested accessibility improvements
Microsoft Word	Standard features: structured headings, captions, alternate text for images MS Word's Accessibility Checker: checks the document and produces a report with suggested accessibility improvements MS Word's Readability Statistics: outputs a readability report using several readability measures/formulas to address accessible language

* This figure captures the most useful and prominent accessibility features for each program based on the instructor's personal experience but is not an exhaustive list.

To serve as a model for students in accessible design, I took great care to use structured headings, captions, alternate text for images, and varied activities to attend to multiple learning styles, as advocated by usability and accessibility scholars in OWI (Borgman & Dockter, 2018; Borgman & McArdle, 2019; Oswal & Melonçon, 2017). I also varied the types of student-instructor interactions by providing both written and audio feedback, video lectures, and a required one-on-one conference that is the newest addition to the course in response to ESCALA's professional development training for inclusive, culturally-responsive pedagogy at an emerging Hispanic Serving Institution (HSI). The required synchronous conference, for instance, was yet another opportunity for formative assessment to gauge student's understanding of course themes and expectations for major projects, which has since led to an unexpected increase in communication with students via email and overall higher grades in the course. It also provided an opportunity to personally connect with students and address any barriers to success, which students would often be reticent to share over email.

As Borgman and McArdle (2019) posit,

> Accessible instruction is about more than setting expectations and making you and your course materials accessible to your students, it's also about creating a community of inclusion in your course and inviting students with all levels of ability to interact with you in a way that works for them. (p. 40)

Even though the major projects were identified before the class begins, the activities and interactions were strategically designed with accessibility in mind through opportunities for optional group work, integration of multiple learning styles, examples of student work for each major assignment, and themed discussion activities about accessibility and confronting ableist structures. In short, I had started to move toward an ideology of inclusion, which starts with the tenets of accessibility and participatory design as asserted by Oswal and Melonçon (2017).

I also attended to structural accessibility components using the tools available in the Canvas LMS. Canvas provides several third-party accessibility programs, such as Panopto and Blackboard Ally, both of which provide screen-reader support and limited file transcription-and-conversion services to students. Panopto includes video captions that can be configured to be integrated automatically or via manual file upload; the video recordings are automatically converted to audio files which can be shared individually or published as an RSS feed for bulk sharing. I also used Panopto for assessment purposes, which appealed to different learning styles by providing feedback in alternate formats, such as a screencast for essay feedback or a podcast for feedback on new media projects. For example, when I used Panopto for video feedback, the file shared with the student was complete with captions and a transcript—operating as both a model of accessibility (for students) and as a natural outcome of accessible pedagogy. And while Canvas has its own proprietary audio and video feedback capability, neither tool attends to accessibility aspects such as automated captions, audio transcript, and screen reader support, which is why an interrogation of the LMS system is so essential to strategic and accessible course design.

Blackboard Ally is another strong tool for strategic and accessible course design. It automatically converts written files to several alternative formats for expanded accessibility support for students (e.g., HTML, ePub, and audio). Additionally, Blackboard Ally runs an accessibility check on all instructor files uploaded to Canvas—such as the syllabus, assignments, and supplemental readings—and scores each file based on its use of structured headings, alternative image tags, and other file attributes. One outcome of using the Blackboard Ally feature has been that online instructors at CWU were given access to the full version of Adobe Acrobat Pro because accessible document elements, like structured headings, are only guaranteed to be preserved when converting files using the full (i.e., paid) version of Adobe Acrobat Pro. (We are still advocating for the software on our personal computers, especially for those of us who teach nearly exclusively online.) The institutional goal is to achieve fifty percent accessible content in each course, but I personally strive for ninety percent or higher—a numerical value I can now make sense of thanks to Blackboard Ally and that I can improve upon thanks to Panopto and Adobe Acrobat Pro. So, I strategically designed the course by uploading assignments in advance to allow myself enough time to address any accessibility issues that could occur, and I announced Blackboard Ally features to students at the start of each quarter, thereby demonstrating Borgman and McArdle's (2019) elements of strategic and accessible course design.

Strategic and Accessible Content (or Examining Your Discussion Board Activities)

The second aspect of a strategic and accessible course is the critical examination of course content. In ENG 310, I focused my redesign efforts on the weekly discussions because I wanted them to become more active, lively, and focused learning spaces because they are always where most student-to-student interaction takes place. In order to create that space, I had to ask some tough questions of myself about the way the class discussion genre functioned, generally speaking, and how I envisioned it functioning in this particular course. Specifically, I approached the class discussion space as a "contact zone" (to borrow a term from Pratt, 1991) that could either work to dismantle or reinforce systems of oppression and overt discrimination.

Table 9.2 shows the weekly discussion topics and activities for a 10-week online, ENG 310 Technical Writing course. Pedagogical goals and accessibility aspects were captured from the researcher's initial course design notes, and the iterative design process was informed by student feedback and university-based training opportunities.

As Cherney (2011) points out in "The Rhetoric of Ableism," ability is a social construct, and ableism is a social practice that is learned over time, and both are reinforced by those around us. Cherney calls on us to name ableism because doing so reveals its systems of power, thereby allowing us to reform those systems and take political action. In response to this call to action, I examined the "norms" of the online classroom, such as the discussion genre because of its assumed stability and appeal to traditional pedagogy that can potentially blind us to its inherent political structures. As is often the case, online discussion is usually limited to a sort of normalized "read and respond" practice, which arguably values written literacies over visual or auditory literacies, thus privileging certain bodies over others. In contrast, I wanted students to begin visualizing the discussion board as a hands-on lab of sorts, where they could practice and model accessible and inclusive document design strategies. Indeed, such a change required the rejection of an ideology of normalcy in favor of an ideology of inclusion (Oswal & Melonçon, 2017).

Table 9.2. Weekly discussion topics and activities in ENG 310*

Week #	Discussion Topic or Activity	Pedagogical Goals	Accessibility Aspects
1	Introduction + Contextualize TW in their careers	Reflection, Community Building, Disciplinary Identity, Research	Positionality, Inclusion
2	Cognitive Approach to Readability: How Readers Actually Read Documents	Reflection, Community Building, Scaffolding	Positionality, Privilege, Inclusion, Usability, Audience-centered
3	Information Design & Usability Testing of Everyday Instructions	Personal Experience, Scaffolding, Community Building, Visual Literacy	Positionality, Usability, Inclusion, Power, Ableism, Audience-centered
4	Use Readability Measures in MS Word on the Instructions Project & Share the Results	Hands-on Activity, Reflection, Scaffolding, Community Building	Positionality, Privilege, Power, Inclusion, Usability, Ableism, Audience-centered
5	Explain a Technical Process using a flowchart (from the instructions project)	Hands-on Activity, Reflection, Compare Contrast, Community Building, Scaffolding, Visual Literacy	Positionality, Power, Usability, Audience-centered
6	Research the Code of Ethics and Ethics-related case or incident from your field	Research, Reflection, Disciplinary Identity, Scaffolding	Positionality, Inclusion, Audience-centered
7	Proposals and Progress Reports, Academia vs. the Workplace	Reflection, Disciplinary Identity, Scaffolding, Compare/Contrast	Positionality, Audience-centered, Usability
8	Use the Accessibility Checker in MS Word on the Occupational Report & Share the Results	Hands-on activity, Reflection, Scaffolding, Community Building, Visual Literacy	Positionality, Privilege, Power, Usability, Ableism, Audience-centered
9	Presentations and Avoiding Death by PowerPoint	Visual Literacy, Reflection, Community Building, Scaffolding	Positionality, Inclusion, Power, Usability, Ableism, Audience-centered
10	Looking Forward. Looking Back: Personal Growth	Reflection, Community Building, Disciplinary Identity	Positionality, Privilege, Power, Usability, Inclusion

Pedagogical goals and accessibility aspects captured from researcher's initial course design notes and iterative design process informed by student feedback and university-based training opportunities.

Table 9.2 captures the planning process used for scaffolding the weekly discussion activities leading up to the two major course projects, including my explicit attempts to incorporate accessibility aspects. I made the process of scaffolding largely public and visible so that students could work together building a sense of community and consensus with regard to identifying ableist texts and practices. Another pedagogical goal of strategic and accessible course content is to increase student interaction and engagement by requiring different, and often overlapping, modes of critical thinking—reflection, hands-on exercises (kinesthetic learning), community building, and disciplinary identity to name a few. These modes have implications for OWI practitioners and PTC scholars since strategic, student-centered course design always includes several active learning domains (Altay, 2014) that must be effectively balanced by the instructor to enhance student learning: *cognitive*, or knowledge acquisition; *affective*, or changing attitudes; and *psychomotor*, or helping students gain new skills in a discipline.

As a PTC and OWI scholar, I must always determine the distribution of active learning domains across the entire course design depending on the alignment between course outcomes and my pedagogical goals for the course. In the case of ENG 310, some of the psychomotor activities included using specialized features in MS Word (e.g., readability statistics, accessibility checker, table of contents generator, structured headings, etc.), but I was equally concerned with students' cognitive understanding of course content and their affective learning domain as it related to accessibility issues and a more general understanding, and appreciation, of technical writing in their respective disciplines.

Extended Discussion Board Example

Figure 9.1 shares a popular discussion activity in the class that required students to run MS Word's Accessibility Checker against a draft of their occupational report and discuss the results with classmates. This discussion board activity was meant to gauge a student's current epistemological state with usability course themes and confront practices leading to ableist texts in terms of structure. Some common discussions between students and opportunities for improvement included adding alternative text for images, improving text contrast (foreground/background), and using MS Word's heading feature so that it appeared to screen readers—issues that were discussed from an accessibility and human advocacy perspective.

This exercise may seem simple enough for PTC scholars and practitioners, but it is a highly engaging activity for new participants seeking entry into our discourse community. The activity simultaneously engages students in all three active learning domains—cognitive, affective, and psychomotor—because the assignment frames other activities and assignments in future weeks of the course and is fundamental in changing students' individual perceptions of accessibility and their active role in dismantling ableist structures.

This discussion activity, likely aided by its public nature, forced students to confront their ableist design decisions in a thoughtful, purposeful, and meaningful way. To be specific, I witnessed first-hand as students became aware of the 3P's: positionality, privilege, and power (as defined by Walton et al., 2019) as they composed and revised their documents. As stated by one ENG 310 student (shared with permission):

> This was a great week of learning for me as I wasn't aware of the accessibility tool before this week, and it's clear that I made several embarrassing assumptions while designing my text for readers [**positionality and privilege**]. The accessibility check is an excellent, important resource . . . I want to assure *equity* of readability in the media I create, and that will require *taking steps* to assure everyone, particularly those with *different abilities*, can read it in their preferred way [**power**]. (my emphasis)

The **Accessibility Check** feature in Microsoft Word is a helpful tool to measure the level of accessibility and usability merits in your document and the items that can be improved. For example, you may have attempted to include descriptive headings and subheadings in your occupational report, but unless you've used MS Word's structured headings feature, the document is NOT accessible. In other words, your document still has an ableist structure: it is not *accessible* or *usable* because it is not *readable* or *scannable* for your intended audience.

Our **call to action** this week is to use this opportunity to improve the accessibility merits of our work by removing any ableist structures that might still exist.

1. Run MS Word's Accessibility Check feature on your report draft.
2. Post a screenshot of your results to discuss with the class.
3. Questions to consider this week: What do the results show in terms of the accessibility and usability merits of your report? How does this activity relate to other accessibility themes in this course (usability, readability, accessibility, universal design, avoiding ableist structures, etc.)? How and where can you improve the accessibility merits of your report (before the final draft is due)? How might you see yourself using the accessibility tool in the future?

The initial post is due **Thursday**. Two responses on or before **Sunday**.

Figure 9.1. Abbreviated version of a hands-on Discussion Board activity in an online, 10-week version of ENG 310 Technical Writing. The complete assignment links to instructions for locating the Accessibility tool in MS Word and for taking screen-shots.

This student, coincidentally, is a major in the B.A. in Professional and Creative Writing, but this reflection is representative of the call-to-action that many students took up in response to the explicit teachings against ableists structures in this course. Students were simultaneously aided by their classmates in their pursuit of solutions to improve the accessibility merits of their final reports, as they all worked toward a shared goal of infusing anti-ableist practices, inclusion, and equity into the online technical writing classroom.

Conclusion

I write this piece as a scholar of PTC, practitioner of OWI, and interested party in student-centered design for learning. And, most importantly, I write this piece as a disabled woman of color, living with a chronic illness and mild vision impairment, who has experienced my fair share of inaccessible and exclusionary online course content as a student. It is my belief that an accessible course is an inclusive course, and instructors focused on inclusive course design have already started the necessary and important work of dismantling systems of oppression.

As Borgman and McArdle (2019) share with readers, "what we were doing in our online courses was architecting an experience for our students and for ourselves" (p. 3). The strategies discussed in this chapter for accessible and strategic design are advocating for just that—architecting an experience. To architect anything, it seems, takes a lot of research, planning, and patience, which is what this chapter calls us to do as practitioners of OWI and PTC. I recognize that institutional training in accessible course design is not as widespread as it should be, which speaks to the need for educational reform and increased professional development opportunities for faculty, even if those opportunities exist beyond the walls of the academic institution we call home.

However, we have an imperative to do so—to reach beyond our institutions for training and support—because failing to do so means the very spaces where we attempt to liberate students, so to speak, could be silencing their voices and reifying oppressive power structures. This chapter outlines my own personal attempt at confronting ableist texts and exclusionary social practices so that the notion of accessibility becomes embedded in the core fabric of the course rather than discussed or treated as an after-thought. I have learned that in order to teach accessibility, the assignments must address the rhetoric of ableism in a coordinated manner alongside practical strategies for overcoming systems of oppression. I must be explicit, intentional, and strategic in these efforts because it is only through the use of rhetoric that "we can reform ableist culture" and move toward political action (Cherney, 2011).

Final Thoughts and Application

This chapter draws on Borgman and McArdle's (2019) accessible and strategic elements of the PARS approach to encourage readers to think strategically about creating accessible courses and learning experiences with their students. In the spirit of this edited collection on practical OWI strategies, I would like to identify some key implications of this chapter to aid readers in both integrating and teaching accessibility in the online classroom.

- Strategic design begins with accessibility. As other scholars have already stated, incorporating accessibility later in the class is more difficult than to just begin with it at the outset (see Table 9.1 for strategies on building accessibility into the fabric of the course).
- To successfully integrate and teach accessibility requires intentionality on your part. And this intentionality will take time (i.e., student feedback and the student-centered iterative design process [see Greer & Harris, 2018]). You must learn to respect and value this process as you do the writing process.
- This new pedagogical approach often requires you to challenge ableist practices and ableist systems of power at your institution, in your department, and within your own classroom. For institutions to ignore access and accessibility issues is not uncommon, so you need to prepare for resistance.
- Educate yourself on the politics of the interface (Bjork, 2018; Oswal & Melonçon, 2014). Technology is not apolitical, which means that your institution's LMS plays a role in reinforcing political structures such as race, class, gender, and ability. You will have to expose them and to teach your students to do the same.
- Consider using a grid or matrix to strategically plan your accessible course design. Doing so will help reveal connections between course outcomes, your unique pedagogical goals, and the accessibility aspects you want to feature in the course (see Table 9.2).
- Evaluate your pedagogy for its accessible and inclusive merits. Some effective practices for strategic and accessible course design include modeling (both of your own and student's work), scaffolding, varying your student-professor interactions, and valuing different learning styles (through varied assignments). This list is not exhaustive, and you are encouraged to seek out specialized training and professional development opportunities when they become available.
- Familiarize yourself with the active learning domains (cognitive, affective, psychomotor) and how they are represented in your overall course outcomes (Altay, 2014). You may need, for example, to shift some of the smaller, privately assessed assignments to the public discussion forum to increase learning, engagement, or to better address one of the three active learning domains.
- Critically examine how you use class discussion, and other routine genres, in your online classroom and whether class discussions can be revised to be more inclusive and accessible. Some strategies for varying class interaction include reflection, hands-on activities (kinesthetic learning), and community building exercises (see Figure 9.1).

- Don't be afraid to blend synchronous and asynchronous activities and assignments, as they make sense for your classroom, in order to create a "community of inclusion" described by Borgman and McArdle (2019). Students will embrace the change if you give them valid reasons.

This list of key implications offers a starting point for those instructors new to accessible and strategic course design or those who are currently undergoing the iterative redesign process. These practical strategies are intended for OWI and PTC practitioners but could likely be useful in other contexts as well, such as online training and development classes, due to the increasing significance of accessibility issues in educational spaces.

References

Altay, B. (2014). User-centered design through learner-centered instruction. *Teaching in Higher Education, 19*(2), 138–155. https://doi.org/10.1080/13562517.2013.827646.

Bjork, C. (2018). Integrating usability testing with digital rhetoric in OWI. *Computers and Composition, 49*, 4–13. https://doi.org/10.1016/j.compcom.2018.05.009.

Borgman, J. & Dockter, J. (2018). Considerations of access and design in the online writing classroom. *Computers and Composition, 49*, 94–105. https://doi.org/10.1016/j.compcom.2018.05.001.

Borgman, J. & McArdle, C. (2019). *Personal, accessible, responsive, strategic: Resources and strategies for online writing instructors.* The WAC Clearinghouse; University Press of Colorado. https://doi.org/10.37514/PRA-B.2019.0322.

Cherney, J. L. (2011). The rhetoric of ableism. *Disability Studies Quarterly, 31*(3). https://dsq-sds.org/article/view/1665/1606.

Greer, M. & Skurat Harris, H. (2018). User-centered design as a foundation for effective online writing instruction. *Computers and Composition, 49*, 14–24. https://doi.org/10.1016/j.compcom.2018.05.006.

Hewett, B. L. & Depew, K. E. (Eds.). (2015). *Foundational practices of online writing instruction.* The WAC Clearinghouse; Parlor Press. https://doi.org/10.37514/PER-B.2015.0650.

Jones, N. N. (2016). The technical communicator as advocate: Integrating a social justice approach in technical communication. *Journal of Technical Writing and Communication, 46*(3), 342–361.

Ko, S. & Rossen, S. (2003). *Teaching online: A practical guide* (1st ed.). Houghton Mifflin College Division.

Oswal, S. & Melonçon, L. (2014). Paying attention to accessibility when designing online courses in technical and professional communication. *Journal of Business and Technical Communication, 28*(3), 271–300.

Oswal, S. & Melonçon, L. (2017). Saying no to the checklist: Shifting from an ideology of normalcy to an ideology of inclusion in online writing instruction. *WPA: Writing Program Administration, 40*(3), 61–77.

Pratt, M. (1991). Arts of the contact zone. *Profession*, 33–40. https://www.jstor.org/stable/25595469.

Walton, R. (2016). Supporting human dignity and human rights: A call to adopt the first principle of human-centered design. *Journal of Technical Writing and Communication, 46*(4), 402–426.

Walton, R., Moore, K. & Jones, N. N. (2019). *Technical communication after the social justice turn: Building coalitions for action.* New York.

Warnock, S. (2009). *Teaching writing online: How and why.* National Council for Teachers of English.

Chapter 10. Negotiating the Hazards of the "Just-in-Time" Online Writing Course

Theresa M. Evans
Miami University

Abstract: Last-minute or "just-in-time" course assignments are "par for the course" for instructors who are contingent and teach online, despite numerous arguments against such practices. Universities and administrators have mythologized online instruction as less labor-intensive and those who teach online as somehow having less expertise than those who teach face-to-face. The reality is that tenure-line faculty resist such assignments without additional professional development compensation and without a guarantee that this labor-intensive and often invisible work will be recognized for tenure and promotion. This chapter takes an anecdotal perspective of a contingent instructor thrust into a full year of "just-in-time" online writing instruction. The chapter details how the instructor developed a strategic, flexible, and reflective mindset to counter the institutional silos and silences she encountered. Her experience serves as an alert to new online instructors and a reality check for administrators who may be unaware of the isolation and frustration of their online teaching faculty, especially those teaching in less-than-ideal contexts. The chapter includes a checklist of the information and resources needed for effective online instruction and a summary of the PARS approach to take with "just-in-time" assignments to help instructors best meet the needs of their students.

Keywords: online writing instruction, contingency studies, writing program administration, OWI professional development, "just-in-time"

This chapter takes my own anecdotal perspective of what it's like to be thrust into "just-in-time" online teaching assignments. The purpose is to serve as a heads-up to new online instructors, to offer some coping strategies, and to provide a reality check for administrators who may be unaware of the isolation and frustration of their online teaching faculty. Because institutions, technologies, and student populations vary so much, no one-size-fits-all remedy is offered here. Instead, I present an exploration into how one instructor developed a strategic, flexible, and reflective mindset to counter institutional silos and silences. My goal is to describe how to make the "just-in-time" online course as personal, accessible, responsive, and strategic (PARS) as possible in less-than-ideal contexts. I have not worked as a writing program administrator, but I have been on the receiving end of less-than-ideal experiences as a writing student and writing instructor in online environments.

The COVID-19 pandemic has highlighted the difficulties of transitioning the on-ground class to online, but "just-in-time" courses are nothing new for contingent faculty. Last-minute course assignments are "par for the course" for those who are contingent and teach online, despite numerous arguments against such practices. Noting the difficulty of finding instructors for in-demand online courses, Rodrigo & Ramírez (2017) emphasized that "it is not enough to train online teachers how to use the institutionally supported learning management system (LMS); training also needs to support pedagogy" (p. 315). Borgman & McArdle (2019) have argued, "Anyone can send an email, anyone can put things on a CMS, but teaching online requires more than using a technology tool to facilitate or enhance your teaching" (p. 3). Yet universities and administrators have consistently mythologized online instruction as less labor-intensive and those who teach online courses as somehow having less expertise than those who teach face-to-face. These attitudes are reflected in what Greer & Harris (2018) call "a heavy reliance on existing systems and instructional design models, which tend to focus on courses as content repositories that can be 'built' once and delivered multiple times" (p. 22). Standardized and linear delivery platforms minimize instructors and treat students as interchangeable cogs.

Citing a 2012 study conducted by the Babson Survey Research Group, Palloff & Pratt (2013) noted that faculty were mostly pessimistic about online instruction; however, they also noted that 75 percent of those surveyed were full-time faculty who did not teach online. In fact, the study found that adjunct instructors were more open to online instruction than those on the tenure track (Babson Survey Research Group, cited in Palloff & Pratt, 2013). Instead of acknowledging the precarious status of adjunct instructors as a potential factor in their openness to online course assignments, Palloff & Pratt (2013) argued that convincing tenure-line professors to participate in online instruction would require fair compensation for the extra time involved. They failed to acknowledge that contingent faculty already are expected to develop and teach online courses with minimal lead time and resources—and for substantially less compensation than any tenure-line instructor. Blair & Monske (2003) noted that efforts to make technologies seamless often erase the course-planning and delivery labor of online instruction, and tenure and promotion have not been adjusted to reflect or respect the work of online educators (pp. 446–448). The lack of incentives for tenure-line faculty to specialize in online education helps explain why much of the online teaching is delivered by contingent faculty, who not only have limited opportunities to conduct their own research, but may also be reporting to administrators who cannot adequately advise them.

If online courses are taught by contingent faculty hired at the last minute—and if contingent faculty get little in the way of professional development before teaching those courses—then published scholarly theories and empirical research are less likely to inform practice than "baptism-by-fire" individual experience and professional development limited to instruction on the LMS. Online writing instructors may have to contend with poorly designed course master templates—or no template at all—and may be denied adequate resources and provided limited guidance as to the chain of command or institutional policies. Sometimes policies specific to online instruction don't exist, or they don't exist in ways relevant to a writing course. Online courses can also make contingent instructors even more invisible to their departments and institutions than they already are. Mechenbier (2015) noted, "Placing an adjunct into an OWC a few days before the semester begins is more common than the academy would care to admit; additional research might help to identify more precisely the frequency and resulting challenges for online writing students" (p. 229). In such a "just-in-time" context, instructors are forced to develop their own theories and reflect on their own experience and observations.

Experience as an Online Student

My first online teaching experiences were informed more by experience than research. To shift to the PARS metaphor, I see research as the caddy in the golf cart who observes and analyzes the game, while offering suggestions to players on the course. Research studies can help instructors to justify what they already know and alert them to strategies that might help them negotiate future roughs, sand traps, and water hazards of the online writing course, just as caddies help golfers with these things on the golf course.

But before I discuss my experience teaching online, I want to briefly describe my experience as an online student, which shaped my approach to online instruction before I had ever taught an online class. I took an online technical writing course in 2007 as a graduate student in a terminal master's program. I wanted to find out what it was like to take an online course, with my curiosity driven by the knowledge that I might be asked to teach an online course at some point. I wanted to make sure I had at least a glimpse of the experience from the student perspective. As a side note, I should mention that I had already been working in virtual environments and on virtual teams since the early 1990s as a freelance copywriter specializing in advertising and marketing communication. I did not come to the online course with a fear of technology or resistance to online instruction.

The online course was invisible to me. With no mandated class meetings or synchronous interactions, and no regular communication from the instructor, the sense of urgency was missing, and I often forgot that I was taking the class. It was taught like a correspondence class: Writing assignments were due once per week, and I received feedback once per week. If I had questions about the writing prompt or my draft in progress, I had to wait several days for an email response. If the answer was unhelpful, I didn't have the time to ask again. In their survey of online writing students, Martinez et al. (2019) found that a majority of online students highly value instructor feedback: "Students value their instructors because of their expertise in writing, they value their instructor's feedback on their writing, and they want and need advice/directions from instructors regularly" (Results & Discussion). The lack of instructor presence made me feel as if I were teaching myself and then sending off my assignments to be judged.

The biggest problem with the course is that I felt so isolated. The course was not set up for any kind of interaction among students; for example, instead of class discussions, the course required weekly multiple-choice quizzes provided by the textbook publisher. Fortunately, I found two students on the roster who were in my graduate school cohort. I connected with them offline, and we began to regularly talk about the course. That helped me tremendously, and I had an "aha!" moment about the social nature of learning: I got as much out of a course from classmates as I did from the instructor. I recognized that peer interaction not only made learning more rewarding, but it also made the instructor's work more effective. I also recognized how important it was for instructors to establish their own social presence. Cunningham (2015) found that two key components of social presence in an online course are "a present and responsive instructor who can provide relevant feedback . . . in a timely manner" and "the ability to work with other students in small groups and on larger projects in ways that are direct and pragmatic" (p. 45). Having classmates to talk with gave me additional support beyond the instructor: I wasn't in this alone anymore, and I didn't have to rely on one person for clarification or even instruction. For future reference, I understood that being present for students in an online course was more important than the technology used to deliver the course.

Scholars who are serious about online writing courses consider how best to adapt writing pedagogy to the online environment; however, institutional reasons for implementing online instruction often have little to do with pedagogy. When it isn't being touted as a potential plug-and-play money-maker, online education seems to be the emergency alternative to finding an available classroom or on-site instructor. Predictably, that means that the pedagogical aspect is not usually well thought out and neither the instructor nor students receive adequate training or lead time before the course begins. Further, although some students do prefer online courses, many students view online options as a way to fit coursework into their busy schedules or to work around limited face-to-face course offerings. Sometimes online instruction is a way to meet unexpected demand for a particular course, which is an important distinction: Even if students prefer a face-to-face classroom, face-to-face is not always an option. Finally, as demonstrated during the COVID-19 switch to remote learning, online instruction can be an emergency response to the unexpected.

PARS as an Ideal for Writing Program Administrators

Although the PARS approach does address the ideal of what an online writing program administrator should be, the ideal is not what instructors will find in every institutional or administrative context. In their advice on Personal Administration, McArdle & Borgman (2019) stated,

> Communication with your faculty is imperative and sharing the student demographics, the school's new online learning initiatives, the available resources for online students really helps support your faculty and allows them to be more successful in their jobs because they get a better picture of the school's goals and a clearer picture of the student learner's needs. (p. 28)

That's the ideal; however, once the course has been assigned, the instructor might not have an accessible administrator—or an administrator who understands online instruction, or an administrator at all! Instructors without a PARS administrator will need to strategically negotiate the lack of access or a lack of understanding about what they need to get the job done.

McArdle & Borgman (2019) defined the three elements of Accessible Administration as "1) helping faculty resolve problems with students, 2) being there to listen to your faculty, and 3) connecting them with technical support" (p. 43). Again, what the PARS approach advocates is not necessarily what instructors will encounter. In practice they may be left to their own best judgment when resolving issues with students. Even those administrators willing to listen might not have the answer to questions, might have little experience with online education, and they will likely expect instructors to contact technical support on their own. Another PARS ideal is Responsive Administration: "Being a responsive administrator means responding to faculty when problems arise and getting your faculty what they need in terms of skills and resources before problems arise" (McArdle & Borgman, 2019, p. 62). If the department has a problem to address, the online instructor may *be* "the skills and resources" the administrator provides as a response to tenure-line faculty who do not have the skills and resources to teach online. Little thought may be given to what an instructor needs to get started, such as obtaining an ID badge, getting email and other university technologies set up, learning how to use the LMS, and becoming familiar with the pre-designed course shell, if one exists. In some cases, instructors may need to quickly design their own online course, which requires that they are provided learning objectives and outcomes and given some sense of what the department values in terms of writing and writing assignments.

Ideally, a writing program administrator would provide Strategic Administration: McArdle & Borgman (2019) suggested, "As administrators, you need to strategize how you'll prepare your online instructors for the student demographic they'll face" (p. 17). In a "just-in-time" situation, an administrator's strategy may simply be to find someone, anyone, who is available to teach at the last minute. If that's the case, the instructor should not expect much in the way of preparation, and may even face confusion about who or what actually *is* the administrator. DePew et al. (2006) noted that "A single [distance education] class can be supported—pedagogically, administratively, financially, technologically—by different individuals and different (micro)institutions with disparate and sometimes competing agendas" (54). Online writing instructors might be bounced from one group to another while searching for answers—and they have to carefully consider their own strategies about what to do with conflicting information.

First Year on the Tour: A Narrative of "Just-in-Time" Online Instruction

What follows is the story of how I negotiated the roughs and hazards during my first year teaching writing courses online. I start by describing the context that led to my first online course assignment in fall 2012 and discuss the steps I took to quickly educate myself about teaching online as a contingent instructor. Next, I explain how I addressed the false starts and new constraints of the spring 2013 semester, when more online courses were assigned to me at the last minute. Following that, I discuss how those initial experiences prepared me to better manage just-in-time online courses by the 2013 summer session and beyond. Finally, I summarize the key issues of online instruction that contingent faculty and administrators need to be aware of and that administrators of distance education programs and traditional writing programs may tend to overlook.

My first online teaching experience was a "just-in-time" assignment offered to me shortly after the start of the school year in 2012. Two face-to-face dual-credit first-year composition classes at a high school had just started, when the instructor suddenly quit. I had just defended my dissertation in August and had no job lined up, so I jumped at the opportunity to step in. Given that I was more than 200 miles away from the high school, the course had to be moved online. Neither dual-credit nor online first-year composition courses were the norm for the writing program at that time—and they were being administered by the distance-education program—so I experienced first-hand the lack of direction commonly experienced by contingent faculty, as university silos led to absent, vague, or contradictory policies. The courses were familiar to me, having taught them for the past five years; however, I had never taught the courses online or to high school students. I reached out to someone who has expertise in online literacy education, which turned out to be a good move. She directed me to some useful resources that allowed me to quickly get a sense of how to design an online course.

This particular course was unusual in numerous other ways:

1. This was the first where my interaction with students was solely through writing: No synchronous technologies were available.
2. My students had expected a traditional face-to-face experience, but the sudden departure of the original instructor left us all negotiating a new online experience.

3. By the time the course started, only 12 weeks were left in the semester to teach it, which resulted in a seat-of-the-pants style of curriculum, focused on the essentials of the course.
4. Some students were taking the course independently, while others were in a teacher-monitored classroom, but I could not immediately determine which students were in which group because the course had to be set up as a Community on Blackboard, with all students listed on one roster
5. After taking the time to develop some YouTube videos, I discovered that the high school blocked access to YouTube. Blackboard could not handle large video files or even PowerPoint files, so I turned all my presentations into PDFs.
6. Due to issues with registration and Blackboard access, several weeks passed before I could determine who was actually supposed to be taking the course. My Blackboard roster included people who were either no longer registered or who were observing the course in some capacity.

Teaching dual-credit classes online was different from teaching regular college courses because I was often unsure of the chain of command. With no written policies or guidelines and so many stakeholders—high school representatives, the university writing program, the distance education program—I found it difficult to know who had authority over any decision I needed to make. For example, I found myself in an odd conversation about whether the grade in a college-level course was going to prevent a senior from graduating from high school.

I needed to know where my agency began and ended from an institutional standpoint to avoid being in violation of the law or institutional policy—or simply to avoid getting the "runaround" or wasting the time of the wrong people with my questions and concerns. I recall asking for clarification on some forgotten issue from the high school representative, who referred me back to the university. When I contacted the writing program, I was referred to distance learning, which referred me back to the writing program. I don't have advice about this except to warn instructors that a lack of coordination among stakeholders is probably not all that uncommon.

After fall semester ended, I figured that was the end of my online assignment. Then, a few days before spring semester started, I was asked to teach the dual-credit composition courses again, along with two sections of second-semester composition for on-campus students. The online sections were by permission only and being offered to ensure spaces for seniors who needed the course in time to graduate that year.

When I telephoned the distance-education office to ask about setting up Blackboard course sites, I recall the person on the other end of the line saying incredulously, "But you don't even have a course template!" Unfazed, I went into overdrive to prepare the syllabi and course sites for the 15-week semester for undergraduates and an 18-week semester for the dual-credit students. The day before class was to start, I was informed that the online course for undergraduate students was on a 10-week schedule. I reworked everything with just hours to spare. Exhausted, but relieved to be ready for class, I sent students an email welcoming them to the course and directing them to the Blackboard site. Soon after, I was overwhelmed with emails from students who could not log into the course site. Thinking this was an IT issue, I was surprised to discover that students could choose their start–end dates any time within the regular 15-week semester, but students could not access the course site until their start date. The technical question was resolved, but now I had 54 undergraduates with 13 different start-end dates (Table 10.1). I had to completely rethink how to manage the course schedule and how to encourage interaction among peers who were constantly coming and going. Further complicating that process was that students were not automatically closed out of the course site after their end date. I discovered that glitch when a few students attempted to submit work after their 10 weeks in the course had already expired. I had to block them from the course until all students finished the course, and then I had to add them back in before submitting final grades, which were due at the end of the regular 15-week semester.

Table 10.1. Student roster for 10-week online course by start-end dates

Start Week	Start–End Date	Combined Rosters
Week 1	Jan 7–Mar 17	[16 students]
	Jan 8–Mar 18	[4 students]
	Jan 9–Mar 19	[3 students]
	Jan 11–Mar 21	[5 students]
	Jan 12–Mar 22	[1 student]
	Jan 13–Mar 23	[1 student]
Week 2	Jan 14–Mar 24	[10 students]
	Jan 15–Mar 25	[1 student]
	Jan 18–Mar 28	[1 student]
Week 3	Jan 21–Mar 31	[5 students]
	Jan 22–Apr 1	[1 student]
Week 4	Jan 28–Apr 7	[2 students]
	Feb 1–Apr 11	[4 students]
Total		54 students

But wait, there's more! In addition to the variable start dates, I also learned that online courses on our campus were self-paced. This nuance was brought to my attention after some students balked at assignment due dates, which, I learned, had to be suggested, rather than mandated. Although most students recognized that they needed due dates to stay on track to complete the course, a few students either resisted or ignored the suggested due dates, and emails to them were left unanswered. Self-pacing is reasonable for a content-driven, self-study course with automated quizzes and tests to measure competency. Writing instruction, on the other hand, requires ongoing writing practice, along with instructor feedback, peer responses, and student revision. Noting the disparity of retention and grades between online and face-to-face courses, Sapp & Simon (2005) found that marginal students in face-to-face classes tend to drop a course early with no impact on their grade, whereas marginal students in online classes tend to disappear without dropping the course, which leads to a failing grade. Those study results matched my experience with a self-paced online course: Some students never "touched" the course or attended briefly and never dropped the course, which resulted in a much higher number of F's than I ever had in a face-to-face classroom. Once I began teaching online courses that gave me the authority to set deadlines, students were better able to recognize early on if they were going to be able to complete the course.

Self-paced online courses seem to offer the promise that students can make up a semester's worth of work at the last minute. The day one cohort of students finished their 10 weeks in the course, I no sooner began filling out the 0's for a student who had been missing all semester, when I received a frantic email from that same student: The LMS must be malfunctioning; after all, there were still a few more hours left in the course! The hard lesson I learned that semester was to make no assumptions about the parameters of an online course or student expectations for that course, even when teaching a familiar course at a familiar institution. By the time summer courses started in 2013, my experiences had prepared me to better manage "just-in-time" online courses: With the help of the writing program, I was able to negotiate a more realistic framework for the course. Students had the same start–end dates and all students had to follow the same course schedule.

Since 2015 I have been teaching online and hybrid courses at my current institution. The courses I teach include technical writing and business communication courses in four-week, six-week, and 15-week formats. I continually build on my pedagogical strategies by reading, pursuing professional development opportunities, trying new approaches, seeking out feedback from students, and reflecting on my experience. I continually adapt to new technologies—including Canvas, Google Slides, WeVideo, Webex, and Zoom—and adjust to new or evolving policies—such as the requirement to include synchronous components in online instruction and the authority to drop students who disappear from online courses.

Although the strategies, technologies, and reasons for delivering online writing courses may change or vary, what remains constant is a lag-time between instructor need and administrator response. What often also remains constant are disconnects between institutional requirements for online course delivery and what is actually going to benefit students. For example, required weekly synchronous class meetings are going to be a surprise to students who think they have signed up for a fully asynchronous online course, based on the course description at registration. Due to student expectations of schedule flexibility, what I have found works best is to facilitate small group meetings rather than meetings with the entire class. The affordances of asynchronous interactions have also led me to re-envision synchronous interactions in terms of their own affordances: as a way to get to know each other, to share ideas, to clear up misunderstandings, and to build trust.

Reflections on the "Just-in-Time" Course

With technologies and pedagogies continually evolving—and with teaching contexts varying so much—no one source can be the final word on how to design and deliver an online course, much less how to take on a "just-in-time" online course. Although not an exhaustive list, Figure 10.1 summarizes the key issues that the instructor of a "just-in-time" course needs to consider and that administrators of distance education programs and traditional writing programs may tend to overlook.

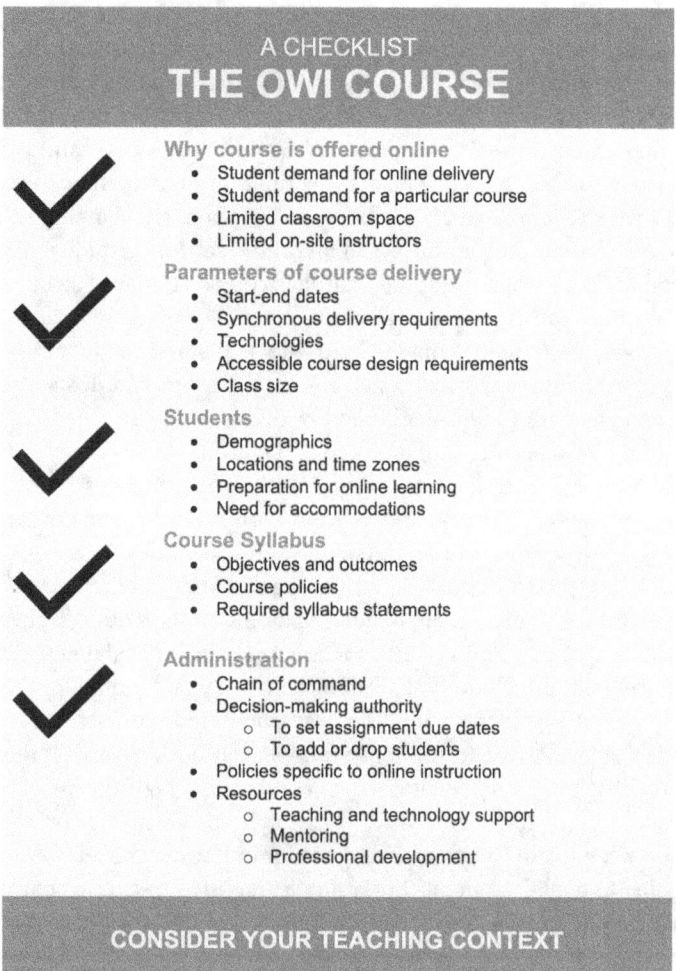

Figure 10.1. OWI course checklist for instructors and administrators.

Instructors who understand the need for the course, why it is being offered online, and how it fits into the departmental and institutional strategy can better anticipate the level of student engagement or resistance. Having some idea of student demographics, including why students take online courses and how the university prepares students for the online learning environment, can help instructors prepare for the logistics of organizing collaborative groups and facilitating student interactions.

Knowing the parameters of the course, including start–end dates for students and policies regarding the course schedule, synchronous interactions, and definition of attendance, can go a long way towards managing student expectations, and can help them make decisions about whether the online course is right for them.

Understanding the chain of command, in terms of who instructors report to, what issues instructors need to report, and who has decision-making authority over specific issues, can help instructors to quickly gain institutional knowledge and build positive working relationships. Designated sites where instructors can find policies, guidelines, tips, or suggestions for online instruction makes that information available at the moment it is needed.

Specific policies addressing online writing instruction can eliminate confusion and missteps. For example, administrators can provide required syllabus statements that appropriately reflect the online mode of delivery, rather than—or addition to—statements about an accessible campus. For example, The Miller Center for Student Disability Services at Miami University recommends the following syllabus statement:

> If you are a student with a disability and feel you may need a reasonable accommodation to fulfill the essential functions of this course, you are encouraged to contact Student Disability Services (SDS). SDS provides accommodations and services for students with a variety of disabilities, including physical, medical and psychiatric disabilities. You are encouraged to contact SDS to learn more about registration and procedures for requesting accommodations.

Other policies may include how much of the course must reside within the LMS, how much control the instructor has over the LMS (e.g., to adjust a mandated course template), and how student access to the LMS course site is managed.

Although some institutions have robust OWI administrations, the fact remains that, for many online instructors, a less-than-ideal administrative context is par for the course: In those situations, instructors can use the PARS approach to make their course as Personal, Accessible, Responsive, and Strategic as possible (see Figure 10.2).

Personal Instruction means taking ownership of the course. If you are working with a course template, then personalize it wherever you can. If that's not possible, be sure to show up in discussions, in peer responses, and in your feedback.

Create your own video announcements and mini-lectures—the polish is less important than the personality. Be personable with all the people you contact throughout the university; developing good working relationships will make your job less stressful.

Accessible Instruction means more than accommodating for students with disabilities. Make sure that all students can easily find their way around the course site, and be as explicit as possible in your instructions. Seek feedback from your students about how they are experiencing the course and the course site. Consider that not everyone may have the same access to technologies.

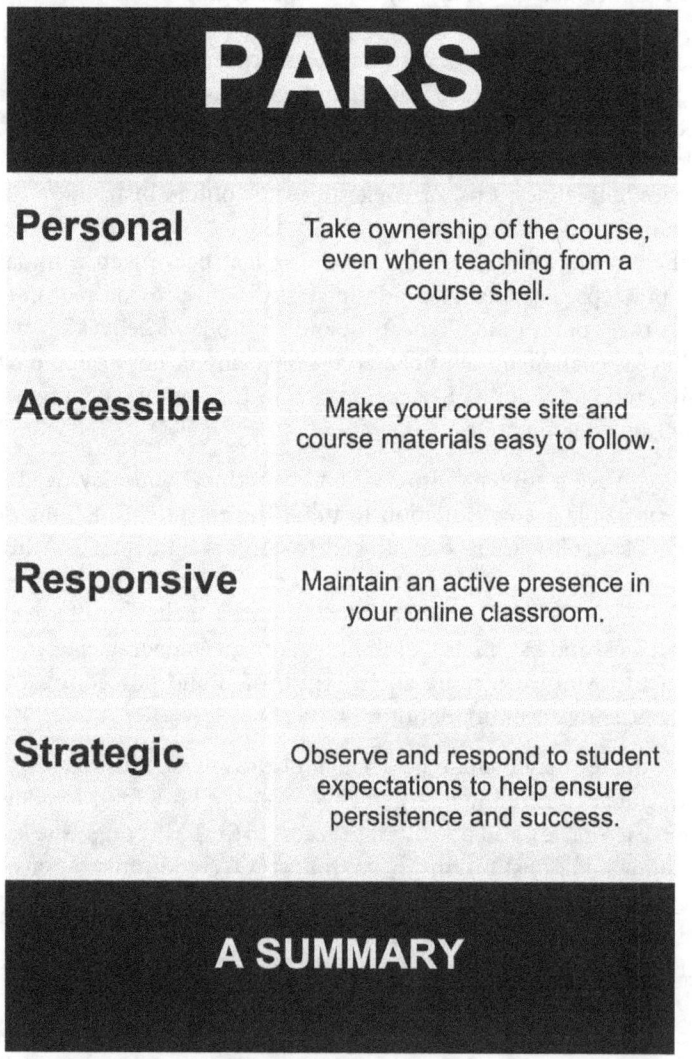

Figure 10.2. Summary of the PARS approach to "just-in-time" online courses.

Responsive Instruction is having a social presence in the online classroom. That means being observant and proactive, reaching out rather than just waiting for the emails. If a student has gone silent, reach out. When students reach out to you, respond quickly. A responsive instructor also facilitates student interactions, helping them to get to know and trust each other.

Strategic Instruction requires an analysis of the rhetorical situation: the purpose, audience, and context of the course, including technology platforms. If you don't yet have all the facts, proceed and prioritize carefully to avoid investing too much time and energy in planning a course that cannot be delivered. Manage student expectations to ensure their persistence in the course and to enhance their overall satisfaction with the course.

Final Thoughts and Application

If you have been assigned a "just-in-time" online writing course, especially if you are teaching online for the first time, you'll need to get your bearings and do a lot of listening and observing and investigating. Your situation is probably not unique, as frustrating as it may seem. You are not alone, and you don't have to figure it out all out by yourself. Reach out to a wider community of colleagues and mentors. If you don't know anyone with experience teaching online, then reach out to a professional organization: The Online Writing Instruction Community (created by Borgman & McArdle in 2015) and the Global Society for Online Literacy Educators (GSOLE) founded in 2016 are a couple of good options. You didn't get much lead time to begin with, so avoid working overtime to create a complete course plan. Instead, set a goal for publishing the first week's activities with an outline of the plan to come. You can adjust the course, once you get a better sense of your students, their expectations, and their needs.

Be present for your students in ways that let them know you are there and you care. Student perceptions about instructor and peer interactions are more important than any fancy technologies or slick course design. How students feel about their experience in the course goes a long way towards fostering engagement, improving retention, and getting the feedback you need to continually adjust the course for a better user experience.

References

Blair, K. L. & Monske, E. A. (2003). Cui bono?: Revisiting the promises and perils of online learning. *Computers and Composition, 20*, 441–453.

Borgman, J. & McArdle, C. (2019). *Personal, accessible, responsive, strategic: Resources and strategies for online writing instructors.* The WAC Clearinghouse; University Press of Colorado. https://doi.org/10.37514/PRA-B.2019.0322.

Cunningham, J. (2015). Mechanizing people and pedagogy: Establishing social presence in the online classroom. *Online Learning, 19*(3), 34–37.

DePew, K. E., Fishmann, T. A., Romberger, J. E. & Ruetenik, B. F. (2006). Designing efficiencies: The parallel narratives of distance education and composition studies. *Computers and Composition, 23,* 49–67.

Greer, M. & Harris, H. S. (2018) User-centered design as a foundation for effective online writing instruction. *Computers and Composition, 49,* 14–24.

Martinez, D., Mechenbier, M. X., Hewett, B. L., Harris, H. S., St.Amant, K., Bodnar, M. I. (2019). A report on a U.S.-based national survey of students in online writing courses. *ROLE / OLOR.* http://www.roleolor.org/a-report-on-a-us-based-national-survey-of-students-in-online-writing-courses.html.

Mechenbier, M. (2015). Contingent faculty and OWI. In B. L. Hewett & K. E. DePew (Eds.), *Foundational practices of online writing instruction* (pp. 227–249). The WAC Clearinghouse; Parlor Press. https://doi.org/10.37514/PER-B.2015.0650.2.07.

Miami University. (2020). Syllabus statements. *Miller Center for Disability Student Services.* https://miamioh.edu/student-life/sds/faculty/syllabus-statements/index.html.

Palloff, R. M. & Pratt, K. (2013), *Lessons from the virtual classroom: The realities of online teaching* (2nd ed.). Jossey-Bass.

Rodrigo, R. & Ramírez, C. D. (2017). Balancing institutional demands with effective practice: A lesson in curricular and professional development. *Technical Communication Quarterly, 26.3,* 314–328.

Sapp, D. A. & Simon, J. (2005). Comparing grades in online and face-to-face writing courses: Interpersonal accountability and institutional commitment. *Computers and Composition, 22,* 471–489.

Section 3: Administration

Welcome to the Administration section of this collection! We selected the above golf course picture to illustrate how administrators see the big picture. They see the water on the right and the sand bunker to the left, but they are also laser focused on the flag at the end of the hole. This section is all about administration. The audience for this section is obviously administrators of writing programs, but that doesn't mean instructors or scholars can't find something interesting in the pages of these chapters because sometimes it helps to view things from another's vantage point.

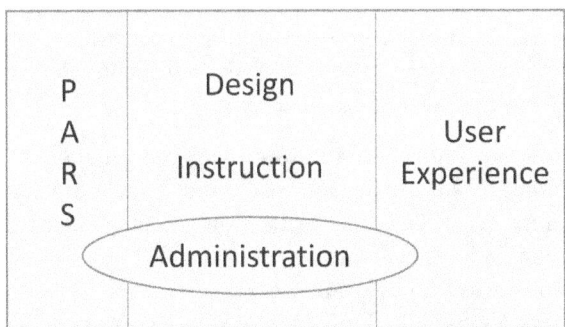

The chapters in this section address some of the challenges that administrators face as previously outlined in other OWI scholarship (Babb 2016; Borgman, 2016; Lente, 2017; Minter, 2015). These chapters illustrate creative ideas on how to be a more personal, accessible, responsive and strategic administrator and they offer ways to mitigate some stress that comes with running a writing program that is all online or includes online courses. These chapters outline how the PARS approach can contribute to training and supporting one's faculty as an administrator and they illustrate how the administration layer of the PARS approach affects multiple aspects of the writing program.

Here are a few things you can do to be a **Personal** administrator because making sure you stay connected with your faculty and staff is essential:

- Be caring and compassionate in your communication with faculty and show you are a human! Support your staff in whatever way you can!
- Have weekly check-ins (meetings or emails) with your staff and remind them you are there for them—don't overload them, but don't disappear!
- Provide online training sessions or lunch and learns to share online teaching/LMS tips and tricks and to talk about what they're doing in their OWCs, or for specific things like managing the workload, how to participate in discussions, and grading expectations, among others.
- Share instructor support resources and student support resources (professional, university, personal).

Accessible administration goes beyond ADA compliance (ada.gov).

- Help your faculty understand what ADA compliance is and host training or work sessions if necessary.
- Create and convey clear expectations for faculty on how to interact with their OWCs—focus on content, grading, and response times.
- Provide faculty with exemplary OWC course examples and/or teach faculty some basic accessible course design best practices associated with the LMS tools/navigation.
- Ensure faculty know how to get in touch with tech support and have access to the programs, software, etc., they will need to do their jobs.

Responsive administration is about setting expectations with your faculty just as instructors set up expectations with their students. Responsive administration comes down to the *how* and the *when*:

- Let your faculty know how and when they can get ahold of you and how long it might take to get a response (post or email out your contact information, response times, and any days off you take during the week).
- Hold virtual WPA office hours
  - When (weekly, biweekly, monthly)
  - Where (Zoom, F2F, Google Meet, Webex, telephone)
- Consider having a department space in your college's LMS, Slack, or Microsoft Teams where faculty can post resources, talk, and help answer each other's questions (you can be a part of it too!).
- Set up a schedule for yourself so you're not working 24/7! Your sanity is vital to the program's success!

Strategic administration brings it all together. Being a strategic administrator includes:

- Planning how your writing program, your course design, and you (as the administrator) will be personal, accessible, responsive and strategic;
- Planning your department orientation, professional development events, mentorship programs, semester long support, etc. so that your faculty get the training they need to be successful online instructors.
- Preparing your online instructors for teaching different student demographics (underprepared, ESL, students with disabilities, first-generation students, and returning full-time working students, etc.).
- Planning out and allocating your time.

The chapters focused on administration in this section will aid you in creating a more PARS-focused administration style. Thomas et al.'s chapter focuses on building personal connections and retaining online students. This multi-authored chapter illustrates how administrators can help their faculty add personal touches to their OWCs in a gradual, sustainable way. Hilliard's chapter illustrates how PARS aids in creating a community of practice (CoP) for hybrid writing instructors. By explaining how to provide training and support to faculty, Hilliard's chapter shows administrators how to implement a PARS-based CoP and support their faculty consistently, not just at the start of the semester.

In their chapter, Jackson and Olinger provide a framework for training graduate students to teach online using PARS letters R (responsive) and S (strategic). They describe how they created and facilitated a mini asynchronous training course to introduce their graduate instructors to online pedagogy. Snart's chapter addresses the challenge of professional development and course design. Snart encourages online administrators to help their instructors think more like instructional designers and to embrace a strategic user experience design mindset. Finally, Wilkes' chapter focuses on training graduate students to teach online by the use of PARS as both the course content (teaching them about the PARS approach), and the approach to designing and delivering the course (using the PARS approach as the course design).

References

Babb, J. (2016) Reshaping institutional mission: OWI and writing program administration. In K. Blair & E. Monske (Eds.), *Writing and composing in the age of MOOCS* (pp. 205–215). IGI Global.

Borgman, J. (2017). The online writing program administrator (OWPA): Maintaining a brand in the age of MOOCS. In K. Blair & E. Monske (Eds.), *Writing and composing in the age of MOOCS* (pp. 188–201). IGI Global.

Minter, D. (2015). Administrative decisions for OWI. In B. Hewett & K. E. Depew (Eds), *Foundational practices of online writing instruction* (pp. 211–225). The WAC Clearinghouse; Parlor Press. https://doi.org/10.37514/PER-B.2015.0650.2.06.

Lente, F. (2017). Navigating the current moment in online teaching & learning: Pedagogy, program administration & professional development. http://composing.org/digitalwrd/teaching-online-administrators-navigating/.

Chapter 11. Create, Support, and Facilitate Personal Online Writing Courses in Online Writing Programs

Rhonda Thomas, Karen Kuralt, Heidi Skurat Harris, and George Jensen
UNIVERSITY OF ARKANSAS (LITTLE ROCK)

Abstract: Building personal connections in online courses is an important part of facilitating learning and retaining students in online programs, as Borgman and McArdle note in their book *Personal, Accessible, Responsive, Strategic: Resources and Strategies for Online Writing Instructors*. Drawing on focus group research collected from students and alumni in three fully online programs located in an independent rhetoric and writing department (a B.A., M.A., and graduate certificate), this chapter describes how teachers and administrators can forge strong personal connections with and among their online students. Students from these programs highlight the importance of creating personalized online learning spaces, as well as techniques for building a sense of community in both the courses and the program. Program administrators comment on how faculty can do the work of adding these personal touches in a gradual, sustainable way.

Keywords: online student retention, connecting with online students, community in online courses, visual design of online courses, online writing programs, independent writing programs, online student focus groups, personalized online instruction, presence in online writing courses, student interaction in online writing courses, online course accessibility, collaboration in online writing courses

Personal connection—the PARS -P element—serves as the foundation for best practice in accessible, responsive, and strategic course design. As Scott Warnock notes in the foreword to *Personal, Accessible, Responsive, and Strategic* (PARS), it "takes strategy and time to show your students how much you care about them" (Borgman & McArdle, 2019, p. viii). To design accessible content, be accessible instructors, and create responsive classes strategically, instructors must first be personal and "personable" instructors (Borgman & McArdle, 2019, p. 4).

Our department has long held making personal connections with students as a core value in course design and program administration, and our experiences and research over the last five years have reinforced that core value.

We first developed our focus on personal connections with students in our on-campus programs, and we wanted to ensure that personal connections were preserved as we developed our online programs.

The Department of Rhetoric and Writing at the University of Arkansas at Little Rock (UALR) has been an independent writing department since 1993 when it split from the Department of English primarily over whether or not full-time, non-tenure track instructors should have voting rights. When the departments split, the new Rhetoric department faculty, composed of lecturers and professors in composition and rhetoric, took with them the first-year composition program and an M.A. in Technical and Expository Writing (which later became the M.A. in Professional and Technical Writing). In collaboration with the university's Journalism Department, Rhetoric and Writing then created an undergraduate major, the B.A. in Professional and Technical Writing, which had two tracks, one in rhetoric and composition (focusing more on technical writing) and one in mass communication (focusing more on journalism). In 2008, the two tracks were redesigned into a single program in Rhetoric and Writing with the option of taking some elective courses in the School of Mass Communication.

Being an independent writing department has afforded our faculty significant freedom in developing curriculum without having to include literature courses or appease literature faculty. Over the years, the department developed four major emphases in its programs: technical writing, editing and publishing, nonfiction, and persuasive writing. When the department redesigned its B.A. in 2008, several undergraduate and graduate courses had already been moved online, and faculty began to talk about possibly developing fully online programs. As these discussions progressed, the department, under Heidi's leadership, also developed the Graduate Certificate in Online Writing Instruction. The freedom of being an independent writing department made this move easier than it would have been if we were part of a more complex unit. (The Department of English, for example, has been slow to develop online courses or programs.)

Even with a faculty open to online instruction, it took Rhetoric and Writing about eight years to launch a fully online version of the B.A. and M.A. programs in Professional and Technical Writing. By 2016, as we were launching three online programs, our university, similar to many institutions across the country, began to experience a loss of enrollments. Because we could market fully online programs, we were able to continue small but steady growth. When the pandemic hit in spring 2020, the department was mostly hybrid or online. We were able to move the fully face-to-face (F2F) classes to an online format seamlessly. The department's experience with online teaching was critical in making this shift, as were our pre-existing efforts to train online faculty and retain online students.

Assessment data from our F2F programs frequently cited the benefits of personal connection between students and professors. When we started offering online courses, we knew that we would need to preserve this strength for our online courses and programs to succeed. Now that we've offered three different programs fully online for four years, the timing seemed right to assess how well our online programs are performing so that we can maintain practices that are effective for our students and our outcomes and make changes where needed. Evaluating the success of our personal connections with online students is an important part of that assessment—and since interacting with students is central to building personal connections, naturally we realized we would learn the most by asking the students and alumni themselves.

In 2016, we received a CCCC Research Initiative Grant to conduct surveys, focus groups, and interview research with students, alumni, faculty, and administrators involved with online course/program development in the rhetoric and writing department. In 2019, we received a second grant from our social sciences college to conduct a second round of research that replicated the survey and focus groups with a different set of students and alumni from the 2016 study.

We four researchers/authors bring a rich variety of perspectives to interpreting the data from these studies, which we share in this chapter to illuminate the importance of strategic implementation (the PARS -S element) of personal connection (the PARS -P element) in course design. Karen joined the Rhetoric and Writing Department in fall 2000, just as the university was offering its first online courses. She served as our department's M.A. program coordinator from 2007–2019 and is now associate dean of the graduate school. George was hired as the department chair in 2004, serving in that role for twelve years; he was an integral part of the development of all our online programs. Heidi joined the department in 2013 and won a college curriculum innovation award for her design of the Graduate Certificate in Online Writing Instruction (GCOWI). She is now the coordinator of all the department's graduate programs. Rhonda is a graduate student who completed both the online B.A. and GCOWI programs. She is currently enrolled in the online M.A. program and was the research assistant for the 2019 study (Melissa Johnson served as the graduate assistant for the 2016 survey and focus group research). As a co-author of this chapter, Rhonda shares her student perspective on personal connection in course design. Feedback from our focus group and survey participants frequently echo Rhonda's experiences.

Why Is the Personal Important?

Being personal in online classes isn't simply having a good personality. Being personable, as Borgman and McArdle (2019) note, means being personal in designing and facilitating your class and, for online writing programs, personal in your administration of online writing classes and work with online faculty.

During both studies, our focus group and survey data suggest that students are more motivated when they feel a "personal connection" to the course and the instructor. We define personal connection as those distinct moments in a course when students recognize links between their ideas and identities and those of the instructor. Personal connection can be fostered by student-instructor interaction, instructor presence in discussion boards, through outcome-driven feedback on student projects, and through instructor accessibility—the PARS -A element.

Student writers in classroom settings often feel they are being judged when they expose their writing to professors and to other students. Many lack confidence in their writing skills and in their ability to contribute to discussions, which is magnified when they move online into what can be experienced as a psychologically unsafe and less personal space. Students need connection and mentorship to thrive, and teachers should make a conscious effort to build connection and mentorship into online settings.

Rhonda explains why connecting with her instructors was important to her development as a writer:

> Writing is personal. It is intimately connected to who we are. When we write, we expose ourselves on all fronts: we expose the quality of our writing and we expose the quality of our ideas. This is particularly true in an online writing class where everything we have to say seems, to some degree, permanently fixed.
>
> As a non-traditional adult returning to college, I had zero confidence in my ability to write academically. There I was, spending an appreciable amount of time writing in my work life, yet stumbling to find my footing in class for two reasons: 1) because I didn't know my writer-self and 2) left to my own devices, I simply couldn't find a bridge between the everyday me and the academic me.
>
> I believe to get the most out of one's education, one must write; and more importantly, one must be comfortable with her identity as a writer. While there are certainly students who have great confidence in their writing, I would stick my neck out and say many students do not; particularly, first year students.

Instructor-student interactions and personal connections, strategically placed throughout a course, can create opportunities to help students connect with their writer-selves through personal engagement. Students in our focus groups echoed the importance of mentorship in helping them develop as academic and professional writers. They identified several factors that made them feel more connected to their professors as mentors:

> Being able to experience the presence of their professors online, to be able to get to know them personally as real human beings.
>
> Being able to interact with professors regularly, both through feedback on assignments and through timely responses to student questions.
>
> Getting the sense that professors actually *wanted* to hear from students, rather than treating their questions as frivolous or burdensome.
>
> Being encouraged to explore, develop ideas, and make mistakes without fear of judgments or penalty (via low grades, critical comments, etc.).

One focus group participant valued that the professors in our online programs gave her "roots" in key writing skills and "wings to go and achieve anything [she] want[s] to achieve." Another remarked, "... this is the first time in any program I've been in where every single professor ... I've had, I trust, and I trust that they are knowledgeable because they are showing me they are knowledgeable, and I trust that they have my best interest at heart ... and I haven't experienced that in other programs that I've had."

As these students explain, when professors take time to add personal elements to their online courses, students then become more comfortable trying new forms of writing and sharing their work and ideas. Even relatively infrequent personal connections can be surprisingly powerful for online students. Rhonda describes some of the techniques that helped her feel most connected to her professors:

> Knowing what my instructor looks like and sounds like (e.g., audio/video) is important to me. Seeing or hearing that my instructor is an actual person and not just text on a screen gives her instant credibility with me. Suddenly this flat, online personality is a real human with observable dimensions. Getting to know my instructor forges that "personal partnership" Borgman and McArdle (2019) talk about.

Focus group participants in our study agreed with Rhonda about the techniques that help them develop early rapport with their online teachers. They cited three main factors that helped them feel connected to their online instructors as people, creating a feeling of safety that made them more willing to take risks necessary to their development as academic and professional writers. Those factors are identified in Table 11.1 and connected with practical suggestions for faculty who want to foster personal connections in their online courses.

Table 11.1. Establishing initial rapport with online students

Students feel personally connected to their online instructors when you . . .	Practical tips:
Help students get to know you as a person.	Include a photo in your course shell. Create short introductory videos to introduce new concepts and assignments. Interact with students on social media. Participate in discussion boards calling students by name; post responses that show students you connect with their goals, ideas, and questions.
Interact with students regularly; convey to students that you want to interact with them.	Provide timely feedback on assignments at predictable intervals. Set up group or individual video chat times. Encourage questions frequently and respond to questions as quickly as possible. Provide multiple means of connecting with students (phone, video, etc.).
Create a safe environment where students can explore and make mistakes without penalty.	Use low-stakes collaborative activities and low-stakes assignments where students earn participation credit but not letter grades. Build in opportunities for learning through revision. Establish guidelines for commenting respectfully and kindly on class member contributions.

Creating Personalized Spaces Where Students Can Succeed

Skurat Harris and Greer (2016) argue that "[t]o teach writing online is to design an environment" (p. 46). This takes forethought, strategy, and commitment. In the F2F classroom, students get a sense of whether they will enjoy the class and connect with their teacher from seeing and interacting with the professor in person. Online, that tone is set and mediated by the class website or LMS shell. Some questions to ask when setting the tone of the online classroom are:

- Does the course look inviting?
- Is the course easy to navigate?
- Are the links and assignments updated and functioning correctly?
- Does the course material support and measure the course learning outcomes? Does the instructor explain how it supports the learning outcomes?

Rhonda reflects on online course designs that worked for her:

> The best writing instructors design learning experiences that help me find direction as a writer. They do this by making a personal connection with me in ways that demonstrate they are genuinely interested in who I am as a person. They find ways to be a bridge between where I am now as a writer and where I want to go with my writing. They also design online writing spaces that don't make me feel as if I'm a temporary guest in their inner sanctum; rather, I'm inhabiting a collaborative space where instructor and student are writing together.

Borgman and McArdle (2019) talk about how online writing instructors need to "make online spaces personal and inviting" (p. 18), because students interact with "inviting personalities" (see Intro, p. ix). Creating a personalized experience for students requires layers of strategic and purposeful communication with each student, applying what Borgman and McArdle (2019) refer to as "multiple means" of interaction. In *Teaching Writing Online: How and Why*, Scott Warnock acknowledges that "the tools of teaching online can seem to create a barrier between you and your students," but that these same tools can "also allow you to expand and shape this personality in highly productive, imaginative ways" (Warnock, 2009, p. 180). In our focus group research, student and alumni comments about the design of online learning spaces clustered around three main areas:

> Inviting visual design of an easy to navigate website or LMS shell.

> Engaging multimodal course materials (with a preference for customized course materials created by the course professor for the specific students in this course at this university).

> Easy to find, fully updated, and functional course materials that explain the purpose for class activities in the context of the learning outcomes.

In the following sections, we identify practical ways that you can implement the PARS method in ways that address these three primary student concerns.

Creating Visually Appealing Spaces

Rhonda explains that visual design is an important part of whether she sees online courses as personal spaces:

> It's obvious to me when I step into an online learning environment whether it exists by design. A big clue is its visual appeal. Borgman and McArdle highlight how aesthetic appeal plays "a large part in the personalization of the online classroom" (2019, p. 20). Indeed, online spaces cannot be devoid of sensory cues:

When they are, they become "sterile and inaccessible to many students" (Ruefman, 2016, p. 5).

For students like Rhonda, sensory cues (the basics of document design, such as fonts, colors, and images) convey nonverbal messages within an online environment that substitute for those messages students have been conditioned to expect in F2F classes (nonverbal communication, modifications in the instructor's voice, eye-to-eye contact, a smile).

Our focus group respondents agreed. "I expect [courses] to be visually appealing, user friendly, and easier to navigate through," said one student. Another noted that in a program that teaches document design and user experience, visually attractive online materials should be the norm; a syllabus that looks like it was typed in the age of DOS does not make a positive impression.

Online instructors should think carefully about these issues to create an intentional design (Skurat Harris et al., 2019 call this "purposeful pedagogy-driven design") for their online courses that conveys the instructor's commitment to the course. The design doesn't need to be elaborate, but it should have consistent elements (i.e., colors, bolding, chunking, labeling) repeated to help students navigate the course easily (see Appendix D for screenshots of an intentionally designed online course).

Creating Engaging, Multimodal, and Customized Course Materials

Just as teachers vary activities in the face-to-face classroom to keep students engaged, online teachers can personalize their courses by adding course materials in a variety of formats, including multimedia course materials that are specifically tailored for a course and its particular students.

Several of our focus group participants shared that personalized videos and presentations are particularly effective for engaging students and helping them feel personally connected. One respondent commented:

> I really like the classes where the professors do a lot of video. I've had some where all they did was give you reading material. And it's just like, here's an article that you gotta read, and you open it up and you look, and the scroll bar is *this* big, and you know it just goes on and on forever. It's very intimidating, very discouraging. So I like when they use a lot of technology and a lot of videos and multimedia stuff, [like] Prezis and different things.

Rhonda adds:

> Instructors who design intentionally tend to create their own resources: a how-to technology video, for example, or a linked point-of-need Google Doc. I imagine there is a bit of front-end

work in designing personalized resources and hand-outs, but over time these instructors are able to provide resources designed with me in mind. When instructors take the time to design in this way, I feel their personal presence embedded in that design.

Not all online teachers have the time, pedagogical freedom, or technological expertise to create large amounts of personalized multimedia content. However, even instructors using pre-designed content can make online courses more personal through welcome announcements, short videos, and explanations of why and how students should complete assignments. In fact, explaining how a course works with the students—even if you're using other people's material—is a personal act, as is including descriptions of the videos that you've chosen and explaining why they are relevant to the class.

Making Courses Easy to Access and Navigate

Personalized course design also requires instructors to make their courses as user-friendly and accessible as possible, showing that the "personal" and "accessible" dimensions of PARS naturally feed into one another. Our student focus group participants explained that they felt their needs and their time were not respected when the online course interface made accessibility difficult.

Accessibility in this instance refers to the ease of getting to materials and the ability to navigate between materials when completing an assignment. Several students complained that instructors sometimes post too many types of materials in too many different places, making it challenging for students to know whether they have located all the assignments and deadlines.

One student explained:

> There was Blackboard, there was Google Hangouts or Google Classroom and Google Discussion. I was confused about where I was supposed to go. I had so many places to go for this one class that I would find myself going, every day, to all of them just to find out where I was supposed to be. . . . [My experience of the course] was just very, very disjointed.

Along similar lines, several students noted that it's possible to have too much uniqueness in course shells. Students can struggle when taking multiple online courses from different instructors, each of whom may use a different style for arranging the course or entirely different online course platforms. "[I]f you're taking four or five classes, it's difficult to remember. Oh, which one is this I am working on? Is there a website? Okay, wait a minute. I've got to stop and pause and regroup," said one respondent. "[D]ifferent instructors hid different things [in] different places," added another student. "I don't think they did it on purpose, but like she said, I found it a little bit difficult."

Courses are also less usable (and feel less personal) when links to materials don't work or aren't regularly updated. Rhonda reflects on this problem:

> Instructors are busy. But I've lost count of how many broken links instructors have given me to online resources selected to *help me* complete an assignment. Sometimes the broken links are out of an instructor's control. Many times, however, it was obvious that an instructor was using the same old, dusty links—semester after semester—simply because it was the easy option. It starts to feel like these instructors are giving *the web* the responsibility of teaching me.

Focus group respondents agreed. For example, one program graduate pointed out that when professors forget to update the due dates on their syllabi and assignment links, not only did students feel the professor wasn't fully present in the course, but it created confusion about when the work is actually due. Another respondent said that seeing mistakes in the course materials actually made him more reluctant to approach his professors:

> I almost felt scared to interact with them at times, especially if I saw the same mistakes over and over, whether it be typos, assignments not opening when they're supposed to open, [etc.]. ... When you ask those questions, you kind of feel like you are bothering them. And then you're scared to do that because you think then it might affect my grade.

Online instructors can show they care for students by structuring accessibility (-A) into their course design. Instructors should:

- Ensure key information and tasks are as accessible and easy to find as possible.
- Post important deadlines and announcements consistently in multiple locations in the course shell (and reinforced through email) to minimize the chance that, in failing to find or look at a single page, students could miss the tasks on which their grades and their learning depend.
- Design through the mindset of novice learners who have not completed a task before, taking care to spell out task steps and make connections between what is assigned and the learning outcomes of the tasks.

Rhonda observes that "it's obvious when instructors have worked through each step in the process for an assignment they've asked me to complete. This is evidenced by how easily all the smaller parts of a larger assignment flow logically in a deliberate direction across time."

Table 11.2 summarizes our recommendations for how online instructors can use visual design and content curation to build personalized online learning spaces where students can succeed.

Creating Connection and Building Community

Of course, the most important aspect of personal connection in any class is the interaction that takes place both between students and professors and among the students themselves. Developing the interactive components in a course requires strong application of the PARS -S element—strategy. Over time, these interactions build a sense of community and belonging that create a safe and welcoming space for learning to take place, increasing the likelihood that students will persist in completing their courses and their degrees.

Table 11.2. Using design to strengthen personal connections with students

The design of your online courses supports personal connection when you . . .	Practical tips:
Use document design to create an inviting, visually appealing space.	Avoid forcing students to read long blocks of tiny text. Use short paragraphs with bold subheadings to label information and increase ease of reading.
	Include color and images that are appropriate to the course content; follow W3C accessibility guidelines for using colors and images (detailed at w3.org).
Create engaging, multi-modal, and customized course materials.	Demonstrate the care and effort you have taken to choose course readings and activities by explaining why you chose those materials. What is unique or special about these materials? Why are they particularly good materials or activities for your students' needs?
	When possible, design personalized videos and handouts to explain assignments and help students succeed in completing assignments.
	Spell out details about how you expect tasks to be completed; make clear connections between tasks and the course's learning outcomes.
Make courses easy to navigate.	Create predictable, easy-to-find links to help students find course materials and complete tasks.
	Use the same organizational structure each week so that students learn where to look for key tasks.
	Post important deadlines and announcements in multiple places so that students can easily find them, even if they forget to look at every page in your shell or website.
	Double check your content for typos and due date errors; always check to make sure that key links are working and up to date.

Our focus group participants told us that the sense of community in the department was vital to their success. "I would say that the first thing that comes to mind when you ask about the Rhetoric and Writing Department is that we're a tightly knit community," said one participant. "I've developed a lot of friends through the program that I would have never even thought I would have had. It's just a very close community feeling, almost like a family." Another respondent echoed this sentiment, saying that a major factor in her satisfaction with the M.A. program was "feeling like you're part of something. The biggest thing I feel like I got out of this program was that I got this whole new group of people that I would have never met in a million years otherwise." Because of the clear interest that professors showed in their students, many of our alumni noted that their connections to the department community have been sustained long after graduation through personal visits, email, and social media.

Interacting with instructors was identified as essential to community building. One student commented that

> The availability of the professors, the openness of all the professors [made me feel valued]. I didn't have a single professor that wouldn't take the time if you wanted to just stop . . . and talk, whether it was about the class or not. They would constantly interact. I think every one of them knew their students by their first name after just a couple of weeks, and it was a very interactive environment.

Yet another student added:

> . . . by emailing my professors and asking questions for clarification, I started a relationship with them, and we began to communicate. And so now most of the professors that I've had . . . I wouldn't hesitate to email them and ask how they are doing. . . . [W]e could have a conversation and it wouldn't be anything unusual.

These remarks show that students clearly value the time that their teachers invest in connecting with them. When they feel seen and appreciated by their instructors, they feel a sense of belonging in the writing course.

Research reinforces the importance of connection and community. Glazier and Skurat Harris (2020) found that when instructors were personable in online classes across the disciplines, retention in those online classes increased by 20–40%. Students in a high-rapport experimental condition were 20% more likely to self-report that they would stay in an online class after only 15 minutes of high-rapport activities.

Building a sense of community online requires two key components:

> Developing a collaborative mentoring relationship between students and professors, in which the professors make an effort to get to know their students and also allow themselves to be known as people.

> Creating opportunities for students to get to know one another and interact in ways that are enjoyable while also promoting social learning.

Rhonda emphasizes the importance of two-way collaboration between instructors and students in forging mentoring connections online:

> Learning is a collaboration between instructor and student, and I learn best when I experience learning as a collaboration. While the student must want to learn and the instructor must want to teach for collaboration to work, it's important to me that the instructor wants to teach *me*, specifically. I need to see evidence of this in the written communications between myself and the instructor. This goes such a long way to making me feel like the instructor understands and appreciates why *I'm* in the class, what *my* goals are. This all boils down to my having confidence that the instructor is present in the online classroom and an equal partner in the learning experience.

Mentoring begins with asking students about their goals and then offering advice related to their goals. Expanding our teaching beyond generalized instruction to include personal mentoring encourages student confidence and persistence.

Instructors can foster mentoring connections by including course activities that help them get to know their students better. For example, including personal introduction icebreakers and getting-to-know-you questionnaires at the beginning of a course allows instructors to find out about students' writing and career goals. One of our focus group participants commented, "One thing that's really important with the online programs [at UALR] is all [my professors] specifically asked at the beginning what we were doing outside of our courses. Then they remembered that and brought that [to the classes they designed]."

As instructors learn about their students' interests and needs, to form a genuine connection, they must also reveal something of themselves. Rhonda observes:

> To cultivate a trusting, constructive interpersonal relationship with me, instructors must also take risks; that is, they must be present and they must be *knowable*. Instructors who take the time to share personal details about themselves beyond the classroom creates positive vibes. Allowing themselves to be known, if only in some small way, humanizes the learning experience for me (Pacansky-Brock, n.d.). I'm suddenly not the only one taking risks. I believe this goes a long way in mitigating what can sometimes feel like an isolating experience.

Personal interaction with students can occur through a variety of mediums, including discussion forums, social media, email, asynchronous video, or synchronous video conferencing. Teachers can share personal details, add photos, make videos, and respond politely to students, including giving prompt and friendly feedback on activities and assignments.

Discussion forums are particularly important, because they not only help instructors connect to students, they also help students connect to each other. They facilitate instructor-student connections because instructors can pose discussion questions that help them assess the class mood and see what students understand. Setting up an ask-anything discussion area creates a space for students to feel comfortable asking housekeeping questions and making comments (including pointing out broken links and asking about missing course materials when necessary).

Discussion forums offer spaces and prompts for students to interact directly with one another (Conceição & Lehman, 2016; Skurat Harris et al., 2016; Warnock, 2009). Students can connect through conversation, activities, and assignments, including low-stakes collaborative assignments that gradually build toward higher stakes collaborations as their relationships and skills develop. "I've learned that I learn just as much from other students [as] I do from the actual coursework," explained one focus group participant. Another described how genuinely interactive discussions were an important part of what made online courses enjoyable:

> I love to go in and see what people have written about, you know, the video this week, and you get to know your classmates a little bit, and, "Oh, she's always got something funny to say," and "Oh, let's look at this raccoon costume." [Personal interaction produces] much, much, much more engagement with my peers and with the professors. You start to get like, favorite people on the discussion board, too. Like you just look for those people, "Oh, my favorite has posted. Let's see."

In the appendices for this chapter, Karen and Rhonda offer more extensive suggestions about how to structure discussions to make them genuinely interactive and enjoyable, rather than a chore that students and professors feel forced to endure. Table 11.3 summarizes our general recommendations on community building.

Making the Personal Sustainable Through Mentoring Faculty

We conclude this chapter by encouraging our colleagues to carry personal connections beyond the online classroom into the way we prepare and support online writing instructors. We want to challenge the view that mentoring online instructors is something that only happens one-on-one between the chair or WPA and an individual faculty member. Mentoring faculty, especially contingent faculty, should be viewed more as creating an inclusive community. When most of the faculty teaches online, the community must necessarily have an online presence. One of the ways we have done this is through a departmental Facebook page where we post announcements about birthdays, faculty publications, student awards, and the work of alums in the world of work. The community should not, however, be entirely virtual. Faculty who teach online can become isolated and may therefore appreciate meeting F2F for training or celebrations. Community should also be conceived of as a set of shared values.

Table 11.3. Building community in online courses

Students feel they belong to a classroom community when you . . .	Practical tips:
Get to know your students as people and show interest in their goals.	Use icebreaker discussion activities or surveys that will help you get to know students early in the semester. Make yourself available for individual interaction with students and clearly communicate that availability. Use assignment responses, discussion responses, and one-on-one conversations as opportunities to mentor students, connecting class materials and activities to each student's personal and professional goals.
Create spaces that encourage students to ask questions, raise their own conversation topics, and have non-academic conversations.	Use open-ended discussion questions that allow students to present their own ideas, such as asking them to apply concepts from the reading to a situation in their own education or workplace. Include discussion spaces where students are regularly encouraged to ask questions about anything in the course. Provide opportunities for students to "shoot the breeze" in video chats or have "off topic" online discussions; give credit for discussion postings that promote social interaction and humor. Let students see your personality shine through in your discussion prompts and responses. Share information about personal hobbies, pets, or kids that will be relatable for students.
Structure discussion prompts and due dates to promote interaction among classmates.	Give students credit for responding to other student discussion posts. Consider moving student discussions to online environments that feel more friendly and personal by nature (for example, social media). For more detailed suggestions, see the appendices on structuring discussion assignments provided by Karen and Rhonda.

The department chair and WPA should pay attention to teacher burnout and stress, especially as teachers move from teaching F2F to online instruction. New online faculty may feel overwhelmed if they feel they have to adopt all these personalization strategies at once. Administrators can encourage faculty to have realistic goals for themselves as they make their classrooms more collaborative and community-focused, especially for first-time online instructors.

The best online courses and programs evolve as faculty and students become more comfortable engaging through digital spaces. The first time a teacher designs or teaches an online course, we recommend that they try one type of interaction that is comfortable for them and do it well. For example, the instructor might be involved in discussion boards, calling students by name, adding and directing conversations, and making announcements that include highlighting good ideas posted by students. In the next semester, the instructor might add small-group synchronous meetings or collaborative writing projects where students learn to use Google Docs (or another cloud-based drafting platform) to write collaboratively.

Just as students need mentoring and encouragement, instructors are more likely to support students if they feel supported. The culture of a department tends to develop top-down. The department chair and the WPA need to regularly talk with instructors about important values, such as student success, not just talk at faculty about the basic requirements for their online classes. They should emphasize sound learning principles rather than specific pedagogies. In other words, they need to speak about the importance of instructor presence while allowing instructors a wide variety of techniques for building presence into their courses. In the appendices to this chapter, Heidi and George describe how our department helped to support online faculty by offering monthly "Tech Jam" workshops that helped voluntary participants develop new skills without drowning them in prescriptive precepts.

Administrators (deans, chairs, and WPAs) need to ensure instructors have adequate resources—both hardware and software. For hybrid and hyflex classes, this will include classroom space that has web cameras—following best practice guidelines that classes be as accessible as possible to as many as possible (the PARS -A element). Administrators should also schedule training sessions in online pedagogy and new technology that go beyond the traditional institutional LMS training.

Finally, instructors will value mentoring students more if their work is recognized in annual evaluations and tenure/promotion decisions. For contingent faculty, encouraging connection and community building can be the center of their reappointment, and successful, student-centered innovation in online learning can be rewarded (Mechenbier, 2015).

We hope that our research will be valuable beyond our department as other departments establish and sustain online classes and programs. Not every instructor will have as much flexibility as we do, and not every student will be as well-versed in online learning as our students tend to be. But implementing any of the above recommendations can help build a strong community and support fully-online students and instructors.

Table 11.4. Taking a personal approach to supporting online faculty

Department chairs and WPAs can support their online writing instructors when they . . .	Practical tips:
Create opportunities for online instructors to interact as a community, both virtually and face-to-face.	Use social media or other online platforms to create group spaces for sharing announcements, accomplishments, birthday greetings, etc. Hold periodic non-mandatory gatherings on campus and/or video meetings for celebrations, professional development, or sharing pedagogy ideas and technology tips (see Appendix C for a detailed example from Heidi and George).
Mentor online faculty to help them develop realistic goals and avoid burnout.	Encourage faculty to develop the personalized aspects of their online courses gradually, rather than taking on too many time-consuming tasks immediately. Suggest that faculty add one new personal or interactive component per semester, giving them time to assess and tweak how each component works for them.
Ensure that faculty have access to resources that support online teaching.	Purchase hardware and software that support effective online teaching and personalization of online courses, including webcams. Provide technology training beyond simply learning the features of the LMS. Discuss sound learning principles and core department values, including student success.
Ensure that the work of online course development and instruction is recognized and rewarded.	Recognize online course development and instruction in annual evaluations and tenure/promotion decisions. Include effective online community building as a criterion for reappointing contingent faculty. Establish awards to recognize and celebrate innovations in personalized online instruction.

Final Thoughts and Application

If you take only three things away from this chapter, they are

- Students engage better in authentic experiences, so design for authenticity.
- Any writing is writing, so design for writing.
- Acts of personal connection facilitate acts of personal connection, so design for personal connection.

Design for authenticity: Design intentionally so that your online writing course feels authentic. Be on the lookout for opportunities to identify any gaps students may have in their writing (see Appendix B) Provide personalized, authentic feedback that facilitates personal connection (-P). Be accessible to your students (-A) and respond quickly and thoughtfully to their concerns (-R). And remember—none of this happens by magic—it takes strategy (-S).

Design for writing: In the online writing class students need to be engaged. Create opportunities for students to write beyond major assignments. Keep in mind that any writing is writing. You can, for example, set up engaging, low-stakes discussions that facilitate instructor-student and student-student personal connection (-P). Experiment with other platforms that lend themselves to variation in engagement and multiple modes of engagement. Find one that works for your teaching style (-S). (See Appendix A.)

Design for personal connection: Instructors are people, too—and like students, instructors also want to feel noticed, valued, and supported. Creating personal connection (-P) extends to connections WPAs make with writing instructors. Set an example: Personally connect with instructors and help them personally connect with their writing students. Be accessible to instructors (-A) and responsive to their needs (-R). And now more than ever, create ways to identify instructor burnout and stress (-S). (See Appendix C.)

References

Borgman, J. & McArdle, C. (2019). *Personal, accessible, responsive, strategic: Resources and strategies for online writing instructors.* The WAC Clearinghouse; University Press of Colorado. https://doi.org/10.37514/PRA-B.2019.0322.

Conceição, S. C. O. & Lehman, R. M. (2016). Students' perceptions about online support services: Institutional, instructional, and self-care implications. *International Journal on E-Learning, 15*(4), 433–443.

Glazier, R. & Skurat Harris, H. (n.d.). How teaching with rapport can improve online student success and retention: Data from two empirical studies. [Manuscript submitted for publication].

Greer, M. & Skurat Harris, H. (2018). User-centered design as a foundation for effective online writing instruction. *Computers and Composition, 49*, 14–24.

Mechenbier, M. (2015). Contingent faculty and OWI. In B. L. Hewett & K. E. DePew (Eds.), *Foundational practices of online writing instruction* (pp. 227–249). The WAC Clearinghouse; Parlor Press. https://doi.org/10.37514/PER-B.2015.0650.2.07.

Pacansky-Brock, M. (n.d.). *Humanizing.* Michelle Pacansky-Brock. https://Brocansky.Com/Humanizing.

Ruefman, D. (2016). Return to your source: Aesthetic experience in online writing instruction. In D. Ruefman & A. Scheg (Eds.), *Applied pedagogies: Strategies for online writing instruction* (pp. 3–16). Utah State University Press.

Skurat Harris, H. & Greer, M. (2016). Over, under, or through: Design strategies to supplement the LMS and enhance interaction in online writing courses. *Communication Design Quarterly, 4*(4), 46.

Skurat Harris, H., Melonçon, L., Hewett, B., Mechenbier, M. X. & Martinez, D. (2019). A call for purposeful pedagogy-driven course design in OWI. *Research in*

Online Literacy Education, 2(1). http://www.roleolor.org/a-call-for-purposeful-pedagogy-driven-course-design-in-owi.html.

Skurat Harris, H., Nier-Weber, D. & Borgman, J. (2016). When the distance is not distant: Using minimalist design to maximize interaction in online writing courses and improve faculty professional development. In D. Ruefman & A. Scheg (Eds.), *Applied pedagogies: Strategies for online writing instruction* (pp. 17–36). Utah State University Press.

Warnock, S. (2009). *Teaching writing online: How and why*. National Council of Teachers of English.

Warnock, S. & Gasiewski, D. (2018). *Writing together: Ten weeks teaching and studenting in an online writing course*. National Council of Teachers of English.

Wiggins, G. & McTighe, J. (1998). *Understanding by Design*. Association for Supervision & Curriculum Development.

Appendix A. Karen's Tip for Personal Discussions

Create more conversational, interactive, and personal discussion assignments using social media.

When I first started teaching online, my courses weren't always as interactive as I wanted them to be, partly because I developed a syndrome I now refer to as "discussion board dread."

I spent lots of time each semester trying to brainstorm creative and engaging topics and prompts for my discussion boards, and I began the semester with fresh energy. I was determined that this semester, I would finally keep up with all the discussion postings and make a point of interacting with every student. But invariably, that energy flagged out after the first four weeks, for both me and the students. Posts I meant to answer but hadn't would accumulate to the point that I dreaded the hours it would take to catch up. Students rarely responded to one another's posts. Interaction slowly but surely died out.

We didn't lose energy because the students didn't have interesting things to say, or that they weren't producing good writing. I could tell they put a lot of thought into their lengthy analytical posts. But because students needed so much reading and thinking time, they usually posted their responses late in the week. No one else in the class had time to read and answer: they were busy producing their own posts. When the following week rolled around, we were all ready to shift our attention to the new material; few of us had the energy to go back and look at the previous week's posts, much less write responses. My discussion boards turned into monologues, not the dialogues I'd intended.

I always wished my class discussions could be more like the social media conversations I saw my students having on platforms like Facebook. On Facebook, you could hear their personalities in the way they wrote. There was much more personal writing, even when they addressed intellectual topics, and much less tortured academic prose. There were memes and jokes and pictures of people's dogs. I enjoyed reading Facebook, and I did not enjoy reading my Blackboard discussions. Why couldn't my discussions be more like Facebook?

In summer 2018, I was scheduled to teach a new topics course in Writing for Social Media—and at the same time, I decided there would never be a better time to try moving my discussion boards out of Blackboard and onto Facebook. I created a private group for the Writing for Social Media class so that students could have a space that was ours alone; they didn't have to interact with the rest of Facebook at all if they didn't want to. Our class made the leap to social media that semester, and the quality of our discussions improved dramatically.

Personal interaction increased immediately, both between me and the students and among the students themselves. Part of the improvement could be attributed to the platform amenities: students got automatic notifications when someone posted to the group, as well as notifications when someone responded to their postings. (This was a big improvement over Blackboard, where people had to remember to subscribe to threads to get email notifications when someone posted.) Facebook's mobile app was also more user friendly than Blackboard's, so moving discussions to Facebook made it easier for students to participate from their phones.

But improved interaction also came from the different conventions of social media. Student postings became less formal, less lengthy, and more conversational. The students and I used a broader range of personalization strategies in our posts, including photos, gifs, memes, emojis, videos, and web links—which created that feeling of variation and multimodality that students in our focus groups noted was important to engagement. Facebook made it easy for us to react to each other's posts, which gave us a way to show we had seen each other right away, even if we didn't post a comment right away—a reinforcing strategy that made many of us feel more seen and valued. For those of us who had already been active on Facebook recreationally, it made interacting with the class much more convenient. We were already there, and it didn't take much effort to respond, so many of us (myself included) were much more present in the class than we had been in other online classes.

These results were not universal, it should be noted. Students who had never been on social media or who actively didn't like social media did not embrace the class Facebook group with uniform enthusiasm. However, feedback from student evaluations suggested that over 75% of students who commented on the experience preferred interacting on Facebook to interacting on Blackboard; they felt it did increase their sense of personalization and connection in the course. I have since shifted all of my online discussions to private Facebook groups with no regrets.

Appendix B. Rhonda's Tip for Helping Students Get to Know Their Writer-Selves

Encourage stimulating, low-stakes, student-student discussions where the instructor is a participant, not a moderator.

Warnock (2009) argues that "[w]e, as writing teachers, are highly empowered in this environment to help channel the natural writing that students are doing anyway into a class experience" (p. 180). I will add to this that, to get better at writing, students need to be writing (and, of course, reading). The discussion forum lends itself well to both activities. As soon as students step into the discussion forum space, they are writing and they are reading (and, in the process, narrowing any gaps they may have in habit or skill in this area).

The main point I'm making here runs parallel with a pet peeve I once had with discussion forum participation; that I put a lot of work into a post and no one reads it—or, at the very least, they only scan-read it. Warnock has a low-stakes exercise that I feel gives respect to the hard work and thought students put into their posts: He has students look back at their peer's posts from previous weeks and has them pick one out to critique. I think this is a brilliant idea: It creates a kind of extrinsic motivator for students to put more into their posts—knowing their classmates will be looking back at and scrutinizing them.

I believe for a student to grow as a writer, reader, and critical thinker, the organization of the self must be challenged and this is precisely what happens in a discussion forum. It's easy to convince ourselves we have this or that figured out when sitting in safe, unchallenging environments of our own design—environments that we control. It is when we step out and into a space where the ideas of others have equal merit that we learn and grow. The discussion forum is an idea platform for students to get practice writing, test their ideas, and learn to have productive conversations with peers.

Appendix C. Heidi's Tip for Fostering Community and Conversation about Online Learning at Faculty "Tech Jam" Fridays

Bring instructors together to build community and learn best practices for online teaching.

We are fortunate to have small, tech-savvy faculty in our department. When I was hired in 2013, one of my favorite activities was to talk about online classes, to see other's classes, and to share teaching tips with those colleagues.

A few years ago, our department began hosting "Tech Jam" Fridays. Once a month, typically before our monthly departmental meeting, some of the faculty brought their lunches and met in our Critical Rhetorics and User Experience (CRUX) lab. The Tech Jams were designed as informal spaces where Rhetoric and Writing faculty could demonstrate different tools they used in their online classrooms. Generally, one person who was pre-selected would start off with a particular tip or tool that s/he used. Then, the floor was open to anyone else who wanted to share. The meetings were not restricted to full-time faculty, anyone who taught in our program could feel free to attend and share, and our remote instructors would come in via Zoom to present their ideas and listen to others.

Tech Jams were very popular for a few reasons. First, they were offered at a time that was generally convenient and easy to remember. Department meetings were held in the same space, so faculty could come, camp out for a few hours, and talk to each other.

Second, they were largely unstructured. A person would start the jam, and then others would join in and share as they wanted. It was less like a formal tech training and more a tech sharing—less like Catholic Mass and more like a Quaker meeting. No one was required to share, but some people shared every meeting.

Third, the ideas shared helped to make our program more consistent and streamlined. If someone demonstrated a new way to use Google Sheets to grade discussion forums, others could do the same and the students would have a consistent experience across classes without top-down mandates.

Tech Jams were opportunities to learn new ways to teach online that were proven to work with our students. However, perhaps more importantly, these sessions developed community and connection with colleagues who were mostly teaching online and didn't see each other as often as they would in traditional faculty positions. Tech Jams allowed us to maintain our departmental community and become better online teachers.

Appendix D. Screenshots of an Intentionally Designed Online Class

This course, taught by Heidi Skurat Harris at UALR, demonstrates how to create student-friendly course spaces. Figure 11.1 shows the course schedule, which includes links to the course website in the first column, links to readings and materials in the second column, a list of assignments (numbered by week and assignment number) in the third column, and the due dates in the final column. Students can—and have—used this schedule as the primary way of navigating their online course. However, they can also navigate the course by clicking links to course materials sent in the weekly welcome announcement (via Gmail), through Blackboard, or through the course webpage.

Figure 11.2 is the landing page for the course shown in Figure 11.1. It showcases the use of color and white spacing for emphasis, includes a photo of the instructor, and gives directions for getting started with the class, including a welcome video that walks students through the features of the course and helps them understand how the course navigation works.

University of Arkansas at Little Rock --- RHET 7373: Writing for Online Instruction
Spring 2018 Course Schedule

This schedule is subject to change at the professor's discretion. **All work is due by 11:59 p.m. CST on the deadlines indicated (unless otherwise specified)**. Note: Central Time (US) is the working time zone for the class.

Readings MUST be read in order to effectively complete discussions and assignments.

Week	Readings/Learning Materials	Assignments	Due Dates
Introductory Materials	Syllabus Course Website Major Project Assignment Description	0.1 View Welcome Video 0.2 Review Syllabus and Course Schedule 0.3 Review Major Project Assignment Description	ASAP
Week One: January 16 - 21 Learning to Read and Write	Week One Workbook: Introduction to Writing for Online Instruction (Your personal copy shared with you through your UALR email account. Create a folder in your Google Drive where you can save this document for easy reference.)	1.1 Discussion Board: Learning to Read and Write	1.1 initial post by **Friday, January 19.** Discussion concludes Sunday, January 21.
		1.2 Workbook Activities: Week One	1.2 complete by **Sunday, January 21**. You do not need to share this with Dr. Harris because she will already have access to your copy.
		1.3 OWI Self-Assessment Grid	1.3 complete by **Sunday, January 21.**

Figure 11.1. Example of a weekly schedule in a writing for online instruction course.

Figure 11.2. Homepage of Google Site for the writing for online instruction course.

Chapter 12. Using PARS to Build a Community of Practice for Hybrid Writing Instructors

Lyra Hilliard
University of Maryland

Abstract: In this chapter, I apply the PARS (Personal, Accessible, Responsive, and Strategic) approach to the hybrid faculty cohort that I facilitate for my writing program. This program responds to and extends OWI Principle 7: "Writing Program Administrators (WPAs) for OWI programs and their online writing teachers should receive appropriate OWI-focused training, professional development, and assessment for evaluation and promotion purposes" (CCCC OWI 2013). Below, I explain how my writing program started offering hybrid courses and how I started coordinating them. I follow this with four sections devoted to each component of the PARS approach. Each section concludes with recommendations for readers in similar positions in their own institutions.

Keywords: writing program administration, online writing instruction, training, support, hybrid

In 2011, my first-year writing program was selected to participate in the University of Maryland (UMD) Provost's Blended Learning Initiative. This highly-publicized initiative was responding to a demand that the campus "pursue an aggressive strategy to promote and introduce blended learning or learning innovations through the use of technology" (University, 2011). UMD's definition of blended courses was broad—"A blended (also referred to as a hybrid) course requires a combination of both face-to-face and online interactions, and involves a rich, collaborative environment embedded with a learning space containing a variety of information sources" (University of Maryland, 2011)—with the understanding that blended courses would replace a portion of in-person class time with online instruction.[1] To prepare for our hybrid redesign of English 101, we attended a two-day hybrid learning retreat with faculty from the other programs. We learned about active learning in large lecture classes. We learned about video lectures. We learned nothing about hybrid learning in small, discussion-based writing classes like ours.

---

1. Because the field of OWI uses "hybrid" instead of "blended," I use hybrid for the remainder of this chapter.

For context, the University of Maryland's Academic Writing Program (AWP) serves approximately 3,800 students each academic year. We offer about 110, 19-seat sections of English 101 each semester that are taught by a mix of contract NTT faculty (about 65%) and graduate students (35%). Our pilot team was led by the AWP director, one of the assistant AWP directors, and three NTT faculty, including myself. Throughout the fall, we worked together to redesign English 101 for the hybrid format in which half of the "seat time" in TTH sections was moved online (we would soon add MWF sections in which one third of the seat time was moved online). While we did our best to design innovative, pedagogically-sound courses, we were hamstrung by a relative dearth in the literature at the time on hybrid writing classes. Our lack of experience in online teaching, either as practitioners or researchers, left us ill-prepared for many of the challenges we encountered in our subsequent pilot semester. As we "trialed and errored" (Borgman, 2016) our way through the following year, we soon faced more challenges: our WPA, who had led our pilot, was replaced by a WPA new to both our institution and to online and hybrid learning. The handful of us still teaching hybrid writing courses were largely working in isolation without opportunities to compare best practices; develop new resources, or mentor new instructors.

In order to sustain the hybrid initiative within our program, we needed someone to lead it. I was nominated to do so and said yes. My primary charges in that first year were to establish core tenets and effective practices of hybrid writing classes and strengthen the community of hybrid writing instructors within our program. Below, I will use the PARS (Personal, Accessible, Responsive, and Strategic) approach to describe how I work with faculty, how I've expanded the hybrid (and online) learning initiative within my writing program, and how you can implement elements of it for your institutional context.

Personal: Building the Community

Identity

I always say that my number one job as an educator is to build a classroom community in which students feel welcome, respected, and supported. The degree to which students are willing to be vulnerable—a necessary criterion to learning—is contingent on fostering a climate of trust (Gitterman, 2008; Neal, 2008). The same goes for instructors: we need a place where we can share what's happening in our classes—including what isn't working—without fear of retribution. So, one of the first things I did was institute more regular meetings for hybrid instructors so we could get together and exchange ideas with each other more frequently. While I didn't have language for it at the time, what I was doing was establishing a community of practice (CoP), which is defined by Lisa Melonçon and Lora Arduser (2015) as a group of people "who share a concern for something they do and learn how to do it better as they interact regularly" (p. 74).

The well-documented loneliness of online teaching (Borgman & McArdle, 2019; Bourelle, 2016; Hewett & Ehmann, 2004; Mechenbier, 2015), is felt in different ways by hybrid instructors. We're still on campus, as instructors are teaching in person once (for T/TH courses) or twice (for MWF courses) a week, so we still occasionally see our colleagues. Yet we do so in an environment that, while not necessarily hostile to online or hybrid writing instruction, isn't necessarily enthusiastic about it, either. The persistent lack of understanding about what hybrid and online writing instruction (H/OWI) is and how beneficial it is to student learning can make H/OWI instructors feel isolated pedagogically and vulnerable professionally (Mechenbier, 2015; Melonçon & Arduser, 2015). This is especially true for contingent faculty who often do not have the experience of being part of a small cohort or learning community that they likely had in graduate school (Borgman & McClure, 2019; Mechenbier, 2015; Penrose, 2012).

Developing a CoP gives instructors a chance to share their success and challenges and work together to solve shared teaching problems (Melonçon & Arduser, 2015; Teagarden, 2018). We're all there to help each other learn—myself included! Second, it gives instructors a sense of institutional belonging. As of the time of this writing, our English Department has 270 instructional faculty in its ranks. It's easy to feel invisible. Having a shared identity with a dozen colleagues dedicated to improving their teaching and who also get to know each other on a personal level goes a long way to helping instructors feel like valuable members of the department (Melonçon, 2017). Everyone needs to be seen—especially instructors whose efforts are otherwise only seen by their students, an audience who may or may not have the ability (or, to be fair, reason) to appreciate the time, effort, and care with which their instructors design and facilitate their learning.

Advocacy

One of the advantages of having an administrator like me who is dedicated to hybrid or online writing instruction (H/OWI) is that I am able to promote my colleagues' many strengths to those in power. I am intimately familiar with my hybrid colleagues' teaching methods because we discuss them in our meetings and also because I observe their classes. I am thus able to highlight their particular areas of expertise to others less familiar with their work. When my WPA mentions, for example, that she wants to plan some breakout sessions on digital writing or peer review at our next professional development day, I name colleagues who have developed particularly successful strategies for teaching their students how to design websites or peer review each other's work in Google Docs. In this way, I demonstrate that my fellow hybrid instructors have a direct hand in shaping and strengthening our writing courses and program (Borgman & McArdle, 2019; Hanson & de los Reyes, 2018; Melonçon, 2017; Melonçon & Arduser, 2015).

Agency

I trust that instructors know what is best for their students and their courses. Each of them, in the words of Melonçon and Arduser (2015), "carries implicit and explicit knowledge about creating courses, crafting assignments, managing the classroom, [and] facilitating classroom discussion and activities" (p. 87), all of which they have to contribute to our ongoing conversations about teaching in new (and familiar) contexts. Instructors in a CoP don't simply receive knowledge about hybrid teaching; they co-construct it (Melonçon & Arduser, 2015).

Because of this, I do not create a standard syllabus or course shell for them to adopt, for I believe that would compromise instructors' agency and impede their ability to cultivate their own hybrid pedagogy (Breuch, 2015; Paull & Snart, 2016; Teagarden, 2018). Instead, instructors in this CoP develop and share their own materials, such as syllabi, assignments, and lesson plans, by adding them to the LMS site I created for this CoP. Many of these materials are annotated to help other instructors adapt them for their own courses. Encouraging faculty to learn from each other and develop their own courses is part of what makes this a sustainable CoP.

This is not to say that I outright oppose course shells and standard syllabi; they work well in other programs and contexts, especially with instructors new to teaching online writing courses (Bourelle, 2016; Rodrigo & Ramírez, 2017) or in programs without dedicated, ongoing mentoring for H/OWI instructors (Borgman 2016). In my case, however, all instructors—including graduate instructors—teaching hybrid sections of our first-year writing course have taught the course face-to-face for at least a year, so they've already developed their own approach to teaching it.

Creating a standard syllabus or course shell would also undermine my approach to building this cohort-based CoP. While I provide formal training for new instructors, which I explain in the next section, my job isn't to tell my colleagues what to do. Rather, my job is to introduce my colleagues to some theory and effective practices, show them how to create interactive learning environments in both online and face-to-face classes, be a friendly source of support, and, most importantly, create spaces for them to come together as a learning community, one in which we all learn with and from each other (Melonçon & Arduser, 2015; Teagarden, 2018).

Takeaways for Personal Administration

- Put people first. This is about your instructors, not you! Listen to them. Ask them what they need and want. Identify what they don't want. Support them without smothering them. Just show up.
- Identify professional development opportunities for your instructors.

If you can't identify them, create them (more on this below). Provide opportunities for them without overburdening them. And then ask your instructors if they want to do whatever it is you've found, e.g., lead a workshop, create a video tutorial, etc. They may leap at the chance to do so; alternatively, they may not be able to take anything else on at this time. And that's okay.
- Trust your colleagues. Most instructors I know are dedicated to their students and passionate about their work. Trust that they'll figure it out. Give your colleagues room to experiment and flounder, for those stumbles nearly always precede a triumphant teaching breakthrough. And then provide them plenty of opportunities to share what they're up to so that you can learn from them, too.
- Be mindful of your positionality. Regardless of how much you design your faculty CoP to be egalitarian, if you have an administrative title, you enjoy a privilege that your colleagues do not. Accept this humbly. And then use your privilege to advocate for your instructors every chance you can.

Accessible: Designing the Training

I'll start this section by pointing out how the hybrid courses in my program are inaccessible to instructors: they can be taught only by those who have been trained to teach them. I was adamant that instructors needed mentoring before they started teaching hybrid, which meant that I needed to build a mentoring structure that went beyond regular meetings. I had to provide access to evidence-based H/OWI pedagogy to those who lacked the resources (e.g., time) to do so on their own. In other words: I needed a training program. It took me three years to design and build customized H/OWI teacher training for our writing program, and it took several iterations for me to become satisfied with all of the modules and activities. Yet even its initial runs were helpful to faculty who were new to hybrid writing instruction. Something is better than nothing, even if it isn't perfect!

And that's the point: despite the fact that we've been teaching writing online for over twenty years (Harrington et al., 2000), most instructors still haven't been a student in an online, let alone a hybrid, course. If an instructor hasn't been an online or hybrid student, how will they know what works—and why? For hybrid courses in particular, how will they figure out how to integrate the online and onsite environments? (Snart, 2015). How will they resist the "course and a half" temptation? (McGee & Reis, 2012). How will they reconcile the problematic binary that assigns social, active learning to F2F environments and independent, reflective learning to online environments, a recommendation that curiously neglects to consider the countless ways in which students can be and are quite social online? (Hilliard & Stewart, 2019).

To address these needs, I developed a three-part, six-week training program. Instructors work in all three learning environments available to them as hybrid instructors: asynchronous online, synchronous online, and face-to-face. This design responds to both what my colleagues specifically asked for and to the scholarship that has long called for OWI teacher training that focuses on pedagogy, not merely technology (Bourelle, 2016; CCCC OWI Position Statement, 2013; Cook 2007; Griffin & Minter, 2013; Hewett & Ehmann, 2004; Rodrigo & Ramírez, 2017; Snart, 2015).

Part 1: Asynchronous Modules & Activities

Instructors are added as students to a course space in our LMS that I created for this training. There, they find the training modules and activities along with sample syllabi, assignments, and activities from current and former AWP instructors. Instructors proceed through the modules as a cohort, just like their students will in their own hybrid classes. Instructors interact with each other (and me) through asynchronous online discussion boards, Google Docs, Voicethread, hypothes.is, and other platforms so that they have experience working with these tools from a student's perspective (Cook, 2007; Hewett, 2015). Here's the overview in the LMS for the August 2018 cohort:

> **August 2018 Cohort Guide**
>
> Welcome to Blended 101!
>
> This ELMS site is grand central for resources related to blended and online teaching, tutorials on some of the more commonly used technologies, and the required online development modules. These modules are designed to help you redesign your 101 course for the blended format. The modules don't cover everything one could possibly learn about blended teaching; rather, they are primarily focused on course redesign, organization, and integrating the online and face-to-face environments.
>
> There are six modules of varying intensities. The first one involves one short page to read and a wiki entry to write. Others, like Modules 3 and 4, are more extensive. I recommend getting through Modules 1 and 2 quickly so that you can get to the more exciting (and time-consuming) ones.
>
> Much of what I'm asking you to do is similar to what you likely do a few weeks prior to every semester: reevaluate your syllabus, revise what isn't working, incorporate new lessons/assignments/activities, etc. The difference, of course, is that a significant part of your teaching is now going to happen online, and you need to figure out how to do that. That's what these modules are for.

Each module has an associated activity that you can complete as soon as you want to get started. Each activity has a due date so that I can provide feedback on your work. The WebEx and on-campus workshops will build on what you learn (and complete!) in these modules.

If at any time you have any questions, please do not hesitate to contact me!

Training Modules	Related Due Dates
Module 1: Blended Training Modules Overview	F, 8/3
Module 2: Learner-centered Teaching	F, 8/3
Module 3: Course (re)Design	W, 8/8
Module 4: Course Structure and Modules-based Organization	F, 8/10
Module 5: Integrated Design for Blended Environments	F, 8/17
Module 5A: Synchronous Teaching	F, 8/17
Module 6: Learning Activities and Lesson Plans	F, 8/24

Figure 12.1. List of training modules and activity due dates.

Part 2: Synchronous Online Meetings

One of the most exciting (or intimidating) elements of our hybrid writing classes is that, for certain classes (those on a T/TH schedule), the online class day and time is locked into students' schedules just like their face-to-face classes. This means that instructors teaching T/TH hybrid writing classes can elect to hold their online classes synchronously via web conferencing should they choose to do so. I piloted this strategy of holding alternating synchronous and asynchronous online classes back in 2012 and have been doing it ever since. I deeply appreciate the ability to bring students online at the same time for certain lessons that include hands-on practice, e.g., learning how to use the library databases, or for activities that benefit from live student-student interaction, e.g., writing a text collaboratively in Google Docs.

As we are well aware, of course, teaching via video conferencing is not easy! It requires an entirely different approach to teaching and learning than those we've developed for face-to-face or asynchronous online teaching. Prior to March 2020, only a handful of my colleagues taught this way with any degree of regularity. It's resource-intensive. It's exhausting. It's intimidating. For many instructors, it's downright terrifying.

Therefore, I require all of my instructors to attend at least one live WebEx or Zoom workshop as part of the hybrid teacher training so that everyone can experience what it's like to interact with peers in an actual synchronous online class, as opposed to passively watching a live webinar (which is what many folks [used to] think of when they thought of synchronous online platforms). I hold 1:1 synchronous online meetings with new instructors to help them learn how to use the technology, and I then give all instructors the opportunity to teach for about 10–15 minutes with the rest of us as their students so that they can figure things out before going live in their own classes (Bourelle, 2016; Grover et al., 2017).

Part 3: Face-to-Face: Digital Pedagogy Day

During one of our early cohort meetings, one of my colleagues said that "we need a full day to talk about all of these ideas and experiment with different tools." I agreed, and we've been doing it twice a year ever since. These "Digital Pedagogy Days" bring all new and experienced hybrid instructors together. New and experienced instructors form mentoring pairs or groups, and experienced instructors get the opportunity to share effective practices from their own classes. Here's an example schedule:

Agenda

Time	Topic	Lead	Time	Topic	Lead
9:00	Icebreaker; Trust & Agency	Lyra	12:25	Increasing Feedback not Workload	Amber
9:30	Maintaining Community	Ellena	12:45	Working w/ UTAs	Lyra
10:10	Peer Review	Adam	12:55	Break	
10:50	Break		1:05	Alternative Assignments	Sayema
11:00	Managing Small Assignments	Lyra	1:30	Mentor Teams	Lyra
11:50	Lunch		1:45	Semester Support/ Wrap-up	Lyra

Figure 12.2. Sample digital pedagogy day schedule.

Having colleagues lead some of the sessions and workshops helps me so that I'm not leading every moment of this five-hour day; more importantly, it helps underscore the fact that I'm not the only person to turn to for advice. I certainly don't expect everyone to teach the way that I do! All of us teach differently, and all of us become better teachers when we have opportunities to teach and learn from each other (Borgman & McArdle, 2019; Bourelle, 2016; Teagarden, 2018).

Takeaways for Accessible Administration

- Put people first. Protect your instructors by reminding your administration how challenging hybrid and online teaching is. This does two things: 1) it protects and promotes your current H/OWI colleagues as expert-practitioners who should be recognized and 2) it helps build the argument for mandatory H/OWI teacher training.

- Make H/OWI training a prerequisite to teaching H/OWI courses. Easier said than done, I know. But if there's even a 1% chance that you can make this happen within, say, five years, do it. Use the CCCC OWI Principles and Effective Practices of OWI (especially Principle #7) to make your case.
- Determine the core things H/OWI instructors need to know. Listen to your colleagues. Figure out what they fear the most about H/OWI teaching before they do it and what they struggle with the most while they do it. Then design your training accordingly.
- Identify existing resources. If you have a campus center for teaching excellence, they may not offer HOWI-specific workshops or support. But they may well have some workshops in backward course design planning and designing accessible LMS sites. You can also look to professional organizations like OLC and GSOLE for webinars and workshops. Figure out what's accessible to you and your instructors before designing everything from scratch.
- Make your teacher training feasible, applicable, and relevant
- Provide instructors with enough theory so that they know that your training is evidence-based without overburdening them by making them read a million articles.
- If you want instructors to produce deliverables, make them things that they can turn around and use in their upcoming courses (e.g., welcome videos, activity prompts).
- Revise the training sequence. And then update it every semester. Keep it fresh!
- Make an online resource hub for your program for instructors to share their syllabi, assignments, and lesson plans. Beg your colleagues to contribute their materials so that new instructors have plenty of examples to pore over.
- Do everything in your power to secure funding for instructors to take the training. And I mean everything. Write recommendation reports. Meet every semester with your Chair. Meet with campus leaders. Be the squeaky wheel. When after six years of making this argument you are told that your institution is philosophically opposed to funding professional development and that's final, tell your colleagues to their faces. And then work on a Plan B, such as formalizing your training into a H/OWI certificate program.

Responsive: Asking for—And Acting on!—Feedback

The H/OWI training and mentoring I provide works because I built the community first—the ongoing mentoring—and then moved backwards to create the formal training for new hybrid instructors. And I did that only after years of listening to my colleagues, listening to our students, listening to my administration, and finding (!) and listening to established and emerging OWI scholars.

Listening to Faculty

Throughout all of its iterations, the hybrid faculty cohort has always functioned as a CoP. Some instructors are part of the cohort each semester and have been for years; others are new. Some instructors attend every meeting I plan; others only attend a few. And that's okay. While I would love to see everyone at every meeting, that's neither feasible nor fair to expect of anyone. This cohort-based model only works if participants find it valuable. And that's something I learned early on and learned how to accommodate over the years.

If you want your overworked and underpaid colleagues to come to meetings on a regular basis, give them a good reason to do so. Some instructors like coming to meetings to simply have the chance to talk with one another about teaching for an hour. I'm one of them. Well, let's be clear: I'm one of them once I'm in the room. Prior to walking (or logging) into the room, I can be as annoyed as anyone else about having *one more meeting* on my calendar! But once I'm in there, I'm happy to be there. I always get something out of it.

Some instructors are more inclined to attend meetings only if there's something new to discuss or concrete to do. At least one of our meetings each semester has this sort of exigence: the one towards the end, when we start planning the upcoming Digital Pedagogy Day. We've also experimented with grading norming sessions and discussions about an article I've shared. After doing a few of these, I got feedback that having to do any extra work on top of everything else people were juggling was simply too much. Yet about a year later, I got some requests for more topical meetings. I ended up combining the two functions into one (packed!) meeting, which worked for that particular cohort in that particular semester. I asked a few instructors to prepare 20-minute presentations on topics that we wanted to follow up on from the most recent Digital Pedagogy Day, like face-to-face Classroom Assessment Techniques (CATs) and activities in Google Docs, and then we used the remainder of the hour for an open discussion.

Listening to Students

I have been administering end-of-semester surveys to all hybrid students in our writing program for as long as I've held my position. That amounts to roughly 2,000 students who have weighed in on what is and isn't working for them in our hybrid classes. From the very beginning, the vast majority of students (85–90%) reported that if they were to do it all over again, they would register for a hybrid version of the course. That was good news. Students also gave us helpful insight into what wasn't working: chiefly, design and organization problems, especially in the early semesters. Learning that gave me the opportunity to focus on these issues in our mentoring meetings over the next year, devote time to it on our biannual Digital Pedagogy Days, and, eventually, create two separate modules on it in the self-paced training sequence. Because I now have years of end-of-semester surveys to analyze, I have been able to track the effectiveness of these interventions and shift my attention to new issues as they've come up. For example, once we had a better handle on course design and organization, I was able to focus more closely on exactly what students were doing in their online classes, which led me to recommend more interactive online classwork for both synchronous and asynchronous online days (Hilliard & Stewart, 2019).

Takeaways for Responsive Administration

- Put people first. Your instructors' collective bandwidth for meetings will change from semester to semester, even when the group members stay largely the same. Check in with them often and adjust as necessary.
- Make it easy for your instructors to come to these meetings. Set your meeting schedule at the top of the semester so that everyone can add the meetings to their calendars well in advance. If you have more than about six instructors, be prepared to hold two meetings per month to accommodate everyone's schedules.
- Survey your students every semester. Design the survey in such a way that you're getting feedback on you and your program, not your instructors. Use the results to inform your programmatic goals over the upcoming year.
- Share survey results with your instructors. Your colleagues are every bit as invested in what students have to say about your hybrid classes, even in the aggregate, as you are. Discuss this feedback as a group to refine your short-term programmatic goals.

Strategic: Planning for the Long Term

When we created my online WPA, or "OWPA" (Borgman, 2016) role, I was asked to write a formal summary of needs and job description for the position. This proved to be one of the most powerful exercises I could have taken, for it allowed me to establish not only what we needed but to envision where we could go. In creating that document, I framed the success of our hybrid FYC classes in terms of student success and campus impact. I was bold, arguing that we had an opportunity to become a model for hybrid learning, both on campus and for writing programs in other universities.

Part of my job description included "research best practices for technology-mediated teaching" to ensure that our hybrid writing course design was grounded in the literature on hybrid and online writing instruction. If I hadn't written that into my job description, I would not have been able to devote as much time as I have on my own research and professional development. I took countless Sloan-C (now OLC) workshops through my institution's membership, took two courses on distance learning through my institution's online sister school, and participated in several webinars on online teaching. I also took myself to conferences to meet OWI scholars before I started presenting at them.

This self-imposed mission to learn everything I could about hybrid and online teaching more broadly and H/OWI more specifically gave me the theoretical background I needed to build customized training for hybrid writing instruction (and, a couple of years later, a second sequence for online writing instruction). When I give feedback on instructors' activities in the modules, lead workshops, and give advice in mentoring meetings, I'm not just drawing from personal classroom experience, as valuable as that may be (Melonçon & Arduser, 2015). I am also drawing from the "highly specialized skillset" that Borgman (2016) argues is needed for anyone in charge of H/OWI courses, one with an "awareness of OWI theory and practice, training in OWI, experience teaching in OWI contexts, OWI course design experience, [and] an ability to create and maintain a support system for OWI faculty" (p. 205).

Perhaps most importantly, I continue to teach at least one course every semester so that I can continue to lead by example and ensure that I am able to apply the latest OWI research and recommended practices in my own classes before encouraging my colleagues to do the same (Borgman & McArdle, 2019; CCCC OWI, 2013, Principle 7 Rationale). My administrative duties have expanded over the past few years, but I have been adamant about retaining my faculty status instead of becoming a full-time administrator. I am a teacher, first and foremost. That's where my heart is.

Takeaways for Strategic Administration

- Put people first. Specifically, start with students first. Frame everything you want to do in terms of student learning and success. No one will argue with you on that fundamental mission.
- Dream big. If you had all the resources and time in the world, what would you want to build? What do instructors need? What do students need? What does your department need? Design that future so that you know what you're working towards at all times.
- Work smart. Break that vision into actionable steps for the short, mid, and long-term. Write it out every semester. Update it annually. This will keep you on track.
- Be collegial. Cultivate relationships with people in the department, across campus, and in professional networks (like the OWI Community!).

- Recognize your limitations. You're one person. You want to do all the things. You also want to do them well and stay sane while doing so. Accept that you'll never accomplish everything you wanted to at the beginning of the year. That's okay. Really. It is.
- Leverage your strengths. The above tip notwithstanding, as an experienced H/OWI instructor and administrator, you have a unique skill set that is invaluable to your institution. Seize every opportunity you can to advocate for your instructors, your students, and for the field—and community—of OWI.

Final Thoughts and Application

As I've outlined above, the PARS approach can help guide you as you create your own H/OWI community of practice, one that focuses on building community (Personal), designing training (Accessible), asking for—and acting on—feedback (Responsive), and planning for the long term (Strategic). While Strategic falls at the end of the acronym, it really comes first: it will remind you why your work matters. Looking back at my proposal for my OWPA job description, I realize that I was never simply making an argument for increased H/OWI support. I was making the case for dedicated English- and Writing Studies-specific pedagogical support. I was making the case for a culture of teaching excellence as a department, regardless of course type or delivery format. I was making the case for fostering a culture of critical digital pedagogy across the entire department (and beyond!), one that recognizes that the success of our students is inextricably linked with ongoing faculty mentoring and support.

References

Borgman, J. C. (2016). The online writing program administrator (OWPA): Maintaining a brand in the age of MOOCS. In E. Monske & K. Blair (Eds), *Handbook of research on writing and composing in the age of MOOCs* (pp. 188–201). IGI Global. https://doi.org/10.4018/978-1-5225-1718-4.ch012.

Borgman, J. & McClure, C. I. (2019). The ultimate balancing act: Contingent online teaching and Ph.D. coursework. *College Composition and Communication, 71*(1), A3-A8.

Borgman, J. C. & McArdle, C. (2019). *Personal, accessible, responsive, strategic: Resources and strategies for online writing instructors.* The WAC Clearinghouse; University Press of Colorado. https://doi.org/10.37514/PRA-B.2019.0322.

Breuch, L. K. (2015). Faculty preparation for OWI. In B. Hewett & K. DePew (Eds), *Foundational practices of online writing instruction* (349–387). The WAC Clearinghouse; Parlor Press. https://doi.org/10.37514/PER-B.2015.0650.2.11.

Bourelle, T. (2016). Preparing graduate students to teach online: Theoretical and pedagogical practices. *Writing Program Administration, 40*(1), 90–113.

Cook, K. C. (2007) Immersion in a digital pool: Training prospective online instructors in online environments. *Technical Communication Quarterly, 16*(1), 55–82. https://doi.org/10.1080/10572250709336577.

Conference on College Composition and Communication Committee for Best Practices in Online Writing Instruction. (2013). A position statement of principles and example effective practices for online writing instruction (OWI). https://ncte.org/statement/owiprinciples/.

Dolan, V. (2011). The isolation of online adjunct faculty and its impact on their performance. *International Review of Research in Open and Distributed Learning, 12*(2), 62–77. https://doi.org/10.19173/irrodl.v12i2.793.

Gitterman, A. (2008). Collaborative learning and teaching. *The Writing Center Journal, 28*(2), 60–71.

Griffin, J. & Minter, D. (2013). The rise of the online writing classroom: Reflecting on the material conditions of college composition teaching. *College Composition and Communication, 65*(1)140–161.

Grover, S. D., Cook, K. C., Harris, H. S. & DePew, K. D. (2017). Immersion, reflection, failure: teaching graduate students to teach writing online. *Technical Communication Quarterly, 26*(3), 242–255. https://doi.org/10.1080/10572252.2017.1339524.

Harrington, S., Rickly, R. & Day, M. (2000). *The online writing classroom.* Hampton.

Hewett, B. L. (2015). Grounding principles of OWI. In B. Hewett & K. DePew (Eds.), *Foundational practices of online writing instruction* (pp. 33–92). The WAC Clearinghouse; Parlor Press. https://doi.org/10.37514/PER-B.2015.0650.2.01.

Hewett, B. & Ehmann, C. (2004). *Preparing educators for online writing instruction: Principles and processes.* National Council of Teachers of English.

Hilliard, L. P. & Stewart, M. K. (2019). Time well spent: Creating a community of inquiry in blended first-year writing courses. *The Internet and Higher Education, 41*, 11–24. https://doi.org/10.1016/j.iheduc.2018.11.002.

McGee, P. & Reis, A. (2012). Blended course design: A synthesis of best practices. *Journal of Asynchronous Learning Networks, 16*(4), 7–22.

Mechenbier, M. (2015). Contingent faculty and OWI. In B. Hewett & K. DePew (Eds.), *Foundational practices of online writing instruction* (pp. 227–249). The WAC Clearinghouse; Parlor Press. https://doi.org/10.37514/PER-B.2015.0650.2.07.

Melonçon, L. (2017). Contingent faculty, online writing instruction, and professional development in technical and professional communication. *Technical Communication Quarterly, 26*(3), 256–272. https://doi.org/10.1080/10572252.2017.1339489.

Melonçon, L. & Arduser, L. (2013). Communities of practice approach: A new model for online course development and sustainability. In K. C. Cook & K. Grant-Davie (Eds.), *Online education 2.0: evolving, adapting, and reinventing online technical communication* (pp. 73–90). Baywood.

Neal, M. (2008). Look who's talking: Discourse analysis, discussion, and initiation-response-evaluation patterns in the college classroom. *Teaching English in the Two-Year College, 35*(3), 272–281.

Paull, J. N. & Snart, J. A. (2016). *Making hybrids work: An institutional framework for blending online and face to-face instruction in higher education.* National Council of Teachers of English.

Penrose, A. M. (2012). Professional identity in a contingent-labor profession: Expertise, autonomy, community in composition teaching. *WPA: Writing Program Administration, 35*(2), 108–126.

Rodrigo, R. & Ramírez, C. D. (2017). Balancing institutional demands with effective practice: A lesson in curricular and professional development. *Technical Communication Quarterly, 26*(3), 314–328. https://doi.org/10.1080/10572252.2017.1339529.

Snart, J. (2015). Hybrid and fully online OWI. In B. Hewett & K. DePew (Eds.), *Foundational Practices of Online Writing Instruction* (93–127). The WAC Clearinghouse; Parlor Press. https://doi.org/10.37514/PER-B.2015.0650.2.02.

Teagarden, A. (2018). Academic freedom, contingency, and the place of professional learning communities. *Teaching English in the Two-Year College, 45*(4), A13-A21.

University of Maryland (2011). *Blended Learning Committee Report.* https://provost.it-prod-webhosting.aws.umd.edu/announcements/Blended_Learning_Report_Final.pdf.

Chapter 13. Preparing Graduate Students and Contingent Faculty for Online Writing Instruction: A Responsive and Strategic Approach to Designing Professional Development Opportunities

N. Claire Jackson and Andrea R. Olinger
UNIVERSITY OF LOUISVILLE

Abstract: This chapter describes a responsive and strategic approach to the development of an asynchronous online mini-course in online writing instruction (OWI) for both graduate TAs and contingent faculty in the University of Louisville's Composition Program. Demonstrating the importance of responding to local contexts, the authors reflect on the conditions shaping their own course design and, based on their experience, provide suggestions for WPAs who are in similar positions. This reflection is organized around seven key questions for WPAs to consider as they design their own professional development in OWI.

Keywords: adjunct, contingent faculty, course design, graduate students, OWI, part-time faculty, professional development, teaching assistants, teacher training, writing program administration

Instructors are often assigned to teach online writing courses (OWC) with little to no preparation for teaching writing in an online environment (Borgman & McArdle, 2019; Bourelle, 2016; Cargile Cook, 2007; Grover et al., 2017). What's more, many writing programs prepare to increase OWC offerings without developing the necessary resources to make sure they are successful (Borgman, 2016). When our English Department moved to increase its OWC offerings, we (Claire, an assistant director of the Composition Program, and Andrea, the director of the Composition Program) wanted to avoid these pitfalls. We thus began developing online writing instruction (OWI) training for the composition instructors—both contingent faculty and graduate students—who would teach our OWCs.

Borgman and McArdle (2019) argue that designing professional development opportunities for online writing instructors is a necessary part of being a responsive administrator, and this includes evaluating what resources one's university already has and what resources the WPA will need to develop (pp. 63–65). Moreover, they advise that WPAs be strategic in their development of these professional development resources in order to both replicate the quality of their face-to-face courses in an online environment and to support their instructors in adapting their teaching practices for OWCs (2019, pp. 81–82). In this chapter, we will describe how our own OWI professional development program at the University of Louisville was developed to be both responsive and strategic to our program's context and our instructors' needs.

Scholarship on OWI has provided a number of models for instructor preparation, including mentoring programs (Jaramillo-Santoy & Cano-Monreal, 2013), graduate seminars or graduate seminars with in-service mentoring and workshops (e.g., Bourelle, 2016; Cargile Cook, 2007; Grover et al., 2017), the requirement to teach "master courses" for those new to online teaching (Rodrigo & Ramirez, 2017), and communities of practice (Cohn et al., 2016; Melonçon, 2017; Melonçon & Arduser, 2013; Stewart et al., 2016). In the Composition Program at the University of Louisville, the constraints of our graduate curriculum prevented us from creating a new graduate course, but we also realized it was important to ensure that our part-time faculty could access the training, as we recognized that they should not be expected to devote significant time to developing online courses on their own (Babb, 2016). While Bourelle (2016) suggests the development of OWI workshops when graduate seminars are not a feasible option, we also felt it was necessary to offer more than a handful of isolated workshops, yet we had limited resources to support instructors to lead mentoring groups for new OWC instructors. Therefore, we decided to offer a six-week, non-credit-bearing mini-course which we officially piloted in the spring of 2020.

We offer this overview to explain how the choices we made in the development of the course were both strategic and responsive approaches to the OWI training given our institutional context and the needs of our instructors. In narrating our course design process, we hope to provide WPAs guidance for designing OWI professional development on their own campuses.

Institutional Context

University of Louisville (UofL) is a public R1 university with around 22,000 students, of whom over 16,000 are undergraduates (University of Louisville, n.d.). It offers over 40 fully online programs—including 12 bachelor's degrees—and many more online courses within departments. Departments at UofL were incentivized to add distance education courses because they received 45% of the income from student tuition, which is more than they received for face-to-face classes.[1] The English Department, under which the Composition Program falls, offered

---

1. This budget model changed in Fall 2020: departments now receive equal amounts back from distance education and face-to-face courses.

its first online course over ten years ago and recently began expanding its selection beyond a few each semester. Over Fall 2019 and Spring 2020, English offered its highest number yet, at 31 online courses: 10 of the 188 first-year composition courses (5.3%), nine of the 23 upper-level composition courses (39%), and 11 of the 93 literature, creative writing, and linguistics courses (11.8%). These courses were taught by instructors of all ranks: four Ph.D. students, seven non-tenure-track faculty, and seven tenured or tenure-track faculty.

Composition courses are taught by approximately 28 non-tenure-track instructors (most of whom are part-time instructors who may teach up to four classes per semester), approximately 23 M.A. and Ph.D. students, and a handful of tenured and tenure-track faculty. Our first-year composition courses (English 101, 102, and 105) have specific learning outcomes, but instructors do not have to follow set curricula (with the exception of M.A. and Ph.D. students in their first year of teaching here, who follow a common syllabus). In general, instructors have a great deal of flexibility in what and how they teach as long as they adhere to those learning outcomes.

Prior to our development of the OWI mini-course that we will describe, composition instructors who wished to teach online were required to complete a short course in online teaching offered by our university's Center for Teaching and Learning (CTL). This course was primarily focused on acquainting instructors from across campus with the learning management software, a common approach of much training for teaching online (Borgman, 2017; Cargile Cook, 2005), and thus provided no instruction in the specifics of teaching *writing* online (Hewett & Ehmann, 2004). Since our department sought to increase the number of OWCs offered, as WPAs we knew we needed a different strategy to prepare our instructors for OWI.

Guiding Questions for Professional Development Design

Because the specific details of our course were responsive to the needs of our instructors and our institutional context, in addition to providing an outline of our OWI course, we have identified the following questions that WPAs should consider as they design responsive and strategic professional development opportunities on their own campuses.

What Should the Curriculum Cover?

The majority of our conversations centered around what we wanted our participants to know about OWI and be able to do in their OWCs. While we envisioned this course as replacing the CTL's option for instructors in the Composition Program, our responsive and strategic design included recognizing the value of the resources already available (Borgman & McArdle, 2019). Claire thus met with a representative from the CTL and the WPA who preceded Andrea to make decisions about what content from the CTL course on online pedagogy to borrow (something that the CTL rep was encouraging). While Claire had felt like the course was mostly just an overview of how to use Blackboard (our LMS) and provided her few resources to think about the specifics of OWI, we recognized that instructors can benefit from instruction in the specific technology they will be teaching with (Hewett & Ehmann, 2004) and that some of that material would still be necessary. We therefore borrowed several modules from our CTL which focused on how to use the LMS or use other technologies, such as VoiceThread, and integrate them into the LMS. Borrowing some of this content saved us additional labor and prevented us from reinventing material we already had access to.

Having decided the length of our course would be six weeks, we sketched the following outline for the course (see Appendix for each week's plan of work and corresponding reading assignments):

Week	Topic	Writing assignments
1	Online Teaching Best Practices	Discussion board posts reflecting on teaching philosophy and teacherly ethos
2	Blackboard Basics	Welcome video; prompt for a major assignment that integrates a digital tool (excluding discussion boards)
3	Developing and Scaffolding Writing Assignments	Mini-unit to provide scaffolding for the major assignment prompt from Week 2
4	Online Discussions	Discussion board guidelines and a discussion prompt
5	Response to Writing	Peer review of syllabus draft; collaborative wiki with peers about benefits and drawbacks of your peer review modality
6	Accessibility in Online Writing Courses	Discussion board post about how the mini-course could be more accessible; exercise to make a Word document accessible; revised syllabus; VoiceThread walkthrough of how you adapted it for the online context; end-of-course survey

We saw a clear order to the content of weeks one through five. We knew we needed to cover accessibility, as it is the overarching principle of OWI (CCCC OWI Committee, 2013) and a necessary piece of OWI training (Breuch, 2015), hence its focus in Week 6. Weeks 1–5 were meant to work through the necessary information instructors needed to design an OWC in order before we addressed this concern. After participants engaged with some theories about OWI and learned the specifics of our LMS in Weeks 1 and 2, Weeks 3 and 4 gave them practice participating in and facilitating online discussions, as well as developing writing assignments specifically for online students, which are skills that are not intuitive and require practice (Bourelle, 2016; Breuch, 2015; Warnock, 2009).

We realized after the pilot, through feedback from the participants, that they wished issues of accessibility had come first, so the accessible principles we discussed could inform their assignment design. As we read this feedback, we recognized the importance of this suggestion, as beginning with accessibility would allow it to be the foundation of the work participants do in designing their course, while saving it for the end made it appear as something extra or optional (see also Coombs, 2010; Oswal, 2015). We advise WPAs to not follow our mistake and either begin with accessibility or weave it into the content throughout.

Because many instructors are skeptical of, or even resistant to, online courses, a key element to the design of our course was working with instructors to recognize their core values as writing teachers and consider how those values could work within, or even be enhanced by, an OWC, as suggested by Breuch's (2015) training exercise on migration (pp. 356–357), which we adapted for Week 1 of the course (see also Warnock, 2009). Not only was this approach necessary for highlighting that OWI does not require "starting from scratch" (Breuch, 2015, p. 353), but it was also responsive to our institutional context in which instructors have a large amount of freedom within the classroom. That is, as mentioned above, instructors are not following a unified curriculum, but are encouraged to develop their own approaches to meeting our student learning outcomes.

It was also important to us that participants have tangible take-aways from the course; thus, assignments typically asked instructors to create their own assignment prompts or discussion board guidelines. The final assignment included a syllabus for an online course with an audio walk-through using VoiceThread (voicethread.com) of how their decisions were informed by the theories and principles of OWI we had been discussing (Grover et al., 2017). We felt the audio walk-through was a better option than a traditional written rationale so participants could experience using sound to connect with their audience (Breuch, 2015). We also adapted Breuch's (2015) training exercise on modalities and media (pp. 375–376) for Week 5. In this exercise, participants engaged in a peer review of one another's syllabi using a variety of modes and media. While participants' time constrained the possibilities of the assignment and we could only ask each pair to engage in one type of peer review—ideally, we would have asked each pair to experiment with multiple modes and media—they then engaged in subsequent collaborative writing about the benefits and constraints of each. This allowed them to reflect on uses of different modes and media for peer review, which, Breuch (2015) argues, is more important than the peer review activity itself.

Who Is the Intended Audience?

While this mini-course did develop out of conversations about the need to add OWI preparation to our graduate curriculum (Bourelle, 2016), we also wanted to be responsive to the needs of our part-time faculty (Babb, 2016), as mentioned above. As we will describe below, these different audiences significantly influenced the format of the course. However, the mini-course still primarily appealed to graduate students. Of the 13 people who enrolled in the course in spring 2020, six were Ph.D. students, three were M.A. students, and four were part-time faculty. Two of these part-time faculty members decided within the first couple of weeks they were too busy to complete the course at this time, and another expressed that the amount of reading required was difficult for her to keep up with. This breakdown suggests to us that we still designed the course with graduate student needs in mind and that inclusion of part-time faculty requires a deeper consideration of the amount of content to include, not just the format of the professional development.

Who Should Design It?

Ideally, the person responsible for designing the professional development would be an expert in OWI (Borgman, 2017). When Claire, an Assistant Director of Composition (ADC), was assigned the task of developing this course, she had had no online teaching experience, but she had recently taken our CTL's online pedagogy course as she planned to teach online in Fall 2019, the semester before she would facilitate the mini-course. Andrea was not yet WPA but had recently taught online for the first time and provided Claire with resources on OWI.

We recognize that having an ADC support the WPA in the design of this course is a benefit of our program structure, as many WPAs do not have an assistant or associate director to collaborate with. However, even if WPAs have no other choice but to design the course themselves, we suggest they consider instructors they know who have online pedagogy experience and ways they can consult with (and compensate) these people.

Perhaps the biggest sacrifice we made in our attempts to be responsive to the time constraints of our instructors was the small amount of interaction they had within the course. While they were asked to respond to each other's work a few times throughout the six weeks, they did not engage in the regular discussions we would expect in an online FYW course. Because students may struggle with the high literacy load of online courses (Griffin & Minter, 2013; Warnock, 2009)—which Cargile Cook (2007) noted the instructors in her OWI training also felt—it may have been beneficial for participants to experience this. In reviewing the participants' discussion board guidelines, which was one of the homework assignments, Claire became concerned that many participants had developed discussion board requirements asking for much longer posts than she would ask of FYW students, and she wonders how that might have changed if participants in the mini-course had experienced the high literacy load of weekly discussions.

Who Should Facilitate It? What Should Facilitation Look Like?

While we originally envisioned our course being facilitated or co-facilitated by Andrea, the WPA, we eventually decided Claire, the ADC, should facilitate the course, both so she could benefit from her work developing the course and receive the teaching experience, but also so Andrea could devote more time to other demands as the new WPA. Because the ADC roles are meant to provide graduate students with professional development and administrative experience, we decided that each spring the course would be offered by an ADC, who has already taken the course and taught online at least once, as part of their job duties (which they receive a course release for). Again, we recognize the ability to have this course facilitated by a graduate student is a benefit not all WPAs will have. We also recognize, however, that WPAs, among their many competing concerns, may not be the people on their campus with the most knowledge about OWI. WPAs might consider advocating for faculty with significant OWI experience to lead the course, thus drawing on the strengths of mentorship models (Jaramillo-Santoy & Cano-Monreal, 2013).

While it definitely increases the labor of the facilitator, running the course involves a lot more than just posting content and commenting on written assignments, but also having a social presence in an OWC in order to make the course feel like a community (Borgman & McArdle, 2019; Breuch, 2015; Warnock, 2009). In many ways, having Claire facilitate the course helped significantly, as she knew the majority of the participants well and often engaged in informal discussions about pedagogy with them in their shared office. Borgman and McArdle (2019) encourage instructors to create a responsive strategy for how and when they'll respond to the students in their courses; for Claire, this involved responding to the weekly work participants had done (e.g., discussion board prompts, blog posts) each Friday and sending out a weekly announcement on Friday as well. Major assignments were typically due Sunday nights, and Claire would devote Mondays to reading and responding to them before attending to other tasks in order to provide participants with written feedback quickly.

Claire's prompt responses and dedicated times set aside for the course created a consistent social presence in the course (Breuch, 2015), and, while we recognize the increasing demands on the time of WPAs, we believe such reliable presence is necessary. This may require instituting a limit on how many instructors can take the course at any given time. We did not create a course cap for our pilot, but when 13 instructors enrolled—making the course almost as large as one of our online FYW courses, which are capped at 15—Claire was concerned about how much time facilitation would take. We therefore recommend an enrollment cap be added in the future.

How Long Should It Last? When Should It Be Offered?

While seemingly a simple question, we feel this is an important consideration when designing professional development that is not a graduate seminar. The professional development needs to balance providing a necessary amount of content for instructors to be prepared for OWI while also not overwhelming their already busy schedules.

Our CTL's online pedagogy course lasts eight weeks, but we decided early on that our course should last six weeks based on an estimate about the appropriate length of a one-credit course, which we initially considered as a model (see below). We planned to offer it in the middle of the spring semester so participants did not have to begin the work until after they had settled into the rhythm of the semester but would be finished before the busy-ness of the end of the semester. The timing of the spring semester was also important, as it allowed first-year TAs to take the course after their required writing pedagogy course in the fall. Some participants expressed that they would have preferred to take the course in the summer, when they would have more fluid schedules, but we questioned if it was ethical to ask contingent faculty to participate in work over the summer, when most are not teaching (especially if this is the only OWI training we provide), and, at the moment, summer course releases for ADCs are on hold.

While the six-week time-frame seemed to be appropriate for us, we suggest WPAs consider the following: Where might this fit into the existing curriculum (e.g., after the required pedagogy course? At the same time?)? How much content can you ask them to engage with in a given week? How much time is necessary for them to experience the online environment (Cargile Cook, 2007)? What competing demands will they be responsible for during the time(s) it is offered?

What Could Incentivize Instructors to Take It?

The primary way we encouraged participation in the course was telling instructors it was a requirement if they desired to teach online but had not yet taken the CTL's course or lacked OWI experience.[2] This requirement was easy for us to make, as we had formerly required either the CTL course or OWI experience for instructors who wished to teach online; however, WPAs in programs that do not have such a requirement may face more pushback for instituting such a requirement. We did, however, advertise the course to all composition instructors as useful professional development focused on teaching writing online, as opposed to the more general online pedagogy course our CTL offered. Presumably as a result of this advertising, some instructors who were not expecting to teach online for us in the future (e.g., second-year M.A. students who were graduating) signed up for the course.

Because of our inability to develop a full graduate seminar—our M.A. and Ph.D. program curricula do not have room for another annual pedagogy seminar—we first began envisioning this course as a one-credit course for graduate students because we wanted to ensure they would receive formal recognition for taking the course. However, at the time, our university's budget model prevented graduate students from receiving tuition remission for online courses, and we knew it was necessary to offer the course online to simulate the experiences of a student in an online course (Cargile Cook, 2007). Moreover, we knew even a one-credit course would be inaccessible to the part-time faculty we were trying to be responsive to: they would have to pay for it or, if they qualified for tuition remission, would have to go through an arduous bureaucratic process. We settled on a no-credit course that offered participants a certificate in OWI for completion of

---

2. We waived this requirement during the COVID-19 pandemic.

the course so their professional development could still be formally recognized and something they could include on a CV (Borgman & McArdle, 2019). In the future, we would like to offer each person a detailed congratulatory letter that they can include in their teaching portfolios (Paull & Snart, 2016). While these may not be the only options to provide formal recognition, we do suggest WPAs provide some such formal acknowledgement of the professional development to further incentivize instructors to take the course.

Should It Be Synchronous, Asynchronous, or Hybrid?

Our discussions of the mode for the course primarily focused on the time constraints of our instructors, and we settled on an asynchronous model because Claire, as a graduate student herself, was worried about the extra demands a synchronous course would place on our already overworked graduate students and contingent faculty. While this rationale was certainly responsive to the constraints on our instructors, we believe a more strategic decision-making process would have started with considering the OWI experiences we wanted our instructors to experience and why. That is, we realize that an asynchronous course was the best decision for our instructors because at the time all OWCs were offered in an asynchronous mode and we wanted instructors to experience what their students would experience (Cargile Cook, 2007). Therefore, we recommend that WPAs structure such professional development opportunities to mimic the types of OWCs they currently offer, which might involve moving between different modes so participants can experience the range of OWC experiences on campus, something we are considering if the synchronous and hybrid courses our department added for Fall 2020 in response to the ongoing COVID-19 pandemic remain after the pandemic ends and university life resumes normal operation.

COVID-19 and the Future of Our OWI Professional Development

Before the pandemic began, we had planned to revise and facilitate the mini-course annually. We saw a continued audience for the course because each year always brings at least 10 new M.A. students and a few new Ph.D. students who will be teaching our composition courses for the first time. In addition, although our part-time faculty are a relatively stable group and we do not do much hiring, not all of them participated in the pilot nor had online teaching experience. However, our program's collective OWI experience—like that of all educators around the world—has skyrocketed in a very short time since March 2020.

When the COVID-19 pandemic hit and our university moved to "remote" instruction, Claire created a copy of the mini-course's Blackboard shell without the instructors' work (e.g., discussion board posts) so that other English faculty and composition instructors could poke around the modules at their own pace (Andrea has also given some colleagues in other departments access to these modules, which fill a need because our CTL's programming has not focused on writing in online courses.) Offering not just a facilitated asynchronous course but also, when the pandemic hit, access to the asynchronous modules (sans certificate) has thus allowed us to be more responsive to instructors' needs for immediate help. Claire and some other instructors with OWI experience also offered to work one-on-one with instructors as they moved their courses online. Over the summer, even more instructors asked for access to the modules, which they could then consult as needed as they prepared for their online courses in Fall 2020.

As we write this in August 2020, Andrea and the new ADCs are incorporating the mini-course into our new GTA orientation, which we have expanded to two weeks in order to make room for OWI preparation. We have selected readings and activities from the units on online teaching best practices, accessibility, Blackboard Basics, and online discussions and have made the rest of the weeks' content available as reference material. In addition, during our program-wide orientation before classes start, we will poll our instructors to find out what kind of OWI professional development they would like in the 2020–2021 academic year to further develop their practice. We envision several different possibilities, including a mini-course 2.0 in spring 2021 that assumes previous experience with online teaching, synchronous teaching circles, and peer-to-peer OWC observations. While COVID-19 and our university's changing plans have made it difficult to pinpoint exactly what form our OWI mini-course will take, they have underscored the importance of being strategic in our design as we work to develop resources that are responsive to the specific needs of our instructors.

Final Thoughts and Application

Because our chapter has centered on the need to design professional development opportunities that are responsive to specific institutional contexts, we resist offering prescriptive suggestions to WPAs as we close this chapter. However, we do encourage WPAs to consider the guiding questions we have used to frame our reflection on the development of our OWI mini-course. In summary, these questions are:

- What should the curriculum cover?
- Who is the intended audience?
- Who should design it?
- Who should facilitate it? What should facilitation look like?
- How long should it last? When should it be offered?
- What could incentivize instructors to take it?
- Should it be synchronous, asynchronous, or hybrid?

By starting with these questions and strategically drawing on the resources at their disposal, WPAs can be responsive to the unique needs of their instructors and students.

Lastly, as the "A" in PARS stands for "accessible," we also stress the importance of ensuring OWI professional development begins with attention to accessibility and weaves issues of accessibility throughout the curriculum. Such an approach avoids our mistake of seemingly tacking this vital consideration onto the end of the course and recognizes that accessibility is the overarching principle of OWI (CCCC OWI Committee, 2013).

References

Babb, J. (2016). Reshaping institutional mission: OWI and writing program administration. In E. A. Monske & K. L. Blair (Eds.), *Handbook of research on writing and composing in the age of MOOCs* (pp. 202–215). IGI Global. https://doi.org/10.4018/978-1-5225-1718-4.ch013.

Borgman, J. C. (2016). The online writing program administrator (OWPA): Maintaining a brand in the age of MOOCs. In E. A. Monske & K. L. Blair (Eds.), *Handbook of research on writing and composing in the age of MOOCs* (pp. 188–201). IGI Global. https://doi.org/10.4018/978-1-5225-1718-4.ch012.

Borgman, J. & McArdle, C. (2019). *Personal, accessible, responsive, strategic: Resources and strategies for online writing instructors.* The WAC Clearinghouse; University Press of Colorado. https://doi.org/10.37514/PRA-B.2019.0322.

Bourelle, T. (2016). Preparing graduate students to teach online: Theoretical and pedagogical practices. *Writing Program Administration, 40*(1), 90–113.

Breuch, L.-A. K. (2015). Faculty preparation for OWI. In B. L. Hewett & K. E. DePew (Eds.), *Foundational practices of online writing instruction* (pp. 349–388). The WAC Clearinghouse; Parlor Press. https://doi.org/10.37514/PER-B.2015.0650.2.11.

Cargile Cook, K. (2005). An argument for pedagogy-driven online education. In K. Cargile Cook & K. Grant-Davie (Eds.), *Online education: Global questions, local answers* (pp. 49–66). Baywood.

Cargile Cook, K. (2007). Immersion in a digital pool: Training prospective online instructors in online environments. *Technical Communication Quarterly, 16*(1), 55–82. https://doi.org/10.1080/10572250709336577.

Cohn, J., Stewart, M. K., Theisen, C. H., Comins, D. (2016). Creating online community: A response to the needs of the 21st century faculty development. *Journal of Faculty Development 30*(2), 47–57.

Conference on College Composition and Communication Committee for Effective Practices in Online Writing Instruction. (2013). *A position statement of principles and example effective practices for online writing instruction.* http://www.ncte.org/cccc/resources/positions/owiprinciples.

Coombs, N. (2010). *Making online teaching accessible: Inclusive course design for students with disabilities.* Jossey-Bass.

Grover, S. D., Cargile Cook, K., Harris, H. S. & DePew, K. E. (2017). Immersion, reflection, failure: Teaching graduate students to teach writing online. *Technical Communication Quarterly, 26*(3), 242–255. https://doi.org/10.1080/10572252.2017.1339524.

Hewett, B. L. & Ehmann, C. (2004). *Preparing educators for online writing instruction: Principles and processes*. National Council of Teachers of English.

Jaramillo-Santoy, J. & Cano-Monreal, G. (2013). Training faculty for online instruction: Applying technical communication theory to the design of a mentoring program. In K. C. Cook & K. Grant-Davie (Eds.), *Online education 2.0: Evolving, adapting, and reinventing online technical communication* (pp. 91–112). Baywood.

Melonçon, L. (2017). Contingent faculty, online writing instruction, and professional development in technical and professional communication. *Technical Communication Quarterly*, 26(3), 256–272. https://doi.org/10.1080/10572252.2017.1339489.

Melonçon, L. & Arduser, L. (2013). Communities of practice approach: A new model for online course development and sustainability. In K. Cargile Cook & K. Grant-Davie (Eds.), *Online education 2.0: Evolving, adapting, and reinventing online technical communication* (pp. 73–90). Baywood. https://doi.org/10.2190/OE2C4.

Oswal, S. (2015). Physical and learning disabilities in OWI. In B. L. Hewett & K. E. DePew (Eds.), *Foundational practices of online writing instruction* (pp. 253–289). The WAC Clearinghouse; Parlor Press. https://doi.org/10.37514/PER-B.2015.0650.2.08.

Rodrigo, R. & Ramírez, C. D. (2017). Balancing institutional demands with effective practice: A lesson in curricular and professional development. *Technical Communication Quarterly*, 26(3), 314–328. https://doi.org/10.1080/10572252.2017.1339529.

Stewart, M. K., Cohn, J., Whithaus, C. (2016). Collaborative course design and communities of practice: Strategies for shared course shells in hybrid and online writing instruction. *Transformative Dialogues: Teaching and Learning Journal* 9(1), 1–21. https://journals.kpu.ca/index.php/td/article/view/1081/541.

University of Louisville. (n.d). *Profile; student enrollment (Fall 2019)*. https://louisville.edu/about/profile.

Warnock, S. (2009). *Teaching writing online: How and why*. National Council of Teachers of English.

Appendix: Mini-Course Weekly Curriculum

Below are weekly plans (inspired by Warnock, 2009) for the mini-course. As mentioned above, the following topics were covered:

- Week 1: Online Teaching Best Practices
- Week 2: Blackboard Basics
- Week 3: Developing and Scaffolding Writing Assignments
- Week 4: Online Discussions
- Week 5: Response to Writing
- Week 6: Accessibility in Online Writing Courses

Week 1: February 10 to February 16, 2020

Welcome to the UofL Composition Program's modules for Online Writing Instruction! This first week we will be thinking about best practices in online writing instruction and developing your teacher persona in an online class. It's a little bit of a heavy week, as we are frontloading a fair amount of material here, but you should have a bit of a break next week!

One thing you'll be reviewing this week, included in the list of readings, is the Quality Matters standards for Online Education. While we won't be explicitly working with these standards much in the course, Quality matters is a nationally-recognized organization whose goal is to ensure the quality of online courses, so it's important for you to be aware of their standards as well as the CCCC principles for teaching writing online.

While it's not in the plan below, please keep in mind your final assignment for this course will be to create a syllabus for an online course and, using VoiceThread, walk us all through your syllabus. Be thinking about this assignment as we progress through the course!

What do I do?	What are the specific instructions? Where do I find the work or the assignment?	When is it due? (Eastern Standard Time)
Watch	Watch the example welcome videos from instructors, found below, and pay attention to the differences in their approach and the way they develop their persona	You'll want to watch these videos by Thursday morning so you can get started on the discussion board requirements.
Write	Before you get started working through the readings, respond to both of this week's discussion board prompts* These prompts can be found on the discussion board.	Please make these posts by Thursday night.
Read	Read the following texts: • CCCC Position statement on OWI • The Quality Matters Standards for online courses • Warnock, Scott. "Teaching the OWI Course." Foundational Practices of Online Writing Instruction. Eds. Beth L. Hewett, and Kevin Eric DePew. Fort Collins, Colorado; Anderson, South Carolina: The WAC Clearinghouse; Parlor Press, 2015. 151–81 • Warnock Chapter 5, "The Writing Course Syllabus: What's Different in Online Instruction"	You'll want to have read by Sunday morning so you can complete the next discussion board activity.
Write	Drawing on the readings above, reply to your earlier discussion post about your teaching philosophy. Once again, the prompt can be found on the discussion board.	Post your responses to yourself by Sunday night

* *The first prompt asked participants to reflect on their process creating welcome videos. The second, in which we adapted Breuch's (2015) activity described above, asked the following:*

> *Before completing this week's readings, write a brief 200-word statement in which you articulate guiding principles that are critical to your writing pedagogy in onsite, face-to-face classrooms.*

Examples might include such principles as "student-centered writing pedagogy is critical to the success of a writing class" or "writing process is foregrounded in every assignment."

Instead of replying to this post, please create a new thread in this forum for your post.

After you have completed this week's readings, please write another 200-word statement articulating how teaching writing online can enhance or mesh with your principles. For example, in terms of student-centered writing pedagogy, you might consider ways online technologies could help foster the goal, such as "students can easily share their writing with one another through electronic means on discussion boards or shared websites." Please refer to the readings as you articulate these beliefs. We will be returning to these posts later in the course.

Week 2: February 17 to February 23, 2020

Congratulations on making it through the first week! For this second week, we'll be thinking about the different ways you can use tools in Blackboard for your online course. I know when I taught face-to-face classes, I only used Blackboard minimally, but since it's where almost all of the interactions in your online courses will happen, it's important to be familiar with what it can do beyond the basics you might have already used. As mentioned last week, I think this will be a lighter week, as you won't have any heavy readings—just a few modules to work through and a couple assignments to practice using some of those tools.

What do I do?	What are the specific instructions? Where do I find the work or the assignment?	When is it due? (Eastern Standard Time)
Complete Modules	Complete the modules from Delphi U found below, each addressing a different part of how to use Blackboard in an online course.	No deadline on these modules this week, but you'll want to finish them before the assignments below.
Create Video	Create a video introducing yourself as a student in this online course. This might be a good opportunity for you to practice using the One Button Studio in the DMS to make a video, or using any other video-making tools you might use in your own online courses. Either upload the video into the Panopto folder or post a link in the thread in the Discussion Board. Be thinking about the persona you said you wanted to portray last week.	Please upload your videos by Sunday night.
Write Assignment	Write a prompt for a major assignment for an online writing course that makes use of one of the tools covered in this module (excluding Discussion Boards). The integration of your digital tool should be clear and purposeful. You'll be asked to develop some smaller assignments that scaffold to this assignment next week, so don't worry too much about the scaffolding right now.	Upload your assignment prompt using the assignment tab by Sunday night.

Week 3: February 24 to March 1, 2020

Week 3 is all about developing effective assignments for online writing courses! You'll start with the assignment you developed this past week and think about how you can scaffold it for students, as this will often look different than it would in an in-person class.

What do I do?	What are the specific instructions? Where do I find the work or the assignment?	When is it due? (Eastern Standard Time)
Read	Read the following texts: • Harris, Melonçon, Hewett, Mechenbier, and Martinez, "A Call for Purposeful Pedagogy-driven Course Design in OWI" • Warnock, Chapter 9 "Assignments: Online, Student Texts Drive Them" • Warnock, Chapter 10 "Peer Review" • Hewett, Chapter 14 Writing Readable OWI Assignments	You'll want to have read by Friday morning so you can complete the blog activity.
Watch	Watch the video from Delphi U and the UofL libraries on how the library can provide research assistance for your online courses.	You'll want to have watched this video by Friday morning so you can complete the blog activity.
Write Blog Post	Drawing on the qualities of effective online assignments outlined in the readings above, develop a small unit (3–5 assignments) to provide scaffolding for the major assignment you developed in Week 2. You may also want to revise the assignment prompt from Week 2 in light of the readings above.	Post your mini-units by Friday night.
Provide Feedback	Provide one of your colleagues with brief feedback on their unit, focusing on its appropriateness and effectiveness for an online writing course.	Post this feedback by Sunday night.

Week 4: March 2 to March 15, 2020 (includes Spring Break)

Now that we've developed some assignments, we'll start thinking about discussions. This is, I think, one of the most difficult, but also most rewarding, parts of online courses. We have a few different readings to think about how to use discussions well and the benefits of online discussions, and I've posted the discussion guidelines I currently use in 101. Your main goal this week is to think about how you will utilize discussions in your online courses.

What do I do?	What are the specific instructions? Where do I find the work or the assignment?	When is it due? (Eastern Standard Time)
Read	Read the following texts: • Seward, "Conversation Starters: Orchestrating Asynchronous Discussion to Build Academic Community among First-Year Writers" • Boyd, "Analyzing Students' Perceptions of Their Learning in Online and Hybrid First-Year Composition Courses" • Salisbury, "Enriching Online Discussions with VoiceThread" • Claire's Discussion Board guidelines (borrowed heavily from Scott Warnock)	You'll want to have read by Friday morning so you can complete the discussion board activity.
Read and Write	Develop discussion guidelines for your own online writing class and at least one discussion prompt (if you included a discussion prompt in your scaffolding plans last week, you can use and refine that one) and post those to the discussion board. Respond to your colleague's posts. A more detailed prompt can be found on the discussion board.	You should post your discussion guidelines/prompt by Friday night. Post your response to your peers by Sunday night.
Write	Don't forget your final assignment in this course will be to walk us through a syllabus for an online course! If you have time this week, you might want to do some work on this syllabus.	End of the course, this is just a reminder :)

Week 5: March 16 to March 23, 2020

This week's focus is on feedback! You have a couple of readings that, you may notice, don't always agree on the best practices for feedback in online classes, so you'll always engage in some practice with feedback yourselves. This week will end with a collaborative writing activity reflecting on the feedback process.

What do I do?	What are the specific instructions? Where do I find the work or the assignment?	When is it due? (Eastern Standard Time)
Read	Read the following texts: • Cox, "Promoting Teacher Presence: Strategies for Effective and Efficient Feedback to Student Writing Online." • Hewett, "Providing Readable Instructional Feedback Online" • Alvarez et al., "The Value of Feedback in Improving Collaborative Writing Assignments in An Online Learning Environment" • The intro to this WPA CompPile Research Bibliography on Audio Response	You'll want to have read by Friday morning so you can complete the peer review activity

What do I do?	What are the specific instructions? Where do I find the work or the assignment?	When is it due? (Eastern Standard Time)
Read and Write	In assigned pairs, engage in online peer review using a draft (however complete) of your syllabus for an online course. Each pair will engage in peer review and be assigned one of the following modalities: • Audio-only peer review • Video-conference peer review • Screencast video peer review Specific instructions will be sent to each pair.	Complete the peer review activity by Friday night.
Write Collaboratively	When you have finished the peer review activity above, work with our entire class to create a wiki reflecting on the affordances and constraints of each feedback modality. A more detailed prompt can be found on the wiki.	The wiki should be completed by Sunday night.
Complete Modules	When you have time during the week, you may want to complete the module on the virtual writing center below.	No specific deadline for these modules.

Week 6: March 23 to March 29, 2020

Congratulations on making it to the final week! We're focused on accessibility this week, and despite the fact that we're getting to accessibility last, you should keep in mind that, as you learned in week 1, CCCC's first grounding principle for OWI is inclusivity and accessibility. With that spirit in mind, I'm hoping you can help us think through how to make this course more accessible.

What do I do?	What are the specific instructions? Where do I find the work or the assignment?	When is it due? (Eastern Standard Time)
Read	Read the following texts: • Oswal, "Physical and Learning Disabilities in OWI" • Miller-Cochran, "Multilingual Writers and OWI" • Gos, "Nontraditional Student Access to OWI"	You'll want to have read by Friday morning so you can complete the discussion board activity.
Complete Modules	Complete the modules from Delphi U on accessibility	You'll want to complete these modules by Friday morning so you can complete the discussion board activity.

Write	Please post a response to the discussion board question for this week. While responses to your colleagues are not required, feel free to respond to them as well!	Post your discussion board question by Friday night.
Complete Assignment	Complete the accessibility assignment, in which you reformat a Word Document to meet accessibility guidelines (found below) and upload in the Assignments tab.	This assignment should be uploaded by Sunday night.
Final Assignment	Using VoiceThread (a link is posted below), upload a walk-through of your syllabus for an online course, explaining how this syllabus has been adapted for the online context.	This assignment should be uploaded by Sunday night.

Chapter 14. Online Writing Instructors as Web Designers: Tapping into Existing Expertise

Jason Snart
COLLEGE OF DUPAGE

Abstract: This chapter addresses the professional development challenge of getting online writing instructors to think of themselves as instructional designers and embrace a strategic user experience design mindset. This, for many, can feel like the formidable task of becoming as expert in the field of design as they have already become in the field of writing studies. This chapter suggests one professional development activity whereby participants tap into their existing web design and user experience expertise by simply reflecting on their own common web experience: banking online, shopping, booking travel, paying bills, etc. What makes these experiences either "easy" or "difficult"? And what can we learn from our own web user experience that might be applied to instructional design? Designing online learning experiences with the user/student in mind and from a user centered focus does not mean learning a whole new field from scratch. Most everybody already has a level of expertise in user experience - just not one we always intentionally tap into.

Keywords: user experience, user centered design, professional development, faculty development

In May, 2020, I began a "Basic Design Principles" online training course offered by the Adobe Education Exchange (edex.adobe.com/pd/course/basic-principles-of-design). Module one of that course states it pretty succinctly: "Understanding the fundamentals of good design is important for any educator who wants to communicate with impact" (Adobe Education Exchange, 2020). In the February 2020 volume of College Composition and Communication Wible (2020) argues that "Integrating design thinking methodology into writing courses can help students to develop creative approaches to problem definition and solution development" (p. 399).

Rewind the clock a couple of decades and you can find more or less the same sentiment offered in foundational texts like Blythe's (2001) *Computers and Writing* article, "Designing Online Courses: User-Centered Practices." There he writes, "Teachers who develop Web-based courses must learn to act like designers" (2001, p. 329). More recently we find an entire volume of the journal, *Computers and Composition*, devoted to the importance of effective and intentional course design. The 2018 special volume is entitled "User-Centered Design and Usability in the Composition Classroom." Among the many user-design focused articles in this volume, Harris and Greer (2018) outline the importance of building "a user-experience mindset into the foundation of online writing instruction" (p. 14). And Borgman and Dockter (2018) discuss how online writing instructors can cultivate "user-centered design in their online courses to accommodate all students with varying learning styles" (p. 94).

In short, we might take it as a truism that to teach writing online is unavoidably, to a greater or lesser degree, also to take on the role and responsibility of web designer: the online writing instructor is, *de facto*, the creator of a "user" experience, even if that user is not the corporate user of so much non-higher ed. professional literature on UX and UCD. Rather, the user, for our purposes, is the student.

And yet, for as unavoidable as it might seem that the online writing instructor is both instructor *and* designer, it can be extremely difficult to get instructors to fully embrace that design mindset, likely because so many of us are already highly trained content experts in a particular discipline, no matter what branch of writing studies that may be: rhet/comp, tech comm, composition studies, etc. The thought of having to become an expert, or what we might *perceive* to be an expert, in a wholly separate field can be intimidating to say the least. Scholarship in this area often suggests deferring to instructional designers where matters of course building are concerned. For example, in McBride's (2010) "Leadership in Higher Education: Handling Faculty Resistance to Technology through Strategic Planning," the author states that as institutions develop online learning, any strategic plan "should include instructional designers who can help transform colleges into learning agile organizations" (p. 2). And many institutions rely on online writing course templates, or master shells, that are not designed by those who are actually teaching the classes. But as Skurat Harris et al. (2019) point out, in many, probably most, cases, "the standardized 'one-size-fits-all' course shell is not serving students nor allowing instructors to teach" ("Next Steps for Purposeful Pedagogy-Driven Course Design").

I am not intending to discount the role that instructional designers play in supporting faculty and online course development. But faculty themselves also need to develop a design mindset and take primary responsibility when it comes to designing their courses. That's why we need to tap into online writing instructors' existing design expertise. It does not serve students (or instructors) when all matters of course design are left to instructional designers. Of course, in some cases deferring to or relying on instructional designers might not even be an option: some institutions may not have staff working in this capacity. Thus, design is by necessity falling within the purview of teaching faculty.

So how, and why, do we tap into that instructor expertise? To pick up the golf analogy that provides the framework for Borgman and McArdle's (2019) *Personal, Accessible, Responsive, Strategic: Resources and Strategies for Online Writing Instructors* text: in asking online writing instructors to become strategic, intentional (and competent) web designers, it is like we are inviting somebody who has not played golf before onto the putting green. Here's a putter, we say. "Now putt." Whether or not that person sinks a few putts (maybe some innate athleticism, maybe just luck), there may be no existing knowledge base or skill set from which they are working. They are functioning as complete novices.

My contribution to the present collection is to offer a professional development activity, which might be used as part of a professional development series or even as a stand-alone exercise, that is designed to reveal the *existing expertise* that almost any online writing instructor will have when it comes to design thinking and usability. The activity does not so much teach participants something wholly new. It actually just brings to the surface a degree of expertise they might not otherwise recognize themselves as already having.

So, to return to the golf analogy, there we are on the putting green with our novice golfer, putter in hand. "Now putt," we say again. But this time we encourage our golfer to think of putting like another sport or activity with which they might already be familiar, whatever that may be. Think of putting like tossing a ball to another person. You don't necessarily have to think about every minute action of the hand, wrist, arm, and body as you go through that throwing motion. You just toss the ball in a controlled way. Or maybe putting is a bit like swinging a baseball bat. Of course, you don't wind up and swing for the fences, but you do stand sideways to your target, you square your shoulders, you concentrate and take an athletic stance, and you follow through. Whatever the specifics, we are looking to reveal some level of existing expertise in our golfer that they might not be connecting with the present, new, activity of trying to sink a putt. In other words, we want to reveal that, despite them maybe never having played golf before, they are far from the complete novice that they may otherwise perceive themselves to be.

Design as Strategy

As Borgman and McArdle (2019) argue throughout their book, "design and strategy are everything in the success or failure of online writing courses and we cannot stress [enough] that you need to pay a lot of attention to these things as you put together distance education experiences for your students" (p. 88). The "strategy" referenced in this quotation—and the S (Strategy) in the PARS acronym—emerges as a foundational pillar, supporting the P (Personal), the A (Accessible), and the R (Responsive), for without any strategy in place, instructors, as content experts but also de facto instructional designers, might only create personal, accessible, and/or responsive experiences for their users—students!—largely by coincidence or fluke. (Sinking the putt by luck, to return to the golf metaphor.)

Instead, as Borgman and McArdle (2019) clearly show, effective writing instruction requires a "plan," a repeatable, iterative process of managing content, designing user experiences, and making revisions as necessary. So how do online writing instructors, particularly those new to the field (or looking to update outmoded training), begin to think about strategy? What expertise might they draw up? Where to even start!?

Perhaps first, we simply acknowledge that yes, to take on the mindset of the instructional designer, the web designer, can seem like an especially intimidating task for instructors. But, having acknowledged that, let's also discover how almost everybody has a level of web design expertise that provides at least a place to start thinking strategically about creating effective user experiences for online writing students. The activity outlined here helps to reveal existing web design expertise in a straightforward, even simplistic way. But it is simplistic by design, because the whole point is to alleviate the sense that to become an effective, or strategic, web designer is to embark on a whole new professional trajectory. Yes, there are myriad things to learn about effective design.

So how to acknowledge that we all have some level of expertise—or at least immediate experience—with web design? Let's first recognize that we are almost all frequent web *users*. We are always part of the UX formula, just not usually as designers. Instead, we are people who use the web for a wide variety of tasks—for most of us on a daily basis: we do online banking, we book travel online, we find directions online, and, of course, we shop. These various web-based activities form the basis of the professional development activity that I offer to colleagues as part of my Teaching Composition Online (TCO) course.

The TCO class is a five-week course that I run through my institution's Teaching and Learning Center. It is in-house training open only to my English department colleagues, both full time and adjunct. We meet synchronously for 50 minutes (usually going a bit over that with questions and collegial conversation), once per week, for five weeks, and there is asynchronous work to do each week as well. The "web design" assignment is built to help instructors overcome that intimidating sense that while they have to be strategic content designers, they might have little to no formal training in that area.

The Assignment

The web-design assignment occurs in week one of the TCO course because, as I stress to my students/colleagues, embracing that design mindset is foundational to effective online writing instruction. So, as we are doing basic introductions, we are also considering what it means to be both writing instructors and UX designers.

The unit objectives include the following:

- Understand "online" writing instruction and its relation to hybrid and fully on-site instruction
- Understand user-centered and UX (user experience) principles as applied to course design

To hit that second objective, I ask participants in the TCO course to first consider basic principles of both user-centered design and user experience, which I introduce in a short lecture portion of our meeting and with reference to Wikipedia entries on "User experience" (en.wikipedia.org/wiki/User_experience) and "User centered design" (en.wikipedia.org/wiki/User-centered_design). (These Wikipedia entries are short enough that workshop participants are—hopefully—not overwhelmed. Assigning books and chapters as we get underway would very likely defeat the purpose of alleviating anxiety!)

So, the readings and my mini-lecture at least get some basic design principles in place. And if nothing else they alert participants to these concepts as fields of study that they *could* explore in much greater depth if they chose to do so. Really, though, it is the *application* of UX and UCD principles that proves most beneficial.

Course participants are asked to reflect on two general types of online/web-based experiences they have on a regular basis, just as part of what they do online all the time: one of these activities should be relatively easy and one must be relatively difficult (or "not so easy" as I have it in the assignment and as I will often say during our synchronous discussion as a way of highlighting how relative these terms are). In fact, we consider at length what terms like easy and difficult even mean, given that they *are* so relative.

Here's an excerpt from the assignment text itself. This is really the heart of the activity:

> In light of what you understand about UCD and UX, now consider a few web-based activities you undertake on a fairly regular basis.
>
> Try to identify one that is particularly "easy" (whatever that term means to you) and one that is not particularly "easy."
>
> Build out a new page in your portfolio (titled "Unit 1—UCD and UX" or something similar) and describe the two "easy" and "not so easy" web activities you have identified.
>
> Try to make connections to user-experience and UCD principles from the readings (and/or other course materials, your existing knowledge, etc.)
>
> For example, for the web-activities that you find "not so easy"— are there specific elements of effective UX/UCD missing. Could they be applied to make your web experience "easier"?
>
> You can compose directly in your portfolio or you can work in a Google Doc or Slide deck.
>
> Please make sure to include screenshots showing some aspects of your web activities/experience.

The discussion around what constitutes "easy" or "difficult" is generally quite fruitful, because it reveals the degree to which one's existing knowledge and experience shapes our perception of difficulty or ease. It's almost laughably simplistic to state, but it's a fact of our student-user experience to keep in mind: once you know how to do something, it seems a lot more "easy" than when you don't know how to do something. So, what is easy for one user can be quite difficult for another user. And the user who finds one thing easy (or difficult) will not always find all online tasks equally easy (or difficult). In fact, it is the variability of user experience and expectation that makes the field of UX different from something like user centered design (UCD): what does the user bring to each activity? What are their likely expectations and assumptions?

In general, I try to frame the "easy" v. "difficult" discussion in terms of any given user's *awareness* of the technology required to accomplish a task. The technology in this case is the intermediary between the user and what the user wants to do. So, a pencil is, for most, an "easy" technology. We don't even think of it *as* a piece of technology (it isn't digital, you don't plug it in, it doesn't cost that much). But that's precisely the point: we perceive the pencil as "easy" to use, to accomplish the task of writing something down, because we don't actually think about the pencil as we are using it. It almost disappears from the act of writing.

Of course, for the average five- or six-year-old, the pencil isn't so "easy." Because they are just learning how to hold a pencil and how to write with it, they are acutely aware of it as a "device" for doing something. Consider, for example, that in her early grades my own daughter was learning how to write with pencil and paper at the same time that she was learning to make slideshows in Google Slides. So, for her, for a time at least, pencil and paper and Google Slides were commensurately "easy" or "difficult" technologies.

As we become *more* aware of the technology—the device or tool as intermediary—that is required to accomplish a task, the more likely we are to perceive that technology or task as "difficult." What button do I click? Where is the options menu? What does this icon mean? Why can't I edit what I've already typed? How do I go back?

These are likely familiar questions to anybody who has used the web before because they reflect our experience, probably a frustrating experience if we have to ask these kinds of questions, because all of a sudden we are aware—painfully aware—of the technology that stands between us and the thing we want to do.

Examples

So, the assignment asks participants in the TCO course to reflect on the various activities they do online and to choose an easy and a difficult one (again, we will have already discussed just how complicated those otherwise common terms actually are). Then, once they have chosen their web activities, course participants must articulate, in as much granular detail as possible, exactly what elements of their online experiences made those experiences user-friendly (or not).

Taking that very granular look at how they, as users, experience certain tasks using the web, opens the door to the most important conversation we need to get to about them understanding themselves *as* instructional designers, and thus ready to implement a design approach that is, explicitly, the "S" of PARS: strategic.

In articulating their various user experiences, participants in the course observe very interesting things about the various web interfaces they use. And it is actually from our negative experiences online that we can often learn the most.

Here are some examples and what course participants had to say. One example looked at a utility bill paying site:

> The user experience gets a little wonky due to the user interface.
>
> Perhaps this [zoom in/out] function works on a website, but I'm using a phone and this website is not designed for a phone app . . . the user experience stinks. I need to keep zooming out and zooming in and rotating my phone so that I can see what each box is so that I can fill in the correct information.

Another talks about building in Google Sites:

> I'm used to menu boxes running across the top and left-hand side of a screen. In sites, google.com, they appear along the right.

Here's another one about a bill-pay site:

> Every time I log on, it seems to purposely take me on a tour of all products they have on sale . . . new TV channels, internet plans, etc. Just let me log in and pay my bill already!

And our institutional learning management system is the go-to example for many:

> Blackboard is very hard to navigate. There are so many boxes that I don't use. The language is hard to understand . . . When I am trying to create new content, it feels clunky. When putting in grades, I can never see the assignment when I scroll down and it is so hard to enter grades.

It's actually somewhat therapeutic to share our "difficult" web experiences with one another, since we all struggle with similarly frustrating websites and user interfaces, whether we face an overabundance of information (like advertising) or multiple options when we just want to do a single, straightforward task, or whether it is the frustration of trying to navigate when menus aren't easily findable and when icons represent certain user options but it isn't very clear what the icons actually stand for.

(One of my favorites along these lines is the "web link" icon in Blackboard: a piece of paper and the earth . . . means web link?)

 ## What does this icon even mean??

Figure 14.1. Icon in learning management system.

As we drill down into what actually makes our various web experiences easy, difficult, or somewhere in between, we begin to uncover web design strategies that we can implement in our own course design and teaching. Of course, we acknowledge that unlike other instances of web design, we are constrained by what the LMS allows us to build.

But through working on this assignment, instructors begin to see that, while they might have no formal training in web design *per se*, they do have an existing knowledge base from which to start. To embrace that sense of being both content expert *and* UX designer is hopefully less daunting after my course participants have thought intentionally about their own user experiences.

Final course reflections indicate that participants are well aware of their dual role as instructor-designer. One of our course objectives makes this explicit: "Understand user-centered and UX (user experience) design principles." Here is a sampling of what course participants had to say about this objective:

> For a course to be effective, the framework of the course must take the user experience into focus.

> If something isn't user centered we aren't thinking about what we are including [in our courses] in the right way.

> Students' emotions, attitudes, and perceptions remain central to user centered and user experience design principles. Prior to this course, I never considered how my students were involved in my course design on Blackboard or how they evaluated it.

This series of comments clearly indicates that course participants are thinking from the student perspective. Further, from final course reflections:

> This objective [about UCD and UX] was a good one for me; I always considered my Blackboard to be updated and organized . . . What could be better? This course taught me that it was organized with what made sense in my head. Students want weekly work organized in one space rather than . . . having to jump all over the place.

> A streamlined experience goes such a long way as far as creating an effective learning experience. It should not be a challenge to submit an assignment simply because the dropbox is in a strange place, for example.

Here again we see course participants drawing that clear connection between basic course organization, the student experience, and, perhaps most important, effective learning. Participants also recognized that simplicity in course design was key:

> My big takeaway for user experience is to keep it simple. Students should easily be able to access and receive what you are trying to communicate without technology barriers.

> The focus should be on simplicity for the user . . . If the framework is designed carefully, students can easily move around the site to find readings, videos, or other resources needed for the student to be successful. Confusion puts stress on the student and the student may feel overwhelmed or alienated by not finding the assignment that needs to be completed. Within my framework, I have simplified the left menu to include only the tabs that students need to use.

These are just a few examples of how participants in the Teaching Composition Online course reflected on our course objective that focused on the design mindset. And to get course participants here, early on we completed the existing expertise assignment outlined above.

By emphasizing that course participants actually *already* had substantial knowledge—even expertise—in the field of web design (as a result of being frequent participants in the myriad web-based activities we undertake everyday), we were able to begin that process of applying existing knowledge to course design, and—hopefully—started to overcome the intimidating sense that we, as content experts, skilled at teaching composition, now need to adopt the mindset of the web designer.

As online writing instructors, we are not just moving our "content" (which is the product of our academic expertise) into a digital space; instead, we are thinking strategically about designing a user experience—a student experience—around that content. As Borgman and McArdle reiterate throughout their book, "design and strategy are everything in the success or failure of online writing courses and we cannot stress that you need to pay a lot of attention to these things as you put together distance education experiences for your students" (2019, p. 88).

By recognizing themselves as daily participants in *many* web activities, instructors begin to see that they actually have much more expertise in the field of web design than they might imagine. Borgman and McArdle (2019) begin their chapter in *PARS* on "strategy" by noting that "So much of online instruction is about strategy" (p. 71). One might push that even further: *everything* about online instruction is strategy, if that instruction is to be successful!

Final Thoughts and Application

The activity I present here is admittedly fairly simple, but, as I hope I've shown, it can be highly impactful in terms of getting instructors to think of themselves as designers who already have some degree of design experience.

As a follow up to the Teaching Composition Online sections I have offered for my colleagues, I invited all course participants to be part of a student-focused research project. I created a very basic survey that asked students just one simple question: "In a paragraph or so, please tell me about your overall experience in this class." I didn't want to ask students specifically about ease of course navigation, course design, instructor presence—all foundational principles in the TCO course. Instead, I wanted to know if students themselves offered insights about these, more or less unprompted. The anonymous and ungraded survey was delivered to students, usually as an online class was wrapping up, by those faculty participating in the TCO course follow-up research project. As of this writing we have almost 60 student responses. I cannot realistically provide them all here (and many students mentioned faculty by name, not to mention signed their own names) but I will offer just a few representative comments that I believe speak to effective course design and user-experience:

> My overall experience with my summer class 2020 was great. Blackboard was easy to navigate.
>
> Well-designed modules.
>
> My overall experience in this class was the announcements and the assignments online were well organized and very understandable to follow the directions on black board.
>
> Course material and Professor were easily accessible.
>
> The professor created YouTube videos to show the step by steps which is amazing and very clear.
>
> One touch that I really liked with this class that you included were the weekly unit videos.
>
> The professor did a great job tying everything together into one cohesive course.

I could go on, as there are numerous comments, that speak to the degree to which students recognize, without really being asked, that their instructors have truly considered the class as a web-based experience for students.

Yes, of course I am hand picking the examples. But I am not cooking the books. Of the 60 or so responses at least half mention something about ease of navigation quite specifically. Holistically, the student feedback is almost entirely positive, and when you are getting student feedback like this . . .

> This class had the BEST online setup. It was super easy and comfortable to use. Other teachers REEEAALLy need to take note on this class.

... you "REEEAALLy" must be doing something right!

To wrap up, it's worth noting that I have presented the instructor-as-designer activity as it exists for me, in my local context, as part of a larger professional development series, the Teaching Composition Online course that I run through my Teaching and Learning Center. Again, that is a five-week course with synchronous meetings and a fairly robust asynchronous component. We use our institutional LMS in depth with discussion boards, posted assignments, videos, slideshow and other "lecture" material. There are even grades! (I don't actually "grade" my colleagues except to demonstrate certain ways in which the gradebook can be used . . .) So, the instructor-as-designer activity I present here has the affordance of existing in a well-developed course framework. We have our course objectives guiding the big picture of everything we do, not to mention a final reflection assignment in which all course participants consider, very specifically, our objective about understanding, *and putting into practice*, UX and UCD principles.

Others may not have this kind of existing framework, like a robust professional development course, already in place. Nor will every department be in the position, even if they wanted to, to design and implement a multi-week course. That being said, I believe the activity outlined in this chapter could still be impactful even as a standalone activity. While I have my course participants actually put into writing the details of their various web experiences (good and bad), it may still be effective and eye opening for instructors to simply have the conversation about what they do online, what activities they perceive as easy or not so easy (and why, exactly), and what might that existing level of experience have to teach them about how they design for their users: students. In other words, I don't think the activity described here necessarily needs an elaborate framework to be successful. It could easily happen in a single department meeting.

So now, to return to the golf metaphor, we are sinking the putt because we are building confidence based on existing expertise and experience. We are successful thanks to skill, not just the occasional stroke of good luck!

References

Adobe Education Exchange. (2020). Basic Principles of Design. https://edex.adobe.com/pd/course/basic-principles-of-design/e/workshop/basic-principles-of-design/step/1.

Blythe, S. (2001). Designing online courses: User-centered practices. *Computers and Composition, 18*(4), 329–346. https://doi.org/10.1016/S8755-4615(01)00066-4.

Borgman, J. & Dockter, J. (2018). Considerations of access and design in the online writing classroom. *Computers and Composition, 49*, 94–105. https://doi.org/10.1016/j.compcom.2018.05.001.

Borgman, J. & McArdle, C. (2019). *Personal, accessible, responsive, strategic: Resources and strategies for online writing instructors.* The WAC Clearinghouse; University Press of Colorado. https://doi.org/10.37514/PRA-B.2019.0322.

Greer, M. & Skurat Harris, H. (2018). User-centered design as a foundation for effective online writing instruction. *Computers and Composition, 49,* 14–24. https://doi.org/10.1016/j.compcom.2018.05.006.

McBride, K. (2010). Leadership in higher education: Handling faculty resistance to technology through strategic planning. *Academic Leadership: The Online Journal, 8*(4), https://scholars.fhsu.edu/cgi/viewcontent.cgi?article=1541&context=alj.

Skurat Harris, H., Melonçon, L., Hewett, B. L., Mechenbier, M. X. & Martiniz, D. (2019). A call for purposeful pedagogy-driven course design in OWI. *Research in Online Literacy Education, 2*(1). http://www.roleolor.org/a-call-for-purposeful-pedagogy-driven-course-design-in-owi.html.

User-centered design. (2020, December 13).In Wikipedia. https://en.wikipedia.org/wiki/User-centered_design.

User experience. (2020, December 17). In Wikipedia. https://en.wikipedia.org/wiki/User_experience.

Wible, S. (2020). Using design thinking to teach creative problem solving in writing courses. *College Composition and Communication, 71*(3), 399–425. https://secure.ncte.org/library/NCTEFiles/Resources/Journals/CCC/71-3/564A09EC-FF4D-49E9-B13D-8807DE1D3C9B.pdf.

Chapter 15. PARS for the Course: Using PARS to Teach PARS in an Online Graduate Seminar

Lydia Wilkes
IDAHO STATE UNIVERSITY

Abstract: This chapter contributes to scholarship on preparing graduate teaching assistants through an online graduate seminar to be online writing instructors. In this chapter I detail the use of PARS as both course content and the approach to designing and delivering the course. I briefly describe the institutional context, student demographics, and student attitudes toward online teaching and learning before discussing the use of PARS to design and deliver an online graduate seminar as a model for English graduate students in a traditional English department. I also discuss students' disparate responses to the centrality of PARS as content, design, and delivery, and their uptake of PARS in their remote crisis teaching. I conclude with a missed opportunity for user testing caused by the COVID-19 pandemic and applications of PARS to remote crisis teaching, which is quite different from OWI, even though the two overlap to some degree.

Keywords: graduate students; online pedagogy; teacher preparation; memes

As more and more students access postsecondary education over distance, online writing courses (OWCs), especially first-year writing (FYW) courses, can be barriers or gateways to student learning and success depending on how they are designed and delivered. For over a decade, this reality has prompted more graduate courses in online writing instruction (OWI) to prepare graduate teaching assistants to design and deliver OWCs that act as gateways. Borgman and McArdle (2019) write that PARS "provid[es] a balanced and supported approach that encompasses the theory and practice from decades of previous research [that] will help to develop a new generation of online writing instructors" (p. 5). In this chapter, I discuss my use of PARS in an online graduate seminar as both the course's featured content and the primary approach used to design and deliver it. I begin by briefly describing the institutional context, student demographics, and student attitudes toward online teaching and learning. I then discuss using PARS to design and deliver this asynchronous course and students' disparate responses to the centrality of PARS as content, design, and delivery. I conclude with a missed opportunity for user testing caused by the COVID-19 pandemic and applications of PARS to remote crisis teaching, which is quite different from OWI, as well as a look to a possible future of OWI informed by PARS.

While I'm no golf pro (to take up Borgman and McArdle's metaphor for OWI), as this graduate-level course might suggest, I expect my performance to be PARS for the course every time I teach writing online! Helping graduate student instructors develop their capacity to do the same was my primary goal for the graduate seminar. Specifically, I wanted to model each element of PARS so that students could draw on the seminar as they designed their own online English courses, most of which were first-year writing courses, and made plans to guide their delivery of those courses. I also wanted to help students avoid many of the mistakes I made as a novice online writing instructor when I, like Borgman and McArdle, began teaching writing online more than a decade ago. In their final papers, students reported using PARS as they quickly put together online materials for remote crisis teaching as a result of the COVID-19 pandemic, though they recognized that remote crisis teaching and OWI differ considerably. Despite this disruption, almost all of the students found PARS approachable and readily applicable to designing user-friendly OWCs that support student learning and success. PARS also enabled some students to navigate the move to remote crisis teaching more successfully than they otherwise would have. Part of that new generation of PARS-trained online writing instructors, they learned to teach PARS for the course and expressed confidence in that approach in their final papers. While the long-term effects of the pandemic on higher education are not yet clear, it is abundantly clear that well prepared online writing instructors are more in demand than ever, and that's an undeniably good thing in a precarious higher education job market.

Institutional Context and Student Demographics for Teaching English Online

The institutional context for this sixteen-week graduate course, called Teaching English Online, was an R3 university in the Mountain West that offers an M.A. program, a TESOL certificate, and the state's only Ph.D. program in English Studies. Both programs attract domestic students from the region and the Ph.D. program also attracts international students who reside in-state. The seminar included students from Nigeria, Wales, and Zimbabwe. Also, secondary school teachers often pursue the M.A. to become credentialed to teach dual enrollment sections of FYW; three secondary school teachers were enrolled in the course. The program advertises itself as emphasizing pedagogy to prepare and place teacher-scholars in positions at two-year and small four-year colleges, which it did at a fairly high rate prior to the pandemic. With pedagogy an emphasis throughout the Ph.D., the practical value of a course in online pedagogy appealed to many students and the course filled quickly.

Pedagogical approaches among graduate faculty members ranged widely on a spectrum of teacher-centered and lecture-based to student-centered and activity-based. Half of tenure-track (TT) and all non-tenure-track (NTT) faculty specialized in literary studies. Other TT faculty specialized in linguistics, creative writing, and rhetoric and composition/professional and technical writing with two faculty in each area and both rhet/comp faculty pre-tenure at the time the course was taught—yet another example of English departments subordinating rhetoric, composition, and writing studies to literary studies (Crowley, 1998; Miller, 1979). Echoing faculty, graduate students pursued literary studies at a very high rate. While many graduate students pursued writing pedagogy with equal interest and passion, some strongly preferred teaching literature to teaching writing. That student preference affected course design in that I offered students the opportunity to develop an online course in literary studies. But, like English graduate students everywhere, everyone was keenly aware that they would teach writing at least some of the time in an academic teaching job, so everyone chose to make an online writing course or secondary school equivalent.

Students' teaching assignments during the semester also ranged widely and affected how they participated in the graduate seminar. Of a total fourteen students, eight were teaching face-to-face (F2F) FYW and communication at the university; two were teaching middle school and high school English language arts; and five Ph.D. students had supervised teaching internships in non-writing English courses above the first-year, sometimes in addition to their FYW teaching assignment. (The numbers do not total fourteen because some students fit in two categories, such as those teaching FYW and working on a supervised teaching internship—four students). Two students did not have a teaching assignment due to fellowship or by choice; one of these students expected to return to teaching high school. Only one student was teaching online and did so as part of a supervised internship rather than as the instructor of record. While I took students' co-curricular teaching into account early on, it became *very* important when the COVID-19 pandemic required all teachers to move to remote crisis teaching, a move I discuss later. Before that, though, students spent a great deal of time thinking and writing about OWI and other online English teaching through the lenses of their co-curricular teaching, a practice I modeled by referring often in videos and discussion board responses to my own co-curricular teaching of an online technical writing course.

PARS for the Course: Assessing and Responding to Students' Prior Experiences

The institutional context, student demographics, and student preferences heavily influenced my responsive course design. Having taught most of the students before in a F2F writing pedagogy seminar, I knew that their levels of experience with and attitudes toward online pedagogy and digital technologies varied considerably. I assessed this variation with a pre-semester survey circulated among teachers of technical writing at Purdue University that I modified for this course (with some language retained verbatim). The survey was used before class began and in the first week of class.

Experience and Skills Inventory

1. What is your name?

2. Have you taken a fully online course before? (Yes/No)

3. Have you taught online before? (Yes/No)

4. How many semesters or years have you been teaching? (Short answer)

5. What course(s) have you taught and where did you teach them? (Short answer)

6. On a scale of 1–5, how comfortable are you with learning new digital technologies? (1=Not at all | 5= Highly: I seek out new digital technologies for work or play.)

7. Where do you expect to teach online? ([This university] or another college/university that uses Moodle | A college/university that uses something else (Blackboard, Canvas, D2L, etc. | A high school | I don't know/I'm not sure, but I do expect/hope to teach online in the next few years | I don't expect to teach online in the next few years | Other:)

8. What do you want to learn in this course? (Long answer)

9. Technology Skills. (Multiple choice grid: see Figure 15.1)

10. Any other technologies that you have experience with that might be valuable?[1] (Long answer)

11. What is a technology, program, or skill you would like to learn more about this semester? (Long answer)

12. Is there anything else that your instructor should know about you? (e.g., special skills, you're looking for a job, applying to a Ph.D. program, working full time, disability status, parent or caregiver, etc.) (Long answer)

Though more than three-quarters of students had taken an online class, over 90% had not taught one. Six students expected to teach online in the near future; another six hoped to do so but weren't sure they would; and two did not expect to teach online in the near future. Of course, no one knew at the time that everyone with a teaching assignment would be forced to teach with digital technologies halfway through the semester in response to quarantine, which I address later.

---

1. Students were not required to answer questions 10 or 12.

Technology Skills *

Mark only one oval per row.

	Expert	Proficient	Novice	I don't know what this is	This scares me, please don't make me try it
Moodle	○	○	○	○	○
Google Suite (Docs, Drive, Forms, Sheets, etc.)	○	○	○	○	○
Powerpoint or other presentation software (Google Slides, Keynote, etc.)	○	○	○	○	○
Screen Recorders (Camtasia, Screencast-O-Matic, QuickTime)	○	○	○	○	○
Survey Software (Google Forms, Qualtrics, SurveyMonkey, etc.)	○	○	○	○	○
Team/Project Management Software (Slack, Trello, etc.)	○	○	○	○	○
Video Conferencing (Zoom, Google Hangouts, Skype, etc.)	○	○	○	○	○

Figure 15.1. This multiple-choice grid yielded especially helpful results that affected the design of the midterm technology review assignment.

Results from the multiple-choice Technology Skills grid (see Figure 15.1) were especially revealing with regard to screen recording and video conferencing, two technologies commonly used in online teaching; these results shaped the midterm assignment, a technology review. While nine students had some degree of familiarity with screen recording software (eight novice, one proficient), three indicated not knowing what it was and two indicated fear and unwillingness to try it. Video conferencing fared better with six indicating proficiency, five at the novice level, two not knowing what it was, and one afraid of it. In response, I modified the midterm assignment to require students to use screen recording software to present their review of an educational technology or LMS tool they had not used before, effectively requiring them to learn two new technologies. Always mindful of modeling, especially when some students indicated fear of screen recording, I made a video example showing them my review of a new-to-me LMS tool, which is similar to "How To" genre of short videos Casey made for faculty members as an online WPA (Borgman & McArdle, 2019, pp. 47–48). Some students included gaining proficiency with screen recording as a course goal during the first week of class because they realized (or already knew) that, as Borgman and McArdle discuss at length, videos in which students can see their teacher personalize an online class.

Three distinct groups—novice, accomplished novice, and expert—emerged from survey results. Three self-identified techies filled out the expert end of the spectrum and three self-identified luddites filled out the novice end with the other eight in the middle as accomplished novices with proficiencies related to online instruction. At the extreme ends were one student with minimal computer literacy and one student with a computer science degree. I used these results to calibrate the course to make it accessible (in Borgman and McArdle's [2019] sense of being useful and removing barriers to learning) to students whose pedagogy was oriented toward lecture, who had little experience with digital technologies, and who were skeptical about the efficacy of online teaching and learning. While this was no small feat, such responsiveness is part of teaching PARS for the course.

PARS for the Course: Design and Delivery

Inspired by learning outcomes for a similar course at Old Dominion University, learning outcomes for Teaching English Online emphasized "teaching students how to read and work with the technologies' affordances" (Grover et al., 2017, p. 246). The course's main readings and activities asked students to learn and apply principles of OWI and online literacy instruction (OLI), and learn and apply the PARS approach as they developed their own OWI materials. I divided the course into two halves with the first four learning outcomes tied to the first eight weeks of class and the remaining outcomes to the second eight weeks. The learning outcomes can be found below.

Learning Outcomes for Teaching English Online

By the end of this course, you will be able to:
- Demonstrate awareness of and be conversant in principles of and approaches to online literacy/writing instruction,
- Situate current practices in online literacy/writing instruction within the historical, political, economic, and social contexts of distance education,

- Apply principles of learning to an existing course syllabus,
- Apply the PARS approach to online course design,
- Explore and evaluate learning technologies based on their user friendliness and appropriateness for your students,
- Create a working online course shell or site based on principles and practices of online literacy/writing instruction,
- Evaluate a peer's online course shell or site as part of usability testing, and
- Evaluate and synthesize principles and approaches to online literacy/writing instruction.

The first eight weeks covered students' backgrounds and experiences with online teaching and learning; the principles of OWI/OLI from the CCCC OWI Committee and The Global Society of Online Literacy Educators, respectively, as well as book chapters and articles by OWI scholars; principles of teaching derived from learning science research in *How Learning Works: Seven Research-Based Principles for Smart Teaching* (Ambrose et al., 2010); the history and theory of distance education from *Teaching and Learning at a Distance: Foundations of Distance Education* (Simonson et al., 2015); and, for four weeks, PARS (Borgman & McArdle, 2019). As I discuss below, spending four weeks on PARS was a strategic decision I made in response to students' prior experiences and experiences in the first two weeks of the course. During this time, students revised an existing syllabus using the principles of teaching from Ambrose et al. (2010) and made plans to use the affordances of their LMS to make their course personal, accessible, responsive, and strategic (PARS).

The second half of the course focused on application and practice. It was to begin with the technology review before moving to structured time to build course shells, usability testing of course shells, revision based on feedback, and a final paper on course design choices and plans for delivery vis-à-vis students' most valued principles of online pedagogy for English courses. I discuss later how the COVID-19 pandemic interrupted the course and forced most students to become crisis teachers using online modalities but not, as they realized, online writing or literature teachers. In the rest of this section I show how I used each element of PARS in the course. Memes and cartoons were central to my personalization of the course and illustration of some concepts, and I discuss them across each element.

Personal

In addition to using personalized videos and an instructor profile that Borgman and McArdle (2019) discuss, I used memes and cartoons to make my online course personal. In a genre native to the internet, memes convey the same humor and playfulness I use to make myself seem human in F2F settings. Most memes I use feature animals that capture students' emotional states at different points in the term (responsively and strategically!). For example, I use a pair of memes strategically at the end of the term in every online course I teach: one of a chipmunk stretching its whole body across a rock and reaching forward with the words "Must . . . make it . . . to end of semester" and, below the link to submit the final assignment, a meme of a squirrel reaching for the sky in a power pose with the words "End of the semester!!" Humorous, playful, emotionally resonant memes make me approachable by showing I understand how students feel during especially stressful weeks. These memes express that I'm a human, too, something Borgman and McArdle (2019) emphasize is important to illustrate to students.

Memes can also be used to illustrate concepts and situations important to the course. One funny meme per week or two that visually conveys a concept is, for me, par for the online course. I know I'm playing the game at a high level when memes serve both purposes. I framed the course's Start Here area with a 1993 *New Yorker* cartoon of two dogs in which "On the internet, nobody knows you're a dog" (not shown) and a 2010 meme update using a cat that addresses anonymity and ethos and provides a glimpse of playful internet culture (see Figure 15.2). Another example of using visuals to illustrate concepts appears in the next section on accessible OWI. My playful humor set a tone and a few students played along by sharing their own fun visuals and, later, including visuals on the course sites they built.

While most of these memes came from Google Image searches, I occasionally made them when existing memes did not meet my needs. I used Meme-Generator.com to make two memes that illustrate the need for balance in responsive online writing instruction, which was a concern shared by everyone in the class that I discuss using the memes in the Responsive section of this chapter (see Figure 15.4).

As always, it's important to consider how cultural differences may affect students' online learning experiences. Animal memes do not resonate across some cultures the way they do in the US. For example, treating companion animals like humans is not common in many African countries and likely did not register as funny or relatable to the same degree for the two students from Africa (as one informed me in a different class). This cultural difference becomes a "friction point" that can impede student comprehension or another aspect of learning (Rice & St.Amant, 2018). This friction point in conveying information effectively across cultures points to the importance of carefully considering international audiences (Rice & St.Amant, 2018) and ensuring that one's teaching practices are culturally sensitive (Parrish & Linder-VanBerschot, 2010) and inclusive.

START HERE!

- Video Introduction to the Course
- Course Syllabus
- How This Course Works
- Video Discussion of Assignments
- Experiences and Skills Inventory

Lolcat online course meme written in lolspeak, circa 2010s.

Figure 15.2. The "start here" section is made personal by a meme. Meme created with Cheezburger.com. Used with the permission of Laura Gibbs.

Accessible

Accessibility was the least familiar concept and practice for students and the topic most likely to overwhelm them with technological minutiae. Although Borgman and McArdle (2019) present a user-friendly version of accessibility, the concept challenged many students to think in an unfamiliar way. I responded to this conceptual newness by including a cartoon about user experience (see Figure 15.3). One of only a few visuals depicting humans, the cartoon shows two white adults standing over a white baby's crib and admiring a toy mobile in one panel while the other shows the baby's view of toy animal butts. The meme jokingly reminds designers (teachers) that they often stop when their needs are met and thus fail to meet the needs of their users (students). Having a visual encapsulate a core idea about accessibility and user experience was tremendously helpful to some students, according to their discussions and reflections from the week.

Figure 15.3. A cartoon humorously illustrates user experience.

Though the visual helped students grasp the new concept, some students in the class tended to think in a teacher-centered manner that was often accompanied by ableist assumptions and ignorance about ableism. These teacher-centered students also tended to let their own mastery of writing in certain rhetorical situations (academic ones circumscribed by standardized American English for academic purposes) lead them to forget the uncomfortable feeling of conscious incompetence—knowing that one doesn't know enough in a specific domain to be competent—experienced by novices, such as first-year writing students (Ambrose et al., 2010). Those entrenched in habituated practice struggled to recall academic writing as a challenge (Anson, 2015) and also tended to be entrenched in unacknowledged ableist assumptions. Although these students also found the user experience cartoon helpful, the word "user" became a barrier to learning for them.

In a discussion of different video captioning options, some students expressed antipathy for the word "user," motivated by their humanistic-inspired rejection of any terms that suggested business or consumption. Unfortunately, a few students were bothered enough by the "user" in "user experience" that they rejected the idea of centering user experience. One student also suggested that first-year undergraduates don't know what kind of user experience they need; the student's peers argued against this perspective and advanced student-centered ideas rooted in user experience, UDL, and Disability Studies. The first student softened their stance as a result. I observed more peer teaching and learning on the topic of accessibility than I did on other topics, which suggests restructuring learning activities to include more peer teaching on accessibility.

Since Borgman and McArdle (2019) approach accessibility from a user experience perspective, I also included Oswal (2015) to introduce students to a Disability Studies perspective. I included links to the Universal Design for Learning Guidelines (v.2.2) and the University of Washington's Course Accessibility Checklist as well. Many students found Oswal's necessarily detailed, complex discussion of assistive devices and technologies overwhelming, and some responded that way to the UDL Guidelines, too. In contrast, local information about the university's or school district's accessible technology services and resources was met with relief. Learning about these services and resources, such as options for adding closed captions to videos, equipped students with resources and eased their anxiety about ensuring their online course would be accessible to all learners.

Responsive

One of the most salient lessons students learned came during the first week from Hewett (2014) and was reinforced throughout the semester by other readings and the students' experiences as online students in my class and another online graduate course: OWI is more time-intensive than F2F instruction. Students worried, and rightly so, about balancing this increased time commitment with other demands on their time. Each was a dedicated teacher committed to their students and knew that being responsive could become a trap unless they maintained boundaries and guarded their time. Their response to being responsive manifested very early as concern about time management and led me to make two animal memes for that week to illustrate the conundrum of responsive online teaching (see Figure 15.4). One meme features a black cat typing on a laptop with the words "Responsive online instructor is responsive" while the other features a French bulldog lying tiredly on a deck and warns of burnout: "Responsive online instructor is too responsive." These memes captured students' concerns about time management apropos of responsive online teaching. I also added a short reading on time management and procrastination, two topics that tended to come up together, and examples of time management plans made by other academics and me.

In addition to struggling with time management overall, students also worried about how to balance a writing teacher's obligation to give helpful feedback with a newer teacher's tendency to over-comment and be too available. In other words, they wanted to know how much feedback was enough. Students debated the use of boilerplate comments to recurring issues in their students' writing and developed a plan for responsive—but not *too* responsive—course delivery. Their plans were either weekly schedules that would recur each week or semester schedules that accounted for busier-than-usual weeks or both. For some, making these responsive plans entailed changing their expectations for themselves as writing teachers in order to guard their time as graduate students and then negotiating their sense that they weren't doing enough for their students. The intellectual and emotional labor of being a responsive online teacher weighed on students as they dealt with the tension between their ideals and the realities of OWI.

Week 6 (Feb. 17-23): PARS - Responsive

Readings and Resources

Week 6 video guide

Responsive

Jessie Borgman and Casey McArdle, 2019, "Chapter 3: Resposive," PARS, 51-69.

Time Management

Charlotte Lieberman, 2019, "Why You Procrastinate (It Has Nothing to Do With Self-Control)," The Ne

Time Management Plans/Maps

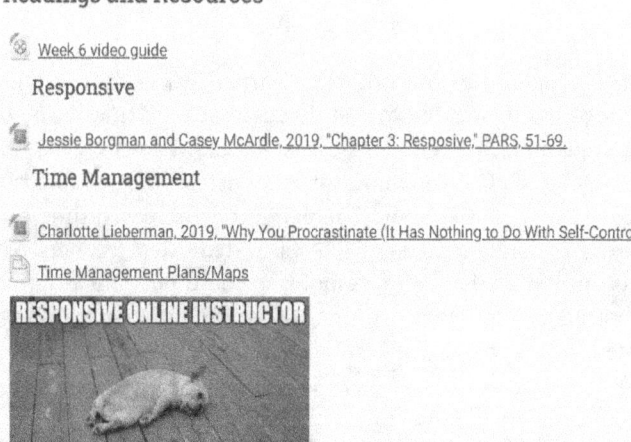

Figure 15.4. Two memes I made to illustrate the balancing act of responsive online teaching.

Strategic

Just as being responsive made intuitive sense to students because they were already responsive teachers, being strategic also made sense and sparked another good discussion. I shared my strategic decision to spend four weeks on PARS, one week on each element, in order to slow the pace of the reading, focus on each element of the approach in depth, increase the number of activities, and allow ample time for reflection. Students appreciated the slower pace but many found themselves in the habit of putting off work for the course until the weekend when it was due—the very habit some of them worried their own students would develop in an online environment.

Since strategic course design must include all students to be sufficiently strategic, teachers must learn about students' demographics, motivations, distractions, and skills, which often vary considerably (Borgman & McArdle, 2019). Like Jessie's students at the community college (Borgman & McArdle, 2019), first-year writing students for whom the graduate students were designing OWCs included adult learners, first-generation college students, military-affiliated students, minoritized BIPOC students, international students, L2/ELL students, refugee students, and students from underfunded rural school districts. These students often have full- or part-time jobs, children, and other caregiving responsibilities, and many are active in their faith communities and reserve weekends for family time. Some students live on a nearby Indian reservation and in other rural areas where they may have to use their smartphones and data plans to access their courses due to a lack of broadband internet infrastructure. In short, they tend to be busy, constrained by limited access to the internet, and in possession of a mix of skill levels, confidence, and anxiety about learning to write in an online environment. Strategically minded instructors work with student feedback that they solicit early and often (Borgman & Dockter, 2018) as part of strategic course design, an approach that creates a positive user experience for students (Borgman & McArdle, 2019).

I modeled one way to solicit student feedback early by sharing an About Me survey that I use in several classes (see below). I did not include the About Me survey in Teaching English Online because most had taken the survey in another course with me and, with other opportunities to share similar information, the survey would have felt redundant. As I noted previously, I changed the midterm technology review after students' answers to the Experience and Skills Inventory. The Technology Skills grid (see Figure 15.1) revealed inexperience with screen recording as well as a desire to learn this technology. Students' early feedback allowed me to make this significant change to a major assignment early in the semester and clearly in response to their feedback.[2]

About Me for English 101

Please answer these questions about yourself. Your answers will be kept private and will be used only to support your success in the course.

1. Your name

2. Your pronouns
    - He/him/his
    - She/her/hers

---

2. The About Me survey is administered during the first week of class.

- They/them/theirs
- Other:

3. Your age
    - 16–24
    - 25–34
    - 35–44
    - 45–54
    - 55–64
    - 65+

4. How many credit hours are you taking this semester?
    - 3–8 hours
    - 9–14 hours
    - 15–17 hours
    - 18 hours or more

5. Do you have a job?
    - Yes, I work part time (20 hours or less)
    - Yes, I work full time (40 hours)
    - Yes, I work beyond full time (40 hours or more)
    - No, I am not employed right now but I am looking for a part-time job this semester
    - No, I am not employed right now but I am looking for a full-time job this semester
    - No, I am not employed right now and I am NOT looking for a job this semester

6. If you have a job, are you allowed to study or do homework at your job?
    - Yes
    - No
    - I don't have a job right now

7. Are you a primary caregiver?
    - Yes, I am a primary caregiver for a child or children, spouse or partner, parent(s), sibling(s), friend(s), grandparent(s), or someone else in my life
    - No, I am not a primary caregiver

8. Which option best describes your access to computer and internet technologies?

- I am using a smartphone as my computer AND for internet access. I have reliable internet access.
- I am using a smartphone as my computer AND for internet access. I do NOT have reliable internet access.
- I am using a personal computer (laptop, tablet, desktop) AND I have reliable internet access at home.
- I have a personal computer BUT my internet access is not reliable at home and I have to go somewhere else for internet access (sometimes or always).
- I am using a library or school computer that I cannot take home AND internet access at a library or school.

9. On a scale of 1–5, how confident are you about reading for college courses? (1= not confident at all | 5 = very confident)

10. On a scale of 1–5, how confident are you about writing for college courses? (1= not confident at all | 5 = very confident)

Thanks for your time. If you have concerns about how your obligations outside of class might affect your ability to succeed in the class, let Dr. Wilkes (email@school.edu) know as soon as you can so she can support you.

The week that students began work on their technology reviews, they were also preparing to host or speak at the annual graduate student conference on campus, an event I neglected to include in my strategy for this course. I polled students during that week about moving the technology review to the next week, to which they agreed with relief, and changed the due date. That Friday, some of us saw each other in person for the first and last times that semester as word of a state quarantine order reached us during the keynote address. At that point, our focus on OWI shifted to a focus on remote teaching during a crisis as students suddenly had a week off from the graduate course, a week they spent preparing to teach remotely.

PARS for the Pandemic

When all instruction became remote in March 2020 due to the COVID-19 pandemic, the seminar became at once more "real" in that students had to use digital technologies to teach remotely and stranger in that they were not able to apply much of what they had just learned in the deliberate, time-intensive way they had learned to apply it. They were engaged in remote crisis teaching, not OWI. Most recognized that strange duality: while they were using digital technologies to deliver instruction, they had not planned their courses as OWCs and did not have enough time to make the switch. One student felt that the seminar was a waste of time because they were not able to apply what they had learned to their teaching; they concluded that online teaching was a matter of trial and error rather than the strategic application of OWI/OLI principles and approaches like PARS. I invited this student to consider in their final paper how they might be engaged in remote crisis teaching rather than OWI, but the student did not do so. However, some students made the transition easily thanks to the PARS approach, and one student who was teaching secondary school shared PARS with her colleagues to their great appreciation. A majority of students expressed gratitude for the seminar and a sense of serendipitous timing. In particular, all students appreciated Barrett-Fox's (2020) plea for instructors to consider how students' radically altered living situations might affect their ability to do academic work and adjust expectations accordingly.

With students suddenly teaching remotely, I scrapped the plan to have them build in an LMS the course they had been designing. Instead, I counted the digitally mediated teaching they did for the rest of the semester in lieu of that course. It's easy to see how one student felt like nothing they learned was applicable: I counted remote crisis teaching as OWI even though the two differ considerably. However, most students understood this difference, and everyone who was teaching appreciated this responsive, strategic adjustment to the course's final assignment. The two students not teaching as well as one student preparing a course shell for the summer completed a pared-down version of the original assignment, including basic user testing and revision (though I dropped the readings meant to guide this work).

While the first seven weeks of this course were on par, the rest were chaotic and tremendously challenging. But a majority of students felt somewhat prepared to take on the challenge of digitally mediated teaching, recognizing that they would have been even less prepared without the course. A few students even excelled as remote teachers! With OWI all the more salient in a pandemic mitigated by physically distancing, the PARS course may not have been as on par as anyone expected, but it was ultimately a valuable learning experience that all students will draw upon in their future online teaching. Even students initially resistant to the notion that "we're all online writing instructors" (Borgman & McArdle, 2019, p. 3) found a way into online teaching, with the golf metaphor serving as the door for some of them. Without the PARS approach, I doubt the course would have been as successful as it was in preparing students to teach writing online.

Final Thoughts and Application

As I write this conclusion, most of the students from Teaching English Online are preparing to teach synchronous, asynchronous, or hyflex FYW OWCs in fall 2020. Having devoted time and attention to learning the PARS approach and applying it to their course design, they are equipped to teach PARS for the course during a fall semester defined by uncertainty. As personal online writing instructors, their instructor presence will say "I'm a human!" to students who want human connections with their teachers. Their OWCs will be more accessible to all students, and those who internalized Borgman and McArdle's (2019) expansive version of accessibility will be better prepared to work with students during a semester likely to contain personal traumas related to the pandemic. Responding to their students within a set of established expectations will help them maintain the human connections they created by being personal. Being strategic in their course design will be a significant challenge in light of uncertainty, but soliciting feedback early and often will help them craft strategic responses to situations as they arise.

While it is not possible to tell how the pandemic will transform higher education, 2020 is poised to be another watershed moment for online education. A generation of online writing instructors trained in the PARS approach could positively affect retention and persistence rates in OWCs by "produc[ing] experiences that exceed the learning potential of face-to-face interaction!" (Hart-Davidson, 2019, p. 96). And these instructors will likely to be more competitive, especially as they amass experience, if they seek teaching jobs in a precarious academic job market. PARS for the course could become PARS for the career!

For busy educators, this list closes the chapter by summarizing key observations and ideas for application.

- The PARS approach worked well as both course content and the basis of course design and delivery in a seminar for graduate students at M.A. and Ph.D. levels who had a range of experience with and attitudes toward OWI.
- This broad applicability suggests that PARS would work well as featured content in graduate courses aimed at many graduate student populations, from secondary school educators pursuing an M.A. part-time to Ph.D. students preparing for an academic career.
- Graduate students' previous experiences as undergraduates in online courses across the curriculum and co-curricular teaching played important roles in how they perceived the PARS approach. Teachers using this chapter to prepare a graduate course or professional development series should allow ample opportunities for participants to reflect on past experiences and co-curricular teaching.
- Peer teaching and learning are especially valuable with concepts like accessibility that may not be familiar to participants.
- The notions of being responsive and strategic in teaching made intuitive sense to everyone who had teaching experience, including those teaching for the first time.

References

Ambrose, S. A., Bridges, M. W., DiPietro, M., Lovett, M. C. & Norman, M. K. (2010). *How learning works: Seven research-based principles for smart teaching.* Jossey-Bass.

Anson, C. (2015). Habituated practice can lead to entrenchment. In L. K. Adler-Kassner & E. Wardle (Eds.), *Naming What We Know: Threshold Concepts of Writing Studies* (pp. 77–78). Utah State University Press.

Barrett-Fox, R. (2020, March 12). *Please do a bad job of putting your courses online.* Any good thing. https://anygoodthing.com/2020/03/12/please-do-a-bad-job-of-putting-your-courses-online/.

Borgman, J. & Dockter, J. (2018). Considerations of access and design in the online writing classroom. *Computers and Composition, 49*, 94–105.

Borgman, J. & McArdle, C. (2019). *Personal, accessible, responsive, strategic: resources and strategies for online writing instructors.* The WAC Clearinghouse; University Press of Colorado. https://doi.org/10.37514/PRA-B.2019.0322.

Conference on College Composition and Communication Committee for Best Practices in Online Writing Instruction. (2014). A position statement of principles and example effective practices for online writing instruction (OWI). http://www.ncte.org/cccc/resources/positions/owiprinciples.

Crowley, S. (1998). *Composition in the University: Historical and polemical Essays.* University of Pittsburgh Press.

Global Society of Online Literacy Educators (GSOLE). (2020). *Online literacy instruction principles and tenets.* https://www.glosole.org/oli-principles.html.

Grover, S. D., Cargile Cook, K., Skurat Harris, H. & DePew, K. E. (2017). Immersion, reflection, failure: Teaching graduate students to teach writing online. *Technical Communication Quarterly, 26*(3), 242–255.

Hart-Davidson, B. (2019). Afterword. In J. Borgman & C. McArdle (Eds.), *Personal, accessible, responsive, strategic: Resources and strategies for online writing instructors* (pp. 95–97). The WAC Clearinghouse; University Press of Colorado. https://doi.org/10.37514/PRA-B.2019.0322.

Hewett, B. L. (2014). Fully online and hybrid writing instruction. In G. Tate, A. R. Taggart, K. Schick & H. B. Hessler (Eds.), *A Guide to Composition Pedagogies* (2nd ed.). (pp. 194–211). Oxford University Press.

Miller, C. R. (1979). A humanistic rationale for technical writing. *College English, 40*(6), 610–617.

Oswal, S. K. (2015). Physical and learning disabilities in OWI. In B. L. Hewett & K. E. DePew (Eds.), *Foundational practices of online writing instruction* (pp. 253–289). The WAC Clearinghouse; Parlor Press. https://doi.org/10.37514/PER-B.2015.0650.2.08.

Rice, R. & St.Amant, K. (2018). Introduction—Thinking globally, composing locally: Re-thinking online writing in the age of the global internet. *Thinking Globally, Compositing Locally: Rethinking Online Writing in the Age of the Global Internet.* Utah State University Press.

Simonson, M., Smaldino, S. & Zvacek, S. (2015). *Teaching and learning at a distance: Foundations in distance education.* Information Age Publishing.

Section 4: User Experience (UX)

Welcome to the User Experience (UX) section of this collection! We selected the above golf course picture to illustrate how the user experience includes all the elements of the course (both golf course and writing course!). From the trees, to the fairway, from the sky to the mountains and the water, all of these elements create the user experience on this particular golf course. Similarly, in an online writing course, the elements of the course, including the assignments, announcements, discussion boards, interactions between faculty and student, interactions between student and student, etc. create the user experience in an online space. The chapters in this section provide various approaches and views on UX research. The audience for this section is scholars and researchers interested in the possibilities that arise from combining best practices in two different fields. While some of the chapters focus on more traditional definitions and approaches to UX, others look more generally at the user experience as a concept to understand the more complex issues that arise when students and instructors act within digital spaces. In their book, Rhetoric and Experience Architecture, Potts & Salvo (2017) argue that "Experience architecture requires that we understand ecosystems of activity rather than simply considering single task scenarios" (p. 4). We believe "Online writing courses are these complex ecosystems of activity, and user-experience design principles should be utilized to develop a more personalized view of learners' experiences and needs" (Borgman & McArdle, 2019). Since we argue that online courses are complex systems and complex user experiences, we feel the chapters in this section are for all three of our targeted audiences: instructors, administrators and scholars. The authors in this section of chapters grapple with the idea of online courses as complex ecosystems of activity and each of the authors illustrate how the PARS approach to OWI creates and facilitates the student and instructor user experience.

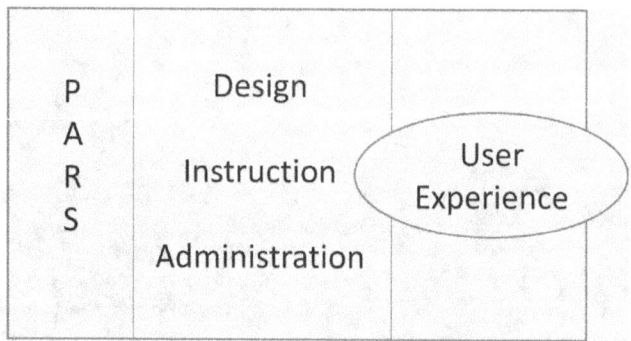

As we said in the introduction to this collection, PARS as an approach spans several layers (design, instruction, and administration) and these layers equal the student user experience (PARS + UX = OWI). The online writing course is a complex ecosystem of activity (Borgman & McArdle, 2019), so it's important that we treat it like one and that we consider all aspects of the user experience.

UX as a methodology became popular in the early 1990s when Norman's (1988) book *The Design of Everyday Things* was released. In this text, he emphasizes ways in which design serves as the communication between product and user, and that designers need to capitalize on that communication in order to make the experience of using the product more pleasurable ("UIUX Trend").

Borgman (2020) notes that, "Understanding connections between the user experience and design of educational materials is fundamental to student success, to teacher satisfaction, and, ultimately, to inclusive and accessible teaching and learning" (p. 55). The principles of UX such as usability comes first, focus on what the users need, factor in accessibility, use simple language, remain consistent, the user is in control (Arctic Leaf Team, 2020) are fundamental to creating, maintaining and ensuring an online course is successful. We hope the chapters in this section will give you the confidence you need to utilize elements of user experience as you design, build, and test your online courses and work to create more inclusive and accessible digital learning spaces.

As you teach and/or administer your online writing courses, you should remain receptive to feedback from students and colleagues on what is working and what is not working in order to create better user experiences. The chapters in this section will help you to keep the user experience as a focus. These chapters illustrate how PARS creates the user experience and is grounded in user experience design principles. Retzinger's chapter encourages readers to put themselves in their students' shoes. This chapter narrates a user experience learning how to play the bass from an online course experience. Retzinger ties together this experience with the student user experience and illustrates the valuable lessons that can be learned from considering how student users experience our courses. Getto's chapter illustrates how PARS can help to create a high-quality student user experience in an online technical communication classroom.

Getto's chapter argues that treating PARS as the definition of a high-quality user experience and incorporating the elements of PARS into one's course can aid facilitating better learning. Bartolotta's chapter is all about usability and illustrates the steps instructors can make to ensure usability in their online courses. This chapter walks readers through the logistics of a simple usability test and encourages them to try more usability tests in their online courses. Stone's chapter focused on how strategy plays a role in creating a more user-centered community engaged course. And finally, Ledgerwood's chapter focuses on how HyperDocs allow teachers to focus on the user experience in a unique way that highlights user-centered design. This chapter illustrates ways to use HyperDocs and how HyperDocs offer a system for strong lesson design that walks students through a process of learning, with students as the focus of the document's design.

References

Arctic Leaf Team. (Jul 10, 2020). *UX design principles.* https://www.arcticleaf.io/learning-center/ux-design-principles.

Borgman, J. (2020). *An investigation of the content practices of online writing instructors and administrators.* [Doctoral dissertation, Texas Tech University]. DuraSpace. https://hdl.handle.net/2346/86509.

Borgman, J. & McArdle, C. (2019). *Personal, accessible, responsive, strategic: Resources and strategies for online writing instruction.* The WAC Clearinghouse; University Press of Colorado. https://doi.org/10.37514/PRA-B.2019.0322.

Potts, L. & Salvo, M. J. (Eds.). (2017). *Rhetoric and experience architecture.* Parlor Press.

UIUX Trend. (2019). What is UX? user experience (UX): Process and methodology. https://uiuxtrend.com/user-experience-ux-process.

Chapter 16. The Bottom End: Transposing Online Bass Lessons to Online Writing Instruction

Dylan "Too Fresh" Retzinger
NEW MEXICO STATE UNIVERSITY

Abstract: This chapter argues that writing programs have the opportunity (if not an imperative) to critically and culturally rethink OWI. One of the existential challenges for OWI is that many of its teachers have never been online writing students. As a result, many instructors have trouble empathizing with the experiences and needs of online writing students and/or are fixated on creating online experiences that resemble the "virtues" of F2F classes. Drawing on user experience theory and employing autoethnographic writing, this chapter explores and transposes the author's experience as an online bass student at an online bass academy to reimagine OWI from the bottom up.

Keywords: user experience, MOOCS, online bass lessons, student experience, design

> I believe deeply in teamwork, community, and collaboration. But most of all, I believe that by being ferociously driven and passionate about ScottsBassLessons I can make a difference to people's lives.
> – Devine, Scott's Bass Lessons, 2020, para. 1

Back at the Clubhouse!

In golf, the clubhouse is a place for coming together and getting better—a place for golfers to reflect on their successes, discuss struggles, share a few tips, and digress (Tiger Woods).[1] When we think about the equivalent for online writing instruction (OWI), the clubhouse is a community of administrators and instructors that are working together to support online students in a way that responds to issues in the world (COVID 19, Black Lives Matter). One of the best ways that our OWI clubhouse can do this is by employing a user experience (UX) driven-PARS (personable, accessible, responsive, and strategic) approach to the instruction, design, and administration of our online writing classes (Borgman & McArdle, 2019). But UX means more than eliciting and responding to user feedback from

---

1. The author would like to thank to Kellie Sharp-Hoskins, Kavita Surya, Jessie Borgman, Casey McArdle, and peer reviewers for their feedback and support.

students—it means being critically and culturally aware of the experiences that shape us as instructors and researchers; and working together means more than providing trainings, resources, and support for individual instructors—it means collaborating on the production of a learning experience that accounts for the diverse (social, political, material, modal, and embodied) needs of students.

Are U Experienced?[2]

Like many, I began teaching online as a graduate student. I was a poet in a program (M.F.A.) with a graduate assistantship (GA) responsible for a hybrid freshman composition course. The pedagogical impetus for the online hour, I later learned, was that in lieu of a lab, it enabled administration to designate it as a four, instead of three-unit course. My OWI training, led by senior GAs, included importing a shell and an instructor intro to the WebCT LMS complete with html tricks. To slide the story on to the fairway <marquee>, from the beginning there was a lack of strategic planning—making a course hybrid for an extra credit hour and allocating the OWI training to tech-savvy graduate students pedagogically trivialized the online component and inadvertently tethered it to those who had strong digital literacy skills. Being html illiterate and having never taken (let alone taught) an online course resulted in my first OWI experience being one of disdain for digital distance.

It was after I graduated when the FOMO (fear of missing out) set in. If I wanted to adjunct, I had to get with online teaching. At first, this took the form of enrolling in tech trainings that guided instructors through the architectural affordances of the new Blackboard LMS and equipped us with the procedural behaviors we would need to do things in-the-system. Later, as a full-time emergency hire at an affiliated community college, I had the fortune of having access to a responsive instructional technology center which provided training and an open space for teachers and students to get one-on-one help with the online dimensions of their courses. Encouraged by the center's director, I enrolled in an online distance education course developed around the Quality Matters (qualitymatters.org) rubric and peer review model, that she was teaching. It was here, in an online course created for aspiring online instructors like me (albeit not OWI specific), where I learned how to design an accessible learning experience and, importantly, had my first experience as an online student and it was personal. I recall the apprehension I felt selecting a profile picture (I ain't professional looking), the anxiety of participating in a choose an animal that represents your personality icebreaker (a donkey, 'cause I'm stubborn), and the time I accidentally insulted another student in a discussion comment (with what I thought was lighthearted joke) and had to walk it back.

With the emergency over (and getting passed over by Ph.Ds. for the business as usual hire), I surmised that I had to doctor my name if I wanted a full-time

---

2. See The Jimi Hendrix Experience (1967), Are You Experienced?

teaching position. Returning to school to pursue a Ph.D. in Rhetoric and Professional Communication, I was a GA teaching online again, but my lean was different now. We had the shiny new Canvas LMS that responded to user feedback, I was engaged in the theory and practice of OWI, and soon enough I was the OGA (online graduate assistant) training new GAs and adjuncts in OWI. Behind the scenes, I was also conducting ethnographic research on identity politics in online learning spaces, or what I like to call interface-to-interface (I2I) classrooms. This project (my dissertation, I2I: The poetics of identification; Retzinger, 2018) was the exigency of my personal experience, my reaction to a student's experience, and what I perceived to be a disciplinary need. One of the reasons I came to like teaching online, after I got the hang of it, is because the interface provided a curtain for me to Wizard of Oz my ethos and conceal my embodied insecurities behind clean-cut sentences and a "white" name. But, as I came to realize, my comfort and privilege wasn't accessible to all. When I asked students to choose an animal that represented their identity, an international student chose a shark because all he wanted to do was swim free with other fish, but he couldn't because his identity was marked and he felt that people were threatened by his presence—even online. Recognizing white privilege at play, I went looking for critical/cultural scholarship on identity politics in distance education and OWI and found myself snapping to a silent count: Not only was there a lack of scholarship, there was an underlying white gaze that didn't account for embodied locations. Or in hook's (1994) words, "The person who is the most powerful has the privilege of denying their body" (hooks, 1994, pp. 136–137). So, I opined, if we were going to promote interactive online learning experiences (Palloff & Pratt, 2007) that were rooted in notions of social presence (Gunawardena, 1995) and crafting a persona (Warnock, 2009) as performances and simulacra of embodied ways of engagement in a society that is wrestling with systemic prejudice, then we needed to account for the locations of our biases in online learning and understand the ways in which identification happened and mattered (Ratcliffe, 2005) on both sides of the interface through names, pictures, ideas, clicks, key strokes, and behaviors (Nakamura, 2002).

I share these experiences and exigencies with you for several reasons. First, because in many ways, my path follows the discoursed terrains and crossroads of distance education literature:

- Issues of administrative agenda and economics being put ahead of pedagogy and instructor training (e.g., Hewett & Powers, 2007; Mechenbier, 2015);
- A digital divide that speaks to literacy and material concerns (e.g., boyd, 2014);
- An existential crisis that reminds us that learning, teaching, and otherwise being online is modally, affectively, and viscerally different (e.g., Haraway 1991; Sunden, 2003; Turkle, 1995);

- Perpetual doubts about the ethos and value of an online education (e.g., Croy, 1998; Woodruff, 2020);
- A pedagogical turn driven by new interactive technology and democratic ideologies (e.g., Goode, 2009; Rosen 2012);
- The lack of situated OWI support and the prominence of LMS workshops and quality standards for training and vetting instructors (e.g., Kerns & Mancilla, 2017);
- And a host of research interests related to all aspects of online learning, such as social presence (e.g., Lowenthal & Dennen, 2017), software politics (e.g., Chambers, 2016; Friesen, 2011; Witte, 2018), cyberpsychology (e.g., Zembylas, 2005), ability (e.g., Borgman & Dockter, 2018), usability (e.g., Bartolotta, et al., 2018); power and identity politics (e.g., Arroyo, 2010; Bomberger, 2004; Chen & Bennet, 2012; Fangfeng et al., 2011).

And second, because both my narrative and the existing literature exposes an existential hole in our course of thinking about distance education, generally, and Borman and McArdle's (2019) UX driven PARS approach to OWI, specifically: Despite my student experience in online distance education courses (e.g., Quality Matters) and for all of my teaching experience, trainings, and research, one of the voids that I face as an online instructor is that I've never been an online writing student.

Who Are U?[3]

User Experience (UX) is the proverbial elephant that we only touch part of (but never the whole), an allochthonous amalgamation (derived and togethered from theories and practices outside of academia), and an improvisation (making it work). Emerging out of industry standards to help designers understand the experiences and meet the technical and affective needs of users, UX has been adopted by distance educators as a vehicle of humanizing systems (Greer & Harris, 2018). While it can be ideologically uncomfortable to identify students as users (Opel & Rhodes, 2018) or even hyphenate them, it does encourage teachers to remember that I2I interactions are different from F2F interactions because they are interfaced and mediated by non-human agents that interpellate students and, I would add, teachers—we are hailed by a machine according to our role. Further, the emphasis on X encourages pedagogues to remember that distance education is more than content or learning management—it is a network of interactions that occurs in digital places, a system that regulates and expects our behaviors in any given location, and a panopticon that administrates and polices our identities. Coupled together, UX is also a compelling framework because it is at once singular and plural, enabling us to move between and address the needs of individual

---

3. See The Who's "Who Are You?" (Townsend, 1978).

students, situated communities, and the larger cultural apparatus, and, like the coupling of students and teachers, UX helps us articulate the political dimensions of the relationship between teacher-designers and student-users. Or in Redish's (2010) words, "We are not our users, and users will always surprise you" (p. 193).

In Personal, Accessible, Responsive Strategic: Resources and Strategies for Online Writing Instructors, Borgman and McArdle (2019) ground their PARS approach to OWI in UX as a way for instructors and administrators to make strategic decisions that respond to the needs of student-users and institutions:

> We know from experience that user research is an important part of success in an online course and degree program. And yet, many do not spend the time to do user research or user testing and the like . . . "UX learning opportunities have the potential to help academic organizations improve customer satisfaction and business strategy, as well as help them better fulfill their mission" (Ghetto & Beecher, 2016, p. 158). We see the PARS approach as a way to apply a user focused approach to your online courses so that your students don't become an afterthought. (p. 89)

To be sure, UX is an important and ethical drive towards on-PARS learning experiences. However, if UX is the theory behind the stroke (praxis), one of the hazards for many online writing instructors (myself included) is that we (older "I"s) don't teach online writing (OW) from a place of lived experience. Unlike the extensive reservoir of F2F experience (i.e., the socio-political, cognitive, embodied, material, spatial, and emotional assemblages of our k-undergraduate education) that we can draw from and use to consciously and unconsciously inform our decisions about the types of experiences that we want to create (and, importantly, avoid) for and with our students in the classroom, our UX as online students (let alone as OW students) is relatively scant or altogether absent. We simply aren't able to empathize with our students or recapitulate UX from a lived place and as a result—out of necessity—many OW teachers, in varying degrees allow/acquiesce and rely on the architectural affordances and values of LMSs, transposing of F2F pedagogy to I2I contexts, and/or scholarship and pedagogical frameworks to anticipate the flattened terrain, map out the route, and become a digital actor. This is not to undermine what these valuable resources and strategies allow us to do, but to remind us that one of the reasons that OWI is so challenging is because we are pedagoging from an existential deficiency—a deficiency that is often filled in and obscured by (if not oriented towards) the experiences that we have and in part shape (for student users) as teacher-designers.[4] Further, because the pre-

---

4. One complication that UX theory presents OWI is that there are multiple (separate and overlapping) locations of experience: Both the instructors' and students' UX of the LMS interacting with their respective hardware and bodies; the students' UX of an

dominant model of OWI (i.e., a single teacher responsible for creating a learning experience for a class of students based on materials and outcomes determined by an administration) is by and large an unapologetic effort to recapitulate the epistemic virtues of F2F learning experiences for I2I students, many OWI instructors are left frustrated by or fixated on fabricating what's lost in the transposition and/or epistemically blind to/economically skeptical of alternative models of online education that more readily embrace online contexts and economies for what they are capable of, such as massive open online courses (MOOCs) and their variants (Krause & Lowe, 2014). In response, in this chapter I use autoethnographic writing to reflect my UX as an online bass (OB) student at an online bass academy and then transpose the implications for OW instructors and administrators through a PARS framework.

Briefly, for those who are curious about my methodological approach to discussing UX, let me begin with Marcus and Fisher's (1999) premise that ethnography "is not the mindless collection of the exotic, but the use of cultural richness for self-reflection and self-growth" (pp. ix–x). Following, the less familiar autoethnography exists in a continuum between objective ethnographic methods and subjective evocation that employs "personal experience as the primary data" (Chang, 2009, p. 49) and allows us to "represent the insider perspective on an experience or a culture" (Canagarajah, 2012, p. 114). In short, I contend that because UXs are at once individual and cultural and because ethnography is a vehicle for community-oriented reflection and growth, autoethnography enables us (you and I, dear reader) to both explore and learn from our personal experiences in order to take action in the world.

Ethnography aside, there is still the bottom end of an elephant obscuring the hole—the subject and field site of my experiences as an online student. Because it is disingenuous for me to pretend to be an OW student, I instead draw upon my experience as an OB student at Scott's Bass Lessons (SBL) (scottsbasslessons.com/). Founded by the British bassist and educator Scott Devine in 2010, SBL is a worldwide online academy for bassists whose mission is to provide a "world-class bass education without boundaries" (Scott's Bass Lessons, 2020, para. 5). Consisting of the SBL academy website, an LMS location, and social media extensions, SBL is a multifaceted music education entity that provides bass lessons and creates an international community for its 85,000 members (Scott's Bass Lessons, 2020), 833,000 + YouTube channel subscribers (Scott's Bass Lessons, n.d.), and some. While there is a dissonance between being an OB and an OW student, I contend that my experiences as a beginning musician (i.e., full of insecurities, unable to read, or keep time) allow me to reflect on my UX through a beginner's eye in ways that my graduate and postgraduate UX in online education courses or trainings wouldn't.

---

instructors' pedagogy; and the UX of an instructor teaching the course [they designed] in relation to the students. And, to be sure, one location informs the UX of another.

Someone Like U[5]

I like iambic pentameter, but I can't keep a beat. I've got big ears, but I can't find the key. I'm not musically talented, but I'm intrigued. At Jefferson Elementary School, the drum and percussion of the Chinese New Year lion dance woke my bottom end up. At Malcolm X Middle School (in the only F2F music class I ever had) I learned some rhythms that I couldn't exactly coordinate with my hands and feet, but the beats still lingered—Dom-ka-da-ka-ka-Dom-Dom. At Berkeley High School, I learned about genre conventions (reggae) and collaboration ("music is music if you want to play music then you can play music if you have people you want to play music with then you can play music" Marley, 1991), but I was too insecure to think that I could. Once, when I did try to sing for fun, I remember being told I sounded like a hoarse mule. On my own, I played a guitar now and then, but aside from the chords a friend taught me, I never really learned the instrument. Altogether, I was uneducated and didn't have confidence in my musical ability, but I had a root. In some ways this is similar to the sentiments of many of the beginning writers that I work with. When I ask them about their identity as a writer—many lack confidence or don't identify as writers, but just as many write more than they think, love all kinds of ink, or realize that writing is a vehicle of power.

I started playing bass seven years ago because I wanted to put some poems to a beat. I bought a used amp, got Too Fresh (the name of the bass) out of my friend's closet, and knew enough to fret a G or groove on a BD. And it was fun, or I had fun but I was clueless. Every now and then, to fill in the gaps, I'd get a book or find lessons on YouTube that interested me. Soon enough SBL videos started catching my attention, e.g., "The most important scale you'll ever learn" (Scott's Bass Lessons, 2014), and at some point I bit on the one free month bait, which was the channel's hook, and checked out the SBL Academy. Upon joining, I was prompted to create a profile (see Figure 16.1) and invited to a synchronous video/chat orientation for new members that was given by Scott himself. Before long, I was navigating the academy website, checking out community discussion threads, and taking lessons. What I initially liked best about SBL was the comprehensive course library (see Figure 16.2), organized by ability level (beginning, intermediate, advanced) and subject matter (e.g., genre, theory, reading, recording), that not only allowed me to personalize my learning experience based on my ability and interests, but also in terms of who I wanted to learn from—Scott or one of the many SBL instructors (see Figure 16.3). Further, unlike the piecemeal YouTube lessons that were available on the SBL channel, in the academy each course was a curated and accessible learning experience complete with sequenced videos, downloadable workbooks, and often backing tracks to practice with. As someone without any real knowledge, the UX was perfect for me—I enjoyed working through lessons at my own pace, according to my level, and finding teachers and topics that resonated with me.

---

5. See Adele's "Someone Like You" (Adkins & Wilson, 2011).

Figure 16.1. My community profile page at SBL.[6]

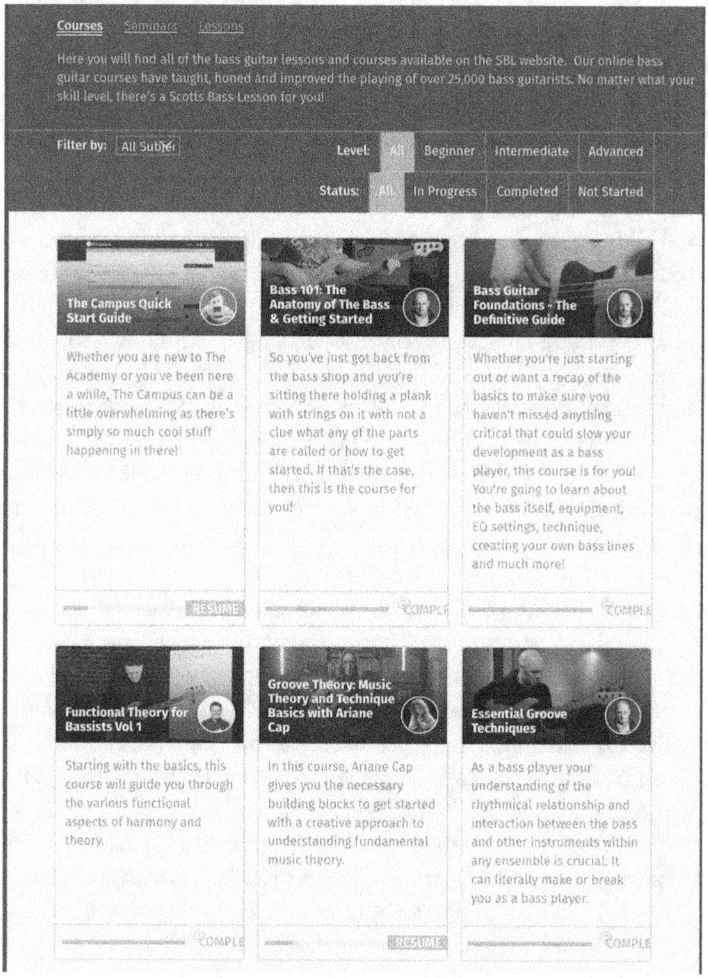

Figure 16.2. SBL's course library.

---

6. Pictures (Figures 16.1, 16.2, 16.3 & 16.4) courtesy of Scott's Bass Lessons.

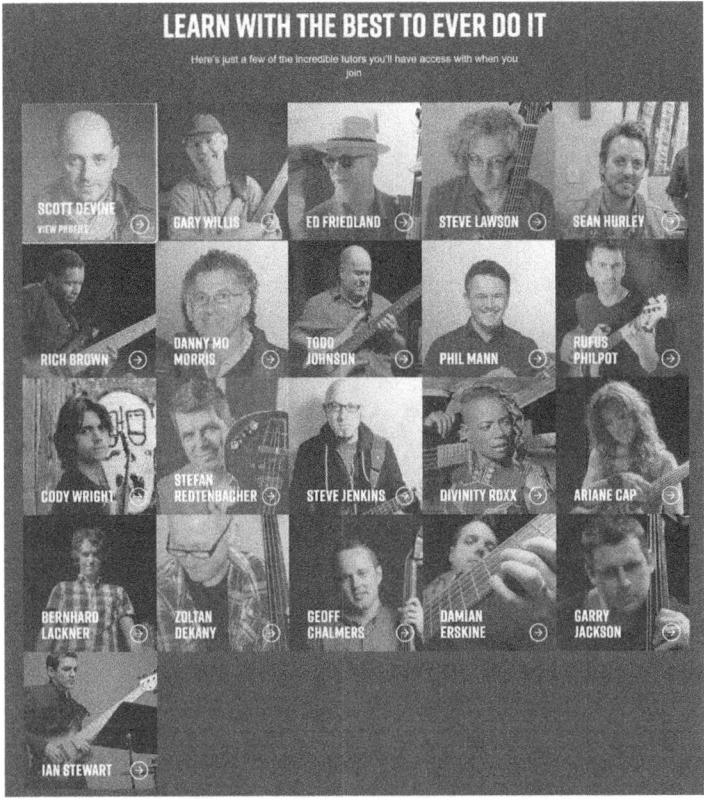

Figure 16.3. SBL faculty.

After the trial ended, I signed up for a year and continued on. I enjoyed SBL and I was learning a lot, but at some point, I kind of hit a wall—the course library got hard and/or the "choose your own adventure" left me indecisive sometimes. It was during this time when SBL, responding to that feeling, introduced "The Bass Technique Accelerator Program," which was advertised as a more familiar asynchronous course (AC):

> For 26 weeks, I'll be your bass tutor.
>
> Every week, we'll have a new lesson.
>
> It will be focused.
>
> It will be deep.
>
> We'll hammer technique.
>
> And at the end, you'll be a different bass player than you were when you started. (Scott's Bass Lessons, personal communication, Sep. 18, 2018).

Having earned my trust, looking for structure, and wanting to get better, I signed up. Conducted through Teachable (scotts-bass-lessons.teachable.com), for twenty-six-weeks I received lessons from Scott that broke down aspects of technique as a series of exercises to practice and build upon. Delivered as weekly modules, the materials included sequenced video with supplemental materials, a discussion board where members could interact with one another or have questions answered by an SBL administrator, and monthly live Q&A sessions with Scott that were then recorded and made available on demand. Soon after this first course, several other courses offered by Scott and other instructors followed—some of which are in their second or third iterations (see Figure 16.4). In many ways these courses are similar to semester-long OW ACs, but there is one key difference—I have access to them for life. In this capacity, each course is like an interactive multimodal textbook (or together like a multimodal library) and while I didn't always finish them on time and found some materials above my level, I didn't mind too much because I can always go back when I'm ready.

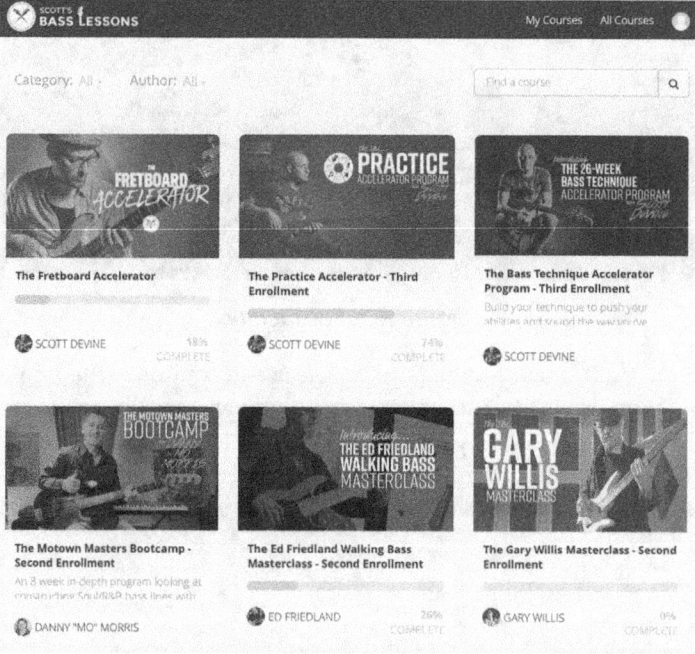

Figure 16.4. SBL's asynchronous course library.

When my year was up, I decided to become a lifetime member and I'm still shedding.[7] I keep tabs on SBLs emails and the YouTube channel to see what's going on; I check in on the community every now and then to get advice on gear, ask questions about lessons, see what others are up to, or share what I'm up to (soundcloud.

---

7. "The shed" is SBL colloquial for practicing bass or doing things in SBL.

com/user-633191931); I've continue to work through the course library; and I keep signing up for the enrolled courses. To be sure, there are still a few features of the Academy that I haven't really used, such as the "Bass Hang" where Scott invites members to submit practice videos for feedback or the recently introduced "Player's Path," which he designed to give students a sense of accomplishment and accountability by progressing through songs at different skill levels. But that is one of the things I like about SBL; it's strategically responsive to the members' needs and there is always something new (or old) waiting for me (when I'm ready)—be that lessons, different instructors, video essays, or pedagogical approaches and utilizations of technology. Further, what this experience has reminded me of is, despite all of the progress I've made and all the practice I've put in, I'm still far from being a competent bassist (or rapper) and it's humbling—like writing, learning the bass is a lifetime craft and some things just take a long time to learn (because they are hard) or don't really make sense until you're ready, but unlike a traditional writing class, SBL is there for me when I am. To be sure, my experience as an OB student has given me a lot of empathy with OW students, and when thinking about the SBL paradigm, my UX has shown me that OWI could learn a lot from SBL. While SBL is by no means a perfect or equivocal model, it offers OW instructors, and importantly, administrators an opportunity to reimagine the status quo in exciting ways. I'll share with you a few—in the key of PARS.

What's the Use?[8]

Scott Devine is a very capable bassist and teacher, but one of the things that made SBL such a personal educational experience was that Scott was just one of the many SBL instructors I was able to learn from. This personalization happened in three ways. At the administration level, SBL strategically selected a diverse group of instructors—each of whom brings their own musical expertise, life experiences, and teaching style—to produce content that they are passionate about. Following, and more familiarly, at the instructor level, each teacher is able to personalize their course and pedagogy. For example, when teaching theory, Scott likes to focus on practical application, while Phil Mann (another SBL faculty) likes to focus on conceptual understanding. And, importantly, at the student level, users are able to personalize their experiences by choosing what they want to learn, who they want to learn from, when they want to learn, and at what pace they want to learn. Transposing this model to OWI, I can imagine English departments, which are often composed of specialists in many fields, leveraging talent to create a passionate and diverse catalog of instructional content—one that includes approaching any given topic from multiple points of view for learners with different needs. For example, grammar and mechanics for ESL students taught by ESL specialists or syntax taught by a Gertrude Stein scholar.

---

8. See Mac Miller's "What's the Use?" (McCormick, 2018).

Of course, creating a personalized catalog of content presents (at least) three other pressing issues in our thinking about PARS: (1) How to make content accessible to students; (2) how to be responsive to students outside of the teacher-LMS-student paradigm; and (3) how to strategically produce this experience? In regard to accessibility, SBL offers a couple of viable answers. First, and structurally speaking, SBL is essentially an online instruction library (OIL) where students are able to access content on demand according to their needs, interest, and learning style. Second, and more familiarly, SBL offers iterative ACs that students can enroll in. Transposing these approaches to OWI, SBL offers two compelling paradigmatic shifts. In regard to the OIL, imagine each university's writing program producing an OIL that students could access on demand to supplement their learning in a particular course or throughout their degree program. And in thinking about ACs, imagine iterative courses that are produced by a department (e.g., a writing program administrator working with graduate assistants and/or colleagues to record lectures [by more than one teacher], develop assignments [of multiple imaginations], and design the course site [with students and teachers in mind]), and then administered by individual instructors who can focus on responding to student work (and, along with students, give feedback or even participate in the next iteration). In looking at both together, the keys here are to see the OIL and ACs as complimentary, where, for example, if a student was in a technical communication AC, where command of APA style was expected but not covered, and they didn't know it, the instructor could refer them to the APA courses in the OIL.

Which leads to questions about responsiveness—who is responding to students in ACs and OILs. In short, an orchestrated team. Breaking down SBL's approach, responsiveness looks something like this:

- Administrators who moderate and respond to discussion board posts and respond to private student questions in ACs and the OIL;
- Instructors (of OIL courses and ACs) who host live Q&A sessions or seminars and (occasionally) invite students to contact them privately;
- Members responding to other members in the OIL community or AC discussion boards.

Transposing SBL's approach to OWI, I can imagine writing programs creating administrators or "librarians" for their OIL, creating schedules for synchronous workshops with instructors of the OIL and ACs, and creating opportunities for students to engage with one another in a community page of an OIL, where for example they could talk about a writing project in their anthropology class (and maybe, in the spirit of writing across the curriculum, one of the OIL librarians is from the anthropology department). Further, at universities with writing centers, I can imagine collaborations where the OIL is integrated into a virtual writing center.

Finally, in response to the strategic production of multimodal OILs and ACs, it goes without saying that this requires a coordinated team effort. When looking at the SBL approach, collaboration is apparent at every step—in the pedagogy (instructors with administrators), in the recorded lectures (instructors with audio/video engineers), in the workbooks and backing tracks (instructors with technical writers and musicians), and of course, the orchestrated effort of updating the website and responding to students. Transposing such a strategic model to the production of OWI courses would be transformative. Instead of each instructor being responsible for producing their own accessible multimodal content, creating and implementing engaging assignments, designing and moderating their own course site, and responding to students' technical questions and writing, which, no matter how you cut it, is a lot to put on one person, writing programs could strategically collaborate on the production of the UX: Administrators working with pedagogues working with audio/video engineers working with technical writers working with web designers working with teachers to personalize learning experiences in accessible, responsive, and strategic ways that make a difference in student's lives.

Final Thoughts and Application

Back at the clubhouse, Bad Bunny[9] (2020) is playing. It sounds interesting, the golfers say, but they're just not sure. It's music from a different culture, in another language, and they weren't expecting it—it's not what we play here. For many instructors, that's what "the internet" is. For many students, that's what academic "English" is. In other words, experience is not only powerful, it's rhythmical. It produces the stories we tell, shapes our expectations about where the story is going, manifests our actions in the narrative in time, and is capable of connecting or dividing us. If there are UX OWI takeaways from this chapter, it's two:

1. To remember that our experiences shape our students' experiences and unless we account for the experiences that shape us as researchers and designers, then we are obscuring our understanding of their experience;
2. Drawing on industry practices, sometimes we need to step outside of our disciplinary values and pedagogies in order to explore the possibility of experience.

Finally, my UX at SBL has transformed my thinking about the possibility of OWI. I'm not sure if it's the economics, values and attachments (to F2F learning), infrastructure and material constraints, a matter of time (current students and future OWI instructors will have lived it), or some combination thereof, but I am certain that now (COVID-19, Black Lives Matter) is the time to explore the possibility of providing students with: personalized learning experience from multiple and diverse instructors who are experts in their field; access to lessons on demand (let students binge learn, learn with topical agency, or learn when they are ready

---

9. Bad Bunny is a musical artist from Puerto Rico.

to learn); a responsive learning community that they are not only recipients of but participants in; and the benefits of a strategic (and passionate and ferociously-driven) collaboration that is in response to the UX of the community and its members.

References

Adkins, A. L. B. & Wilson, D. (2011). Someone like you [Song]. On *21*. XL Colombia.

Arroyo, A. T. (2010). It's not a colorless classroom: Teaching religion online to Black college students using transformative, postmodern pedagogy. *Teaching Theology and Religion, 13*(1), 35–17.

Bartolotta, J., Bourelle, T. & Newmark, J. (Eds). (2018). User centered design and usability in the composition classroom [Special issue]. *Computers and Composition, 49*, 1–106.

Bomberger, A. (2004). Ranting about race: Crushed eggshells in computer-mediated communication. *Computers and Composition, 21*, 197–216.

Borgman, J. & Dockter, J. (2018) Considerations of access and design in the online writing classroom. *Computers & Composition, 49*, 94–105.

Borgman, J. & McArdle, C. (2019). *Personal, accessible, responsive, strategic: Resources for online writing instructors*. The WAC Clearinghouse; University Press of Colorado. https://doi.org/10.37514/PRA-B.2019.0322.

boyd, d. (2014). *It's complicated: The social lives of networked teens*. Yale University Press.

Canagarajah, A. S. (2012) Autoethnography in the study of multilingual writers. In L. Nickoson & M. P. Sheridan (Eds.) *Writing studies research in practice: Methods and methodologies* (pp. 113–124). Southern Illinois University Press.

Chambers, M. L. (2016). A rhetorical mandate: A look at multi-ethnic/multimodal online pedagogy. In D. Ruffman & A. G. Scheg (Eds.), *Applied pedagogies: Strategies for online writing instruction* (pp. 75–89). Utah State University Press.

Chang, H. (2009). *Autoethnography as method*. Routledge.

Chen, R. T.-H. & Bennett, S. (2012). When Chinese meet constructivist pedagogy. *Higher Education 64*, 677–691.

Croy, M. (1998). Distance education, individualization, and the demise of the university. *Technology in Society, 20*, 317–326.

Fangfeng, K., Chávez, A. F., Causarano, P.-N. L, & Causarano, A. (2011). Identity presence and knowledge building: Joint emergence in online learning environments? *Computer-Supported Collaborative Learning, 6*, 349–370.

Friesen, N. (2011). *The place of the classroom and the space of the screen: relational pedagogy and internet technology*. Peter Lang.

Goode, L. (2009). Social news, citizen journalism, and democracy. In M. Mandiberg (Ed.), *New media society* (pp. 287–305). New York University Press.

Greer, M. & Harris, H. (2018). User-centered design as a foundation for online writing instruction. *Computers & Composition, 49*, 18–24.

Gunawardena, C. N. (1995). Social presence theory and implications for interaction and collaborative learning in computer conferences. *International Journal of Educational Telecommunications, 1*(23), 147–166.

Haraway, D. (1991). *Simians, cyborgs, and women: The reinvention of nature*. Routledge.
Hewett, B. L. & Powers, C. E. (2007). Guest editors' introduction: Online teaching and learning: Preparation, development, and organizational communication. *Technical Communication Quarterly, 16*(1), 1–11.
hooks, b. (1994). *Teaching to transgress: Education as the practice of freedom*. Routledge.
The Jimi Hendrix Experience. (1967). *Are you experienced?* [Album]. Track Records.
Kearns, L. R. & Mancilla, R. (2017). The impact of quality matters professional development on teaching across delivery formats. *American Journal of Distance Education, 31*(3), 185–197.
Krause, S. D. (2014). MOOC assigned. In S. D. Krause & C. Lowe (Eds.), *Invasion of the MOOCS: The promise and perils of massive open online courses* (pp. 122–129). Parlor Press.
Krause, S. D. & Lowe, C. (Eds.). (2014). *Invasion of the MOOCS: The promise and perils of massive open online courses*. Parlor Press.
Lowenthal, P. R. & Dennen, V. P. (Eds). (2017). Social presence and identity in online learning [Special issue]. *Distance Learning, 38*(2), 137–140.
Marcus, G. & Fischer, M. (1999). *Anthropology as cultural critique: An experimental moment in the human sciences* (2nd ed.). The University of Chicago Press.
Marley, R. N. (1991). Talkin' [Song]. On *Talkin' Blues*. Polygram Records.
McCormick, M. J. (2018). What's the use? [Song]. On *Swimming*. REmember Music.
Mechenbeir, M. (2015). Contingent faculty and OWI [online writing instruction]. In B. L. Hewitt & K. DePew (Eds.), *Foundational practices in online writing instruction* (pp. 227–249). The WAC Clearinghouse; Parlor Press. https://doi.org/10.37514/PER-B.2015.0650.2.07.
Nakamura, L. (2002). *Cybertypes: Race, ethnicity, and identity on the internet*. Routledge.
Ocasio, B. A. M. (2020). *YHLQMDLG*. Rimas.
Palloff, R. M. & Pratt, K. (2007). *Building online learning communities: Effective strategies for the virtual classroom* (2nd ed). Jossey-Bass.
Woodruff, J. (2020, May 14). *Will college campuses reopen in the fall? Cal State's chancellor weighs in*. PBS NewsHour. https://www.pbs.org/newshour/show/will-college-campuses-reopen-in-the-fall-cal-states-chancellor-weighs-in.
Ratcliffe, K. (2005). *Rhetorical listening: Identification, gender, whiteness*. Southern University Press.
Redish, J. (2010). Technical communication and usability: Intertwined strands and mutual influences. *IEEE Transactions on Professional Communication, 53*(3), 191–201.
Retzinger, D. H. (2018). i2i: The poetics of identification (10983783). [Doctoral dissertaiton New Mexico State University] ProQuest Dissertations & Theses A&I.
Rosen, J. (2012). The people formerly known as the audience. In M. Mandiberg (Ed.), *The social media reader* (pp. 13–16). New York University Press.
Scott's Bass Lessons. (n.d.) *Home* [YouTube channel]. YouTube. https://www.youtube.com/channel/UCWTj3vCqkQIsrTGSm4kM34g.
Scott's Bass Lessons. (2014, December 12). *The most important scale you'll ever learn* [Video]. YouTube. https://www.youtube.com/watch?v=PWlv4NPyRIo&t=2s.

Scott's Bass Lessons. (2020). *About* [Video]. YouTube. https://scottsbasslessons.com/about.

Sunden, J. (2003). *Material virtualities: Approaching online textual embodiment.* Peter Lang.

Turkle, S. (1995). *Life on the screen: Identity and the age of the internet.* Simon and Schuster.

Townsend, P. (1978). Who are you? [Song]. On *Who are you?* Polydor Records.

Warnock, S. (2009). *Teaching writing online: How and why.* National Council of Teachers of English.

Zembylas, M. (2005). Levinas and the "inter-face": The ethical challenge of online education. *Educational Theory, 55*(1), 61–78.

Chapter 17. Ensuring High-Quality Student User Experiences: PARS and the Technical Communication Online Writing Class

Guiseppe Getto
East Carolina University

Abstract: When teaching online, our students are functioning not only as learners within our courses, but as users of the technologies and resources we utilize to facilitate their learning. User experience design (UX) can thus be a useful process for teachers of online writing classes, especially those that are teaching classes in technical communication. The UX Process invites teachers to develop classes that are usable and useful through preliminary research, prototyping, usability testing, and maintenance. These are processes that teachers of online writing classes already use in some form or another, whether they realize it or not, but this chapter illustrates the full UX process for course development, with PARS as the definitive goal of an online student user experience. Treating PARS as the definition of a high-quality user experience for student users of online writing classrooms means ensuring that online courses are developed, implemented, and continuously improved in the direction of being personal, accessible, responsive, and strategic. PARS-committed instructors, like their UX counterparts, need to be willing to shift and change over time as well, always remembering that the primary goals is the best student learning experience we can deliver.

Keywords: user experience, technical communication, course development, instructional design

When teaching online, our students function not only as learners within our courses, but also as users of the technologies and resources we utilize to facilitate learning. This is never more the case than when teaching an online technical communication class. In such a class, students often face not only technological hurdles, such as navigating a course website or learning management system (LMS), but also hurdles that involve technical knowledge-making, such as how to build a website of their own or how to draft a technical report that uses Plain language. In all online courses, we must think about the experiences students have as users of our courses. In online technical communication courses, however, it is often the difference between success and failure for many students.

In this chapter, I will lead readers through the user experience (UX) process, with PARS as the definitive goal of an online student user experience. The central term for UX work beyond the classroom is the UX Process or UX Lifecycle, which can be defined as the sum total of activities that need to occur to ensure a high-quality user experience (Hartson & Pyla, 2012). These stages typically include preliminary research, prototyping, usability testing, and maintenance. Treating PARS as the definition of a *high-quality user experience* for student users of online writing classrooms means ensuring that online courses are developed, implemented, and continuously improved in the direction of being personal, accessible, responsive, and strategic. This will involve a brief discussion of PARS and how it intersects with UX, an exploration of the UX Process, and finally a road map of how PARS can be practically applied at each stage of the UX Process during course development. Sprinkled throughout will be actual examples of my own teaching strategies to illustrate key points. And I will also emphasize how instructors with no background in UX can fold this process into their regular course development activities, and how, in fact, it will benefit them to do so.

PARS Meets UX Process

UX can be defined as the sum total of activities needed to create a high-quality user experience. Although intersections of UX and online pedagogy, such as universal design for learning (UDL), have developed a strong history in education research as approaches to accessible pedagogy for all learners (Coyne et al., 2017; Hall et al., 2012; Meyer et al., 2013), and though the field of technical communication has demonstrated dedication to UX and universal design for over a decade (Dolmage, 2009; Melonçon, 2013), practical approaches to UDL, such as PARS, in technical communication classrooms are scant with a few notable exceptions (i.e., Borgman & McArdle, 2019; Walters, 2010; Williams et al., 2013;). In their previous book, *Personal, Accessible, Responsive, Strategic: Resources and Strategies for Online Writing Instructors*, Borgman & McArdle (2019) define the following goals of the PARS process, when applied to instructional and course design strategies (p. 7):

- Cultivating relationships virtually with students (Personal)
- Creating an identity and presence as an online instructor (Personal)
- Setting boundaries for instruction/grading/virtual availability (Responsive)
- Handling the extra written communication (Accessible/Responsive/Strategic)
- Responding to student writing in digital environment (Responsive/Strategic)
- Creating an entire course prior to the class ever meeting (Accessible/Responsive/Strategic)

- Being strategic in pedagogy and facilitation of a course (Personal/Strategic)
- Cultivating support from the WPA or department chair (Personal/Responsive/Strategic)

In other words, courses that are personal, accessible, responsive, and strategic (PARS from here on) should involve all the above activities. In the world of UX beyond the classroom, we would call these goals *requirements*. When UX specialists begin work on a product or service, you see, they begin by defining what the requirements are for the product or service, both from the standpoint of an organization's goals and from the standpoint of users. In the case of online course development, the touchstone we are seeking is between the institution's standpoint, the teacher's standpoint, and the student's standpoint. Online writing courses are a service offered to students (users) who are seeking to learn some aspect of writing. Teachers offer them because they are required to by their institutions and/or because they fit their pedagogical goals. Institutions benefit from these courses by providing required classes to students in an accessible manner that doesn't require physical space. UX happens where these student goals, teacher goals, and institutional goals meet.

Like learning, UX is both a process and a product (Allabarton, 2019). It is a process in that it provides a roadmap for the process of creating digital experiences that ensure a high-quality experience for users. And it is a product in that the outcome of the UX process can be defined as a product called *a high-quality user experience.* So, just as students who engage with an online technical communication course (or any online course) need to have certain experiences to successfully navigate the course, their combined experiences in that course are a product of all the activities, technologies, and interactions they encounter. When seen this way, PARS becomes a list of requirements for balancing the goals of institutions, teachers, and students within an online course. And UX specialists excel at designing digital experiences based on requirements.

Like learning, UX can also seem more complex than it actually is. What follows is a rather technical description of the UX process to give a sense of what it entails. UX is formally practiced in higher education, but is far more prevalent outside of academia, where web designers, mobile app developers, and creators of other IT products and services regularly use it to increase usability and usefulness. It's important that all practitioners of UX have a firm grasp of these basic concepts.

As mentioned previously, the central term that UX specialists use to define their design process beyond the classroom is the UX Process or UX Lifecycle, which can be defined as the sum total of activities that need to occur to ensure a high-quality user experience (Buley, 2013; Garrett, 2003; Hoober, 2014; Hartson & Pyla, 2012; Morville, 2007). This process is typically depicted as a series of stages that a designer (or more often: group of designers) goes through to produce a digital product or service for a specific community of users. These stages are:

1. Preliminary research
2. Prototyping
3. Usability testing of prototype
4. Maintenance

Essentially, designers start by doing preliminary user interviews, preferably conducted in the context in which users will be using an application. These interviews might be followed up with observational sessions in which UX specialists note common work practices, technology usage, and other elements of the users' context. From this contextual data, a rough prototype of the application (i.e., a simulation of one or more features of the final product) is developed. In the past this has commonly started with the development of a paper prototype—which is still the case according to my anecdotal interactions with UX practitioners—but often quickly proceeds to the development of a low-fidelity, or simple and low-tech, clickable prototype that can be used in usability testing. This prototype is then refined through succeeding rounds of usability testing until it reaches high fidelity, or very similar to the final product, and then is finally launched as a product or service. Maintenance of the product or service often entails updates, design tweaks, and content strategy for the product, with the design process beginning again in earnest when an exigence for major changes arises, such as changes to web standards or organizational goals.

If that sounds like a lot of work, it is! And if the UX process seems overwhelming, that is also a common concern. However, instructors who have taught online before may also recognize some of their own course design process described above. Many of us have done lots of preliminary research, even talking to students about their needs, while designing our courses. And we have *all* created prototypes of our online courses before they ever launch, whether that is a combination of a course website, a syllabus, a list of activities, a learning management system, or all of the above! Many of us then share these prototype classes with our colleagues for testing. That's why for the remainder of this chapter, I'm going to illustrate each stage of the UX Process and how it can be applied to the design of online technical communication courses, or any online course. For each stage, I will also highlight how the list of PARS requirements I mentioned above can be implemented. At the end of this chapter, readers should have a much firmer grasp on how to apply the UX Process to their course design and will hopefully be convinced that this will help them produce better online writing courses.

Preliminary Course Research and Development

The most important step in developing an online writing class that will include PARS learning goals is understanding the mental models and overall expectations of students who will take the course. Nielson (2010) reminds us that what a user believes about a system, like the collection of people, technologies, and interactions that make up an online writing course, affect how a user is able to use that system. The collection of these beliefs and expectations is called by UX designers a mental model. Assessing the mental model of incoming students is particularly important in a field like technical communication where students often come to classrooms with little to no knowledge of the specific workplace contexts being explored.

And anyone who has ever taught a class has assessed the mental models of their prospective students, whether they realize it or not! Whenever we begin to design an online class, we teachers think about things like:

- What introductory experiences will students need to familiarize themselves with the course materials (Personal/Strategic)?
- What technologies will help students best communicate with the teacher and with each other (Personal/Accessible)?
- What challenges might students face as they begin to work on course activities, including those related to technology, social interaction, and learning style (Strategic/Accessible/Responsive)?
- What biases might students enter the class with that should be addressed (Personal/ Accessible)?

These are all questions similar to those that UX designers ask their users when building a new application.

Often, designers will interview prospective users to gather data on their individual mental models. They then code this data to look for patterns amongst their user base and display this data as personas, or archetypal users (Goltz, 2014). That often isn't realistic for teachers, however, whose students don't engage with a class until it launches. That's why I recommend to teachers that they come up with what are sometimes called "assumption personas," or personas that are based on what the designer, or in this case the teacher, thinks their users will be like. Much of the information for an assumption persona can be gleaned from our institutions which share information with us like our students' demographics, majors, and career goals. Such personas should contain info like the following:

> Name
>
> Photo (can be gathered from online student records)
>
> Demographics (age, race, gender, location, occupation)
>
> Story: what makes them a want to take this class? What values do they bring to the class?
>
> Goals and Challenges: what is the student-user trying to accomplish with the help of this class? What pain points might they experience that can be alleviated through experiences they have in the class?

How I Can Help: what can I (the teacher) build into the course to help this type of student-user achieve their goals and alleviate their pain points?

Note the above use of the phrase "this type of student-user." Users are all different. There is no rule about how many personas represent a given user base, but there are typically more than one. For an example student persona and more tips about how to create one, please see Getto and St.Amant (2014).

Some good starting personas to think of are students with some experience in the course material, students who have no experience whatsoever in the course material, students who will struggle heavily with the course material, and students who will struggle with the technological aspects of the course. Planning for these four basic personas will help teachers create welcoming, usable online course environments that can cater to a broad array of student-users.

Some scholars and practitioners have expressed concerns that personas can promote biases by underrepresenting already underrepresented student groups. This is a danger *if personas are not representative of your actual students,* which is why it's important to craft personas for the students in your actual course, rather than using predefined ones. After the course launches, it's important to update your personas based on the students you're actually teaching. Once teachers have an idea of who their student users are, it's time to prototype a course environment!

Prototyping Online Tech Comm Courses

After a basic, PARS-oriented student user experience has been defined, instructors need to assemble a collection of technologies that will enable them to bring that student user experience to life. This will most likely include some combination of:

- Learning management systems (LMS; i.e., Moodle)
- Content management systems (CMS; i.e., WordPress)
- Social media platforms (i.e., Twitter, LinkedIn, Tumblr)
- Proprietary resources (i.e., online textbooks, peer review systems, etc.)

The most important part of this step is ensuring that all technologies used form a coherent technological environment that actively enables PARS-related goals mentioned at the beginning of this chapter. Too often, we load our online courses down with the latest and greatest technologies only to find that there might be an older, more reliable one, such as email, that would solve problems more simply (PARS: Strategic/Accessible). Sometimes our institutions require the use of some technologies over others. There are always limitations as we build online course environments, just like in the private sector when UX designers are subject to budget limitations, deadlines, organizational goals, and other project specifications.

Prototypes are used by UX designers to create a simple version of an application for testing before designing the whole thing. The goal is to spot problems early on so they don't spread throughout the whole application (Cerejo, 2010). A great way to start this process is to think about the first three or four interactions a student-user might have with an online course. These interactions might include:

- Introducing themselves to the teacher and other students (Personal/ Responsive)
- Completing and submitting their first assignment (Accessible/ Responsive/Strategic)
- Collaborating with their peers on a shared assignment (Personal/ Responsive)
- Asking for help when they get lost and don't know how to proceed (Personal/Responsive)

Teachers might create a learning environment that enables such interactions in order to look at things from the student's point-of-view. Many LMSs include the ability to launch a course with a test student user account that can only access what students will see, for example. Regardless, teachers should create a simple prototype of their course *before designing the entire course* to try to spot usability problems early on, before they get built into the entire workflow of the course. It's a lot easier to fix an online interaction that occurs once than it is to fix that interaction if it has been embedded dozens of times. Once teachers have a simplified course environment that they think will meet the needs of prospective student-users, it's time to do some usability testing to improve the prototype before launch.

Usability Testing Online Tech Comm Courses

The development of every PARS-enabled online course should also include some level of usability testing, but to manage this process as part of an already-complex course development process can be challenging for online writing instructors. In the private sector, UX designers often do small batches of usability testing with an average of five users throughout a product development cycle (Nielsen, 2012). In order to fold regular usability testing into the course development process, then, instructors can do two different types of usability testing:

1. Initial testing of a simplified prototype of the course before launch (Accessible/Strategic).
2. Using student reports of problems or issues from the initiation of contact (i.e., pre-course surveys or introductory emails) as opportunities to improve the course (Accessible/Responsive/Strategic).
3. As far as the formal process of usability testing, it is relatively simple (see Figure 17.1):

For a full assignment sequence that includes a list of sample usability test questions, please visit guiseppegetto.com/engl3040/module-4-2/.

This is the process as it is practiced by UX designers. Instructors of online courses (both tech comm courses and otherwise), should feel free to adapt the process as needed. They might get some past students to usability test a course they're developing, for example, or they might go through the prototype themselves and really try to see it from the perspective of different student personas.

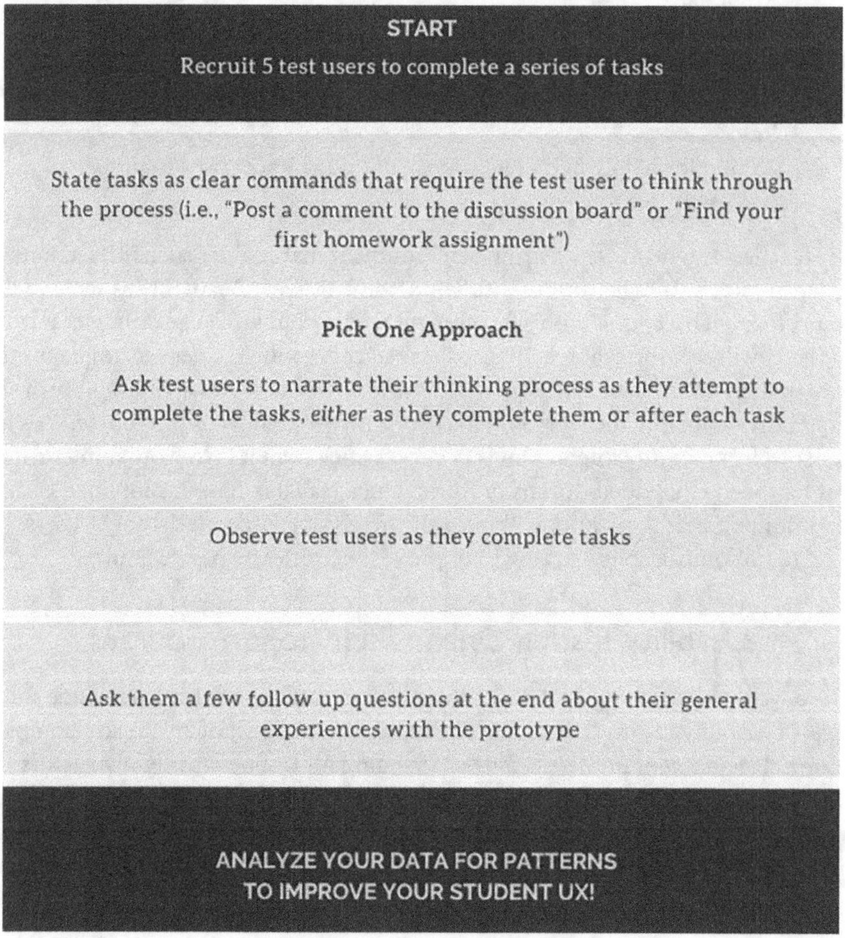

START
Recruit 5 test users to complete a series of tasks

State tasks as clear commands that require the test user to think through the process (i.e., "Post a comment to the discussion board" or "Find your first homework assignment")

Pick One Approach

Ask test users to narrate their thinking process as they attempt to complete the tasks, *either* as they complete them or after each task

Observe test users as they complete tasks

Ask them a few follow up questions at the end about their general experiences with the prototype

ANALYZE YOUR DATA FOR PATTERNS TO IMPROVE YOUR STUDENT UX!

Figure 17.1. Usability testing process.

Maintaining Online Tech Comm Courses Over Time

Rather than a series of discrete stages, the UX process as applied to the development of PARS-enabled online courses should be thought of as a series of heuristics that guide decision-making over the entire lifecycle of course development, including after the course is taught more than once. UX designers in industry work to continually improve the products and services they are responsible for, and online writing instructors should be no different: the process of research, prototyping, and testing should become a natural part of online writing pedagogy. As instructors solve problems reported by individual students, for example, these solutions should then be prototyped as potential course-wide solutions that can be tested more broadly, thus gradually improving the course over its entire lifecycle.

I still have many of the original prototypes I created years ago when I first began teaching online. And I have many student personas, snippets of feedback, and comments from evaluations that continue to guide me. The goal of UX is never really fulfilled because, just as it is in teaching, the needs of users shift and change over time. PARS-committed instructors, like their UX-counterparts, need to be willing to shift and change over time as well, always remembering that the primary goals is the best student learning experience we can deliver.

Maintaining online writing classes should include activities like the following:

- Reflecting on overall course design, including individual assignments, assignment sequences, and technologies used, each time a course is taught (Responsive/Strategic)
- Adapting courses to new students, learning outcomes, and institutional goals (Accessible/Responsive/Strategic)
- Ensuring that best practices in course technologies are followed, meaning all technologies follow institutional guidelines and are updated, accessible, and responsive to student needs (Accessible/Responsive)
- Doing additional usability testing of new prototype assignments and other course activities (Accessible/Responsive)

Maintenance is the easiest part of UX to neglect. What worked in a past iteration of a course will probably work this time. This is a mantra we often tell ourselves as teachers, but the reality is that student goals, teacher goals, and institutional goals are changing all the time. We have to continually adapt our OWLs to produce new student user experiences that align with these different interests.

This isn't to say that maintenance requires a fresh start every semester, of course. An important part of UX is also avoiding analysis paralysis where we are afraid to do the same thing even if it has been successful because we haven't tested it with a specific group of students. It's better to prioritize testing new assignments and activities, as these are the most untested and hence the most likely to fail. That being said, we must also use reflection time between courses to look for blind spots in our courses. Are there elements of courses we have kept around because they serve our goals but not institutional or student goals? Or, are their elements that are popular with students, but don't serve institutional or teacher goals? Are institutions mandating language or policies that don't align with learning goals? These are the kinds of questions OWL instructors should be continually asking themselves.

Final Thoughts and Application

When applying the UX process to online writing classes, teachers should think of UX as an additional tool kit to assist with course planning, development, and revision, not as an additional burden to these processes. We all have questions that arise when planning an online writing class, whether we are teaching the course for the first time or for the fiftieth. These questions might include:

1. Which assignments were most successful and which were least successful?
2. Were any intended learning outcomes neglected? If so, why?
3. Were all student needs met? If not, why not?
4. Were there particular aspects of the course (i.e., communication, assignment sequencing, accessing technology, etc.) that many students struggled with?
5. What issues with course design came up repeatedly in student evaluations?
6. How do I (re)develop this course to meet student expectations while also implementing institutionally-mandated learning outcomes?

UX can help us answer these questions by helping us test out our solutions to problems before we implement them. Specifically, the following elements of UX described in this chapter can help with the following questions from above:

> Question 1: Usability testing of prototype
>
> Question 2: Preliminary research
>
> Question 3: Preliminary research
>
> Question 4: Usability testing of prototype
>
> Question 5: Preliminary research
>
> Question 6: Maintenance; Prototyping

The UX process, you see, is never finished. Only when a product or service is retired due to obsolescence can we stop adapting it to user needs. As long as we are teaching an online writing course, we must continually adapt it to align student goals and institutional goals with our own. When we notice areas of misalignment, we should begin the UX process over again by inventing a new prototype and testing it with current users. This is how the best technology companies in the world continue to provide exceptional experiences to their customers. And likewise: as teachers we must strive, year after year, semester after semester, day after day, to provide exceptional experiences to the student users whom we serve.

References

Allabarton, R. (2019, June 27). What is the ux design process? A complete, actionable guide. Career Foundry. https://careerfoundry.com/en/blog/ux-design/the-ux-design-process-an-actionable-guide-to-your-first-job-in-ux/.

Buley, L. (2013). *The user experience team of one: A research and design survival guide*. Rosenfeld Media.

Borgman, J. & McArdle, C. (2019). *Personal, accessible, responsive, strategic: Resources and strategies for online writing instructors*. The WAC Clearinghouse; University Press of Colorado. https://doi.org/10.37514/PRA-B.2019.0322.

Cerejo, L. (2010, June 16). *Design better and faster with rapid prototyping*. Smashing Magazine. https://www.smashingmagazine.com/2010/06/design-better-faster-with-rapid-prototyping.

Coyne, P., Pisha, B., Dalton, B., Zeph, L. & Cook Smith, N. (2017). Universal design for learning in pre-k to grade 12 classrooms: A systematic review of research. *Exceptionality: A Special Education Journal, 25*(2), 116–138.

Dolmage, J. (2009). Disability, usability, universal design. In S. Miller-Cochran & R. Rodrigo (Eds.), *Rhetorically rethinking usability: Theories, practices, and methodologies* (pp. 167–190). Hampton.

Hall, T., Meyer, A. & Rose, D. (2012). *Universal design for learning in the classroom*. The Guilford Press.

Garrett, J. (2003). *The elements of user experience: User-centered design for the web*. New Riders.

Getto, G. & St.Amant, K. (2014). Designing globally, working locally: Using personas to develop online communication products for international users. *Communication Design Quarterly, 3*(1), 24–46.

Goltz, S. (2014, August 6). A closer look at personas: What they are and how they work. *Smashing Magazine*. https://www.smashingmagazine.com/2014/08/a-closer-look-at-personas-part-1/.

Hartson, R. & Pyla, P. (2012). *The UX book: Process and guidelines for ensuring a quality user experience*. Morgan Kaufmann.

Hoober, S. (2014, May 5). The role of user experience in the product development process. *UX Matters*. http://www.uxmatters.com/mt/archives/2014/05/the-role-of-user-experience-in-the-product-development-process.php.

Melonçon, L. (Ed.) (2013). *Rhetorical accessibility: At the intersection of technical communication and disability studies*. Baywood.

Meyer, A., Rose, D. & Gordon, D. (2013). *Universal design for learning: Theory and practice*. CAST Professional Publishing.

Morville, P. (2007, July 23). *User experience strategy*. Semantic Studios. http://semanticstudios.com/user_experience_strategy/.

Nielson, J. (2010, October 17). *Mental models*. Nielson Norman Group. https://www.nngroup.com/articles/mental-models/.

Nielson, J. (2012, January 3). *Usability 101: Introduction to usability*. Nielson Norman Group. https://www.nngroup.com/articles/usability-101-introduction-to-usability/.

Walters, S. (2010). Toward an accessible pedagogy: Dis/ability, multimodality, and universal design in the technical communication classroom. *Technical Communication Quarterly, 19*(4), 427–454.

Williams, J., Rice, R., Lauren, B., Morrison, S., Van Winkle, K. & Elliott, T. (2013). Problem-based universal design for learning in technical communication and rhetoric instruction. *Journal of Problem Based Learning in Higher Education*, 1(1), 161–175.

Chapter 18. Usability Testing for OWI Instructors

Joseph Bartolotta
HOFSTRA UNIVERSITY

Abstract: This chapter explains how online writing instructors can test for the usability of their courses. Drawing from PARS principles (Borgman & McArdle, 2019), testing for usability becomes a pedagogical enhancement in an online writing course for students and instructors alike. Designing and deploying a usability test can seem daunting, but this chapter will offer the basics for setting up a simple usability test and will prepare instructors to eventually develop their own usability approaches for future classes. The usability testing I describe in this chapter will help instructors identify a specific task that they want to explore for usability, and then introduce a procedure whereby students themselves act as the testers of their own course while also writing toward an assignment for their class.

Keywords: usability, OWI design, student feedback, online education

This chapter explains how online writing instructors can test for the usability of their courses. Drawing from PARS principles (Borgman & McArdle, 2019), testing for usability becomes a pedagogical enhancement in an online writing course for students and instructors alike. Designing and deploying a usability test can seem daunting, but this chapter will offer the basics for setting up a simple usability test and will prepare instructors to eventually develop their own usability approaches for future classes. The usability testing I describe in this chapter will help instructors identify a specific task that they want to explore for usability, and then introduce a procedure whereby students themselves act as the testers of their own course while also writing toward an assignment for their class.

Usability testing is defined by the International Organization for Standardization (ISO) as "extent to which a system, product or service can be used by specified users to achieve specified goals with effectiveness, efficiency and satisfaction in a specified context of use" (Standardization, I. O., 2019, p. 3). That's a lot to dissect. For now, think of usability as the extent to which your students are able to complete the goals you have created for your online writing course. I don't mean their ability to write a paper, but their ability to find the resources (such as readings, assignment prompts, and other supporting items) that will help them effectively complete their work in class. This chapter is meant to be a brief introduction to usability testing that online writing instructors can quickly use in their courses. There are many other topics related to usability testing that can make the experience more rigorous and enriching that this chapter will only briefly touch upon. Resources identified in the References and Further Reading sections make excellent follow-up reading if you'd like to learn more about this tool. What follows is meant to show how a simple usability test can be an instructive opportunity for students and instructors alike and can help reshape the design of a course to be more accessible for all students.

PARS and Usability Testing

The PARS approach lends itself nicely to usability testing. I see alignment with all of the PARS letters and usability testing. For example, when we invite students to write about their personal interactions with the course design, it allows teachers to respond on a personal level. Usability testing can capture issues with access so we know when students are not able to interact with our tasks. A good usability test is responsive when we examine the data our students create and make changes to our courses. Finally, usability testing is strategic in that research shows that just 4 to 7 testers can uncover most usability issues (Sauro & Lewis, 2012). This number is probably much lower than the number of students in most OWI courses. The PARS approach can work well for instructors who want to deploy usability testing to be able to assess the student experiences completing different tasks in a writing course.

One of the things that first drew me to usability testing was that it offered me a mechanism to find out if my students were having the sort of experience in my class that I was envisioning and designing for them. Early in my teaching career, I heard from a student that, while she did have a computer at home, she did not have a reliable internet connection. She had to go to the local library and download my videos and assignments and then take them home if she wanted to work. This information changed how I designed the online components of my course. Still, I never would have known this had she not told me about her situation, which is why usability testing for online courses is so important. While user testing invites students to tell their teachers about their experiences interacting with the course, teachers may also get some hints about the contexts in which students access our courses. When we know more about *how* they interact with our courses, we can better conceptualize how to design a course for them. Our assumptions about instructional design as teachers is limited by our imagination about what the student experience is like. When we value the experiences our students are bringing to our classrooms and keep an open mind about what those experiences could look like, we can design in ways that are more thoughtful and responsive to their needs.

Usability testing done thoughtfully can be a way to let the diversity of student experiences become apparent. Adam Banks (2006) argues that, due to the fact that race and gender can be hidden online, "in cyberspace, it is finally possible to completely and utterly disappear people of color" (p. 1). We need to resist this erasure by centering the experiences of our students, especially students from historically marginalized communities, when we think about designing for usability. While we cannot rely on usability testing to do all the work of addressing racism and microaggressions built into our online platforms, it can allow instructors to identify and remedy issues quicker than doing nothing. When teachers reconceptualize and redesign their courses to meet their students' experiences, they can also aid in not isolating entire groups of students who do not have computers or internet access at home.

It is also important to take note that each student's report about their experience is personal, and user-testing should be seen as a reflection of their individual interactions with the course. As instructors, we need to honor the personal nature of a user test. We cannot simply look at a usability failure as an error on the student's part. We need to look at their individual issues and try to creatively resolve them. It may be possible that out of a group of 60 students, only five will report a usability challenge. As instructors with this data, we have to make decisions about how we respond. If we adjust the design of the task, do we risk more students have a different set of issues? Is it worth the time to overhaul the design to address an issue faced by just 8% of students? These are questions instructors must grapple with when they consider their course designs.

While discussing accessibility in OWI, Borgman and McArdle (2019) observe that, "it is good and right to create an accessible and inclusive space for students. However, many instructors struggle, or avoid, consideration of this principle because they lack the knowledge and experience on how to make things accessible" (p. 36). These next few pages offer online writing instructors the sorts of knowledge and know-how to incorporate usability testing into the classroom in a way that is instructive and useful for both the student and the instructor.

Task-Based Usability Testing

The first step toward understanding the usability of our courses is to become more focused on what concerns us. We may be so preoccupied by the fear that our courses are difficult to use that we lose sight of the places where these difficulties can actually emerge. The trick to creating more usable interactions for students is to think smaller than the whole course itself. Instead of thinking about making the whole course itself more usable, think about making tasks students have to complete more user-friendly. Usability experts agree that the way towards designing strong usability testing involves thinking about user experience at the task level (Barnum, 2011; Krug, 2014; Rubin & Chisnell, 2008). The International Organization for Standardization (ISO) (2019), implores designers to consider three things when drawing up plans for an interactive system: the users (in our case, students), the environment (in our case, an online LMS or instructor-designed site), and tasks. Thinking about usability at a task level gives us the ability to work more nimbly in enhancing how our students interact with our courses.

We might not realize it, but a lot of our web experiences outside school and work is task-based. We go to retrieve what we need and then do not return to the site until we need something similar again. Consider if I wanted to find the scores for a recent golf tournament; if I am sitting in a dentist's office and the sports section of a newspaper is nearby, I might pick it up and after a little searching find what I am looking for. In this case, due to the context, the newspaper was arguably more useable because it was within an arm's reach, and I could get the information easily. Now, if I did not have the newspaper nearby, I might reach for my cell phone to get the information. First, I unlock my phone, then I look for the proper application, then I find the "scores" area on that application, and unless there was a major tournament in the past few days, I'll probably have to tap on the "scores" button and search through a drop-down menu and then click on the "golf" button to be taken to a page dedicated to golf scores. Assuming there aren't too many tournaments going on, I should be able to get the information I want and move on with my life.

Yet, in searching on the phone, every step I mentioned is an opportunity for a usability failure. Each step was a task I had to complete, and the ease with which I accomplished them helps app designers monitor the usability of the app. For instance, when I look at the drop-down menu under "scores," were the sports listed in alphabetical order? How far do I have to scroll before I get to "Golf?" Do I have to scroll past Archery, Baseball, Basketball, Bobsledding, and so forth to get to the "Golf" button? Or, is the information listed by league, so I need to get down to PGA, which would be even further down the alphabetical list? Or, do the designers redesign the menu so the golf scores are closer to the top when a major tournament is ongoing? This approach could be good for one weekend but it would also mean the menu is subject to change in the future, so a user could not rely on using the same strategies to find the score two weeks later. These are just a sample of the sorts of decisions designers must make to satisfy their users. We can also see that the usability of a website or app can be held up at any number of tasks as our users try to achieve their goal. The role of thinking about tasks gets a little trickier when we extend it to OWI.

Baselines Constraining Usability in OWI

If we are using Learning Management Systems (LMSs), our students may be used to an interface but have several different teachers organizing information within those sites differently. To that end, students have to learn a new way of accessing information on the site, and different ways to complete the same task, at the start of each class and keep that structure in mind as they interact with each course site. Trickier still, some LMSs have rigid design structures that do not allow instructors to make substantive changes to the site that could enhance usability, while others are so flexible that students find it difficult to apply procedural knowledge they know from one course to the next. Some instructors insist on making their own sites using What You See is What You Get (WYSIWYG) structures such as WordPress. Here again, students must navigate an unfamiliar site and learn its architecture in much the same way they find their classroom in a new building on campus. Due to the structures imposed by LMSs or WYSIWYG website templates, it may be difficult to imagine what sort of tasks you actually have control over designing. You may be surprised to learn that even though you cannot change the layout of your course site easily, you still have a lot of control over how students interact with the content you post. As online course designers, we can help enhance the usability of our courses by designing experiences that come close to our student's intuitive interaction with our course sites, no matter where we operate them.

One thing we must remember is that we do not need to see students encounter a design failure to consider something to have a usability issue. A design failure in one place on the site could have a relatively catastrophic consequence for our students. They may not be able to complete their assignment, or access important information. However, catastrophes are rare and when they do occur, students are usually quick to point out the issues. To borrow from a golfing metaphor, catastrophes are like taking a shot that ultimately goes into the water and results in a penalty and a second shot, a re-do. When it comes to online course design we have to go in and fix things so that students can start again, which, while embarrassing, is usually easy enough. The things that worry me are the smaller usability issues. The ones that make a student sigh and mutter "now I have to do this again" under their breath. They know how to complete the task before them, but they find some part of it is convoluted, tedious, boring, or unclear. These are exactly the places where I think students are more reluctant to reach out with their concerns. To that end, we, as instructors, must be proactive in identifying the annoying and upsetting problems in our courses. Usability testing helps us better understand what is and is not intuitive for our students.

What Usability Could Look Like in OWI

Here is a common scenario you may encounter: You want students to write a discussion board post about a recent reading, but you'd like them to connect their response to a text they read two weeks ago. Students need to be able to access both readings so they can pull quotes and reference information in the discussion board post. You have placed your readings in folders corresponding to which week number it is in the course. It is week 9, but students need to connect the week 9 reading to a week 7 reading. Here is a potential usability problem: how easy is it for students to find the reading from week 7? Will they need to check the course schedule to remember which week they read the week 7 text? Does the schedule offer a breakdown of which week is which? In a lab, we could do the work of giving students a task and observing in real time what they do to accomplish that task. Five students may demonstrate three different paths to retrieving the week 7 reading, and as user researchers, we could examine each path to find out which one is the most efficient or productive toward their goal (efficiency is not always the standard by which we want to measure usability, but I'll get to that later). This data is invaluable to designers as we get a sense of what the intuitive user experience looks like, and we can adjust based on what our users do.

What I just described is an example of a potential challenge that can be tested for usability. A few years ago, I, along with Julianne Newmark and Tiffany Bourelle (2018), designed and carried out a usability test for an online introductory technical writing course. We recruited students from an upper-division technical writing course to test a "Start Here!" module that all students would go through at the beginning of class. We had four different versions of the course and divided up the student-testers so we had an equal number of testers for each site. All we did in designing the usability test was ask the student-testers to click on the "Start Here!" button and see how long it took them to get through the first module and observed places where they had trouble. We were not interested in seeing which teacher's design was "best." Usability testing should never be a competition—it should always be formative. Moreover, usability testing should not be seen as a way to train students about how to use their course interface. What instructors should be interested in is how new data about usability might impact our course designers.

While we (myself, Bourelle, and Newmark) wrote a couple articles about the testing, we deployed a rather time and labor-intensive setup to get our information. In our protocol, I had to sit and moderate each student's 30-minute usability testing session. A few years later we (now working with Michelle Stuckey) tweaked the protocol so we could have students perform the tests remotely, so we would not have to personally observe each student as they worked through the testing. Remote usability testing is used widely by online shopping platforms (although they still use traditional user testing from time to time as well). Customer-testers download apps such as dScout, follow instructions and then make short videos describing their experience completing their assigned tasks (they are also paid for this work). The information they share is invaluable to designers, and without the restrictions of having to observe each tester individually designers can pull from a much larger collection of data to help inform their design choices.

Online writing instructors can take a page from the remote usability testing setup without having to spend the sort of money on testing that companies must invest in this process. Moreover, online writing instructors can creatively collect data about how students interact with a course website while also contributing to learning objectives in class. The next section of this text sets out a procedure to accomplish both.

Your First OWI Usability Test

Try to choose a task that is relatively novel to the course; something the students may not have done before. For this reason, it is probably best to have students perform their tests early in the term. Students are good at learning how to navigate websites, and if they have already learned the ins and outs of your LMS or course site, they may interpret what they have learned as marking an easy user experience. There are other papers to be written about the value of learnability and its relationship with the design and usability in the context of OWI, but I won't engage that here. For now, strive to find the most novel user experience students will engage at this point in the course.

Find a Task to Test

Unless students make clear that they are struggling with a particular part of an online class, it may be hard to figure out what task to have them test. Do not worry too much about finding the best task to test right now; focus on something simple so you comfortably build up your confidence in usability testing.

When selecting a task, think of the specific actions students need to take in class. To name a few examples; students might "post" to a discussion board, "access" a class reading, "download" a rubric, "record" a video, "find" information about the writing center, and so forth. For this activity, I am going to use this task: "Make an appointment with the writing center." It's a real concern for me as an online writing instructor. Figure 18.1 is a screenshot of my course LMS home page. See if you can spot where the link is that gets students to make an appointment with the Writing Center:

I am sure some readers found the link with ease. Others will say that there may be better ways to draw students' attention to the Writing Center. Usability testing will help me better understand if my design choice was useful to the students or not.

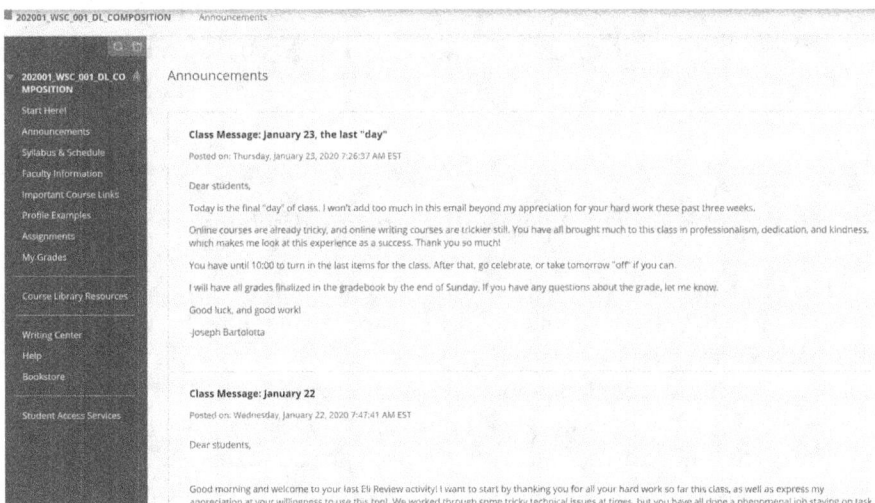

Figure 18.1. Can you find where students are supposed to access the Writing Center in this page?

Note Your Own Assumptions

It's important to note what sort of assumptions you are basing your design strategies from as you enter a usability test. Acknowledging your own assumptions gives you a point of departure as you imagine ways improve your course's design. You can turn your assumption into a user experience map as well, a visual representation of the major points on your student's journey to complete the task you identified in the previous step.

I have a link to my institution's writing center on the left navigation bar of my LMS homepage. I would make a note to myself that I would expect the user experience journey for my students would be broken into smaller sub-tasks, most likely looking like this:

1. Find the link to the "Writing Center" link on the left navigation of the LMS homepage.
2. Once on the writing center's homepage, click on the "Make an Appointment" box on the right side of the screen.
3. On the next screen, fill out the requisite information to make an appointment with the Writing Center

Usability experts would turn this into a user experience map to help visualize the route users take to complete an activity. This is what my very brief user experience map from the scenario I described looks like:

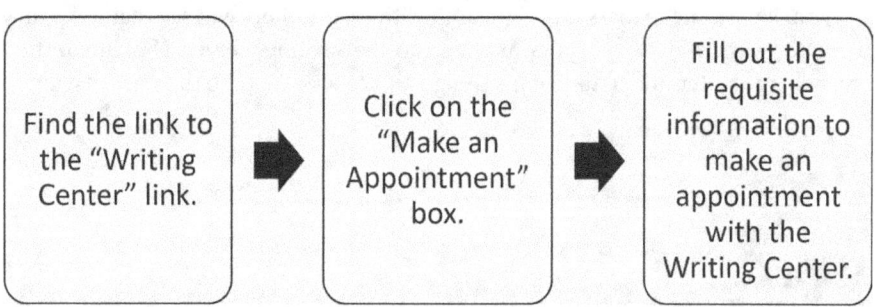

Figure 18.2. A simple activity map with sub-tasks.

It is short, but that is the point; introducing students to user testing practices does not need to be overly complex. It is also important for teachers to keep track of what their assumptions are going into the activity, as this will help uncover some underlying assumptions about design in general.

Naturally, we could we imagine several ways students might make this journey, but focus on what you think is most likely for now. This will be important for later as you evaluate how your assumptions aligned with student experiences. You may find that students have skipped a step or found themselves adding more steps you did not foresee.

Instruction on detailed prose

The best user experience data is usually the most detailed. This offers usability researchers precision in knowing which design elements need the most attention. Consider perhaps having students first write about a simple task, such as writing a set of instructions teaching a new student how to walk from some place on campus to the nearest off-campus pizza parlor. Ask students to share their descriptions of the journey someplace where other students can see it; perhaps on a discussion board or a shared file.

Students will write their directions with varying degrees of detail. Some may write street names and exact measurements of distance, while others may use campus landmarks to help their audience navigate the route. Later, students can look at what their peers wrote and start to have a discussion about what sorts of details were necessary for the instructions.

Modelling

Consider offering a model where you perform a speak-aloud protocol describing your own user journey while navigating a website. Of course, you will want to avoid the same task that you are asking your students to perform. I suggest modeling how you look for a book in the campus library. I am a big fan of screen capture technologies such as Camtasia and Screencast-O-Matic. Those technologies are particularly helpful if you are trying to teach students how to navigate something on a website. Using screen capture technology, and starting on your own browser, show students what steps you go through to get access to the book. Tell them what you are looking at as you make decisions about where to click. This activity will surely take more time than you would usually spend completing the same task, but that's the point; it is important to let students know that they are making many decisions when they interact with online systems. What they click, what they decide not to click, where they search for information; these are all important components of their journey.

It can also be useful to mention what items on the screen you find helpful. If there is a big blue button that lets you know how to best search for a book in a particular way. As we know, having a sense of what works in writing and design is just as useful as knowing what does not. Get students into the habit of commenting on both the shortcoming and enhancements of the designs they interact with.

The Students Test

Finally, it is time to have students perform their own usability test. Give them a task. In my case, I want them to get to the website where they make an appointment with the writing center. Invite students to find creative ways to make notes about their journeys. If students have a phone with a voice recorder, they could record their thoughts as a similar speak-aloud practice as they complete the task. Once students feel they have completed the task, have them write up a detailed summary of their experiences and submit them to the instructor.

Debrief

Find a way to debrief students about their work. Collect all of their writing and take some notes about what you see. Was there a typical journey students took? What were the major deviations from each other? Go back and look at your own assumptions about the student's user journey—did students take a similar path to what you described.

Most importantly, let students know how you plan to incorporate their feedback into your course design. Be self-effacing about the effort; let students know about your design decisions in the context of design and writing being an iterative process. Show students the way professionals respond to feedback and give them a sense of how their work could make the course better for both themselves and future students.

Final Thoughts and Application

PARS gives us some nice theoretical frame so we can articulate some approaches to using the best practices in designing and carrying out our online writing courses. I like to think that usability testing can be one of the tools we use to put the ideas presented in PARS into practice. Usability in the Strategic Golf Bag of OWI, if you will. Perhaps, in keeping with the golf metaphor that helps us understand PARS, we can think of usability testing is one of the many clubs in the OWI golf bag. Each club represents a tool we have in shaping effective and inviting courses for our students. I like to think that usability testing is like the sand wedge; it gets us out of bunkers. Over 18 holes even the most seasoned professionals find themselves stuck in a bunker. The wedge can get us out of the sand and back on track to making PARS.

However, we must remember that the club is only as good as the golfer. When you sit down with the student responses, start to explore if some of the challenges students are facing are deeper than simply completing course work. If students are having issues connecting to the internet, do not have access to the textbook, or find the amount of time it takes to complete a task to be too much, you may need to think deeper about adjusting some of the larger parameters of the course. This can be a challenge, but it is also a way to design a course that is more accessible and welcoming to your students, and helps you revise your future courses more strategically.

What I have put forth here is an activity designed to introduce students to descriptive writing practices and letting them see how writing and design are iterative processes. User testing helps to make your courses more strategic and accessible. Usability testing can help you can get the sort of feedback that can make you more thoughtfully consider your design choices while also engaging students in responding to your course design. As you become more comfortable with the method of usability testing presented in this chapter, you can start to tiptoe into more complex practices like having students test more complex tasks or splitting them into groups to face different designs that you are working on in the course (this would be a form of A/B testing). There are many more exciting and pedagogically rewarding ways to engage students in your course design.

References

Banks, A. (2006). *Race, rhetoric, and technology: Searching for higher ground.* Routledge.

Barnum, C. M. (2011). *Usability testing essentials: Ready, set . . . test!* Morgan Kaufmann.

Bartolotta, J., Newmark, J. & Bourelle, T. (2018). Engaging with online design: undergraduate user-participants and the practice-level struggles of usability learning. *Communication Design Quarterly Review,* 5(3)63–72. https://dl.acm.org/doi/abs/10.1145/3188173.3188180.

Borgman, J. & McArdle, C. (2019). *Personal, accessible, responsive, strategic: Resources and strategies for online writing instructors.* The WAC Clearinghouse; University Press of Colorado. https://doi.org/10.37514/PRA-B.2019.0322.

International Organization for Standardization (2019). *Human-centered design for interactive systems* (ISO 9241-210). https://www.iso.org/standard/77520.html.

Krug, S. (2014). *Don't make me think, revisited: A common sense approach to web usability.* New Riders.

Rubin, J. & Chisnell, D. (2008). *Handbook of usability testing: How to plan, design, and conduct effective tests.* Wiley.

Sauro, J. & Lewis, J. R. (2012). *Quantifying the user experience: Practical statistics for user research.* Morgan Kaufmann.

Additional Reading

Courage, C. & Baxter, K. (2005). *Understanding your users: A practical guide to user requirements methods, tools, and techniques.* Gulf Professional Publishing.

Redish, J. G. (2007). *Letting go of the words: Writing web content that works.* Morgan Kaufmann.

Chapter 19. Aiming for the Sweet Spot: A User-Centered Approach to Migrating a Community-engaged Course Online

Erica M. Stone
MIDDLE TENNESSEE STATE UNIVERSITY

Abstract: Aiming for the Sweet Spot: A User-Centered Approach to Migrating a Community-engaged Course Online illustrates how the PARS approach helped facilitate the migration of a community-engaged writing course from a synchronous face-to-face format to an asynchronous online format. Using a personal, accessible, responsive, and strategic (PARS) approach to course redesign, this chapter makes specific recommendations for hitting the sweet spot in online writing instruction through user-centered instruction and place-based user experience architecture.

Keywords: Community-engaged course, community engagement, modality, service learning, user-centered instruction, place-based user experience architecture

As argued by Borgman and McArdle (2019) in their recent book *Personal, Accessible, Responsive, Strategic: Resources and Strategies for Online Writing Instructors*, the principles and practices of user experience can (and should) be applied to online course (re)design approaches. In fact, user experience (UX) design and user experience architecture (XA) are expanding well beyond the fields of software design and computer programming and into larger ecosystems, like online writing instruction (Borgman & McArdle, 2019; Moore, 2017; Potts & Salvo, 2017). In an effort to attend to Potts and Salvo's (2017) call to move UX/XA "beyond isolated tasks of writing, designing, and programming" (p. 5) and build on Borgman and McArdle's work, this chapter demonstrates how the PARS approach can be used to migrate a community-engaged writing course from a synchronous face-to-face format to an asynchronous online format.

Using a localized, case example from my time as an adjunct instructor at the University of Missouri-Kansas City (UMKC) in Fall 2017, I argue that the "sweet spot" in online writing instruction (OWI) is treating students as the central users of instructional spaces and documents (Blythe, 2001; Borgman & McArdle, 2019; Greer & Harris, 2017).[1] In the game of golf, the "sweet spot" is a specific area on

---

1. The student work in this chapter belongs to Abigail Birkner who took my Discourse 300 course as an honors student in Spring 2018. Abigail consented to her work being shared in this edited collection, and no compensation was awarded for her work.

a golf club face that should be hit for optimal results (i.e., a hole in one; or at the very least, meeting or beating par). For online writing instructors, the possibility "hitting the sweet spot" can vary based on the needs of the student population as well as course outcomes, department expectations, and the presence of a community or industry partner. While keeping mind the expected course outcomes, departmental policies, and community partner goals, this chapter uses my recent experience at UMKC to provide a model for prioritizing the needs of students as the central users of a community-engaged writing course during an instructional modality change and subsequent course redesign. Following Borgman and McArdle's (2019) praxis-based chapter structure, I discuss my course redesign process in three sections:

1. First, I describe the context of my localized case at UMKC in Fall 2017, and I provide a brief overview of the general education curriculum.
2. Next, I illustrate how the PARS approach helped facilitate the migration of a community-engaged writing course from a synchronous face-to-face format to an asynchronous online format. I also explain the exigency for an online community partner, and I provide examples of assignment templates and student work.
3. Last, I reflect on my course migration and redesign process, and I provide broad recommendations for shifting a community-engaged course online during times of austerity and crisis. I also preview how the community-engaged online course discussed in this chapter led to the development of additional online courses and interinstitutional partnerships.

Course Context: Localizing the PARS Approach

For nearly ten years, the University of Missouri-Kansas City's general education curriculum required students to take a three-course sequence in writing and speech called Discourse (catalog.umkc.edu/course-offerings/undergraduate/disc/). (Note: This program is currently undergoing a "teach-out" as UMKC has revised its general education curriculum to increase transferability and cohesion with the UM System.) The first course in the sequence, Discourse 100: Reasoning and Values, focused on social, professional, political, and community discourse. The second course, Discourse 200: Culture and Diversity, engaged directly with academic research and the research process with an emphasis on individual, institutional, and cultural identities. The third course, Discourse 300: Civic and Community Engagement, sought to put the rhetorical and research skills from Discourse 100 and 200 into practice in an

---

I'm thankful for her excellent contributions to this chapter and her willingness to share her coursework with the WAC community.

interdisciplinary and intercultural service-learning project with a designated community partner.

Discourse 300 was taught as a "linked" speech and writing course where students enrolled in an "anchor" class that covered specific subject matter (e.g., anthropology). While an anchor faculty member served as a subject matter expert in a specific discipline, a Discourse 300 instructor would provide writing and public speaking instruction and guidance on a discipline-specific project that focused on community-engaged writing and/or public speaking. In 2016, discourse classes were delinked from anchor courses, and community-engagement placements and logistics became the responsibility of discourse instructors, which were largely contingent faculty and graduate students.

During my tenure as an adjunct faculty member at UMKC, I taught 13 sections of Discourse 300, most of which were face-to-face. But, in Fall 2017, I was asked to develop a fully online and asynchronous section of the class. While this was a daunting request for a part-time instructor, I had over six years of experience teaching online, and I had close ties with community organizers and nonprofit organizations across the Kansas City metropolitan area because of my work as a community organizer (Austin & Stone, 2020; Stone, 2019). Since this important groundwork was already laid, I was able to focus less on coordinating outside community connections and more on designing an online course that benefitted my central users: undergraduate students from over 15 different majors. In other words, I focused on "hitting the sweet spot" by putting the PARS approach into practice.

Hitting the Sweet Spot: Operationalizing the PARS Approach

In order to develop an online, community-engaged writing course that centered the needs of students, I used the PARS approach. Admittedly, the Borgman and McArdle's book wouldn't be published until 2019, but Borgman had shared details about the four-part approach during our Ph.D. classes and professional development sessions at Texas Tech University. Like Borgman and McArdle (2019), I believe that instructors should be personal, accessible, responsive, and strategic in the design, facilitation, and administration of their online writing courses. As an instructor of Discourse 300 at UMKC, I had the additional responsibility of ensuring students had the opportunity to create meaningful relationships in the Kansas City community and build a writing and learning community all within an asynchronous online space (Warnock, 2009). In the four sections below—aptly named for each part of the PARS approach—I illustrate how the PARS approach helped facilitate the migration of a Discourse 300 from a synchronous face-to-face format to an asynchronous online format. I also explain the exigency for an online community partner, and I provide examples of assignment templates and student work.

Personal

According to Borgman and McArdle (2019), personalized online writing instruction often focuses on developing a recognizable course presence, approachable instructor profiles, and sometimes, respective administrative practices. I extended Borgman and McArdle's definition of personalized online writing instruction to meet the individual, and sometimes disciplinary, needs of students. To make the content and assignments of my online Discourse 300 personal and user-centered, I developed an online, pre-course survey for students to complete upon registration. I asked questions about the genres of writing they used in their discipline (e.g., engineers use technical reports), and I inquired about the kinds of practice skills (e.g., usability testing) they were interested in gleaning from the course. In their responses, students emphasized their desires to learn practical skills and make connections within the greater Kansas City community that might help them obtain jobs or internships. Based on this data, I worked with our community partner, Code for Kansas City (codeforkc.org), to develop accessible course assignments and community interactions that would benefit each students' individual goals and meet the objectives of the course.

Accessible

On the most basic level, an accessible writing online writing course is "universally inclusive" and ethnically addresses the needs of all learners (Borgman & McArdle, 2019, p. 36). But I take up Borgman and McArdle's invitation to expand the definition of access further to include removing unnecessary barriers like the cost of course materials or the modality of a community engagement site. Redesigning a community-engaged course for an online learning environment meant ensuring my students had an accessible community partner who could allow them to complete their service-learning projects completely online and asynchronously. Since students often choose online classes for their "convenience and access" (Salter, 2012, p. 213) and because UMKC serves a primarily nontraditional student population with multiple time commitments and often inflexible schedules (Austin & Stone, 2002), my users (students) were to partner with a fully online community partner. Over the summer, I had collaborated with one of the core team members of Code for Kansas City, a brigade chapter of Code for America (www.codeforamerica.org) that is dedicated to bridging the digital divide through civic hacking and open data. Using Moore's (2017) heuristic for place-based user experience architecture, I met with the Code for Kansas City core team and its community coders to determine the kinds of digital, field-based projects my students might be able to work on. Together, we chose CommunityKC (codeforkc.org/#project-list), an asset mapping project that connects people and resources across Kansas City. Since the site was already existing and needed some additional user experience research and content development, it was a great project for advanced online writing students to practice place-based experience architecture (Moore, 2017) through low-stakes, online field research and usability testing. I discuss the UX project and how the students interacted with Code for Kansas City more in the section on Strategic OWI course redesign.

In addition to securing an accessible community partner, I increased the accessibility and affordability of the course by using all open educational resources, including textbooks, coding tools, and software. While my course required a considerable amount of time for writing, speaking, and community-based projects, students were not required to spend any additional money on course materials. We used the first iteration of Suzan Last's (2019) open-access textbook, Technical Writing Essentials (pressbooks.bccampus.ca/technicalwriting/), to learn about the basic concepts of technical communication, and I relied on other open educational resources like Usability.gov (usability.gov) to help students understand the basic principles of user experience and practical frameworks for usability testing.

Similarly, students retained the intellectual property rights to all of the deliverables they produced in collaboration with our community partner. To combat the tendency for service-learning courses to become hyper pragmatic and focused only on the deliverables for the community partner (Scott, 2004), a significant portion of the course was spent on reflective, collaborative work where students focused on articulating our iterative and agile development process, not just with one another, but with our community partner. When their schedules permitted, online Discourse 300 students were invited to join the community coders at Code for Kansas City during their weekly hack nights to work on the CommunityKC map synchronously and in-person. As my undergraduate co-author, Jasmine Amerin, and I discussed in a recent Intercom piece (2019) about the benefits of Code for America as a service-learning site, it's important to follow Scott's (2004) "suggestion to use participatory design principles and an intercultural inquiry process that mirrored the values of cultural and community rhetorics" (p. 30) to ensure a mutually beneficial collaboration.

Responsive

Responsive online writing instruction and course (re)design have a lot to do with habits of mind, time management, communication patterns, and student feedback (Borgman & McArdle, 2019). All of these components are infinitely important to student success and satisfaction in an online writing course. Another facet of responsive online writing instruction is addressing the complications that can arise when migrating an online writing course from face-to-face format to an online format. As Warnock (2009) argues, it's simply not enough to port over face-to-face materials into an online writing classroom. Similarly, Borgman & Dockter (2018) point out that "this act of migration can be troublesome when online teachers don't consider the unique opportunities that exist within the online domain. The assumption is what works in in one teaching context will work equally well in another" (p. 96). During my initial course redesign, the shift in location and modality caused some concern—not just for how I might maintain the authenticity of the assignments, but also for how an online learning modality might impact our relational work our community partner, Code for Kansas City.

As mentioned in my introduction, the sweet spot in online instruction is treating students as the central users of our instructional spaces and course documents. But, accommodating a shift in instructional location and modality is not always a part of the online course design process. All too often, writing studies departments and writing program administrators will construct one predesigned version of a course for all contingent faculty or graduate teaching assistants to teach instead of allowing instructors to incorporate their expertise and located ethos (Simmons, 2010; Stone & Austin, 2019;). Because UMKC recognized the importance of faculty expertise, ethos, and academic freedom, I was able to be responsive to the needs of my students when I migrated Discourse 300 online. Keeping my students in mind as my central users, I made adjustments to the course foci to accommodate the location change, as outlined in Table 19.1.

Table 19.1 illustrates how a shift in course location and instructional modality warrants a shift in the course foci and community engagement site. In other words, an online course requires a more easily accessible, online space for community-engaged coursework. In previous semesters, my face-to-face Discourse 300 students had been required to engage synchronous, face-to-face version of Discourse 300 required students to engage with a local community problem or issue in Kansas City (e.g., food insecurity) through a specific community-oriented nonprofit organization. Oftentimes, students would partner with an organization they were already connected with or one that was facilitated by their anchor course faculty. In my Fall 2017, asynchronous, online version of Discourse 300, my students engaged in a user experience and usability analysis of CommunityKC, an online community and nonprofit resource mapping site designed by local community-based coders. This responsive approach to community engagement and service learning in an online writing course helped facilitate an impactful learning experience for my online Discourse 300 students.

Table 19.1. Course foci adjustments to accommodate location change

	Face-to-face, Community-engaged Class	Online, Community-engaged Class
Course Focus	Engaging with a local community problem or issue in Kansas City (e.g., food insecurity) through a specific community-oriented nonprofit organization	Engaging in a user experience and usability analysis of an online community and nonprofit resource mapping site designed by local community-based coders

Strategic

Strategic online writing instruction and course (re)design are "focused on the user experience of the students" (Borgman & McArdle, 2019, p. 71). By shifting my online Discourse 300 students' required servicing-learning component from face-to-face environment to an online space, I was able to accommodate their schedules while maintaining the integrity of the community-based course. Because I was working from the liminal space of a community-engaged adjunct (Long, 2008), I was able to strategically restructure my course by creating opportunities for my students to engage in a civically engaged project that was built for and works in an online community space. This attention to user-centered design principles in my course redesign process improved student learning outcomes and provided a pathway for future scenarios where I might have to relocate community-engaged projects and/or classes . . . like the COVID-19 pandemic just a year later (more on this experience in my Final Thoughts and Application section).

To accommodate the shift in instructional modality (from face-to-face to online), I made strategic changes to the assignment design and structure in my Discourse 300 class, as illustrated in Table 19.2.

Table 19.2. Assignment structure changes to accommodate shift in instructional modality

Assignment Description	Synchronous Face-to-Face	Asynchronous Online
Preliminary Assignment	Project proposal	User experience (UX) exploration and analysis
Speech 1	Defining specific community problems	Instructional video about the community site
Midterm Assignment	Research project progress report	Existing organization profile update; creation of new organization profile
Speech 2	Advocating solutions for a particular population	Progress report
Reciprocal Contribution to Community Partner	Public writing for self-identified community group	User experience (UX) recommendation report for website
Summative Assessment	Community-focused research paper	Community-focused research paper

All assignment redesigns were done in collaboration with core team members of Code for Kansas City, specifically the community coders who were working on the CommunityKC map. Using Moore's (2017) heuristic for place-based experience architecture to create opportunities for students to conduct place-based field research about the people, places, and resources of Kansas City, I was able to extend

Potts and Salvo's (2017) call to move UX/XA "beyond isolated tasks of writing, designing, and programming" (p. 5). Because building an place-based XA in "local communities requires familiarity with the tempos and geographies of the citizens" (Moore, 2017, p. 155), my working knowledge of Code for Kansas City, as both a community organization and a community of knowledge-workers, was beneficial to the students enrolled in my online, asynchronous section of Discourse 300. As part of their collaboration with the CommunityKC mapping team, my online students were able to learn about the diverse communities and lesser-known organizations within their neighborhoods and around the UMKC campus. Maintaining a place-based and geographical connection to the Kansas City community, even while working in a completely online environment, was important for a course whose history was rooted in civic and community engagement.

As outlined in Table 19.2, Discourse 300 students in both the face-to-face and online course formats completed six major writing and/or public speaking projects. The objectives for each project remained the same; only the location and modality shifted. I'll spend the next few paragraphs outlining each assignment in the online version of Discourse 300, being careful to identify how each assignment engaged in strategic learning activities and outcomes. When appropriate, I will link and discuss assignment templates and student examples from a student who took the second iteration of my online Discourse 300 class (see Author Note).

First, online Discourse 300 students worked individually to conduct a user experience exploration and analysis report of the CommunityKC site. They composed a report intended for the community coders that provided observations of how the site functioned for a first-time user who was unfamiliar with its purpose and audience. This assignment engaged all four of the PARS elements, but most specifically, it was personal. During the pre-course survey, students has requested to learn new skills that would help them in their future jobs or internships, and user experience exploration and analysis certainly fit that request. Not only is user experience a growing career field, but nearly all businesses and nonprofits benefit from having someone on staff with a working knowledge of usability testing and user experience design. Appendices A and B offer examples of the assignment template used for this report (Appendix A) as well as a completed student example report (Appendix B). After submitting their reports, the students discussed their findings as a class in an asynchronous discussion board where they identified portions of the site that needed additional instructions, which informed the second assignment: an instructional video about the site.

Because discourse students were also required to produce 18+ minutes of polished public speaking, two digital speeches needed to be integrated into the design of the online course. In small groups, students produced an instructional video and corresponding transcript for the site users that gave additional directions for portions of the site that were identified as troublesome. For example, one student created an instructional video for how to search for a specific community project on the CommunityKC mapping site, while another student showed site users how to search by project type, as shown in this student example video at youtube.com/watch?v=1TJP-jGqMqo. A full transcript for this video can be found in Appendix C. This project taught students how to design accessible deliverables through a hands-on, creative process. Each instructional video was provided to the community coders, and with students' permission, they have been able to use the instructional videos on their site. As mentioned in the previous section, students maintained the intellectual rights to all of their deliverables, and none of their work was used by the community partner without proper attribution.

As part of their community-engaged research assignment for the class, each student interviewed a community partner featured on the website to update their contact and organizational information. Moore's (2017) step-by-step instructions for how to teach and implement a place-based XA were extremely helpful as I worked to navigate this new instructional modality and occupy the liminal space of both a community volunteer for Code for Kansas City and an instructor-collaborator. Additionally, students were responsible for locating one new Kansas City organization that was interested in being featured on the site. Students interviewed a member of the new organization and helped them create their own organizational and project-specific profile on the site using a Google Form which fed into a spreadsheet for the Code for Kansas City coders to access. Students were invited to attend optional and ungraded coding meetings to work on data input, troubleshooting, and the like.

While the audience for the first speech was the community coders and eventually the CommunityKC website users, the audience for the second speech was me: the instructor. I asked students to schedule a synchronous meeting with me to deliver a short progress report speech. This assignment required students to compose a progress report where they reflected on their course progress toward curriculum-specific objectives as well as how the course was meeting their expectations for an online, community-engaged course that worked with a community partner in a nontraditional, mostly asynchronous, space. This assignment allowed both me and my students the opportunity to engage personally and responsively with one another. During these informal speeches, I learned where students were struggling the course as well as how I could improve my course design, facilitation, and assessment.

In an effort to ensure a reciprocal contribution to our community partner, students composed a memo intended for the community coders that provided recommendations for how to improve the site for its intended users: citizens of Kansas City. This recommendation report included observational and field data from all of their interactions with the site users as well as their own extensive use and testing of its features. For example, one student suggested that CommunityKC should have an events calendar added to their site, which has since been implemented by the Code for Kansas City coders. This aspect of the course was strategic because it combined all of the students' previous work on CommunityKC content and required them to engage with a vested audience. Additionally, this memo gave students the opportunity to see what it might be like to work directly with a client in a future job or internship.

As their final assignment for the course, students conducted a formal research project on a systemic problem identified by one of the community partner organizations featured on the CommunityKC site. For example, one student had been working with a site user who focused on mitigating neighborhood blight, so her research project focused on Kansas City's history of racism and redlining in residential real estate. Another student had created a new community profile for a faith-based group during the midterm assignment, so his research project investigated how faith-based groups in Kansas City support the work of other nonprofit organizations. While this last assignment did not interact specifically with Code for Kansas City or the CommunityKC websites, it strategically fulfilled the requirement for students to complete an academic research paper by the end of the course.

Final Thoughts and Application

As I reflect back on my user-centered migration and redesign of Discourse 300, I see many implications for our current time of increased austerity and crisis in the field of writing studies, in higher education, and around our fractured country. The COVID-19 health crisis as well as sustained civil unrest have left most of us feeling drained, at best. If I were to repeat this migration and redesign process during this precarious time—or make general recommendations to another faculty member who is considering migrating a community-engaged writing course online—I would prioritize students as the central users of online spaces and documents through a PARS approach.

In order to design a course that is personal and responsive, develop an online survey for students to complete when they enrolled in the course that asks about their goals and preferences. If you're contemplating a course survey to center students' lived experiences, consider surveying students throughout the course to increase agency and respond to student concerns about instructional content, course pacing, or assessment practices. Once you've reviewed the students' responses, you can share them with the class to demonstrate that you're listening and justify any changes you might make to the course design based on their feedback.

To create an accessible and affordable online course, use all open educational resources, including textbooks, coding tools, and software. I understand the concept of open educational resources can be overwhelming, but adapting and adopting open educational resources can be incremental. The open access movement is not all-or-nothing, as evidenced by the WAC Clearinghouse's (wac.colostate.edu/about/) incremental approach to supporting and growing open access research within our own field! As a first step, consider adopting ready-made textbooks from resource sites like Open Stax (openstax.org), the Open Education Network's

Open Textbook Library (open.umn.edu/opentextbooks/), or one of the many titles available through Press Books (pressbooks.com). When you're comfortable adopting an open textbook, you might consider using open courseware or open source software (St.Amant & Still, 2007).

Antiracist and Inclusive Pedagogical Changes

While there are many choices I would repeat in a subsequent, user-centered course migration and redesign, there are some pedagogical changes I would make if were to repeat this migration and redesign process in 2020 and beyond. I describe a few in this section; although, I'm sure I will think of additional changes after this book has been published. After all, user-centered course (re)design is iterative, reflective, and ongoing.

As someone who is sincerely invested in the work of recognizing, revealing, rejecting, and replacing (Walton et al., 2019) racist practices, policies, and pedagogies that harm Black, Indigenous, and People of Color (BIPOC), I would work to recenter the lived experiences of multiply marginalized populations in my online, community-engaged classes. As a first step, I would be explicit and intentional in my syllabus, readings, and assignments about the social, economic, and racial contexts that undergird students' access to technology (Haas, 2012) as well as their exposure to digital literacies (Byrd, 2019; Kynard, 2013). In my face-to-face Discourse 300 course, I taught about Kansas City's racist history (e.g., redlining) and the systemic inequality that remains as a result. When I shifted the course online, this important sociocultural context slowly slid out of focus, especially as more of my energy and time went to coordinating with our community partner and managing the online components of the course.

But pedagogical practices don't only exist within instructor-created documents; exemplars and templates are imbued with the values and lived experiences of their authors. To further center BIPOC experiences and cite inclusively when discussing UX/XA, I would assign exemplar texts authored by public-facing scholars of color to highlight the kinds of technical and professional communication (TPC) that exist outside of the academy. Specifically, I would assign Iyamah's (2019) article that maps space-making and the lived experiences of Black people onto the five phases of the UX design process (define, research, synthesize, design, implement). I would also assign McKoy's (2020) digital dissertation chapter that uses her theoretical framework, Amplification Rhetorics, to increase the value and exposure of public-facing TPC genres and practices (e.g., TrapKaraoke) that are typically confined to historically marginalized communities.

By adapting Moore's (2017) heuristic for engaged in place-based experience architecture, I pushed the boundaries of XA and encourage reflective practices and projects within a community-engaged online writing classroom. In addition to using Moore's heuristic, I would build upon Hurley's (2018) concept of spatially-oriented course (re)design. Even if an online writing course doesn't engage with a *community map*, like my online Discourse 300 class *did*, a spatially-oriented course makes "the intersections among spatialities visualities, technologies, subjectivities, and communication practices more apparent" (Hurley, 2018). Admittedly, Hurley's methodology wasn't published at in Fall 2017, the semester I migrated my community-engaged writing course online. However, my willingness to continue to read and reflect on my own course over time reiterates both how and why a user-centered course (re)design is iterative, reflective, and ongoing.

Iterative, Reflective, and Ongoing Application

In alignment with the iterative, reflective, and ongoing revisioning process of user-centered courses, the migration and (re)design of Discourse 300 in Fall 2017 led to the development of additional community-engaged online courses at UMKC (see Amerin & Stone, 2019; Stone 2019) and one in-process, interinstitutional research project with Antonio Byrd at UMKC. Just one year before I left Kansas City to begin my new role at Middle Tennessee State University (MTSU), Antonio was hired at UMKC as an assistant professor where he has continued the English Department's collaboration with Code for Kansas City, specifically within ENGL 430WI: Advanced Technical Writing. Following Simmons' (2010) model for extended community writing projects, Byrd and I have continued to work together to consider how community-engaged technical writing courses can be designed iteratively across semesters, institutions, and student populations. Meanwhile in Murfreesboro, I've been making inroads with Code for Nashville (codefornashville.org) as a potential community partner for MTSU's new Bachelor of Science in Public Writing and Rhetoric (PWR). When the MTSU writing studies team begins to design community, digital, and technical writing courses for the PWR major, I will refer back to this chapter to ensure our online PWR courses are inclusive, user-centered, and (okay, I'll say it . . .) hit the "sweet spot."

Acknowledgments

Thank you to Jessie and Casey for including me in your first (of many, I'm sure!) edited collection about the PARS approach to online writing instruction (OWI). I've enjoyed participating in the OWI Community (owicommunity.org) for the last three years, and I'm humbled to be included in your collection.

I'd like to extend my sincere thanks to my brother, Steven Mote, for his thorough lesson in golf terminology during the drafting of this chapter. Despite reading Jessie and Casey's first book several times—I know absolutely nothing about the game of golf. I suspect his favor of the term "sweet spot" in my title and as a metaphor for user-centered online writing instruction is just one more little brother jab!

References

Amerin, J. R. & Stone, E. M. (2019). Purposeful partnership: Code for America brigade chapters as a professional development network for technical writers. *Intercom, 66*(2) 28-31.

Austin, S. E. & Stone, E. M. (2020). The ethos triad for contingent composition faculty: Location, modality, and WPA Support. *Forum: Issues about Part-time & Contingent Faculty, 47*(3), A9-16.

Blythe, S. (2001). Designing online courses: User-centered design. *Computers and Composition, 18*(4), 329-346. https://doi.org/10.1016/S8755-4615(01)00066-4.

Borgman, J. & Dockter, J. (2016). Minimizing the distance in online writing courses through student engagement. *Teaching English in the Two-Year College, 44*(2), 213-222.

Borgman, J. & McArdle, C. (2019). *Personal, accessible, responsive, strategic: Resources and strategies for online writing instructors.* The WAC Clearinghouse; University Press of Colorado. https://doi.org/10.37514/PRA-B.2019.0322.

Byrd, A. (2019). Between learning and opportunity: A study of African-American coders' networks of support. *Literacy in Composition Studies, 7*(2), 31-55.

Greer, M. & Harris, H. S. (2018). User-centered design as a foundation for effective online writing instruction. *Computers and Composition, 49*, 14-24.

Haas, A. M. (2012). Race, rhetoric, and technology: A case study of decolonial technical communication theory, methodology, and pedagogy. *Journal of Business and Technical Communication, 26*(3), 277-310.

Hurley, E. V. (2018). Spatial orientations: Cultivating critical spatial perspectives in technical communication pedagogy. A. M. Haas & M. F. Eble (Eds). *Key theoretical frameworks: Teaching technical communication in the twenty-first century* (pp. 9-113). Utah State University Press.

Iyamah, J. (2019). Black people have always been UX designers: Space-making is an iterative design process. *Medium*, https://medium.com/black-ux-collective/black-people-have-always-been-ux-designers-space-making-is-an-iterative-design-process-fcefe4cce846.

Kynard, C. (2013). Literacy/literacies studies and the still-dominant white center. *Literacy in Composition Studies, 1*(1), 63-65.

Last, S. (2019). *Technical writing essentials: Introduction to professional communications in technical fields.* Press Books.

Long, E. (2008). *Community literacy and the rhetoric of local publics.* Parlor Press; The WAC Clearinghouse. https://wac.colostate.edu/books/referenceguides/long-community/.

Mckoy, T. T. (2019). *Y'all call it technical and professional communication, we call it #ForTheCulture: The use of amplification rhetorics in black communities and their implications for technical and professional communication studies* (Doctoral dissertation, East Carolina University). https://thescholarship.ecu.edu/handle/10342/7421.

Moore, K. R. (2017). Experience architecture in public planning: A material, activist practice. In L. Potts & M. J. Salvo (Eds.), *Rhetoric and experience architecture* (pp. 143-165). Parlor Press.

Salter, D. W. (2012). Online student retention. In A. Seidman (Ed.), *College student retention: Formula for student success* (pp. 211–228). Rowan and Littlefield.

Scott, J. B. (2004). Rearticulating civic engagement through cultural studies and service-learning. *Technical Communication Quarterly, 13*(3), 289–306.

Simmons, M. (2010). Encouraging civic engagement through extended community writing projects: Rewriting the curriculum. *The Writing Instructor.* https://files.eric.ed.gov/fulltext/EJ890596.pdf.

St.Amant, K. S. & Still, B. (2007). *Handbook of research on open source software: Technological, economic, and social perspectives.* Idea Group Inc.

Stone, E. M. & Austin, S. E. (2020). Writing as commodity: How neoliberalism renders the postsecondary online writing classroom transactional and ways faculty can regain agency. *Basic Writing Electronic (BWe) Journal, 16*(1), 1–23.

Stone, E. M. (2019, May 10). Exploring social advocacy through community-engaged, public-facing technical communication. In J. Jiang & J. Tham (Eds.), *Sweetland Digital Rhetoric Collaborative's blog carnival on multimodal design and social advocacy,* https://www.digitalrhetoriccollaborative.org.

Walton, R., Moore, K. R. & Jones, N. N. (2019). *Technical communication after the social justice turn: building coalitions for action.* Routledge.

Warnock, S. (2009). *Teaching writing online: How and why.* National Council of Teachers of English.

Appendix A. Usability Report Template

To: Erica Stone
From: YOUR NAME
Subject: CommunityKC User Experience Exploration and Analysis Report
Date: FILL IN SUBMISSION DATE

Website Impressions

Based on your first impression, what is the purpose of this website? How would you use it if you stumbled upon it during an internet search? Be specific and feel free to use any of your salient points from our first two discussion boards.

Positive Attributes

What are some positive attributes of the website? Be specific and feel free to use any of your salient points from our first two discussion boards.

Negative Attributes

How and where does the website need improving?

Which features are confusing? Describe, in detail, the issues that you encountered?

On average, how many minutes did you spend using the website before getting frustrated?

Be specific and feel free to use any of your salient points from our first two discussion boards.

Recommended Users
Who do you know that would like this product? How would they use it? Be specific and feel free to use any of your salient points from our first two discussion boards.

Summary of Feedback for CommunityKC
Based on your responses above and your discussions with classmates, share your initial recommendations for the CommunityKC developers. Be professional and specific. As with the other sections, feel free to use any of your salient points from our first two discussion boards.
I will share this section of your report with the team lead, and we will use these parameters to help us determine the work we will do on the site this semester.

Appendix B. Example Usability Report

To: Erica Stone
From: Abigail Birkner
Subject: CommunityKC User Experience Exploration and Analysis Report
Date: 10 February 2019

Website Impressions
   Based on my first impression of the website, I would say that the purpose of the website is to connect people or organizations to community service opportunities and efforts to revitalize neighborhoods in Kansas City. I would personally use it to increase my awareness of projects and needs in the community and learn how to get involved to meet the needs of people in my community better. I would also potentially use it to direct other people who want to get involved to the needs in their community and projects they can engage in.

Positive Attributes
   The site has a really great backbone and the beginning of some good ideas. I appreciated the map because it saves people time of looking up event locations in relation to where they are. It helps to make the site more interactive and engage others as well. I also appreciated how they list all of their projects, and within the listing, give the background and contact information for organizations or the organizing person for the project. They have a color scheme for the website, and it is organized with tabs containing different fields of information. Overall, the idea for the website is wonderful, and it could be incredibly impactful for service projects and collaboration between different organizations and people with some restructuring.

Negative Attributes
   While I love the idea of the map, I think that it slightly distracts from highlighting the purpose and use of the website by being the front page. I felt that the

website seemed to lack some personality/heart, and I think the map being the front page does not help with it being personal and engaging from an understanding of the depth/purpose of the website. And while it has a backbone, I feel as though it is slightly bare from an aesthetic perspective, which is why I felt like it lacked a personal experience. The events/projects are also seemingly outdated, so if there were some way to keep it updated, I think that that would be a good draw for people because they would not have to sift through so many outdated projects, which would have frustrated me had I been using it to find a project. I also feel like it lacked being personal to me because the "about" page includes a very general email and number. There is no information about the founders or why it is important to them or how to contact them, so I feel like the heart does not seem as though it is there, which is what would draw me to an organization or something like this website personally.

Recommended Users

I personally think this website would be incredible for collaboration between non-profit organizations and other groups who exist for community service/to meet the needs of the community. I also feel it could be incredibly beneficial for mentor/mentee programs like the Kansas City Public School's Success Mentoring Program to get involved in. They could advertise the program on CommunityKC, but they could also use it for mentors/mentees to get involved in together. It would really help mentor/mentee relationships to grow while serving the communities that the mentees live in together. It serves as a way to help the students in the program who are at risk of dropping out, failing out, etc. in a more holistic manner.

Summary of Feedback for CommunityKC

While the purpose for the website is wonderful and the backbone is there, it seems to be lacking a personal draw. By updating the projects/adding more current ones and finding a way to make the "about" page and aesthetic of the website more personal, you could potentially increase viewer draw and retention time on the website. In conjunction to that, moving the map to another tab on the website could help to decrease confusion and focus in on the purpose so that visitors can understand and appreciate the purpose and then engage at a greater depth. Overall, the purpose is wonderful and could be incredibly impactful for the local community with some restructuring to increase clarity, draw, and retention.

Appendix C. Student Example Transcript

Hi there! Today, I am so excited to be giving a tutorial on CommunityKC's website. And I'm so excited because this website CommunityKC is a fantastic tool that aims to connect projects, people and resources. Its vision is for the revitalization of local neighborhoods. Some that might even be in your neck of the woods, which is why I had to give you a tour that will spark awareness and engagement for CommunityKC's mission and for the betterment of the local communities in Kansas City. If you follow along with my career. So I hope you'll see that this homepage contains this map here. And this map here is a wonderful tool that they have created to help show you the regions in which the projects are located. And then as you can see, there's a key right here to the right, which tells you about the project types.

You have a little guide here telling you about the recently added projects, oops, sorry for that. And you have up here, their logo, their slogan, and the little sections that tell you all of the information that is located on this website. So, it tells you about this map right here. You can see events and you can add the event. You can view all projects out a project and see some frequently asked questions and an about page. We will go over all of these tabs at one point in a moment. Um, you can also see that you can log in to add the event or register to get more information and things of that nature sound here. You have three of the main people who helped to start this website and are working on it. Now, I want to tell you about more about CommunityKC and what it is and what they do.

So, this mapping tool was created to design and was created and designed to help connect people with each other because after all, when you're working on community projects and you're volunteering, things like that, you're better together. When you can add your resources, it will help to go much further than alone. And so they are really trying to identify potential partners and pair them up for greater collaboration within the community. It also helps local people to become more informed of their local projects and the initiatives going on in their neighborhoods or neighborhoods of, out of them. This will help to avoid duplication of efforts, animal help, to network and share information about what's going on so that you can better serve the community. And again, it helps to show you that there are so good things in the world and good people who are just wanting to help people.

It is really just such a great mission and being to be a part of. So, as you can see, I just went over all of this kind of stuff. And there's more about the map and how it was launched when it was launched. You can read more about upcoming and events and what they plan to do next with the website here at this link. And then you can also see that the community projects in this range there from large products, completely redevelop neighborhoods or small projects like community gardens. They really honestly, um, have such a wide range to fit the skills and abilities of people in the local community. Um, really the, the projects highlighted in this map, as you can see here, engage and empower residents to make a difference in the community. Cause honestly, if we can come together and be engaged, we are more likely to do better.

The, the communities in which we live and the ones that are neighbors to us, um, sparks a chain reaction of positive change. And as you can see here on the "about" page, they also have information. So, they have an email that is info@communitykc.org. Again, that is info@communitykc.org that you can contact them with questions, or you can call them at eight one six five zero two nine two eight or nine five eight, four, I'm sorry. That is nine five eight four. So again, that number is (816) 502-9584. And when you can speak to someone about more questions than you have about this website, you can also visit their FAQ page as shown and you can access it on the link from the about, or you can access it at the top at the taps. And these frequently asked questions are about who should use it.

What is considered a CommunityKC project? How do you use the mapping tool? How can this help my organization to collaborate? Who developed the tool and what are future plans for the tool? And so I'll just run over briefly each of the sections. So who should use it. This map was created for any organization working in the community neighborhood revitalization. So that includes, you know, people who just want to get involved, civic groups, faith-based groups, and computer community improvement districts, and even funding organizations. So it's really just anyone who is looking to engage or has an organization or knows of an organization that is really working to better.

Community projects are ones that occur on a regular basis. To some extent, either annually or monthly or things of that nature. A lot of things, these ones are not. And just once one time, they're really trying to invest in the community. So they should be projects that are occurring on a regular basis. Some examples of that are cleanup events. There are community gardens to help, you know, throughout through the use of a garden that can educate kids who may not have the best access to food or things of that nature on how to grow good produce, and it can help. So that are the communities that don't have as great access to resources. And again, literacy projects, cultural skills, training, things like that. Those are considered community projects. You use the mapping tool. I will give you a little brief overview of it in a second.

And again, it really helps to collaborate. And I really want to highlight that the people who divulged CommunityKC, the majority of them are all are working on this on a volunteer basis. They have a real passion and a heart to invest in this, and they are so excited about it. And I am excited about it too. And to be telling you about it today, now I'm going to give you a brief little tour of the website. So again, on the home page, do you have the map on the map? You can click on any of the numbers and then it will help them spread and show different projects that are within that region. Again, they are color coded and some of them have more than one project type under the events and add an event. You can add an event here. So, your login or your register with one of the following, will help to submit an event and create one that can turn into a project.

And now they have, if the map is kind of like fuzzy for you to work in, they have a project listing, which I love, because if you go, I'll show you the last page of it. There are 11 pages of projects that are going on. And if you click on them like this youth leadership development, one, it gives you the organization type. It gives you the address, the lead person. So name of someone that you can contact and their email address, which is really great. It really helps to connect you directly to the people who are working the projects. And, and it tells you again, whether it's annual, what kind of project it is like the sole focus is on education and sports programming for Metro kids. The city participants now operate sports leagues and afterschool programs, and they conduct workshops and health nutrition, really serving to be mentors to better the community.

Now I would like to show you how to search for a project by project type. So if we go back to the map, there's a key here that tells you different types of project types. So you can search for a project type. If you're looking for like a capacity building the red ones, as you see here, and, or you can go right here and you can search by say, you want a public health and safety project to work on and be involved in and you can hit, um, I accidentally hit gun map for you. I'm so sorry. You can plug in that project type right here. And you can hit submit when you hit submit once will pop up. So the yellow is public health and safety. And as you see this, the gives the project type listing right here, and the public health and safety is also healthy living or physical activity.

So, it can have different categories and different product types. Like this one is listed under public health and safety. It's a neighborhood crisis response team is something that works on CPR, fire safety, and crime prevention in local communities. That is such an awesome thing to be knowledgeable, knowledgeable about and be conducting workshops on. So it's super exciting. And just, again, as a reminder, the project types can be more than one. So if you see a color, you're not thinking that's what it is. It probably is there. And like this project right here is also public health and safety it's, um, garden farm, which is really awesome. Again for the betterment of the community. Now, if you down like the map, you can go to the list view right here, or you can have you all projects. So I'm going to click go to the list view.

And on the last few, you can do the exact same thing. Public health and health and safety hits the net and the projects will pop up and improve deliverability. You have safe routes to school or things of that nature. Um, again, in the emergency response team, community, garden, redevelopment, crosswalk, and healthy campus, different things that are really aiming to spark change in the communities. And so, again, this is the CommunityKC website. I just really want to reiterate to you on their "about" page, that the project highlighted are to engage and empower residents, to make a difference in their community. These people are volunteers they're truly wanting to connect people and resources and to spark change and create a better life for future generations. If you have any, if this tutorial like left gaps or questions or things like that, please feel free to contact us at info@communitykc.org. Again, that is info@communitykc.org or call at (816) 502-9584. Again, that night number is (816) 502-9584. I really appreciate you watching this and I hope you will. I hope this has helped to increase your awareness about the projects going on in local communities in Kansas City. Thank you. Have a great day!

Chapter 20. PARSing out the Course: User-centered Design through HyperDocs in Online Writing Instruction

Kathleen Turner Ledgerwood
LINCOLN UNIVERSITY

Abstract: HyperDocs is a term coined by Highfill et al. who developed a system for using the Google Suite in K–12 education classrooms. Although the idea of HyperDocs was originally created with the use of Google products, since that time Microsoft 365 and Box now provide many of the same tools for collaboration and sharing that Google does. Additionally, this concept may have originated in lower levels of education, but I find that it is very applicable to OWI and meets all four of the PARS standards for effective OWI. As Highfill et al. conceive of HyperDocs, they are more than just a document with links. Instead, HyperDocs offer a system for strong lesson design that walks students through a process of learning, with students as the focus of the document's design, a focus on UCD. HyperDocs allow teachers to focus on the UX in a unique way that highlights UCD. At the same time, the use of HyperDocs in either individual lessons or in whole units is at once personal, accessible, responsive, and strategic. This chapter will outline the ways that using HyperDocs in OWI helps students by meeting PARS criteria and using multimodal composition practices, and it will provide multiple ideas for using HyperDocs in online writing classes.

Keywords: HyperDocs, Google Docs, collaboration tools, lesson design

All of the discussion of user-centered design (UCD) aligns well with the idea of using Borgman and McArdle's (2019) PARS (Personal, Accessible, Responsive, Strategic) approach in designing online writing instruction (OWI).[1] Due to my experience with after school technology seminars and my research on HyperDocs, I've been using them in my online courses because they are very applicable to OWI, utilize all four or the PARS elements, and meet the standards for effective OWI. Although the idea of HyperDocs was originally created with the use of Google products, since that time Microsoft 365, Drop Box (dropbox.com), and Box (box.com) now provide many of the same tools for collaboration, commenting, and

---

1. For access to multiple resources discussed in this chapter and more, please visit this Google Drive folder https://bit.ly/2PiKYWc

sharing. Additionally, this concept may have originated in K–12 education, but I find that it is very applicable to OWI and meets all four of the PARS standards for effective OWI. This chapter will outline the ways that using HyperDocs in OWI helps students use multimodal composition practices, and it will provide ideas for using HyperDocs in OWI. This chapter will also illustrate how the use of Hyper-Docs allows instructors to use all four elements of the PARS approach.

HyperDocs is a term trademarked in 2016 by Highfill et al. who developed a system for using the Google Suite in K–12 education classrooms (Hilton, 2020). Their goal was to use the Google Suite to move beyond simple documents with hyperlinks in them to documents that create interactive lessons to help build learning and critical thinking. HyperDocs is a system of using the collaborative tools within Google's features in order to create engaging lessons. (See further definitions and examples at hyperdocs.co). HyperDocs grew out of a desire by teachers to focus on usability and creation by the students, and therefore they place the focus on student choice and student voice. As a writing teacher, these concepts and goals immediately resonated with me as a way to help guide students through digital literacy and content creation. In *Multiliteracies for a Digital Age*, Stuart Selber (2004) argued for "three subject positions connected to the literacy landscape: students as users of technology, students as questioners of technology, and students as producers of technology" (p. 25). Selber essentially claims that students need functional, critical, and rhetorical literacy. Selber's call for helping students become digitally literate in these three areas aligns well with HyperDocs and the idea that this system is "making it possible for us to flip our role and the role of our students, from consumers to creators" (Hilton, 2020). Thus, HyperDocs is a call to place the end user, their learning process, and the online environment itself front and center in our lessons using a collaborative model for teaching.

What are HyperDocs?

As Highfill et al. (2016) conceive of HyperDocs, they are more than just a document with links; instead, Hilton (2020) defines HyperDocs as "An interactive Google Doc that replaces the worksheet/lecture method of delivering instruction" (hyperdocs.co/courses/62). Instead, HyperDocs offer a system for strong lesson design that walks students through a process of learning with a focus on UCD. Highfill et al. (2016) state,

> The reason HyperDocs work is because each one begins with a strong lesson design, curates quality instructional content, and packages learning in a way that engages learners. A HyperDoc shifts the focus from teacher-led lectures to student-driven, inquiry-based learning, allowing students to actually learn through exploration. (p. 7)

HyperDocs invite students to write together and collaborate with one another in the same document, allowing for a non-linear conversation in which they can comment on and add to each other's work. HyperDocs allow a lot of choice and curation of digital content to package either an individual lesson or an entire unit in OWI. HyperDocs promote learner-centered design (LCD) using a seven-step process.

The Basic HyperDoc Lesson Plan Template[2] (see Figure 20.1) explains the seven-step process created by the HyperDocs team and has boxes that anyone can fill in.

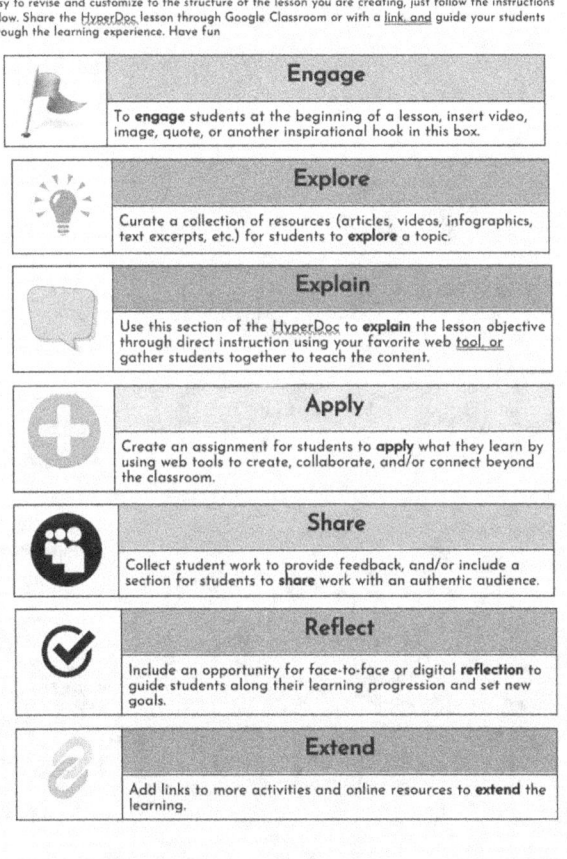

Figure 20.1. Basic HyperDoc lesson plan template.

---

2. Visit https://docs.google.com/document/d/1FF848DW78iE-Ht9M0JVDyp0N5N3jN9UuXssl_qTb1fo/edit

When I first started using HyperDocs, I thought it was a great way to outline a road map for students for an essay project from beginning to end. I created a road map with links to all of the resources for writing. I used a road map template that is in an open Google folder for teaching writing and reading. The template, originally designed by Genevieve Pacada, created a HyperDoc road map for an informative essay assignment. I took this template and idea and created an Argument Essay Road Map (see Figure 20.2).

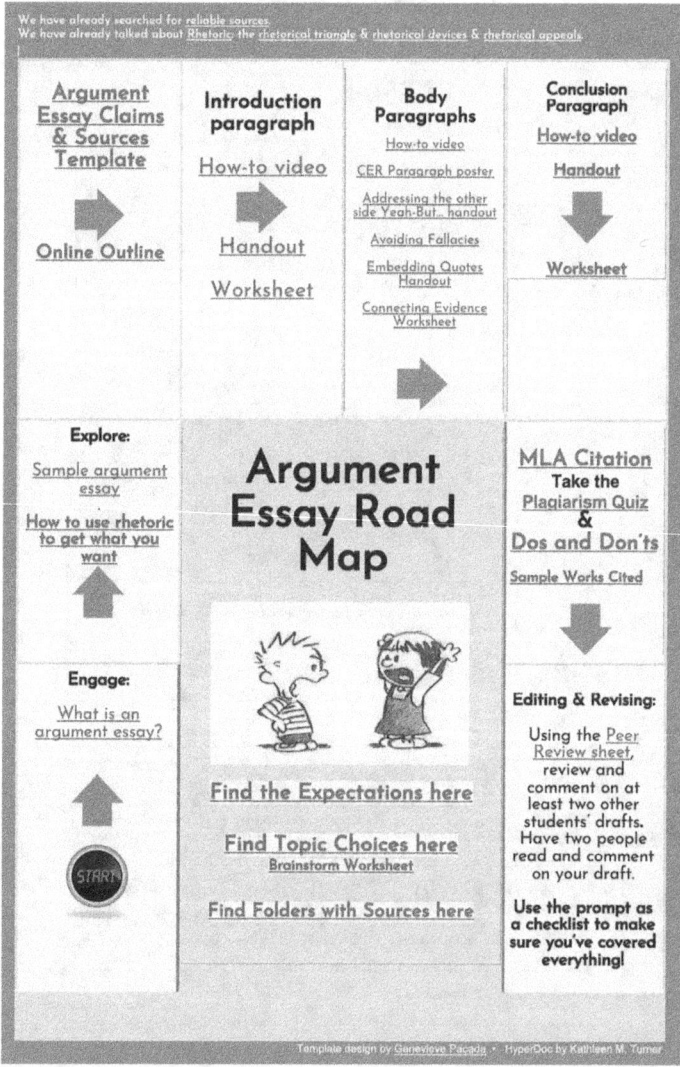

Figure 20.2. Argument essay road map (View the road map at https://docs.google.com/document/d/1iJojZlEFH3ujNleape83tt2FrS4TTueokdb_nqleMW4/edit)

HyperDocs Aligns with PARS

Personal Elements and HyperDocs

HyperDocs focus on using collaborative digital tools and in so doing, this approach to designing elements for a course lend themselves to a very personal experience for the student. As Borgman and McArdle (2019) note, making OWI personal means that we do not have students engaging in passive learning, instead we build a social sense of community, paying attention to the entire experience of the students and being certain to engage all of their senses. The use of HyperDocs helps create "robust, sensory rich environments and engaging activities that bring students into contact with one another" (Ruefman, 2016, p. 8). HyperDocs focus on having students weave collaboration into the process of learning. This focus on collaboration means that through using a HyperDoc approach, teachers can engage the community of the class and reflect on their learning as they proceed through a lesson or unit.

HyperDocs also allow us to curate or create content in order to provide directions in multiple formats, including written directions and audio/video overview. HyperDocs can be useful in an OWI class because students can write comments and questions on the instructions or prompts, and the questions and answers can be seen by any student. The conversations can occur in the exact space that the ideas are formed. Students can also collaborate with each other, ask each other questions, offer resources or ideas, and discuss options right in the document itself. HyperDocs also allow the opportunity to reinforce content (have multiple formats to make content accessible). And we can build in multiple moments for constructive feedback within the HyperDoc, including using digital tools that might allow for screen capture, audio, and video feedback. HyperDocs allow us to package learning that engages users. HyperDocs shift the focus away from the teacher and toward the student by opening the assignment itself to questions and comments that students make. As Borgman and McArdle (2019) state, we want to make our instruction personal and engaging in order to move students "into a more dynamic and collaborative learning space" (p. 22). Using HyperDocs facilitates this kind of LCD and moves students into working together in collaborative spaces. This is one way we can invite "students to engage in a more developed learning community and to help reduce the teacher student power dynamics" (Borgman & McArdle, 2019, p. 22). Using these kinds of collaborative writing spaces helps students see their learning as more personal and helps them develop more personal connection to each other and to the instructor. For example, when I teach about peer review, I use a HyperDoc to get students to think through and research peer review strategies, then the class works together to come up with a list of guidelines and ideas that they want to keep in mind as they peer review each other's work (see Figure 20.11). Students created the guidelines together through comments and revisions that they began when I first introduced the idea of peer review. After each peer review, we revisited and revised the chart, adding more about what the students wanted out of their peer reviews. This kind of a living document can easily be made using collaborative software, like Google Docs, and the comment feature proves valuable to revision and discussion on the document itself. Another example of collaborative writing from a professional development seminar where teachers collaborated on bringing their knowledge of HyperDocs together (see Figure 20.3). In their book on HyperDocs, Highfill, Hilton, and Landis (2016) offer a link to a list of different online collaborative tools one might assign to students in a HyperDoc (p. 48).

How are you already using Hyperdocs in your classroom/school?	What do you need to know more about to get started with HyperDocs?	What concerns do you still have regarding HyperDocs?
I'm not using it... yet. My students do all of their 'explorations' in google slides - they are hyperlinked to online resources, have videos in the slides, etc - but ALL of their work is on their slides, not collaborative with other students. I think creating a Hyperdoc would be every better.	I need the steps - I know there are different 'stages' to a HyperDoc- I need to learn how to think through those and tie them into my content.	Just making it work. I've seen them as full units worth of learning or just one day - I wonder which is better? I work in slides a lot, but I never seem to find great resources for high school social studies.
I've only used one Hyperdoc during my current SS unit on government.	I need tools that will help elementary students use Hyperdocs with better ease.	Keeping elementary students on task and not getting hung up on commenting on other people's posts.
I created	How do I put a hyperlink into a doc?	
I haven't used it in school, but did use it in college and in my student teaching.	I'd like to know how to present it to the teachers at my school, since I am the media specialist.	Math. Getting math to work with hyperdocs. I think the math teachers would like it, but the programs they use to create formulas may not be compatible.
I have never used it before, but see this as a great tool.		When using someone else's hyperdoc, what if a link doesn't work or isn't available at your school? Can you edit it?
I have used three hyperdocs this year. Looking to add many more. I love the idea of taking everything that I use and putting it in one place.	How to take it to the next level... the difference between and ok HyperDoc and a great one!?	GRADING?? Seems like I can not simplify grading all the different parts.

Figure 20.3. HyperDocs collaborative writing.

Accessible Elements and HyperDocs

When you begin to use this HyperDoc system, there are many ways in which you can adapt lessons and units for accessibility. Beginning with an accessible design is key to making sure to reach all OWI students. Additionally, in the case of OWI, as Borgman and McArdle (2019) state, "You must find a way to utilize the environment in which the course resides" (p. 39). HyperDocs are an excellent way to utilize the online environment and engage learners. If your university subscribes to Google products and every student has an account, like mine do, then it is easy to incorporate this environment from their university accounts. However, I've also taught at universities where they give everyone Box accounts (www.box.com/home) and my current university is in the process of switching to Office 365 products, and currently now faculty have Office 365, but students have Google. So, when I create materials for teaching faculty and professional development, I use Office 365 products, but I use my personal Google account to build materials for my students. I find all the same tools are available in almost all of the university cloud systems.

While it is important to remember that "each user interacts with multimodality differently" (Oswal & Melonçon, 2017, p. 70), we also must remember that students come to us with different levels of knowledge and at different places in their growth as writers. For example, I work at an open-enrollment HBCU which purposefully draws students from lower SES and from schools where many of my students have not written an essay of more than one-page in length. In order to reach a variety of backgrounds and knowledge in my first-year writing classes, I know that I must be able to cater to different skills. I'm able to build that into the HyperDocs, leaving students room to begin where they are comfortable and can call upon their apriori knowledge. One example of how I build in what I like to call a "choose your own adventure" in HyperDocs is in my Peer Review Hyper-Doc[3] (see Figure 20.4).

Experiences with Peer Review
Follow one in the chart below

I've never done Peer Review before	Watch this brief video about what peer review is and how it helps writers
I've done peer review, but haven't had the best experiences	Watch the first video at Writing Commons here
I'm a pro at peer review; I love it!	Read this brief article or watch the video about improving peer review here

Figure 20.4. Peer review experiences choices.

This document asks students to begin with different introductory material depending on their experience with peer review. Some of my students have never participated in a peer review, so they start with a more basic video. Many of my students have completed peer reviews, but didn't feel that it was a useful exercise, so they have a different video they can watch about the benefits of peer review.

---

3. Visit https://docs.google.com/document/d/1NkgXdBmyz3MlUWawOk5NyPYyDpvdTIvWVA0EXNsW0Bw/edit

And the last box allows students who enjoy peer review to read or watch some tips for improving peer review. An example I used recently in a professional development session with high school teachers was a HyperDoc I created about using HyperDocs (bit.ly/2UJlYL4). Early in this HyperDoc I had a slide in which the teachers could go to resources depending on their familiarity with the concept of HyperDocs (see Figure 20.5). Each of the images on this slide is a link to more information about HyperDocs. This is another way in which we can bring accessibility to students and offer additional support to their learning journey.

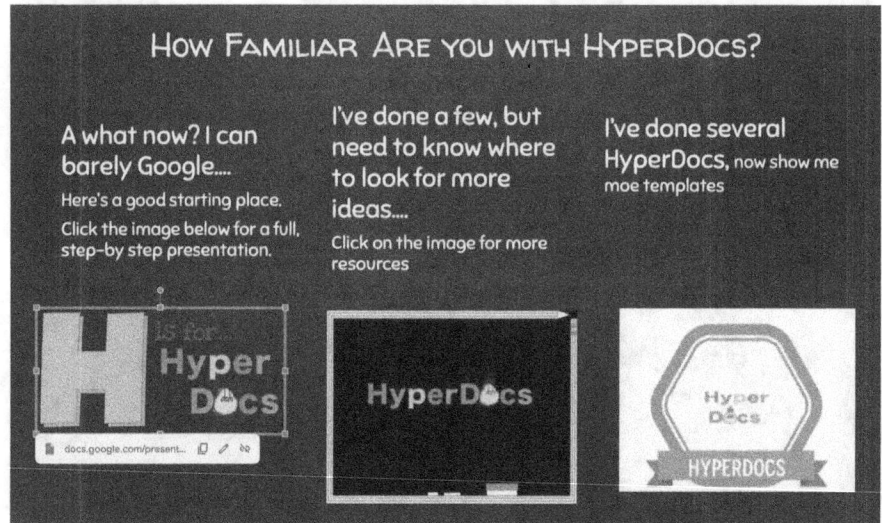

Figure 20.5. HyperDocs.

One benefit of HyperDocs is that it is an easy way to invite students into dynamic learning spaces and to get them to become content-creators. For example, the last item on one of my HyperDocs introducing the idea of linguistic justice asks students to find sources related to what we've been discussing online and curate content for each other (see Figure 20.6 for a picture of the HyperDoc directions and Figure 20.7 for the linked document that students add content to).[4] The collaborative nature of HyperDocs allows my students to ask questions and directly comment on my assignment and on the work of their peers; through the use of the collaborative nature of the HyperDocs, they enable students to be resources for each other in building their digital and multimodal repertoires. As Greer and Harris (2018) state, "If students see themselves as collaborators in the course design process, they are more likely to remain engaged and to begin to grasp the complexity of the tasks and processes they need to complete in order to learn and grow as writers" (p. 17). HyperDocs allows us to invite students into

---

4. View SAE and Code Meshing at https://docs.google.com/document/d/1s36spoQ o_repA7rz9dHy2yAypVoAhHH1g5kvlXLJkoo/edit

spaces to create materials for the class to use. An example of this is when I have students begin a persuasive essay: I start by having them brainstorm all their topics together in one Google Doc, Google Slides, or on a Google JamBoard. This way they can comment on each other's ideas, ask questions, and discuss all in one space. I also go in and add to the document, asking questions, helping to narrow topics, offering resources and ideas. We have a giant class collaboration space to write with each other about our ideas, thoughts, opinions, and knowledge. Students really love being able to interact together like this. And one beauty of it is we can do this asynchronously, checking in on the document, and figuring out how one broad topic might break down into many essay topics.

Apply	Your Task
Find and read something else online about Code Switching (Code Meshing) or Black Language. This can be a video, podcast, article, infographic, or any online source that extends and adds to our conversation.	Post a link to what you found here and fill in the chart for your source.

Figure 20.6. Directions from Linguistic Justice HyperDoc.

After finding your own source, fill in your information and ideas in the chart below.

Name	Title and link to what you found about this broader topic (you might look up code switching, Black language, code meshing)	What are your thoughts on this issue of language and whose language is used in writing and education

Figure 20.7. Whole class Doc for student collaboration and sharing.

Responsive Elements and HyperDocs

Borgman and McArdle (2019) suggest that one thing you can do if you are tech savvy is to have a Google Document for your whole course that you can update as needed. That you can "give them a learning hub to navigate your class and mitigate confusion" (p. 46). You could strategically build a system of HyperDocs that lead students through the course. One aspect I really like about using HyperDocs in the writing classroom is that I can add and make changes to an assignment as we go through it. So as students ask questions, I can use the HyperDocs to place answers and extra help so that the whole class can see it, rather than just using one-to-one communication channels, like email. I often enable comments on my HyperDocs for students, so they can type questions right into it and I can answer any questions that they may have for the whole class. (See Figure 20.8 for an image of an assignment with sample student questions and my responses to their questions.)

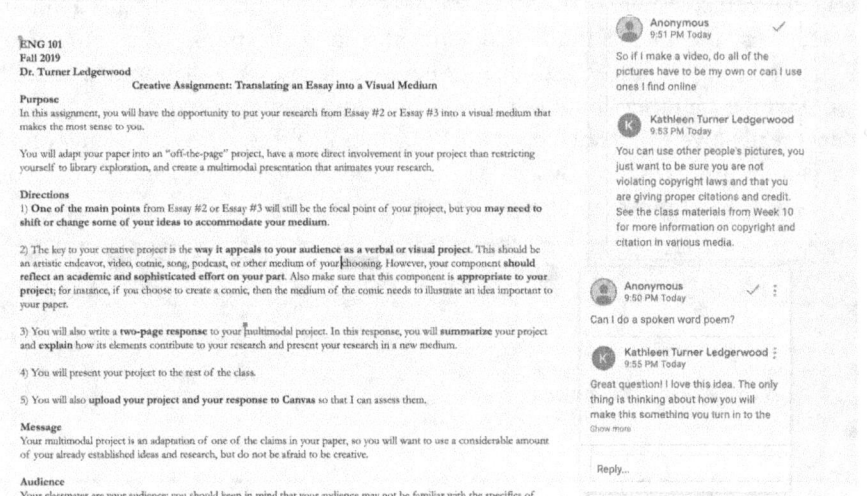

Figure 20.8. Assignment with student questions and instructor responses.

This is one way in which we can think about the amount of time we spend responding to students and how we can be more effective. McArdle explained that after being flooded with student emails, "He started to choose quality over immediacy" (Borgman & McArdle, 2019, p. 54). Using Google Docs or Slides and giving students the ability to comment on the document can be an effective way to think about how we respond to students as a whole class, rather than responding to the same question through individual emails.

I also find that using HyperDocs is helpful in OWI because I can help students know when and how I will be interacting and commenting on their work. In both the instructions and a collaborative Google Doc, I'll often include information about how and when I will be looking at what they add. I want them to know exactly how I will interact with their work and when, so that they can go back and look through the comments, questions, and suggestions I add to their work. This methodology also helps to establish "yourself as an audience for your students," which is "actually a design issue" (Borgman & McArdle, 2019, p. 56). Also, having students use more collaborative environments opens them up to considering their audience to be more than their instructor, which builds a more authentic writing situation into the course. Instructors can design places where students create and write content that they know will be seen by many writers. Often this encourages a different kind of community of learners, where students collaborate and help each other on more than just their peer review assignments.

Strategic Elements and HyperDocs

Because of the nature of building HyperDocs, they force instructors to be strategic in creating content and plan lessons for student learning. In order to build a HyperDoc, I have to know the learning outcome and use backward design (Bowen, 2017) to walk through steps to teach a concept or skill. (See Figures 20.9, 20.10, 20.11, and 20.12 for a model of how to use strategic backward design through Hyperdocs.) The package of the HyperDoc forces me to be strategic as I think through that seven-step process. This helps instructors begin to think about designing for the learners in the classroom. Using HyperDocs allows me to plan an entire semester in one schedule on a Google Doc, I can organize modules linked off of this schedule, thus creating a central hub for my students. Students report preferring this because they can set their Google Drive to access files offline, conserving data plans and maintaining access when WiFi is unreliable. Additionally, students report this as easier to navigate than the LMS because their instructors often take such different approaches to organizing it.

Processes
Students should be able to

- Practice writing as a recursive process, that is, an ongoing process that allows writers to later invent and rethink as they receive feedback and revise their work

Figure 20.9. Learning outcome statement.

Gearing up for Peer Review

Experiences with Peer Review

Follow one in the chart below

I've never done Peer Review before	Watch this brief video about what peer review is and how it helps writers
I've done peer review, but haven't had the best experiences	Watch the first video at Writing Commons here
I'm a pro at peer review; I love it!	Read this brief article or watch the video about improving peer review here

Read this article on Peer Review and Commenting on writing

Read "How to Write Meaningful Peer Response Praise" by Ron DePeter from Writing Spaces

Engagement Activity

Go to this Google Doc and add ideas to the chart about effective peer review

© HyperDocs created by @lsgivets

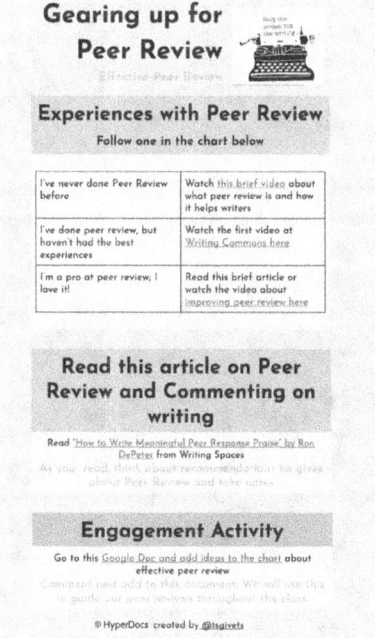

Figure 20.10. Peer review HyperDoc.

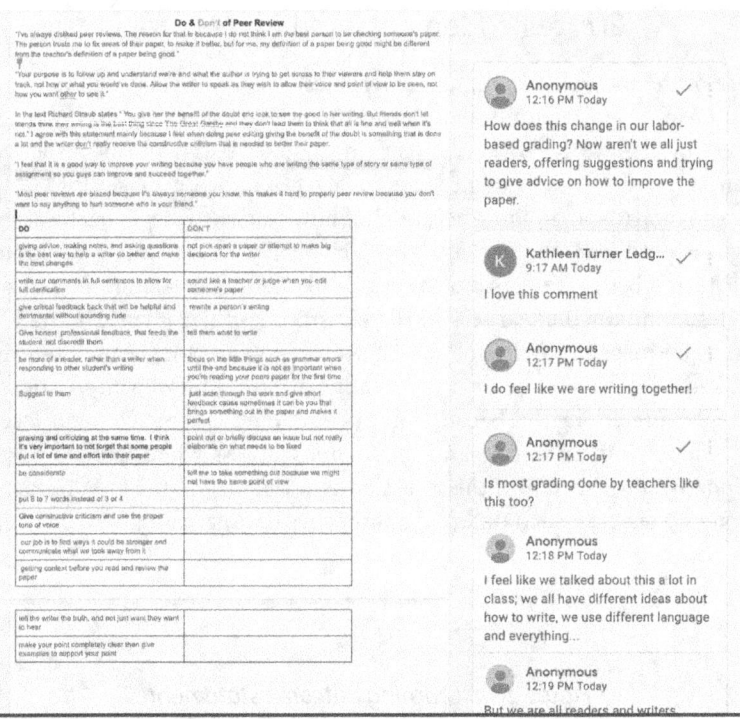

Figure 20.11. Collaborative Google Document.

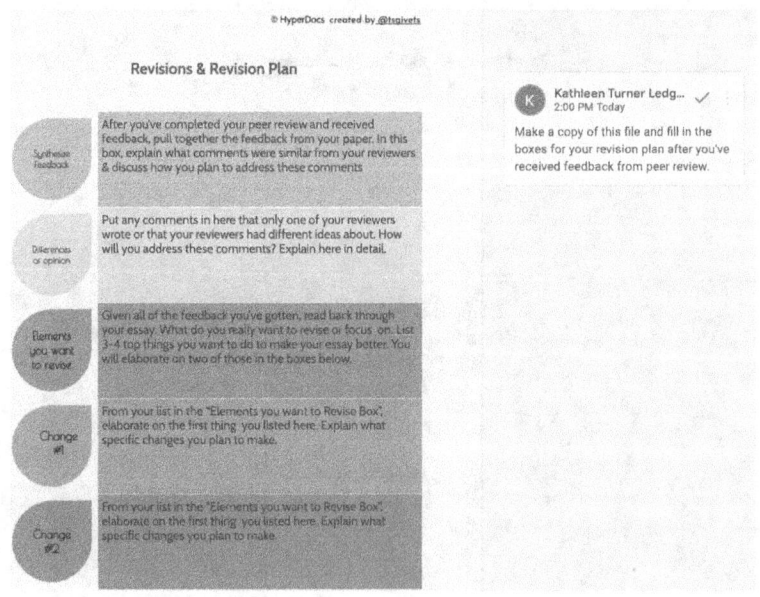

Figure 20.12. Revision plan (following peer review).

Ever since I created my first HyperDoc to put all of the resources for a single essay assignment, I use HyperDocs to be strategic for all sorts of little lessons or big thoughts we return to throughout class, as well as for whole units. I often allow students to choose topics or readings that are different to give them some choice in what they discover. Then they turn around and create content for students who read something different from what they did. In OWI, options allow students to have choice that makes the lesson more personal, it makes them take control of teaching one another, and they become collaborators in the teaching and learning process. The collaborative nature of HyperDocs fits so well in the context of a OWI because "Both instruction and learning to write are a collaborative process, a team effort of give and take" (Borgman & McArdle, 2019, p. 10). We can strategically design more collaboration in OWI.

PARS & HyperDocs

In OWI, keeping the PARS approach in mind as you start to try new tools and approaches can be very helpful. HyperDocs add to this framework by allowing students the ability to explore, and we need to keep the learning process in mind as we create and curate content for students. Highfill et al. (2016) emphasize that HyperDocs "create learning experiences that highlight how students learn rather than simply emphasize what students learn" (pp. 12–13). My students report that designed documents with short and easy directions or bulleted points are more appealing to them, which aligns well with UCD information design to "chunk" information to reduce cognitive load. I always make sure to ask students for feedback on the documents they are using, which helps me adjust my assignments, lessons, and units to better assist students.

HyperDocs, like the OWI Community (owicommunity.org) offers an online community and a wealth of resources to help generate ideas, get started, and use templates from other teachers. So far most of the HyperDoc lessons and units are made for K-12 students, but there is great potential for more discussion and research in higher education around OWI and course design. Hyperdoc templates have been helpful in getting me started, but as my confidence expands, and my use of PARS expands, I can see how I can improve the docs and my teaching by making each doc more personal, accessible, responsive, and strategic.

Training students on HyperDocs

When I first use a HyperDoc in a class, I have found that the first introduction is best used as a training tool. I adapt a Google Slide presentation that was initially created by Nicole Beardsley.[5] This walks students through what to expect and do

---

5. View How to Hyperdoc at https://docs.google.com/presentation/d/1BW_DTi4PSn-Mu5ReJruhXUiGt4m_zpA-1Q9_qtEzh8eY/edit#slide=id.g35f391192_00.

with a HyperDoc. It's always important to keep in mind that students will come to documents with a variety of skills and comfort levels, so I always try to provide an introduction to the design of the document before I assign the first one. This one that Nicole Beardsley created can be copied and changed to suit the teacher's personality and the students or university where you're teaching. Emili Sabourin and I presented a bit of a different version of this original Slides presentation at the MOREnet conference in 2018.[6] This works well if you want to introduce the idea to your faculty or talk through how your writing program might use HyperDocs. (See Figure 20.13 for a screenshot of a slide from the presentation.)[7]

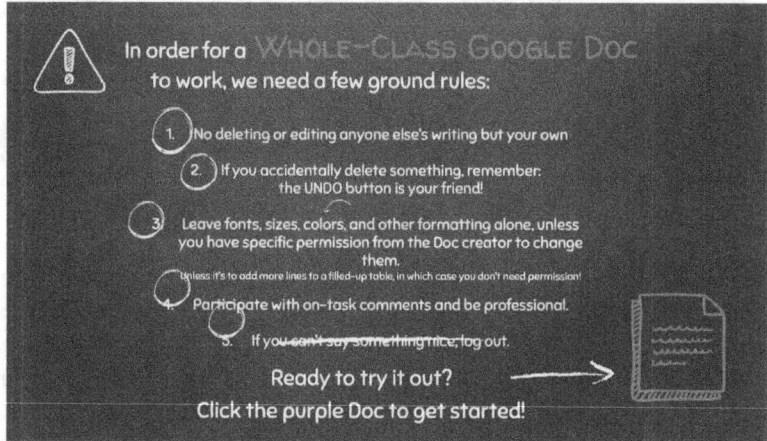

Figure 20.13. Rules for a whole-class HyperDoc.

I think it's important to show students how HyperDocs might look and to help them understand that they will need to click to read, watch, and create as they work through a HyperDoc. In OWI, I create videos that accompany the HyperDoc and walk students through what they should see, what they can comment on, and how the HyperDoc works. Not all of my students need to watch the video as they work through the HyperDocs, but some have reported that they really appreciate having the video to accompany the work. I like to do this as a screensharing video with my face still in a little video box to make sure that I reach that personal side of communicating with students.

---

6. View How to Hyperdoc MOREnet at https://docs.google.com/presentation/d/1qbVi9z2l7BPm5YV5i6e_K1vgctGFL8HZhFpcXsbB9eI/edit#slide=id.p1.

7. Like all the other HyperDocs, we made these available for public access for any teacher to copy and use.

Conclusion

In order to truly prepare effective materials, we need to focus our pedagogy on students and student learning outcomes. The September 2018 special issue of Computers and Composition was dedicated to thinking about what it means to have a "usability" and "user-designed" pedagogy when we consider computers and writing (Bartolotta et al., 2018). Indeed, UCD and UX have an important role to play in teaching rhetoric and composition. Just as we ask students to consider their audience in writing assignments, we too need to consider and put students as users and audience at the forefront of our design and pedagogy. This becomes even more important when we talk about design for OWI as Borgman and McArdle (2019) point out with PARS. The PARS approach and HyperDocs allow OWI teachers to consider our students in terms of thinking about how we design our classes and learning for students. Both offer instructors a framework grounded in best practices for OWI and for pedagogy in general, which can only help instructors be more strategic in their teaching. In The Hyper-Doc Handbook: Digital Lesson Design Using Google Apps Highfill et al. (2016) quote a high school senior student (Jordan Moldenhauer) at the beginning of the book who says,

> I want to be given facts that can help me think for myself. And when I form an opinion, I want my teachers to have the courage to hear me out, not tell me I am wrong . . . The real world is a test. And we are all taking it. (p. 5)

What this student is clearly articulating is that LCD must be taken into consideration in designing all pedagogical materials and that she wants a PARS approach in her education.

As technology moves toward collaborative platforms, OWI should include collaborative spaces for students to write together about topics or to generate ideas. As Highfill et al. note, "When you package the latest collaboration tools in a HyperDoc, you give all of your students the opportunity to have conversations, listen, respond appropriately, discuss topics, build on ideas or comments, ask questions, and work together toward a shared goal" (p. 48). Ultimately, collaborative tools will also help prepare students for their futures in an increasingly technologically-based society. HyperDocs is one way to engage students in collaborative writing and discussion in online platforms that they will use after OWI.

Final Thoughts and Application

HyperDocs can provide engaging and meaningful writing and critical thinking for students. If you think you might be ready to foray into HyperDocs, you might start small with just one activity or a simple lesson. It can be helpful to think about HyperDocs as a design package for material you want to teach in a writing class. Alternately, you might try making one document that links everything for a paper or unit, adding more resources as students ask questions. I often have one central HyperDoc for general writing-related resources: some explanations of writing concepts, ideas to get students started on an essay, or help for someone who gets stuck on just one part of writing. My students report that they appreciate these documents to go back to and find all the links to all of the writing aids. They might just need a reminder on introducing quotations or effective transitions. You also might just consider incorporating just some elements of HyperDocs to start, for example letting students write comments and questions directly on an assignment as a way to save time on answering questions.

References

Bartolotta, J., Bourelle, T. & Newmark, J. (2018) Co-Editors' welcome to the special issue on usability and user-centered design. *Computers and Composition, 49,* 1–3. https://doi.org/10.1016/j.compcom.2018.09.001.

Borgman, J. & McArdle, C. (2019) *Personal, accessible, responsive, strategic: Resources and strategies for online writing instructors.* The WAC Clearinghouse; University Press of Colorado. https://doi.org/10.37514/PRA-B.2019.0322.

Bowen, R. S., (2017). Understanding by design. Vanderbilt University Center for Teaching. https://cft.vanderbilt.edu/understanding-by-design/.

Greer, M. & Harris, H. (2018). User-centered design as a foundation for effective online writing instruction. *Computers & Composition, 49,* 18–24.

Highfill, L., Hilton, K. & Landis, S. (2016) *The HyperDoc handbook: Digital lesson design using Google Apps.* Elevate Books.

Hilton, K. (2020). What is a HyperDoc? HyperDocs. https://hyperdocs.co/courses/62.

Opel, D. S. & Rhodes, J. (2018). Beyond student as user: Rhetoric, multimodality, and user-centered design" *Computers and Composition, 49,* 71–81. https://doi.org/10.1016/j.compcom.2018.05.008.

Ruefman, D. (2016). Return to your source: Aesthetic experience in online writing instruction. In D. Ruefman & A. Scheg (Eds.), *Applied pedaogies: Strategies for online writing instruction* (pp. 151–181) Utah State University Press.

Selber, S. (2004). *Multiliteracies for a digital age.* Southern Illinois University Press.

Conclusion: Moving Day!

Jessie Borgman
ARIZONA STATE UNIVERSITY

Casey McArdle
MICHIGAN STATE UNIVERSITY

As you read the title to this conclusion, you may be thinking, "huh?" Why are the editors talking about moving in relation to online writing instruction? But stay with us for a minute.

As you know, we love golf! The PARS approach was created out of a shared love for the game of golf and we've capitalized on various golf terminology and golf concepts throughout our first book, our workshops, and in various parts of this collection. Our collection authors even joined in and used some golf references and golf puns/play on words in their chapters.

The reason we use golf as a metaphor is that we truly do see some solid connections between OWI and golf. We thought it was awesome and exciting that some of our authors picked up on the golf terminology because it showed how others can see the connections between golf and OWI like we can. There are so many ways to apply golf concepts to the teaching and administering of online writing courses and programs. So, with that, we'll conclude our collection with another golf concept, "Moving Day."

Professional golf tournaments normally consist of a four-day event that begins on Thursday and ends on Sunday. During the first two days, Thursday and Friday, the entire field of golfers who have qualified for the tournament, or been invited to the tournament, play. At the end of Friday's round, a cut is made where the top

65 golfers, plus those who tied, advance to the weekend. The cut is made from how good the players played on Thursday and Friday. Essentially, the best golfers for that week move on to the weekend. Thus, golfers tend to see Saturday as the day when the tournament really begins, which is why they call it "Moving Day."

On this day, golfers begin to position themselves to make a big move to hopefully win the entire tournament on Sunday. They practice different shots on the range, they work on their putting, develop a new strategy on how they will play the course and certain holes on the course, they reexamine clubs that will support that strategy, consult with their coaches or caddies, and anything else they think will help them make the "moves" they need to make to be successful and win the tournament. Each course is different, so strategies can vary depending on skill set, weather, and confidence.

Instructing online writing courses and managing online writing programs can be as complex as playing a different golf course. Every semester, like every golf course, is different, but you, like the golfers, can rely on the fundamentals you've put in place, practice hours you've put in, and your experience.

We view this book to have the potential to be your Moving Day. You can think of our first book as days one and two of the tournament where you were trying out things, getting your game ready, practicing and strategizing. Now you have made the cut! You have made it to the weekend! So, it's moving day and you have looked around to see what has worked, what has not worked, and what new things might you do to get your online writing class going.

We hope the chapters in this book help you make the moves you need to make to be successful in your courses. Each chapter explores different ways you can work on your OWI game and refine your skills. Some chapters have you work on your short game, others ask you to look at your long game, some are mostly mental and ask you to rethink how you approach the game entirely. All of these come together in a way that gives you the options you need to win, you just have to make the move!

And don't worry, after this tournament, or after this school year/semester/class, there will be more opportunities to work on your game!

Cheers,
Jessie and Casey

Website: owicommunity.org
Facebook Group: facebook.com/groups/owicommunity
Twitter: @theowicommunity
Google Group Discussion Forum: TheOWIC@googlegroups.com

Afterword: Re-Mapping the Global Context for Online Education

Kirk St.Amant
LOUISIANA TECH UNIVERSITY AND UNIVERSITY OF LIMERICK

As of this writing, some 4.8 billion persons worldwide have online access (Internet World Stats, 2020). From an education perspective, these individuals include roughly 77 million students in the US (U.S. Census Bureau, 2019), 270 million students in China (Guet et al., 2019), and 260 million students in India (Trines, 2018). Yet these numbers fail to show the full scope of online education today. In truth, every individual with online access is a learner—someone who goes online to learn something they do not know. These leaners account for 60+ percent of the world's population and represent individuals from almost every background imaginable.

It is a context where online learning has become lifelong learning as multiple generations regularly consult online sources to acquire the knowledge they need and skills they desire. This connected context of lifelong learning represents the new normal for most individuals born in the lasts three decades and for perhaps every generation to come. It is a situation of great potential for online education worldwide. The question becomes: How do we realize these opportunities? The answer involves understanding content creation—or composing of texts in order to convey ideas, create conversations, and establish communities when online.

Infrastructure and Education

For decades, the hard infrastructure—or physical requirements—needed for large-scale online education have existed (St.Amant, 2017a). Over the last two

DOI: https://doi.org/10.37514/PRA-B.2021.1145.3.2

decades, hardware and software have evolved the point that online interactions are a regular part of the daily lives of many individuals around the globe. Likewise, telecommunication technologies and network infrastructures have advanced to the point that a growing number of persons worldwide can access the Web with reasonable consistency. Thus, the prospects for a massive, global shift to online education has been available for some time. Historically, however, that opportunity has remained largely unrecognized on both a local and a global scale.

The limitations to realizing the potential of online education were due primarily to soft infrastructure—the cultural attitudes, perceptions, and behaviors affecting how individuals viewed online education (St.Amant, 2017a). It is this soft infrastructure that clouds opinions of online programs and skews perceptions of their students and graduates. It is soft infrastructure that has prompted many students and educators to opt for the more familiar yet often less convenient on-site classroom over the online learning environment. As a result, global forays into online education have remained relatively "ancillary" with the core focus of education worldwide remaining on-site instruction.

Shifting Paradigms

These perspectives shifted drastically in the spring of 2020 when an unprecedented number of students around the world found online offerings to be the only educational option available (Li & Lalani, 2020). Suddenly, students in multiple nations were thrust into online learning situations with many of them having little experience and even less preparation for this transition. The same was the case for many of the world's educators, who were suddenly confronting a situation several had previously avoided or relegated to secondary status (Anderson, 2020). The transition was far from perfect anywhere. Yet it was one of the greatest paradigm shifts in the history of modern education.

A lack of familiarity with digital pedagogies, a limited understanding of what one could (and should) do in virtual classrooms, and an inconsistent grasp of how students and instructors should use technologies created confusion, miscommunication, and frustration at the start (Anderson, 2020; Li & Lalani, 2020). The situation did, however, increase exposure to and participation in online education in a way not previously possible. That exposure has led to widespread familiarity with online options for education. Large-scale online learning quickly moved from an abstract concept to a global reality where students and teachers alike had to navigate unfamiliar spaces in what was often a "learn-as-you-go" style.

With that familiarity came adaptation to new venues and, in many cases, an appreciation for what these contexts could offer (Schleicher, 2020). For many individuals, this level of familiarity also brought a paradigm shifting revelation: By removing the limitations of physical space, online education opened classrooms to instructors from across the nation and around the world. It allowed for new, large-scale collaborations ranging from regular guest lectures by experts in other nations to innovative co-teaching across a region. It also created an unprecedented opportunity for students in different countries to interact via collaborative activities and projects. The paradigm of pedagogy as tied to physical space had shifted greatly; the challenge became how to successfully recognize this potential. The answer involves a focus on writing.

Centrality of Content Creation

At its core, online education is about content creation—composing texts (content) to convey information in virtual spaces (St.Amant & Rice, 2015). In online educational settings, written communiques like emails and text messages are central to providing regular updates and notifications. Similarly, the online venues where individuals share ideas and debate concepts—discussion boards, chat rooms, and online forums—also rely heavily on written messages for exchanges. Even in situations where the mechanism for interactions seems visual in nature (e.g., a graphic user interface), the use of such media often requires corresponding written texts explaining how to operate a technology in order to access educational content and participate in related exchanges.

Essentially, interactions usually done orally in face-to-face classrooms must be re-cast in textual form to create parallel exchanges in online spaces. This dynamic means the importance of writing to pedagogical method and educational success in online contexts is not confined to certain disciplines. Rather, the centrality of writing to online education ripples across every field and program where online instruction occurs. Thus, recognizing the potential of online teaching and learning writ large depends upon how effectively individuals use writing to facilitate learning experiences. Individuals engaged in the teaching of writing are poised to play a central role in this process. These individuals have the opportunity to re-shape pedagogy to solidify the importance of writing and the teaching of writing across disciplines and on a global scale.

Realizing these opportunities involves addressing three interconnected factors known as the "3Cs":

- Contacting: The ability to access others—instructors or students—via online media. Online, text is essential to such access, for individuals need information (e.g., texts) making them aware of available opportunities and instruction (texts) on how to participate in such situations.
- Conveying: Rendering ideas in a format that allows them to be shared with and viewed/read by others. As online spaces often limit the modality of engagement, conveying often means creating texts (written content) in order to share, review, consider, and critique ideas.
- Connecting: Interacting with others to process information, reflect upon ideas, and engage in exploration where multiple perspectives discuss concepts to foster understanding. As such interactions often occur in

text-based forums online, writing is central to these processes. (St.Amant & Rice, 2015, p. v-x)

These 3C factors generally exist as abstract concepts around which educators must often struggle when shaping practices for teaching and learning. The PARS approach examined in this collection provides teachers with a key a mechanism for addressing such challenges. The entries in this collection also provide effective examples of how to implement these 3Cs ideas in different ways, via different technologies, and for different audiences. Moreover, PARS's focus on writing and writing instruction maximizes the content creation core of online education and helps individuals integrate the practice of and teaching of writing in different ways across a range of classes, curricula, and programs.

The PARS Advantage

The PARS framework focuses on usability as connected to the experiences of those who will read (use) texts. This focus allows PARS to help educators realize writing involves more than putting words on a (digital) page. Rather, to successfully foster connections, meaningfully convey ideas, and effectively connect with others, writing must focus on how, where, and when learners access, review, and engage with online texts. It is a question of usability—both in terms of the texts provided and the technologies used to access and interact with them. In this way, educational content creation must account for how texts fit into the lifestyles of the learners who use them.

The modern context of lifelong, globally distributed consumption of educational content requires a deep understanding of who the users of that content are and the experiences they bring to the learning process (see Moore & Hodges, 2020). By focusing on four variables central to such practices, the PARS approach helps educators across disciplines better understand, map out, and create strategies for addressing these complex usability expectations in a manageable way. Central to this framework is how PARS helps educators humanize learners by focusing content creation on

- Who learners are
- Where they interact with educational content
- How they engage with ideas
- What technologies they used to create content to convey ideas

It is a view that places learners at the center of the content-creation processes in online education.

PARS focus on the personal (P) and the accessible (A) reminds educators that no one approach works for all (Moore & Hodges, 2020; Will, 2020). It also reminds educators that their expectations of how to contact, convey, and connect are not universal—both in terms of texts used or technologies involved. Such awareness prompts the reflection and investigation needed to produce texts with the user (audience that uses text + technology used + contexts where used) in mind (St.Amant, 2017a). It also leads to the development of content that can help learners use texts and technologies to create as well as consume content when sharing, discussing, and debating in online spaces.

PARS's focus on the responsive (R) and the strategic (S) prompts online educators to engage in reflection on how learners in a subject are user of subject-related content. Essentially, both face-to-face or online interactions are based on expectations of how to act, react, and interact. When mapped into online environments, such expectations can become hazy (Moore & Hodges, 2020; Will, 2020). When distributed across globally dispersed lifelong learners, meeting such expectations can become challenging (St.Amant, 2017b). The solution, as the RS part of PARS teaches, is to craft experiences and create content that help learners understand the patterns used to foster interactions in online educational spaces. Doing so involves passive approaches to content creation (e.g., modeling how to do by doing one's self) and active instructions for writing (e.g., providing instructions for how to engage in certain interactions).

Through these four PARS elements, educators learn that there is no single approach to creating usable content for fostering effective education online. Rather, like usability, it is a continual process of

- Identifying who users (leaners) are
- Researching and understanding their experience-based expectations
- Creating content that can help them use (access and engage with) texts to create meaningful learning experiences (St.Amant, 2018)

In this way, PARS helps online educators continually adapt and expand their practices to meet the changing needs of learners. By examining these ideas across different contexts, this collection provides examples for how to use content to contact, convey, and connect effectively in online educational environments. By using PARS as a guide to achieving the 3Cs, educators can enhance their content to meet the needs of lifelong learners in global contexts.

Final Thoughts

Every challenge presents an opportunity to reflect, explore, and create. As more individuals around the world gain online access, the challenges for educators teaching in online contexts will only grow. It is an environment of continual opportunity for educators across all disciplines and institutions. Realizing such opportunity as it evolves requires a framework for understanding the ever-changing nature of

- Who users of online educational content are, and
- How their experiences shape their expectations for online education

The PARS approach can play a major role in meeting these challenges and creating opportunities for all involved. By applying it to address the 3Cs of global online education, individuals can establish the pedagogical practices essential to success in today's educational paradigm of globalized lifelong learning.

References

Anderson, J. (2020). The coronavirus pandemic is reshaping education. *Quartz*. https://qz.com/1826369/how-coronavirus-is-changing-education/.

Gu, M., Michael, R., Zheng, C. & Trines, S. (2019). Education in China. *World Education News + Reviews*. https://wenr.wes.org/2019/12/education-in-china-3.

Internet World Stats. (2020). The internet big picture: World internet users and 2020 population stats. https://internetworldstats.com/stats.htm.

Li, C. & Lalani, F. (2020). The COVID-19 pandemic has changed education forever. This is how. *World Economic Forum*. https://www.weforum.org/agenda/2020/04/coronavirus-education-global-covid19-online-digital-learning/.

Moore, S. & Hodges, C. B. (2020). So you want to temporarily teach online. *Inside Higher Ed*. https://www.insidehighered.com/advice/2020/03/11/practical-advice-instructors-faced-abrupt-move-online-teaching-opinion.

Schleicher, A. (2020). *The impact of COVID-19 on education: Insights from education at a glance 2020*. Paris; Organization for Economic Co-operation and Development.

St.Amant, K. (2017a). Of friction points and infrastructures: Re-thinking the dynamics of offering online education in technical communication in global contexts. *Technical Communication Quarterly*, 26(3), 1–19.

St.Amant, K. (2017b). Of scripts and prototypes: A two-part approach to user experience design for international contexts. *Technical Communication*, 64(2), 113–125.

St.Amant, K. (2018). Contextualizing cyber compositions for cultures: A usability-based approach to composing online for international audiences. *Computers and Composition*, 49, 82–93.

St.Amant, K. & Rice, R. (2015). Online writing in global contexts: Rethinking the nature of connections and communication in the age of international online media. *Computers and Composition*, 38(B), v-x.

Trines, S. (2018). Education in India. *World Education News + Reviews*. https://wenr.wes.org/2018/09/education-in-india.

United States Census Bureau. (2019). Census Bureau reports nearly 77 million students enrolled in U.S. schools. https://www.census.gov/newsroom/press-releases/2019/school-enrollment.html.

Will, M. (2020). Expectations for online student behavior vary during coronavirus school closures. *Education Week*. https://blogs.edweek.org/teachers/teaching_now/2020/04/during_virtual_classes_how_much_should_school_rules_be_enforced.html.

Contributors

Authors

Joseph Bartolotta is Assistant Professor in the Department of Writing Studies & Rhetoric at Hofstra University. His work examines the training and application of usability and user experience principles in writing programs and for students in TPC. He further explores the ways schools and industry organizations define best practices, competencies, and ethics in their respective contexts, and looks for ways to bring both together for generative discussions.

Bianca Batti is a Marion L. Brittain Postdoctoral Fellow and Online Developer for Teaching and Learning in the Writing and Communication Program at the Georgia Institute of Technology. She received her Ph.D. in literary studies with a graduate concentration in Women, Gender, and Sexuality Studies from the Department of English at Purdue University. Her research interests include online pedagogy, feminist game studies, and the digital humanities. Her work has been published in scholarly journals like The Popular Cultural Studies Journal and Kairos: A Journal of Rhetoric, Technology, and Pedagogy, and also in Haywire Magazine, Not Your Mama's Gamer, and edited anthologies.

Libby Chernouski is a doctoral candidate in the English Language and Linguistics program in the Department of English at Purdue University. She conducts interdisciplinary research on reference theory and the linguistic semantics of natural language processing.

Kristy Liles Crawley is a full-time member of the English faculty at Forsyth Technical Community College, where she has taught online, hybrid, and face-to-face courses for more than a decade. Her research on pedagogy and rhetorical studies appears in *Teachers, Teaching, and Media: Original Essays about Educators and Popular Culture*; *Prose Studies*; *Routledge Companion to Literature and Class*; and *Teaching English in the Two-Year College*.

Bradley Dilger, Associate Professor of English at Purdue University, is co-lead of the Corpus & Repository of Writing (Crow, writecrow.org), the first learner corpus linked to a repository of pedagogical texts. With Neil Baird, he studies writing transfer.

Theresa M. Evans (Tess) is Assistant Teaching Professor in the Department of English at Miami University of Ohio. She teaches courses in the Professional Writing Program, including face-to-face, hybrid, and fully online sections of Technical Writing and Professional Communication for Business. She became interested in online writing instruction in 2012, shortly after defending her dissertation in Rhetoric and Composition, when she spent a year teaching online sections of first-year writing and research courses. Other teaching and research interests include professional and technical writing, commercial rhetoric, and contingency studies. Her work has been published in *Rhetoric Review*, *The Proceedings of the Computers and Writing Conference*, and *Online Literacies Open Resource (OLOR)*. Tess serves on the executive board of the Global Society of Online Literacy Educators (GSOLE), transitioning in 2020 from Secretary to Treasurer.

Thomas M. Geary (Ph.D., University of Maryland) is a Professor of English at the Virginia Beach campus of Tidewater Community College, where he teaches face-to-face and online composition, rhetoric, technical writing, developmental writing, and humanities courses. Tom serves as the editor of *Inquiry*, the peer-reviewed journal for faculty, staff, and administrators in Virginia's community colleges, as well as a member of the MLA Delegate Assembly. Tom has several forthcoming book chapters and articles, and his research interests include sonic rhetoric, electracy, online writing instruction, podcasting, digital storytelling, open educational resources, community colleges, and compassionate pedagogy.

Guiseppe Getto is Associate Professor of Technical and Professional Communication at East Carolina University and is President and Founder of Content Garden, Inc., a digital marketing, content strategy, and UX firm: contentgarden.org. His research focuses on utilizing user experience (UX) design, content strategy, and other participatory research methods to help people improve their communities and organizations. His co-edited collection, *Content Strategy in Technical Communication*, is currently available from Routledge. The findings of his research have been published in peer-reviewed journals such as *IEEE Transactions on Professional Communication*; *Technical Communication*; *Computers and Composition*; *Rhetoric, Professional Communication, and Globalization*; *Communication Design Quarterly*; and *Reflections*; as well as conference proceedings for the Association for Computing Machinery's Special Interest Group on Design of Communication (ACM SIGDOC). His work has also appeared in industry-based publications such as *Intercom* and *Boxes and Arrows*. He has taught at the college level for over fifteen years. During that time, he has consulted and formed research and service-learning partnerships with many non-profits and businesses, from technical writing firms to homeless shelters to startups. He is also a poet. His first book, *Familiar History*, is currently available from Finishing Line Press at guiseppegetto.com/poetry. Read more about him at guiseppegetto.com.

Heidi Skurat Harris is Associate Professor and Graduate Coordinator in the Department of Rhetoric and Writing at the University of Arkansas–Little Rock where she oversees the Graduate Certificate in Online Writing Instruction. She currently teaches online writing instruction, technical writing, and creative nonfiction at UALR. Her publications focus primarily on research into effective online program development & sustainability and creating community and rapport with online students.

Lyra Hilliard is Senior Lecturer in the Department of English at the University of Maryland, College Park. She teaches hybrid and online writing courses for the Academic and Professional Writing Programs and coordinates the internship program for undergraduate teaching assistants in English courses. In her role as Blended and Online Learning Coordinator, she co-developed and co-directs the department's online and hybrid teacher training program. She has led the Academic Writing Program's hybrid faculty learning community since 2013.

N. Claire Jackson is a Ph.D. Candidate in Rhetoric and Composition at the University of Louisville. Her research interests include writing program administration, writing teacher development, online writing instruction, labor, and translingualism. As Assistant Director of Composition at UofL, she developed a professional development course in Online Writing Instruction for graduate students and faculty.

George H. Jensen is Professor in the Department of Rhetoric and Writing at the University of Arkansas Little Rock, where he teaches courses in rhetorical theory and creative nonfiction. His books include *Personality and the Teaching of Composition* (with John K. DiTiberio, 1989), *Storytelling in Alcoholics Anonymous: A Rhetorical Analysis* (2000), and *Identities Across Texts* (2002). In addition to these scholarly books, he has written *Some of the Words Are Theirs: A Memoir of an Alcoholic Family*, which was published with Moon City Press in 2009. With Heidi Skurat Harris, he is drafting a book on Norman Maclean's revisions to "A River Runs through It."

Alisha Karabinus is Assistant Professor of Writing and Digital Studies at Grand Valley State University. Her research interests are in digital publics and technical and professional communication, particularly with regard to games.

Karen Kuralt is Associate Dean of the Graduate School at the University of Arkansas at Little Rock. She was the M.A. program coordinator in the Department of Rhetoric and Writing for 12 years. She teaches graduate and undergraduate courses in business and technical writing both on campus and online. A winner of the College of Social Sciences and Communication Faculty Excellence Award for Public Service, Kuralt has worked as a science editor and workplace writing trainer with a variety of organizations including the National Center for

Toxicological Research (NCTR), the Arkansas Department of Human Services, the Arkansas Department of Environmental Quality (ADEQ), and the University of Arkansas Cooperative Extension Service. She serves on the board of directors at Wildwood Park for the Arts in Little Rock.

Angela Laflen is currently a faculty member in the English Department at California State University, Sacramento. She teaches in the Writing Program, in the areas of digital writing, online writing pedagogy, and professional writing. She has been teaching online courses since 2007. Her published work focuses on digital and multimodal literacies and writing response practices, and her work has appeared in *Computers and Composition*, *Assessing Writing*, and the *Journal of Response to Writing*, among others.

Kathleen Turner Ledgerwood is Assistant Professor of English and the Writing Area Coordinator at Lincoln University in Missouri. As a teacher-scholar-activist, she is very interested in equity-based, antiracist, and decolonizing teaching practices. This interest has led to research in how students deal with affect in regards to writing feedback and revision. In her spare time, you'll also find her studying and writing about popular media, especially film and television.

Cat Mahaffey is Senior Lecturer in the Writing, Rhetoric and Digital Studies (WRDS) Department at UNC Charlotte. She teaches first-year writing and courses such as Digital Design Theory and Practice and The Rhetoric of Digital Design. Her research interests include online privacy, accessibility, digital rhetoric, and technical and professional writing. Her work and research are published in *Next Steps: New Directions for/in Writing about Writing* (2019) and *Emerging Technologies in Virtual Learning Environments* (2019).

Christine I. McClure is Instructor in the Humanities and Communication Department at Embry-Riddle Aeronautical University, Daytona Beach, and teaches face-to-face Speech and hybrid Technical Report Writing and humanities courses. Christine is a Ph.D. candidate at the University of Central Florida in the Texts and Technology program focusing on Scientific and Technical Communication. Her research interests include online and hybrid pedagogy, and instructional technology and design as a co-discipline to Technical Communication. Her publications include "Experiencing COVID-style Classroom Teaching," "Creating a Robust Course in Canvas," "Information in the Making: Information Behavior Theory and the Teaching of Research-Writing in the Digital Age," and forthcoming "The Me Too Movement: A Qualitative Content Analysis of News Featuring #MeToo."

Andrea R. Olinger is Director of Composition and Associate Professor of English at the University of Louisville, where she studies disciplinary writers' representations and practices of style, WAC/WID, and writing teacher development.

Nitya Pandey is a Ph.D. student in rhetoric and composition at Florida State University. Her interests include online writing instruction, affect, virtual communication, social media, and digital multimodal composition. She received her master's degree in Professional Writing and Editing from West Virginia University.

Cynthia Pengilly (Ph.D., Old Dominion University) is an Assistant Professor of English and Co-Director of the Technical Writing Program at Central Washington University. She teaches courses in technical and professional communication, visual rhetoric, medical/health rhetoric, and cultural studies. Her research explores rhetoric, technology, and activism with a particular focus on competing representations and articulations of identity in online spaces. She also specializes in digital rhetoric and innovative pedagogical strategies in online writing instruction (OWI) and online tutoring. Dr. Pengilly has several forthcoming articles and book chapters.

Dylan Retzinger is a technical and professional communication instructor at New Mexico State University. Too Fresh is a reggae bass from Berkeley, CA.

Alex Sibo is a Ph.D. Candidate in English at Pennsylvania State University. Their research interests include pedagogies of composition and literature, online writing instruction, and disability studies. They teach first-year composition, technical communication, and advanced technical writing for Penn State's University Park and World Campuses and currently serve as a graduate WPA for Penn State's Program in Writing and Rhetoric.

Mikenna Leigh Sims is Teaching Associate and graduate student in the English Department at California State University, Sacramento. She teaches first-year composition and has taught both face-to-face and online. Her research interests include labor-based contract grading and second language writing instruction, and she has presented her research at conferences such as the Conference on College Composition and Communication (CCCCs) and California Teachers of English to Speakers of Other Languages (CATESOL).

Jason Snart is Professor of English at the College of DuPage and is Chair of Literature, Creative Writing, and Film. He is also editor and founder of the *Online Literacies Open Resource*, one of two peer reviewed journals published by the Global Society of Online Literacy Educators. His books include *The Torn Book: Unreading William Blake's Marginalia* (2006), *Hybrid Learning: The Perils and Promise of Blending Online and Face-to-Face Instruction in Higher Education* (2010), and *Making Hybrids Work: An Institutional Framework for Blending Online and Face-to-Face Instruction in Higher Education* (2016).

Allegra W. Smith is a Ph.D. candidate in Rhetoric and Composition at Purdue University. A professional and technical communication teacher-scholar, her work focuses on improving technological experiences for diverse populations. Her research has appeared in the Journal of Global Literacies, Technologies, and Emerging Pedagogies (JOGLTEP), the proceedings of the Association for Computing Machinery Special Interest Group on Design of Communication (ACM-SIGDOC), and Communication Design Quarterly.

Kirk St.Amant is the Eunice C. Williamson Chair in Technical Communication at Louisiana Tech University (US) and a faculty member teaching with the online technical communication programs at the University of Limerick (Ireland) and the University of Strasbourg (France).

Mary K. Stewart was an Assistant Professor and the Assessment Coordinator for the English Department at Indiana University of Pennsylvania during the drafting of this chapter. She is now/currently Associate Professor and the General Education Writing Coordinator in the Literature & Writing Studies Department at California State University, San Marcos. Beyond her institution, she serves as the Webinar Co-Chair for the Global Society of Online Literacy Educators and a co-editor for Writing Spaces. Her qualitative and quantitative research focuses on collaborative and interactive learning, writing pedagogy and online writing instruction, and antiracist writing program administration and assessment.

Erica M. Stone is Assistant Professor of English and Associate Director of General Education English at Middle Tennessee State University. As a teacher-scholar, she works at the intersection of technical communication, public rhetoric, and community organizing. Erica's writing can be found in *Kairos: A Journal of Rhetoric, Technology, and Pedagogy*; *Forum: Issues about Part-time & Contingent Faculty*; *Basic Writing Electronic (BWe) Journal*; *Spark: A 4C4Equality Journal*; *Community Literacy Journal*; and various edited collections. Read more about her community-based work at ericamstone.com. Contact her at erica.stone@mtsu.edu or on Twitter @ericamstone.

Rhonda Thomas is a Graduate Teaching Assistant in the Department of Psychology at the University of Arkansas at Little Rock. Her academic work is in professional and technical writing, online writing instruction, and instructional design. She considers herself a career lifelong learner and an online learning veteran. Her professional background is in business, professional, and technical writing, website authoring and design, and data management. Her research interests include digital rhetoric and adult learning theory. She is a published songwriter—having won several songwriting awards—and is a member of Broadcast Music Incorporated. Pre-pandemic life included making music with her husband and friends. In her spare time, you can find her pulling weeds in her garden and working on a memoir about her life growing up on Blytheville Air Force Base. rhonthom.com

Lydia Wilkes has taught online writing courses for over a decade at a variety of institutions, most recently as an assistant professor of English at Idaho State University. She has published on anti-Black racism in online writing instruction in the *Proceedings of the Computers and Writing Annual Conference, 2016 & 2017*. Her work has also appeared in *Composition Forum* and the *Journal of Veterans Studies*.

Editors

Jessie Borgman has taught both face-to-face and online since 2009. She has several published articles and book chapters and has presented at conferences including, *CCCCs*, *C&W*, and *TYCA*. She has served on the *CCCC* OWI Standing Group in multiple capacities. Her research interests include online writing instruction, instructional design, content strategy, user experience, two-year colleges, and writing program administration. She is an instructor in the Writers' Studio at Arizona State University.

Casey McArdle is Associate Chair for Undergraduate Studies in the Department of Writing, Rhetoric, and American Cultures at Michigan State University. He is an advocate for accessibility in and out of the classroom and has been involved with OWI for many years via publications, presentations, and research teams that focus on OWI.

Together, in 2015, Borgman and McArdle co-created a resources website and community for online writing instructors called, The Online Writing Instruction Community (owicommunity.org). They co-authored a book which was released in the fall of 2019 titled, *Personal, Accessible, Responsive, Strategic: Resources and Strategies for Online Writing Instructors* which is based on their PARS approach to online writing instruction.[1] They host professional development workshops on online writing instruction and the PARS approach.

---

1. View the book at https://wac.colostate.edu/books/practice/pars/.

www.ingramcontent.com/pod-product-compliance
Lightning Source LLC
Chambersburg PA
CBHW071228070526
44583CB00017B/2091